# THE EARTH
## FROM THE AIR

Yann Arthus-Bertrand

# THE EARTH
# FROM THE AIR

THIRD EDITION

Thames & Hudson

For Anne, Tom, Guillaume, and Baptiste,
with love.

*This vision of the world would not have been possible
without the help of UNESCO, Fujifilm, Air France, and Eurocopter.
I am grateful for their trust and their friendship.*

*The captions for the photographs in this 2005 edition have been edited
and updated by Isabelle Delannoy, Nathalie Chahine, and Marie Renault.*

Translated from the French *La terre vue du ciel*
by David Baker, Simon Jones, and David H. Wilson

First published in the United Kingdom in 1999 by
Thames & Hudson Ltd, 181A High Holborn, London WC1V 7QX

www.thamesandhudson.com

Third edition 2005

British Library Cataloguing-in-Publication Data
A catalogue record for this book is available from the British Library

ISBN-13: 978-0-500-54306-1
ISBN-10: 0-500-54306-2

Printed and bound in France

Yann Arthus-Bertrand has been part of my publishing life for twenty-six years. In 1979 I brought out his first book with Hachette Réalités. He and his wife, Anne, were just back from two years in Kenya, and his lion photographs caused a sensation. Not a year has passed since then without our publishing one or more books together. It has been a great experience, following his progress through the years, his combination of brilliance and hard work, as he traveled the globe in search of humanity and himself.

Maturity is a concept I can't really define, but I do know that with this book, Yann has reached the end of a journey to which he committed himself so fully that he deserves our respect. It has meant ten years of work, hundreds of thousands of photographs taken and miles traveled, stepping out of one airplane and into another, from country to country, juggling flight schedules all the way. But all of this would be nothing without his incomparable eye, which always finds the detail that makes a photograph better. His eye catches humanity in its finest light, without ever making concessions. His eye is always generous as well, as no one can fail to agree.

Let there be no mistake: this book is not simply a series of photographs. It is a work of art, the testimony of a citizen of the world at the dawn of the third millennium, who wants to show his vision of the Earth, its beauty as well as its failures. But behind his enthusiasm lies a certain anxiety. He worries about this changing planet, caught between demography and industrialization.

In 1999, when the first edition of this book was published, no one could have imagined that the book, along with the touring exhibition that accompanies it, would become a legend. Almost 3 million copies have been sold in twenty-five countries, and tens of millions of people have visited the exhibition as it expands all over the world. An unimaginable success, from such a simple idea: the Earth, the human race, the environment.

Now, several years later, nothing can stop this phenomenon that has grown beyond its author. Nothing can stop this movement, this growing awareness that we ourselves are the planet Earth. And it is we, the men and women of this world, who have ruined the very thing that gives us life.

Here is a new edition, even more committed, even more relevant, with striking new images and detailed new texts. A work of art; a collection; a legend.

Yann is more than just an author; he is a friend. I know him better than anyone and I can testify to his charisma. This work (and work it surely was) required the cooperation of an incalculable number of people, but he kept on asking them and they kept on saying yes, drawn by his will and his powers of persuasion. This book is also the most beautiful form of thanks that he could ever give them.

Hervé de La Martinière

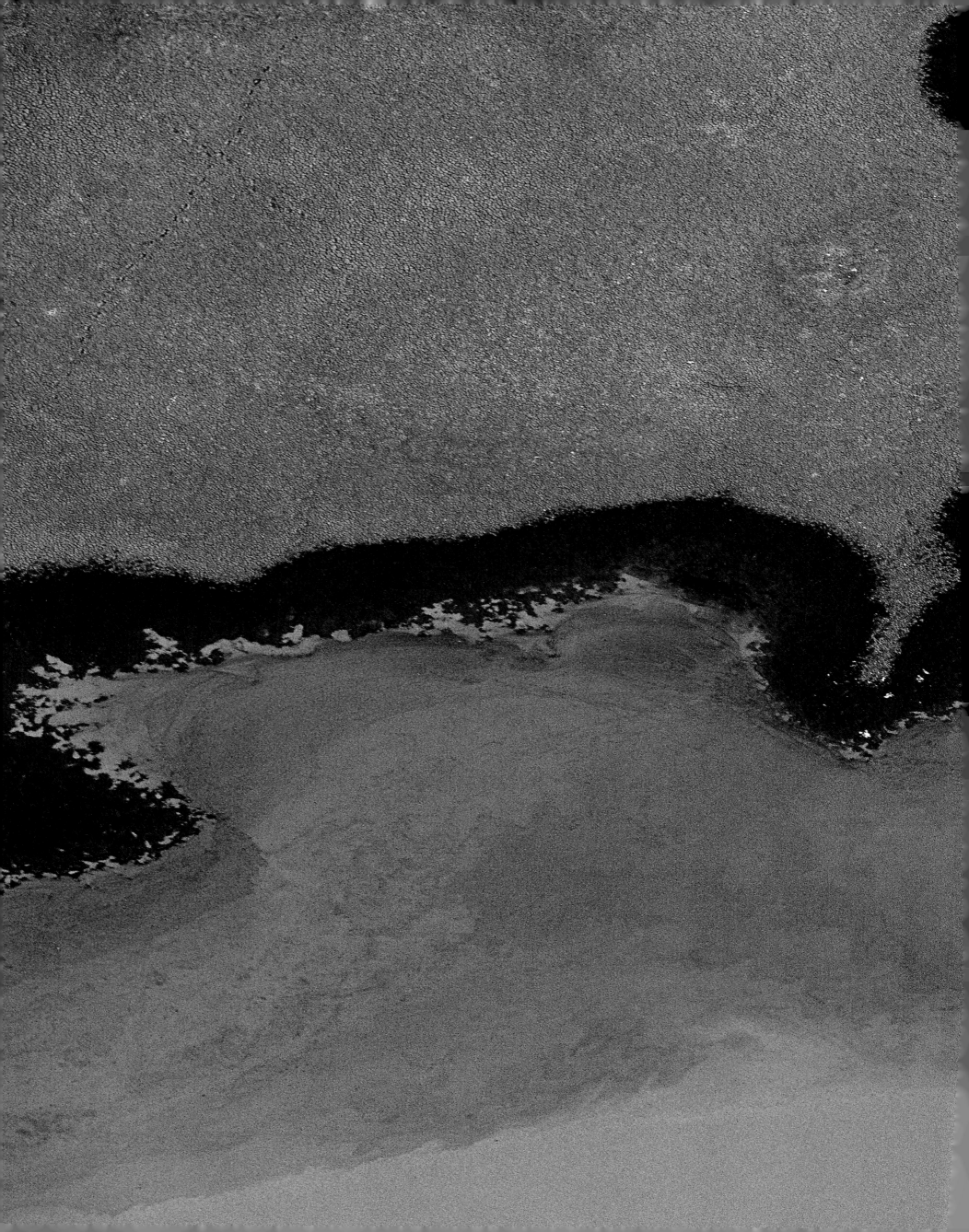

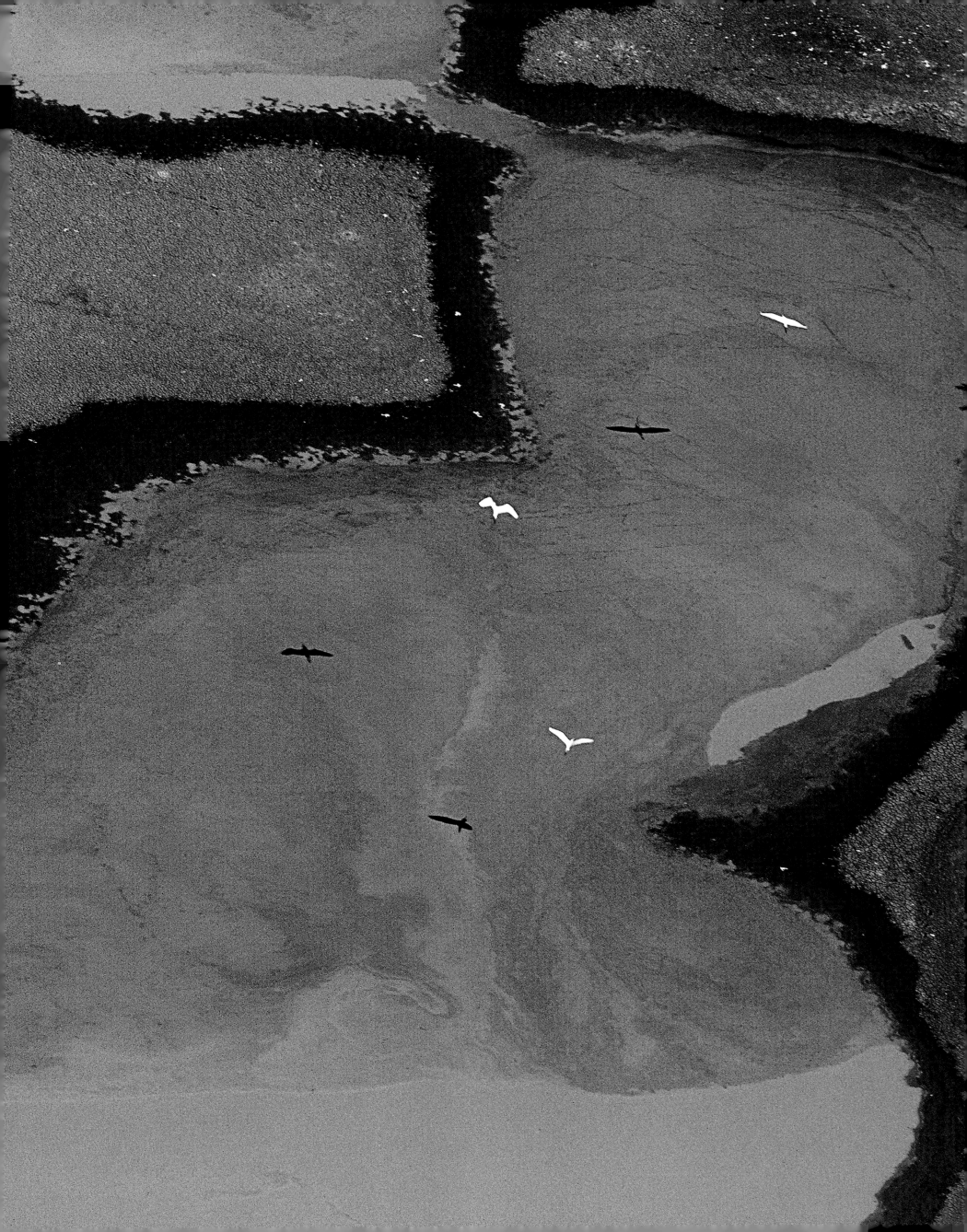

8

# CONTENTS

# BUILDING AN ECO-ECONOMY

All over the world, the limits of the planet's ecosystem are being tested.
The unbearable pressure that the human race is exerting on the Earth
is causing enormous imbalances and endangering millions of human lives.
In the face of this ecological destruction, there are two paths open to us:
either to continue as we are, and move inevitably towards economic
and social disaster, or alternatively, to adopt a new economic model,
in which the quest for profit at all costs is replaced by the taking
into account of ecological realities.

As world population has doubled and as the global economy has expanded sevenfold over the last half-century, our claims on the Earth have become excessive. We are asking more of the Earth than it can give on an ongoing basis, creating a bubble economy. We are cutting trees faster than they can regenerate, overgrazing rangelands and converting them into deserts, overpumping aquifers, and draining rivers dry. On our cropland, soil erosion exceeds new soil formation, slowly depriving the soil of its inherent fertility. We are taking fish from the ocean faster than they can reproduce.

We are releasing carbon dioxide ($CO_2$) into the atmosphere faster than nature can absorb it, creating a greenhouse effect. As atmospheric $CO_2$ levels rise, so does the Earth's temperature. Habitat destruction and climate change are destroying plant and animal species far faster than new species can evolve, launching the first mass extinction since the one that eradicated the dinosaurs 65 million years ago.

Throughout history, humans have lived on the Earth's sustainable yield—the interest from its natural endowment. But now we are consuming the endowment itself. In ecology, as in economics, we can consume capital along with interest in the short run, but in the long run it leads to bankruptcy. It is time to abandon Plan A—business as usual—and turn to Plan B. This new strategy will involve reducing our demands on the Earth, cutting our $CO_2$ emissions, narrowing the gap between rich and poor, and creating an economy that reflects ecological truth.

Humanity's demands on the Earth have multiplied over the last half-century as the world population has grown from 2.5 billion in 1950 to over 6 billion today. Population growth and rising incomes together have tripled world grain demand over the last half-century.

To satisfy this swelling demand, farmers have plowed land that was highly vulnerable to erosion—land that was too dry or too steeply sloping to sustain cultivation. Each year billions of tons of topsoil are being blown away in dust storms or washed away in rainstorms, leaving farmers to try to feed some 70 million additional people, but with less topsoil than the year before.

Demand for water has also tripled as agricultural, industrial, and residential uses have climbed, outstripping the sustainable supply in many countries. As a result, water tables are now falling and wells are going dry. Rivers are also being drained, to the serious detriment of wildlife and ecosystems.

Raising land productivity will be an ongoing battle for the foreseeable future as cropland per person shrinks. In a world where literally billions of people want to diversify their diets, one way to raise land productivity is to produce animal protein more efficiently. Replacing grain with agricultural residues to feed ruminant animals such as cattle, sheep, and goats can create a sort of second harvest from the grain crop, decreasing grain demand and increasing land productivity. Shifting consumption to more grain-efficient forms of animal protein can also raise land productivity. This means moving from feedlot beef and pork to more poultry and herbivorous species of farmed fish, such as carp, tilapia, and catfish. Planting legumes as a cover crop with grains is another method of adding nutrients to the soil, while also preventing erosion.

A related challenge is to eliminate overgrazing on rangelands. Growing numbers of livestock remove vegetation, and their hoofs pulverize the protective crust of soil that checks wind erosion. Here the solution is to shift to stall feeding of animals, cutting the forage and bringing it to them.

Shifting from the use of fuelwood to renewable energy sources—everything from solar cookers to geothermal electricity—can reduce erosion and decrease pollution. Protecting the Earth's remaining vegetation also warrants a ban on clearcutting forests in favor of selective cutting, because clearcut land suffers heavy soil losses until the forest regenerates. With soil erosion, we have no choice but to reduce the loss to the rate of new soil formation or below. The only alternative is a continuing decline in the fertility of soils, cropland abandonment, and increasing desertification.

Water scarcity will be a defining condition of life for many this century. The simultaneous emergence of fast-growing water shortages in so many countries requires a wholly new approach to water policy, a shift from expanding supply to managing demand. Managing water scarcity will affect what we eat, how we dispose of waste, and even where we choose to live.

This will require extending primary education to all children, promoting good nutrition and reducing hunger, providing vaccinations and basic health care, and offering reproductive health care and family planning services in all countries. Slowing population growth is the key to eradicating poverty and its distressing symptoms, and, conversely, eradicating poverty is the key to slowing population growth. We now have the knowledge and the resources to reach these goals. In an increasingly integrated world, we also have a vested interest in doing so.

Throughout most of recorded history, the indirect costs of economic activity, the sustainable yields of natural systems, or the value of nature's services were of little concern because the scale of human activity was so small relative to the size of the Earth that they were rarely an issue. But with the sevenfold expansion in the world economy over the last half-century, the failure to address these market shortcomings and the irrational economic distortions they create will eventually lead to economic decline.

Our only hope now is rapid systemic change—change based on market signals that tell the ecological truth. Unless we can get the market to send signals that reflect reality, we will continue making faulty decisions as consumers, corporate planners, and government policymakers.

We can build an economy that does not destroy its natural support systems, a global community where the basic needs of all the Earth's people are satisfied, and a world that will allow us to think of ourselves as civilized. The goals are absolutely essential and the technologies are already available.

The choice is ours—yours and mine. We can stay with business as usual and preside over a global bubble economy that keeps expanding until it bursts, leading to economic decline. Or we can adopt Plan B and become the generation that stabilizes the population, eradicates poverty, and stabilizes the climate. Historians will record the choice, but it is ours to make.

LESTER BROWN

---

⌂ **LAS PURGAS MARKET, SANTO DOMINGO, DOMINICAN REPUBLIC** (18°28' N, 69°53' W)

In the southwest of Santo Domingo, at the little market of Las Purgas, Dominican and Haitian stallholders put up brightly colored parasols to shelter their wares. The atmosphere is warm and colorful. Electrical goods, furniture, clothing: almost anything can be bought, sold, or exchanged here, whether the goods are new or used, authorized or improvised. Markets of this kind are becoming more common on the island, a reflection of the growth of the informal economy, which provides a living for 7 of every 10 Haitians and almost one in two Dominicans. The rise of the informal economy in the countries of the southern hemisphere is strongly linked to labor surpluses and migration to cities. In addition, in recent decades more and more women have begun to work, either by choice or necessity. With more restricted access to education, women are often less qualified than men and so have less easy access to capital, credit, and professional training. They are therefore vulnerable to discrimination of all kinds and end up in less valued jobs.

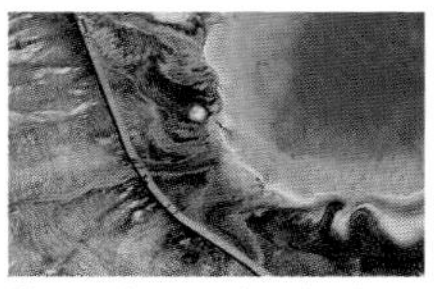

**PAGES 16–17**
GRAND PRISMATIC SPRING, YELLOWSTONE NATIONAL PARK, WYOMING, UNITED STATES
(44°26' N, 110°39' W)

Situated on a volcanic plateau that straddles the states of Montana, Idaho, and Wyoming, Yellowstone is the oldest national park in the world. Created in 1872, it covers 3,500 square miles (9,000 km²) and contains the world's largest concentration of geothermic sites, with more than 10,000 geysers, fumaroles, and hot springs. Grand Prismatic Spring, 370 feet (112 m) in diameter, is the park's largest hot pool in area and third-highest in the world. The color spectrum for which it is named is caused by the presence of cyanobacteria, which grow faster in the hot water at the center of the basin than at the periphery where the temperature is lower. Declared a Biosphere Reserve in 1976 and a UNESCO World Heritage site in 1978, Yellowstone National Park receives an average of 3 million visitors per year. The continent of North America, which contains the five most visited natural sites in the world, is visited by between 80 and 90 million tourists per year—11 percent of world tourism in numbers, but almost 18 percent in revenues.

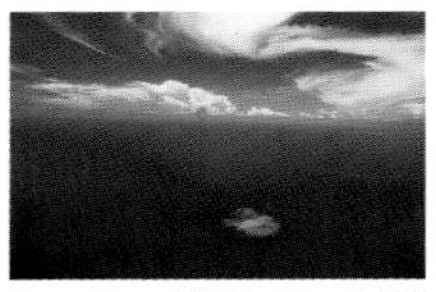

**PAGES 18–19**
ISLET IN THE SULU ARCHIPELAGO, PHILIPPINES
(6°05' N, 120°54' E)

More than 6,000 of the 7,100 Philippine Islands are uninhabited, like this islet in the Sulu Archipelago, a set of 500 islands that separate the Celebes and the Sulu seas. Their extraordinary biodiversity is under threat, not from distant industrial sites but from the effects of global pollution. These islands, which barely rise above the surface of the water, are among the first potential victims of global warming and are certain to disappear when the sea level rises. The oceans, which maintain our planet's equilibrium, play a major role in our climate, storing up heat from warmer times and releasing it later, transporting it in its currents, providing the water for rainbearing clouds through evaporation, and trapping and absorbing carbon dioxide. This vast mass of water is inhabited by fauna whose diversity is scarcely imaginable and which, through the food chain—from plankton through fish to the marine mammals—plays an enormously important role in human subsistence.

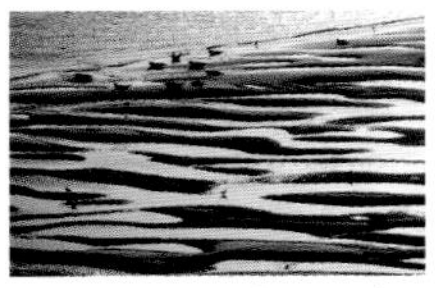

**PAGES 20–21**
COMMON SEALS IN THE BAY OF THE SOMME, FRANCE (50°14' N, 1°33' E)

For a distance of more than 40 miles (70 km) along the English Channel, land and sea intermingle at the heart of a vast coastal wetland—the maritime plain of Picardy, famed for its rich bird life. Some 340 species of birds either nest there or use it as a stopover during their great autumnal migration to warmer climes. Here you will also find the largest colony of common or harbor seals (*Phoca vitulina*) in France, with a population of over seventy. Summer is the season of births. At ebb tide the seals come with their pups to rest on the sandbanks which the tide has uncovered. This tranquillity is essential, for if the seals are disturbed, they will rush back to the sea, and the pups, which have not yet been weaned, may lose their mothers in the chaos and thus be condemned to almost certain death. The maritime plain of Picardy is one of the largest natural wetlands in France, and such fragile ecosystems are among the most fertile on Earth, even though they only cover a small area. During the last thirty years, half of France's wetlands have disappeared or suffered heavy pollution.

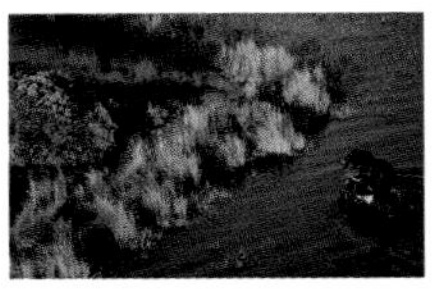

**PAGES 22–23**
ELEPHANTS IN THE OKAVANGO DELTA, BOTSWANA
(19°26' S, 23°03' E)

African elephants (*Loxodonta africana*) cover many miles in their search for the 220 lb to 440 lb (100 kg to 200 kg) of food that they need every day. In single file, they follow the dominant female, communicating by movements of the trunk and ears, scent, touch, and a wide range of deep sounds that are beyond human hearing. Relentlessly hunted for their ivory, these animals are now in danger of extinction. Their population dwindled from 2.5 million in 1945 to 500,000 in 1989, the year in which the ivory trade was banned. Today they number around 300,000, and are mainly concentrated in game reserves which are often too small to provide enough food for them without ruining the ecosystems and harvests of countries which are already suffering from malnutrition. Despite these hardships, eleven Central and West African countries have tried in vain to maintain a total ban on the ivory trade, with a view to curbing the incidence of poaching and providing a joint solution to the problem of saving the elephant. The means used to control the ivory trade, however, are inadequate, and the resumption of international trade—even if it is restricted—has given the poachers free rein.

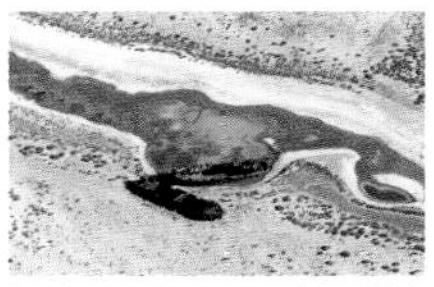

**PAGES 24–25**
GROUNDED BOAT, ARAL SEA, ARALSK REGION, KAZAKHSTAN
(46°39' N, 61°11' E)

In the early years of the 20th century, when the Aral Sea in Kazakhstan covered an area of 26,000 square miles (66,500 km²), it was the world's fourth-largest inland body of water. After the construction in the 1960s of dams that feed a vast irrigation network for the cultivation of cotton in the region, the flow of the Amu Darya and Syr Darya rivers, which feed the Aral Sea, diminished to a disturbing degree. The sea lost 50 percent of its area and 75 percent of its water volume, and its shores shrank 40 to 50 miles (60 to 80 km)—leaving behind the hulls of small boats that had once fished its waters. As a direct consequence of the diminishing water, the salinity of the Aral Sea has continually increased over the course of the past thirty years, today reaching about 1 ounce per quart (30 grams per liter), three times its original salt concentration, causing the disappearance of more than 20 species of fish. Salts carried by the winds burn all vegetation within a radius of hundreds of miles, contributing to the desertification of the environment. Although the Aral Sea is among the best-known examples of this effect, it is far from unique: 230,000 square miles (600,000 km²) of irrigated land all over the world, 75 percent of it in Asia, have excessive salt, which reduces agricultural productivity.

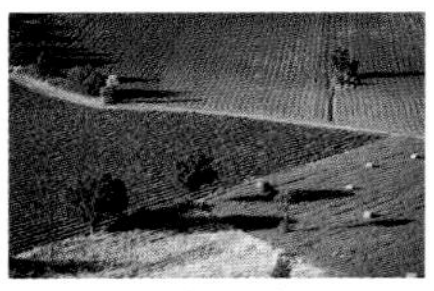

**PAGES 26–27**
LANDSCAPE OF BRIGHTLY COLORED FIELDS NEAR SARRAUD, VAUCLUSE, FRANCE (44°01' N, 5°24' E)

On the Vaucluse plateau, an arid limestone upland in the east of the *département*, lavender fields blossom in the Mediterranean summer heat. Cultivation of fine lavender began about 1920; the crop was distilled to produce an essential oil for perfume and aromatherapy. Now, however, it faces competition from lavandin and synthetic products. By 1992, annual production had dropped to 25 metric tons (one-sixth of production totals in 1960). This decline was all the more worrying because lavender cultivation, which makes use of arid land, supports rural communities in mountainous areas where agriculture is in decline. A program to relaunch and modernize this industry was started in 1994. In 2001, over 13,000 metric tons of essential oil of lavender and lavandin were produced from land totaling over 23,000 hectares. France is the top producer, supplying 70 percent of the world's lavender, of which 90 percent is exported to the US. The perfumed, purple carpets that are strewn over the landscapes of Haute Provence are also a considerable asset for tourism in southeast France.

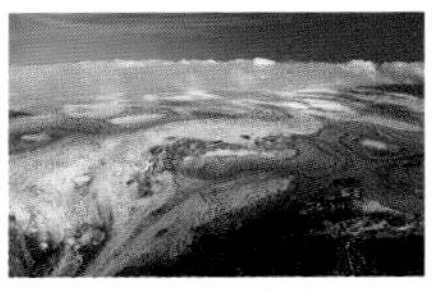

**PAGES 28–29**
FOLGEFONNI GLACIER ON THE HIGH PLATEAUS OF SØRFJORDEN, NORWAY
(60°14' N, 6°44' E)

The Folgefonni glacier, hemmed in between two fjords, Hardangerfjorden and Sørfjorden, in southern Norway, is the third-largest of the country's 1,500 glaciers, occupying an area of 83 square miles (212 km²). A plateau glacier typical of those found in temperate regions, it slides on a film of water formed between the rock and ice. In summer the partial melting of ice supplies the water of the fjords with silt and clay, giving them a very unusual green tint. Regardless of seasonal variations, the volume of glaciers is being reduced by global warming, and particularly by emissions of greenhouse gases. Despite these alarming signs, the United States, which has 5 percent of the world's population but emits 25 percent of greenhouse gases, refuses to ratify the Kyoto Agreement, a first step in the bid to encourage industrial nations to reduce their greenhouse gas emissions, which came into force on February 16, 2005. Aware of the economic benefits that the possession of technology designed to reduce or contain greenhouses gases will bring in the future, the United States nonetheless remains the top investor in this sector.

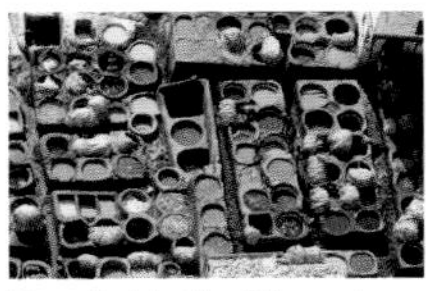

**PAGES 30–31**
DYER'S VATS AND WORKSHOPS IN FEZ, MOROCCO
(34°05' N, 4°57' W)

Founded in the 9th century and home to the oldest university in the world, the city of Fez had its golden age in the 13th and 14th centuries, when it was Morocco's capital. The buildings and monuments of the Medina, a UNESCO World Heritage site since 1981, date from this period. The dyers' district of Fez has hardly changed since those days, and the same traditional coloring techniques have been used for centuries. Tanned hides and textiles are submerged in dye vats with ceramic surfaces, known as fullers, and are trodden down by the craftsmen. The coloring is derived from natural pigments: poppy, indigo, saffron, date nuts, and antimony are used to obtain red, blue, yellow, beige, and black, respectively. The dyed materials are used to make the world-famous carpets and leather objects that are the principal handmade Moroccan exports. Some of the processes used are harmful both to the environment and to the craftsmen themselves, who work without protective masks. The local council is currently trying to relocate the workshops that cause pollution to an area outside of the city, equipped with treatment installations, while allowing the non-polluting workshops to remain inside the Medina.

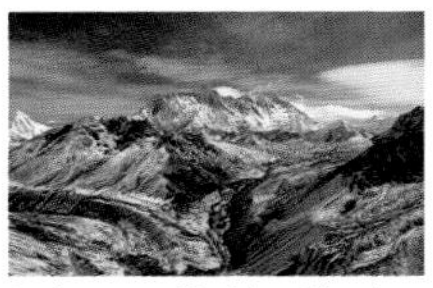

**PAGES 32–33**
MOUNT EVEREST, HIMALAYAS, NEPAL
(27°59' N, 86°56' E)

In the massif of the Himalayas stands Mount Everest, the highest point on the planet at 29,028 feet (8,848 m). In Nepali the mountain is called *Sagarmatha*, "He whose head touches the sky," and in Tibetan it is called *Chomolongma*, "Mother Goddess of the world." The name Everest comes from the British colonel George Everest, who in 1852 was commissioned to map the landscapes of India. It was not until May 29, 1953, that the "roof of the world" was climbed by the New Zealander Edmund Hillary and the Nepalese Sherpa Tenzing Norgay. Although they may seem invincible and unchanging, the Himalayas are actually in the midst of profound ecological change. The rise in temperatures in the region (+1.8°F, or +1°C since 1970) is causing the glaciers to melt and the mountain lakes are filling so quickly that some forty of them are in danger of overflowing within five years, threatening the lives of millions of people in the valleys below. At the current rate, the glaciers of the Himalayas, like all mountain glaciers worldwide, could disappear within 40 years. The consequences would be enormous; mountain areas provide water for half of the world's population.

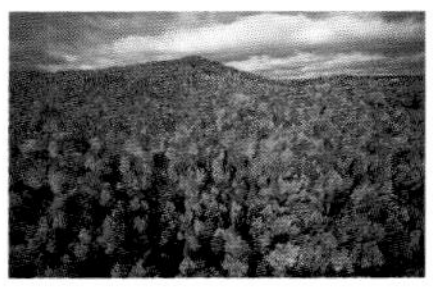

**PAGES 34–35**
AUTUMN FOREST IN THE REGION OF CHARLEVOIX, QUEBEC, CANADA
(47°40' N, 71°02' W)

The hills of the Charlevoix region along the Saint Lawrence River in Quebec province are dominated by a mixed forest of deciduous trees and conifers. In 1988 UNESCO declared 1,800 square miles (4,600 km²) of this region a Biosphere Reserve. The Quebec forest, boreal in the north and temperate in the south, covers nearly two-thirds of the province and has been exploited for lumber since the end of the 17th century. Today it contributes to the economic prosperity of Canada in the worldwide production of newsprint paper, paper pulp, and timber, as well as Christmas trees and maple syrup. The Canadian forest has long been overexploited and has also been decimated by parasitic insects and acid rain, resulting in a considerable reduction in its total area. However, the forest today still covers almost 144.6 million hectares (84.6 million in Quebec), around one of million of which is cut down every year. Since 1992, Canada, a world leader in sustainable forest management, has been striving to introduce sustainable practices, and to reconcile the various environmental, economic, social, and cultural demands being made on its forests.

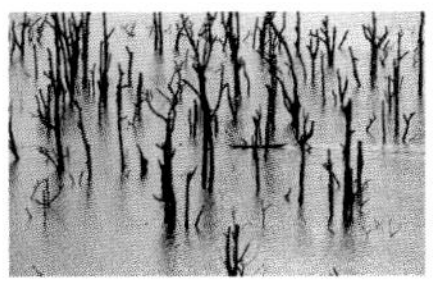

**PAGES 36–37**
FISHERMAN ON LAKE KOSSOU, NEAR BOUAFLÉ, CÔTE D'IVOIRE
(7°06' N, 5°45' W)

Lake Kossou, which spans 585 square miles (1,500 km²) in the center of Côte d'Ivoire, is an artificial reservoir designed to regulate the flow of the Bandama River and facilitate the construction of a hydroelectric dam. The lake was built between 1969 and 1971, at the cost of 75,000 displaced people, who benefited from resettlement and development measures. Hydroelectric dams, which produce renewable energy from the flow of water, are in principle non-polluting. However, they always create major upheavals in the environment: the diversion of rivers, the flooding of fields and forests, the destruction of natural habitats, and the displacement of whole populations who, in the long term, gain very little from the move. The dams block the flow of silt upstream, and so deprive the soil downstream. The vast size of such reservoirs can also be dangerous in the event of earthquakes, and there is always a serious risk of conflict over them in cross-border basins. The negative consequences of such projects have proved inescapable, and experts now advise the construction of dams and reservoirs on a much smaller scale.

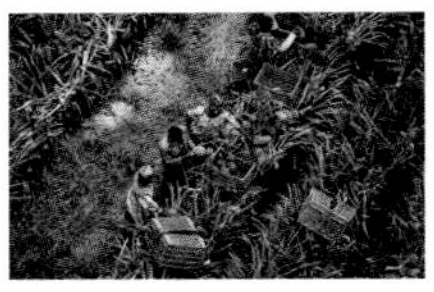

**PAGES 38–39**
PICKING PINEAPPLES, ABIDJAN, CÔTE D'IVOIRE
(5°19' N, 4°02' W)

Although Côte d'Ivoire is the biggest exporter of fresh pineapples to the European Union, the sector is suffering a crisis. Latin American countries are competing fiercely, and the EU is demanding higher standards in the traceability and level of chemical residues. Moreover, producers claim the Pineapple and Banana Trading Office is contributing to the continuing fall in prices, to the point that in 2003 they were lower than production costs. Worse still, since September 19, 2002, the crisis has been exacerbated by the country's civil war, not only because roads are closed but because farmland lies at the root of the conflict. Since 2001, Ivorians have angrily accused immigrants, chiefly from Mali and the Republic of Burkina Faso, who make up 30 percent of the population, of enriching themselves on their land. In the Bonoua district, immigrants have even been asked to stop growing pineapples, which are the area's chief resource.

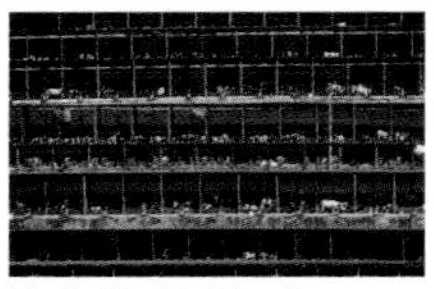

**PAGES 40–41**
CATTLE-RAISING NEAR FUKUYAMA (EAST OF HIROSHIMA), HONSHU, JAPAN
(34°31' N, 133°20' W)

Until World War II, most Japanese farmers devoted themselves chiefly to crops, only keeping two or three cows. Over the last fifty years, however, milk has become the country's second-biggest agricultural product after rice. With limited land available, most of it in valleys and on the outskirts of towns, Japan's farmers have concentrated on milk production and made it increasingly intensive, to meet growing consumer demand. Between 1975 and 1990, the number of cows rose by 160 percent while the number of farms, which became increasingly specialized, declined continuously. A Japanese cow today produces about 1,850 gallons (7,000 liters) of milk per year, while a French cow produces 1,438 gallons (5,450 liters). This trend is widespread in richer countries. It damages the rural economy, the diversity of food products, and the environment. Medium-sized farms are disappearing, and livestock farming is becoming separate from crops, breaking the natural cycle that returns to the soil the organic matter that animals took from it when feeding.

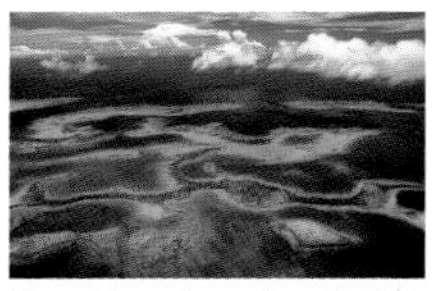

**PAGES 42–43**
NEUIKA CORAL REEF, NEW CALEDONIA (FRENCH OVERSEAS TERRITORY)
(22°50' S, 167°25' E)

The string of coral reefs that girdles the deep blue lagoon of New Caledonia is under threat. It is turning pale and dying, attacked by pollution generated especially by nickel extraction on Grande Terre, the territory's chief island. Every year, New Caledonia's opencast mines produce 118,000 metric tons of this metal—the tenth biggest production in the world. The industry is the archipelago's main economic resource, but it is a threat to the lagoon. Rainwater runs off from the mines into the sea, bringing waste that then settles on the surrounding coral. Many residents also suspect that the nickel treatment plants dump toxic waste and metals in suspension into the lagoon, and that these poison the coral reefs. These reefs are precious. Although they cover only 0.09 percent of the planet's seas and oceans, they are home to 2 million animal and plant species. But more than half are being damaged by human activities such as pollution, removal of coral, and dynamite fishing.

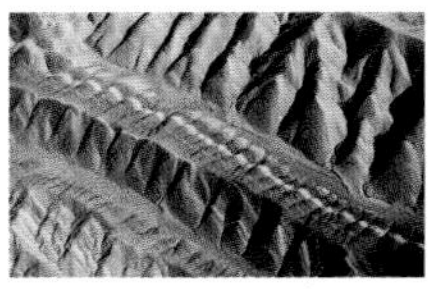

**PAGES 44–45**
MOUNTAINS IN GURVAN SAIKHAN NATIONAL PARK, IN THE ÖMNÖGOV (SOUTH GOBI), MONGOLIA
(45°30' N, 107°00' E)

The Gurvan Saikhan ("Three Beauties") national park owes its name to three groups of peaks, the "Beauties of the East, Center, and West" which tower over this ancient mountain range. Partly of volcanic origin, the range appeared between 550 million and 235 million years ago, like the Hercynian (that is, the Black Forest or central German) ranges in Europe or the Appalachians in the United States. These mountains are exceptionally rich in flora and fauna. Medicinal plants are plentiful, and two-thirds of the plant species endemic to Mongolia grow there. They are also home to fifty-two mammal species—eight of which are on the "red list" of Mongolia's threatened species, including the argali, the snow leopard, and the Siberian ibex—as well as 240 species of birds. Today, the chief threat to this fragile ecosystem is mining, for the Gobi is rich in coal, tungsten, copper, iron, gold, fluorite, molybdenum, anthracite, and semi-precious stones.

Failure to stop the fall in water tables will lead to the depletion of aquifers, an abrupt cutback in water supplies, and the risk of a precipitous drop in food production. With water emerging as the limiting factor for food production, productivity can no longer be thought of simply as yield per hectare, but also as yield per ton of water. One approach to improving water productivity is to use more efficient technologies, such as overhead sprinklers or drip irrigation. Another method is to shift to more water-efficient grains, such as from rice to wheat. Similarly, shifting animal-protein production to fish and poultry can raise the efficiency of grain use, and therefore the efficiency of water use.

Nonfarm water use is dominated by the use of water simply to wash away waste from factories and households or to dissipate heat from power plants. The use of water to disperse wastes is an outmoded practice that is getting the world into trouble. The current "flush and forget" system for human waste has four inherent problems: it is water-intensive; it disrupts the nutrient cycle; most of humanity cannot afford it; and it is a major source of disease in developing countries. Toxic industrial wastes discharged into rivers, lakes and wells can permeate aquifers, making water unsafe for drinking. They are also destroying marine ecosystems, including local fisheries.

The time has come for us to learn how to manage waste without discharging it into the local environment. For cities, the most effective single step to raise water productivity is to adopt a comprehensive water treatment and recycling system, reusing the same water continuously. In rural areas, composting toilets can prevent water waste and, in addition, will produce a rich, safe form of fertilizer that can then be returned to the land.

As the world moves into an era of scarcity, the challenge for governments is to take the politically unpopular step of adopting prices for water that reflect its value. Charging for water encourages greater efficiency by all users, from the farm to the factory to the kitchen sink. Pricing water to encourage efficiency without hurting low-income users is possible with a graduated pricing schedule, such as South Africa's lifeline rates, whereby each household receives a fixed amount of water for basic needs at a low price. When water use exceeds this level, the price escalates, ensuring that basic needs are met while discouraging waste.

Although stabilizing atmospheric $CO_2$ levels is a staggering challenge, it is nonetheless achievable. Detailed studies by governments and by various environmental groups are beginning to reveal the potential for reducing carbon emissions while saving money in the process. The accelerating rise in the Earth's temperature calls for simultaneously raising energy efficiency and shifting to renewables in order to cut carbon emissions in half.

Government mandated efficiency standards for household appliances, automobiles, and the construction of new buildings would be an easy first step, taking advantage of readily available technologies.

More complex is redesigning urban transport systems. Most systems, now automobile-centered, are highly inefficient, with the majority of cars carrying only the driver. Replacing this with a more diverse system that includes light-rail complemented with buses, and that was bicycle and pedestrian-friendly could increase mobility, reduce air pollution, and provide exercise, and former parking lots could be prime targets for city revitalization projects.

Greater use of clean, renewable energy sources, such as wind, solar, and geothermal, would significantly reduce carbon emissions, but the current market has not generally favored their development. Wind in particular offers a powerful alternative to fossil fuels. Abundant, inexhaustible, cheap, widely distributed, climate-benign, and clean, wind has been the world's fastest-growing energy source over the last decade. Advances in design have brought wind energy prices down below 4¢ per kilowatt-hour at prime sites, on par with fossil fuels.

The transport sector is a leading source of carbon dioxide emissions, second only to power generation. Fortunately, the technology to halve automobile emissions is already available in the form of gas-electric hybrid engines. These "hybrids" can get 55 miles to the gallon [23 kilometers per liter], and as gasoline prices rise, they are quickly gaining popularity.

Next is to add a plug-in capacity and a second battery to the gas-electric hybrid model. By increasing its electricity storage capacity, motorists could do their daily commuting, shopping, and other short-distance travel largely with electricity. This could easily lop 20 percent off gasoline use in addition to the initial 50 percent cut made by shifting the U.S. automobile fleet to gas-electric hybrids. This combined with investing in wind farms across the Unites States to feed cheap electricity into the grid would enable us to power our cars largely with clean wind energy.

Each year the taxpayers of the world underwrite $700 billion of subsidies for environmentally destructive activities, such as fossil fuel burning, overpumping aquifers, clearcutting forests, and overfishing. Shifting these subsidies to environmentally friendly, climate-benign energy practices, makes both economic and ecological sense. For example, shifting subsidies from road construction to rail construction could increase mobility while reducing carbon dioxide emissions. Incentives for growth in the renewable energy market could come in part from simply restructuring global energy subsidies—shifting the $210 billion in annual fossil fuel subsidies to the development of renewable energy production.

Along the same lines, it would make eminent sense to reduce income taxes while raising taxes on climate-disrupting energy sources. This form of tax shifting helps consumers understand the full costs of burning fossil fuels, and garners multiple dividends. In reducing taxes on income, labor becomes less costly, creating additional jobs while protecting the environment. This switch to more energy-efficient technologies and renewable sources of energy reduces carbon emissions and represents a shift to more labor-intensive industries. By lowering the air pollution from smokestacks and tailpipes, it also reduces respiratory illnesses and health-care costs. Tax shifting also helps countries gain a lead in technology development and deployment.

If developing countries add nearly 3 billion people by mid-century, as projected, population growth will continue to undermine efforts to improve the human condition. Stabilizing population is central to avoiding economic breakdown in countries with large projected population increases that are already overconsuming their natural capital assets. The challenge now is to create the economic and social conditions that will lead to population stability worldwide.

**POWER STATION AT HVIDOVRE ON THE BALTIC SEA, DENMARK** (55°39' N, 12°29' E)

Completed two years ago, this plant on the Baltic coast southeast of Copenhagen produces energy from renewable sources such as wind, but also from fossil fuels such as oil and coal. Although these produce pollution, the plant's builder claims that it uses new technologies that reduce toxic emissions by up to 80 percent. Power stations and cars are the chief sources of manmade air pollution. Children, the elderly, and those already n poor health are most at risk. According to the World Health Organization (WHO), almost 3 million people die every year from the effects of pollution. In Europe, half of these deaths are thought to be linked to vehicle emissions. Many countries, notably in South America, limit car use in large cities.

## ❯ MATERIAL GROWTH

The economic world of today is based on the exploitation of resources. Consequently, when an economy grows, its consumption of those resources undergoes a proportionate increase.

**GROWTH AND THE CONSUMPTION OF RESOURCES**
In less than a century, the number of objects around us has increased more than tenfold.
Between **1900** and **1995**, the average ecological footprint per individual in the industrialized countries multiplied by **5**.

**THE RESULT OF OUR CONSUMPTION: PRODUCTION OF WASTE**
The industrialized countries discharge into the environment, in the form of waste, between one-quarter and three-quarters of the natural resources they use.
In the industrialized countries, the volume of waste per person has tripled over the last **20 years**.

## ❯ THE USEFULNESS OF THINGS

**DOES MORE CONSUMPTION MEAN A BETTER LIFE?**
With the same standard of living, the ecological footprint of an American will be **double** that of a European. In the United States, each individual produces an average of **1,587 lb (720 kg)** of domestic waste a year, or **4.4 lb (2 kg)** a day.

**THE THROWAWAY SOCIETY**
In the industrialized countries, more than **80%** of products are discarded after being used just once.

**UNDERUSED GOODS**
The effective life of products is vastly inferior to their potential life. A drill, for example, may be used for **30 minutes** a year, but its lifespan could be **10 years**.

## ❯ THE HIDDEN FACE OF CONSUMER GOODS

Embodied energy: this is the amount of energy required for the life cycle of a product or service (extraction of raw materials, production, packaging, storage, distribution, transport, disposal, recycling).

**MIPS (MATERIAL INTENSITY OF A PRODUCT OR SERVICE): THE QUANTITY OF RESOURCES DAMAGED OR LOST IN THE MANUFACTURE OF A PRODUCT (INCLUDING ENERGY, RAW MATERIALS, WASTE)**
Gold ring weighing **5 g ≈ 2 tons** of raw materials
Pair of jeans weighing **0.6 kg ≈ 32 kg** of materials and **8,000 liters** of water
Computer ≈ from **8** to **14 tons** of non-renewable resources

Energy: producing **1 ton** of fuel requires the extraction of **1.25 tons** of crude oil
Transport: a journey of **15,000 km ≈ 1,260 liters** of fuel consumed
Food: producing **1 kg** of beef ≈ **2 liters** of fuel consumed
Electrical goods: the manufacture of **1** dishwasher ≈ **98 liters** of fuel consumed

## ❯ CHANGING THE BALANCE BETWEEN ECONOMIC GROWTH AND EXPLOITATION OF RESOURCES

**ECO-DESIGN: DESIGN THAT MINIMIZES THE ENVIRONMENTAL DAMAGE CAUSED BY A PRODUCT THROUGHOUT ITS LIFE CYCLE**
In the countries of the OECD (Organization for Economic Cooperation and Development), the building industry is responsible for consuming **25** to **40%** of energy, for **33** to **50%** of flow of products, and for large amounts of waste from construction and demolition.
"Housing of high environmental quality" is an increasingly popular approach which limits the environmental impact of construction or renovation while still ensuring that the interiors of buildings remain sanitary and comfortable.

**INCREASE THE PRODUCTIVITY OF RESOURCES**
Divide by **4** over **20 years** (factor 4), and by **10** over **50 years** (factor 10) the consumption of resources used for products and services.
Factor 4 applied to cars: a car would weigh **300 kg** rather than **1.2 tons** and it would use an average of **1.87 liters** of fuel instead of **7.5 liters** to cover 100 km.
Factor 4 is feasible even now for a large number of products.

**INDUSTRIAL ECOLOGY: INDUSTRIAL PRODUCTION DESIGNED TO REDUCE THE FLOW OF MATERIALS, ENERGY AND WASTE**
In Kalundborg, near Copenhagen, **5** industries (electricity generating station, oil refinery, pharmaceutical and chemical factories, cement works, and farming) draw some of their energy resources and raw materials from the waste produced by other industries. The annual savings are **45,000 tons** of oil, **15,000 tons** of coal, **600,000 m³** of water, and **175,000 tons** of $CO_2$.

## ❯ THE ECO-ECONOMY IN PRACTICE

**ECO-PRODUCTS**
A Patagonia PCR (= post-consumer recycled) Synchilla sweater: **90%** of the product can be made from recycled material. For one sweater, this would mean a saving of **1.12 liters** of fuel and **3 kg** of toxic waste that would otherwise pollute the atmosphere. A compact fluorescent light bulb lasts **5 times** longer than a standard bulb. For **15,000 hours** of light, a standard light bulb will cost **$120**, while an energy-saving bulb will cost **$35**: 3.4 times less.

**SHARING, NOT HOARDING**
A car spends on average **92%** of its time standing still.
Car-pooling would save the average person **57%** on fuel costs.

**MODERATION**
When we do not consume, we do not destroy resources or produce waste. Can we learn to distinguish between what we want and what we need?

**SUBSTITUTION**
**15,000 km** by car = **1,260 liters** of gasoline or 15,000 kWh. Using the bus, overground or underground trains, cycling, or simply walking instead of driving will save between 10,000 and 15,000 kWh a year, or **20** to **35 times** the annual cost of lighting a house.

---

❯ **BUDDHIST TEMPLE AT BAMIYAN, AFGHANISTAN** (34°49' N, 67°31' E)

On March 10, 2001, the Taliban, in their determination to remove all traces of any faith other than Islam, blew up the two famous sandstone Buddhas, sculpted more than 1,500 years ago, in the rocks overlooking the town of Bamiyan. These statues, 125 ft (38 m) and 180 ft (55 m) tall, stood in niches that protected them from erosion. Five flights of steps led the faithful up to the Buddhas' heads, which they could walk around using galleries inside the rock, decorated with frescoes. These in turn led to caves laid out as places of prayer or ceremony, with ceilings covered in plasterwork and paintings. In the 6th century about a thousand monks settled in the Bamiyan Valley, and Buddhism and Islam coexisted until the 9th century. The Buddhists of Bamiyan survived for another thousand years and more, but they had no defense against the Taliban. Today, all that can be done is to shore up the rocks shattered by the explosions, and to protect the paintings and the rest of the site against vandalism and looting. Shortly after their destruction, the remains of the sculptures were found on the art market.

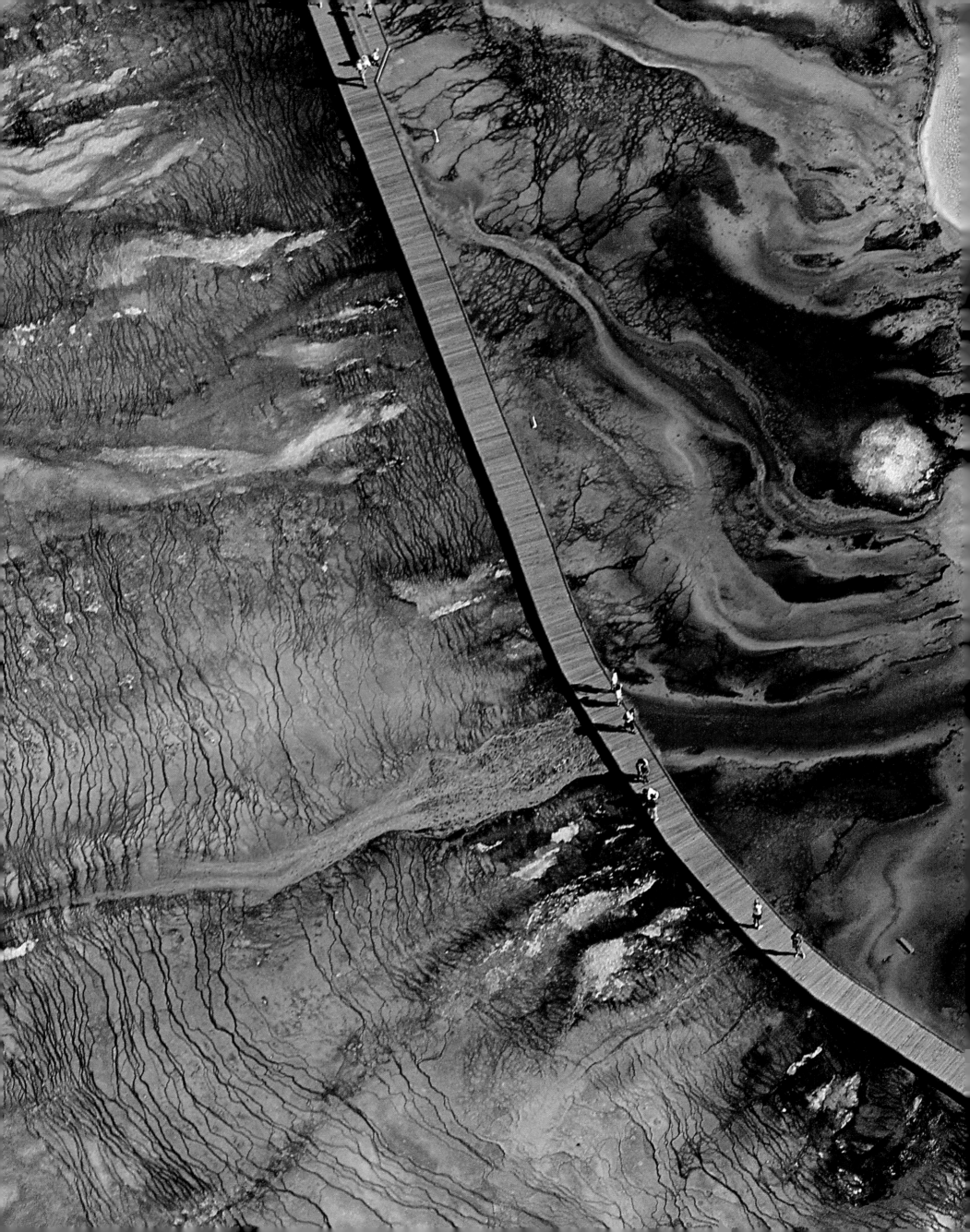

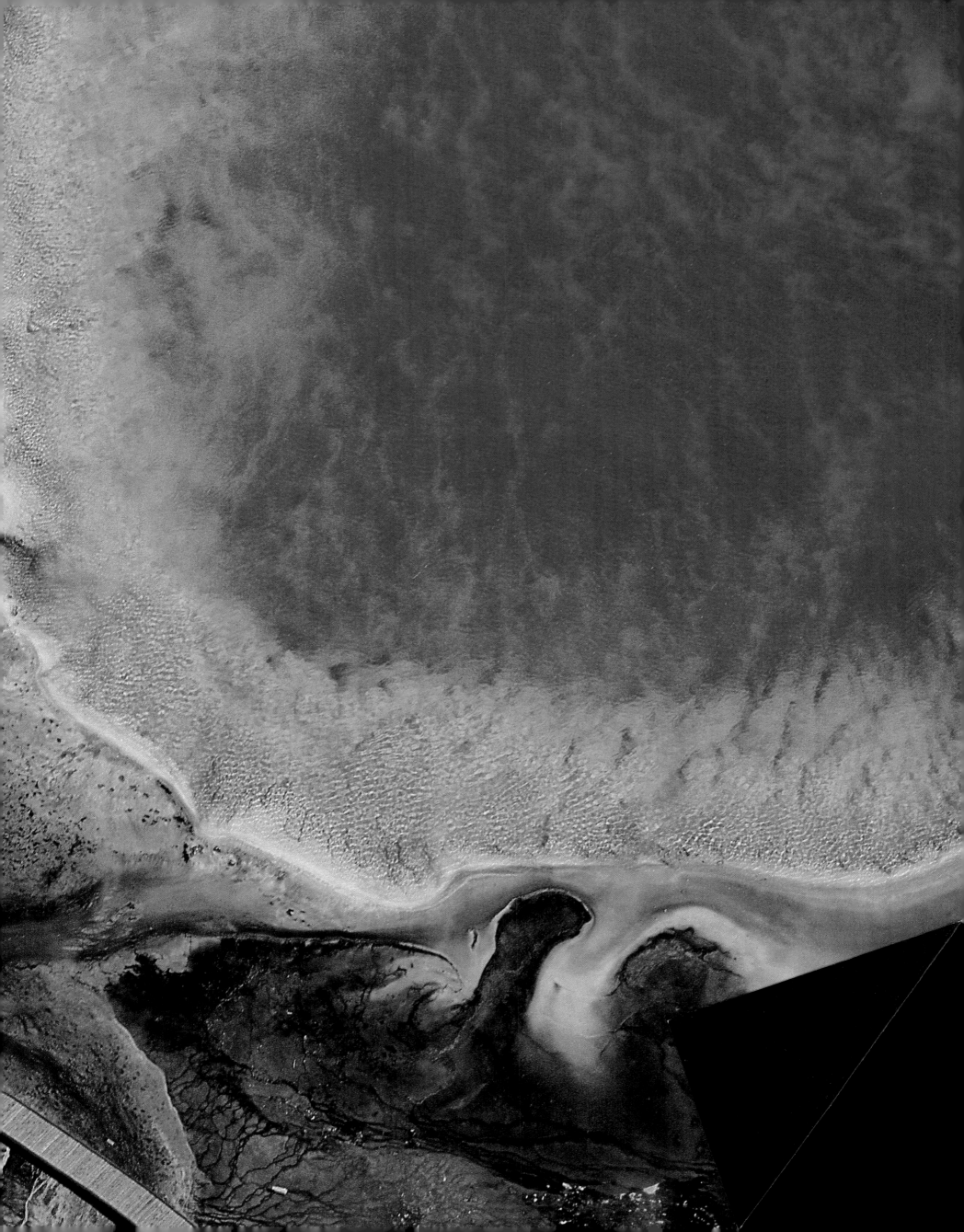

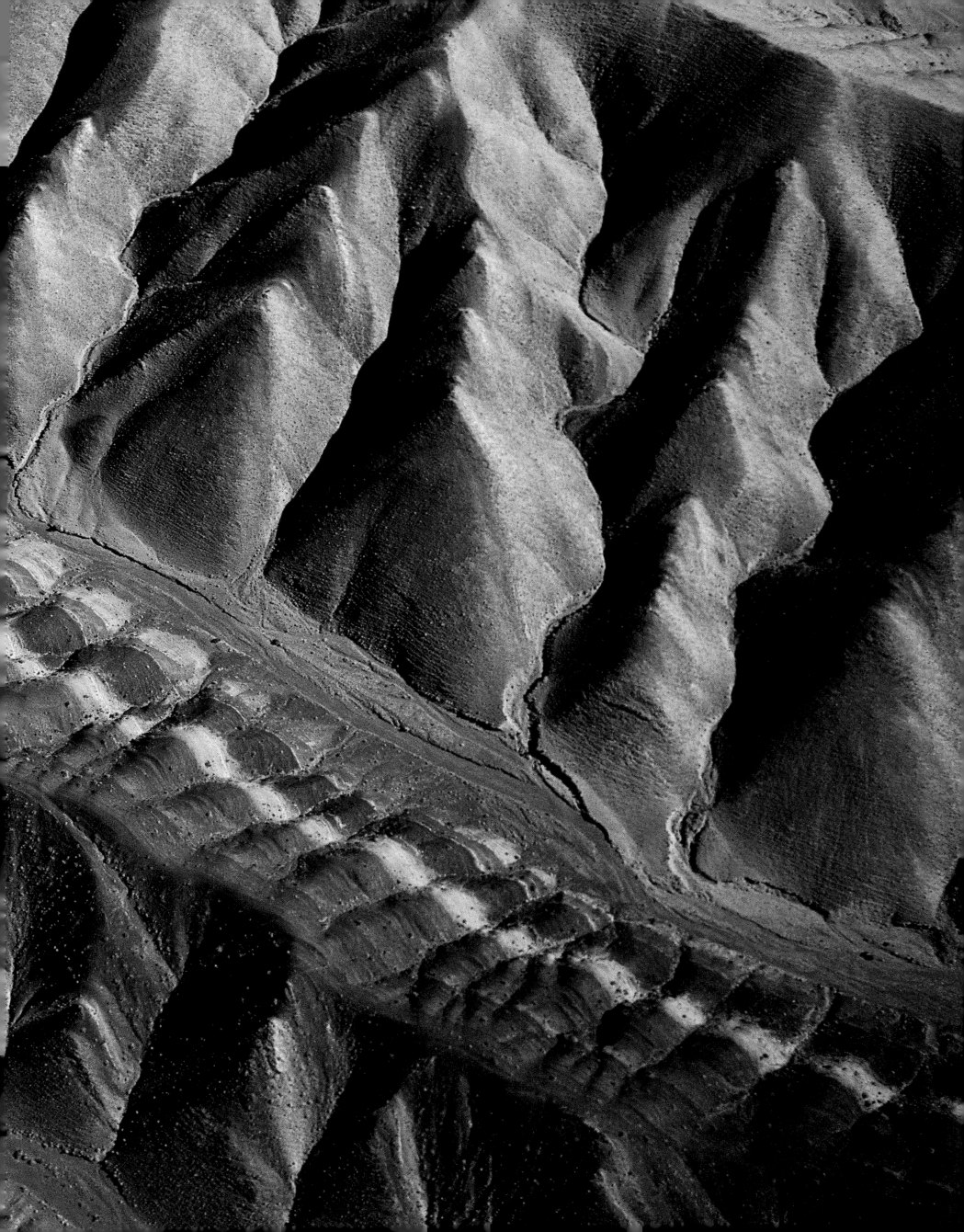

# WORLD POPULATION
# AND THE ENVIRONMENT

In the space of a century, population patterns have changed.
People have concentrated not only in cities but also along coastlines,
in the valleys of great rivers, and in metropolises. Observations on a finer
scale show the complexity of the relationships between people and
their environments. Political, economic, and social characteristics each
play an important role locally, which on the global scale grow even greater.

In the Roman period the world was inhabited by about 250 million people. Not until the Renaissance, fifteen centuries later, would the population exceed 500 million. The 1 billion mark was reached much more quickly, around 1810; 2 billion by 1930; 4 billion in 1975. Today we number more than 6 billion. Growth has therefore proceeded at an accelerated pace that has justly been called, since the 1950s, a demographic explosion. However, since 1970 the growth rate has slowed: from 2 percent in 1975 to 1.2 percent today. According to the United Nations, this gradually accelerating decline could lead to a stabilization of the population at 8 billion by about 2040. The deceleration is as surprising and abrupt as the acceleration that preceded it. It is also unique for a living species in that it does not result from an increase in the death rate but rather from an increasingly effective control of fertility.

When rapid growth occurs within an animal population, it is referred to as a "disruption," to indicate clearly that the species has briefly escaped the control of the forces that maintain it in balance with its environment. Usually order is restored by a high death rate, which returns the population to its habitual level, often called its "carrying capacity." Sometimes the environment is irremediably changed—as occurred with the introduction of dogs, rats, and rabbits in Australia and the Pacific Islands—and a new balance is established between living species. The human situation is different. This species has invaded the entire world, to the point of global disruption. Our species thus avoids the sword of mortality. In fact, instead of a rise in the death rate, for the past fifty years we have experienced a dizzying drop in the

death rate: the global life expectancy was 50 years in 1960; it rose to 60 years in 1980; and it is now 65.

Humans' relations with their surroundings are thus much more complex than those of other species. The first reason for this is the extreme heterogeneity of human populations, in terms of living standards, density, dietary habits, and consumption. To cite just a few examples, a Laotian emits as much greenhouse gas as a German, because of the deforestation and slash-and-burn farming common in Laos. Conversely, Bangladesh, which holds 120 million people squeezed onto 55,600 square miles (144,000 km²) (slightly smaller than the state of Wisconsin), emits less greenhouse gas than the city of Chicago alone. The relationships between population density and environmental preservation are paradoxical. Twenty or thirty nomads pushing their herds to overgraze in the Sahel will seriously alter an ecosystem that is already fragile and contribute to the desert's encroachment, whereas several hundred residents per square mile in the rice fields of Java or the Philippines manage to live in a delicate balance with nature.

The second reason for the loss of contact between nature and humans is the means of production of material goods and food and their increasingly global nature. Local cultures, which maintain contact with the immediate environment, are profoundly changed by the current globalization. To understand, for instance, the pillaging of the Amazonian forest, we must first take into account Brazil's social system, in which poor peasants are constantly pushed into new lands on the "frontier," they become burdened with debt, and then sell the land back to large companies that finish the job of soil exhaustion through intensive farming. These companies are following the rules of the world market: sorghum and corn are harvested for livestock in North America, and coffee is sold to the entire world. We thus see how, in the final analysis, the social and political systems on the national or global scale are responsible for establishing—or, rather, upsetting—relations between people and their surroundings. These systems must be questioned in order to understand the current evolution of population, the death rate, and fertility.

We can point out four large classes of populations with highly defined traits and problems: Communist nations; Subsaharan Africa; the most developed countries; and emerging nations.

[<] **EROSION ON THE SLOPES OF A VOLCANO NEAR ANKISABE, NEAR ANTANANARIVO, MADAGASCAR** (19°04' S, 46°39' E)

The origins of the Malagasy people are little known; the first residents apparently settled on the island a mere 2,000 years ago, arriving from Africa and Indonesia in successive waves of migration. For centuries the island has practiced traditional farming by slash-and-burn cultivation, known as *tavy*, which has been particularly devastating for the natural environment. Intensified overexploitation in recent decades, due to major demographic growth (the island's population has almost tripled in less than 30 years), has led to anarchic deforestation, wiping out more than 80 percent of the primary forest that once covered 90 percent of the island at the turn of the century; every year nearly 600 square miles (1,500 km²) of forest are destroyed. Deprived of vegetal cover, the humus and loose earth are stripped away by the rains, uncovering a layer of clay that is permanently infertile and digging networks of ravines, known as *lavakas*. Faced with the disappearance of arable land, the Malagasy peasants also exploit steep, hilly regions. However, Madagascar's biodiversity offers enormous potential for development; 98 percent of the island's mammals and 68 percent of its plants do not exist anywhere else. For example, the unique pink periwinkle is used by the pharmaceutical industry to produce treatments for leukemia.

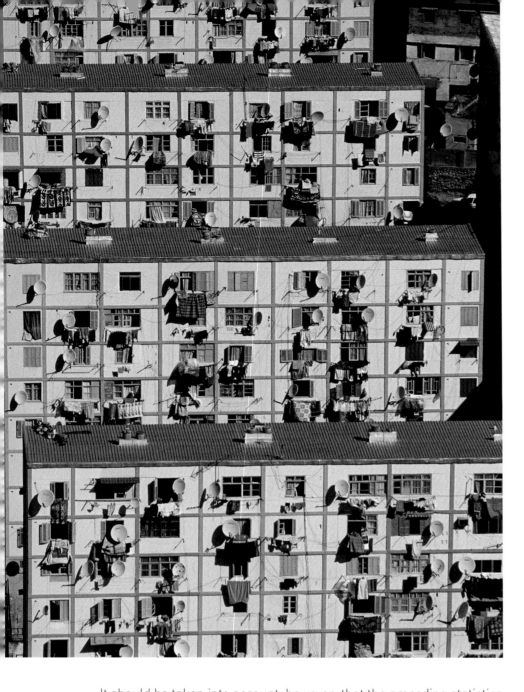

well as in production allowed people to concentrate not just in cities but along coastlines, the valleys of great rivers, and in metropolises, urban blankets that can extend for more than 60 miles (100 km). The record for size is held by two Japanese urban areas, Kansai (comprised of Osaka, Kobe, and Kyoto) and Kanto (Tokyo and Yokohama), which each have a total population of 35 million. The region of all of Provence, in southern France, must be broken up to understand its population patterns: the coastline has 1,600 inhabitants per square mile (1,000 per km²); the next 6 miles (10 km) inland have 160 residents per square mile (100 per km²); and the next area has fewer than 16 people per square mile (10 per km²); whereas the region of Haute Provence has fewer than 3 inhabitants per square mile (2 per km²).

This new pattern of concentration creates pollution problems. In Los Angeles, for instance, the air at low altitude is trapped in the shoreline basin and does not get renewed, in the absence of wind, so pollution builds up and directly affects the climate. This also occurs in Alsace, in eastern France, and in the neighboring area of Baden, Germany, squeezed between the Vosges Mountains and the Black Forest. Athens also suffers low-altitude pollution; "nephos" is their term for the greenish cloud of pollution that blocks the atmospheric layer (known as "atmospheric inversion," because in theory warm air is supposed to rise) and masks nearly all sunlight over the city one day out of five. To make matters worse, these population densities are found in spaces that are often sensitive and ecologically important, such as ecotones (transitional areas between two different ecological systems), maritime coasts, and regions with complex hydrological systems of great rivers (which are popular locations for metropolises).

It should be taken into account, however, that the preceding statistics on population refer to states that are often immense, such as the 1 billion Indians or the 300 million Americans. Yet contact between humans and the environment occurs on a far smaller scale, on the level of communities. Unfortunately, local data are inferior to national data, because statistics remain an instrument of nations, which are primarily interested in their own functioning and survival as organized, centralized states. In an examination on a smaller scale, different problems appear. Population distribution in space, more than its total volume, becomes a key factor. In one century the population distribution has been transformed. Since time immemorial the world had been characterized by a landscape populated but, only here and there, densely concentrated in cities. In 1700 Edo (the future Tokyo), with 800,000 inhabitants, was the largest city. Advances in transportation as

A century ago the German geographer Friedrich Ratzel published *Anthropogeography*, in which he stressed the importance of the links between a population and its territory. We started with some figures on global population, but to gain a better sense of the problems we face today we must observe environmental interaction on a local scale. In the final analysis, individual cultures play a critical role. Population numbers and technology are perhaps less decisive factors than the cultural traits that govern the relations between humans and their environment. Education, cultural diversity, and adaptability are more crucial than raw demographic numbers as we struggle to maintain a beautiful, diverse Earth.

HERVÉ LE BRAS

**APARTMENT BLOCKS ON SIDI M'HAMED HEIGHTS, ALGIERS, ALGERIA**
(36°45' N, 3°1' E)

The satellite dishes on these apartment blocks are turned toward Europe, in order to pick up French and other European TV channels. On the other side of the Mediterranean, in the suburbs of French cities, the same dishes are turned toward Algeria. The Algerian diaspora promotes cultural unity by sharing the same television news from all over the world. This phenomenon is now widespread in cities, although the countryside is less well equipped. With the growth of satellite TV, radio and the Internet, sounds, words and images now travel at incredible speeds and city-dwellers all over the world have access to the same products of culture. Although this has made world culture more homogeneous to some degree, it has also made it richer and more cosmopolitan: through developing technologies and democratization of the media, communities are setting up their own channels in their own languages, and spreading their culture internationally.

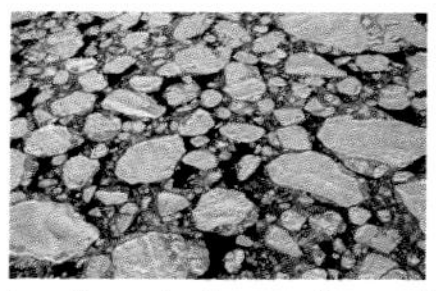

**PAGES 54–55**
LANDSCAPE OF ICE, NUNAVUT TERRITORY, CANADA
(75°57′ N, 92°28′ W)

Ice floes in the Arctic melt and break up into round blocks—a sign that spring has arrived in Nunavut, which means "our land" in the language of the Inuit. Whales and other marine animals can now make their way through the blocks of ice. This combination of archipelago, water, and ice has protected the Inuit civilization for some 5,000 years, across an area of 750,000 square miles (2 million km²). Generation after generation of Inuits have learned to read the ice, but their hunters are now faced with the increasing effects of global warming on their territory, and it is no longer safe for them to travel across the ice floes without information provided by satellite technology. Since 1960 the average thickness of ice in the Arctic has been reduced by half, and temperatures have risen by more than 36°F (20°C). "The Earth is literally changing beneath our feet," said a member of the ICC (Inuit Circumpolar Conference) in 2003.

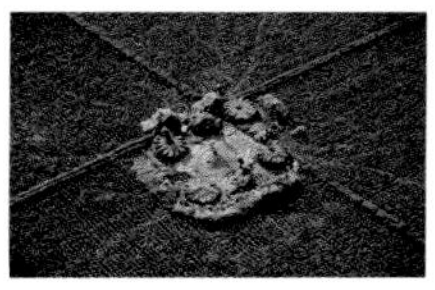

**PAGES 56–57**
WORKERS IN THE FIELDS BETWEEN CHIANG MAI AND CHIANG RAI, THAILAND
(16°41′ N, 100°11′ E)

Rice plantations occupy nearly 15 percent of Thailand, dominating the country's landscapes as far as the valleys of the north, around the cities of Chiang Mai and Chiang Rai. Rice is generally harvested in small family farms in the traditional manner: it is beaten by hand in the fields before it is carried into the villages, where it is stored and then sold. Thailand is the leading exporter of rice in the world. Every year the country sells 8 million tons abroad, one-third of its annual crop. Nearly 120,000 varieties of rice exist throughout the world, but the expansion of modern commercial agriculture, which favors monoculture of high-yield crops (one crop only is grown on two-thirds of the rice fields of Southeast Asia), is gradually reducing this agricultural diversity. In China almost 3,000 local varieties of rice have been lost in the past thirty years. This means the loss of genetic potential for the improvement of cultivated plants, while increasing the risk of poor harvests because of the uniform vulnerability of crops to new illnesses and pests. Rice constitutes the basic foodstuff for more than half of the Earth's population, and Asia provides 92 percent of the annual harvest worldwide.

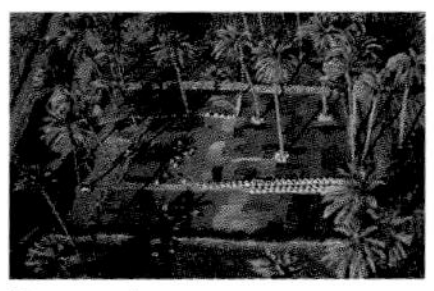

**PAGES 58–59**
DRYING DATES IN A PALM GROVE SOUTH OF CAIRO, NILE VALLEY, EGYPT
(29°43′ N, 31°17′ E)

Date palm trees are grown only in hot, arid areas with water resources, such as oases. Five million tons of dates are produced each year worldwide. Most of the production from the Near East and North Africa is intended for each country's domestic market and only 5 percent is exported. Egypt, the world's second-leading producer, after Iran, harvests more than 800,000 tons of dates each year, which are consumed locally at a rate of 22 pounds (10 kg) per person per year. These dates are generally preserved in traditional ways. Fresh-picked, yellow or red depending on the variety, the dates slowly turn brown as they dry in the sun, protected from the wind and water by a small wall of earth and branches. They are then kept in baskets woven from palms. Although most of the dates produced go on the table, several derivatives (including syrup, flour, dough, vinegar, sugar, alcohol, and pastries) are made from the fruit, either manually or industrially.

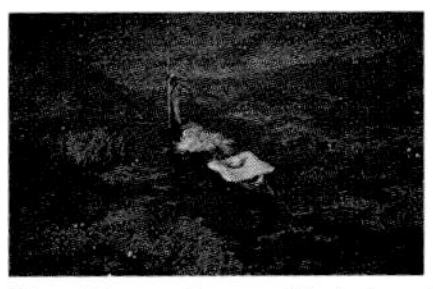

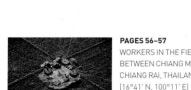

**PAGES 60–61**
PIROGUE ON THE NIGER RIVER IN THE GAO REGION, MALI
(16°12′ N, 0°01′ W)

The Niger river, which has its source in the massif of Fouta Djallon in Guinea, is the third-longest (2,600 miles, or 4,184 km) river in Africa, and flows through Mali, Niger, and Nigeria. Crossing through Mali for a length of 1,050 miles (1,700 km), it forms a large loop that rises to the southern border of the Sahara, watering major centers such as Timbuktu and Gao. In Mali, life revolves around the Niger: economic activity is confined to its shores, and 80 percent of the population live on fishing or on agriculture, which depends on irrigation. The river is also the most common means of transport for a population of 13 million, 65 percent of whom live below the poverty line. But as well as being under threat from desertification and pollution, the Niger has for several years been invaded by a beautiful and deadly flower—the water hyacinth, which literally asphyxiates the fish. Mali and the other countries along the river are doing their utmost to fight this green pest. Having already been hard hit by a plague of locusts in 2004–2005, the country is now all the more dependent on the good health of its river.

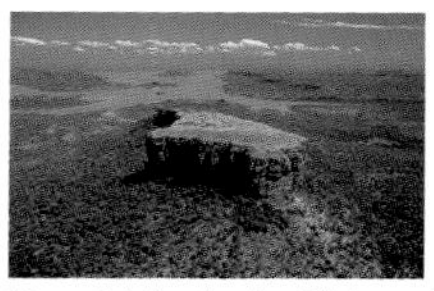

**PAGES 62–63**
MOUNT TRAFALGAR, PRINCE REGENT NATURE RESERVE, WEST KIMBERLEY, AUSTRALIA
(15°16′ S, 125°03′ E)

The wild Kimberley Plateau, between the Timor Sea and the Gibson Desert, is one of the most thinly populated areas on the planet. It is the true outback: the remote upcountry of western Australia whose vast area—occupying almost one-third of the country, an area five times the size of France—is home to just 1.8 million people. UNESCO has designated the basin of the Prince Regent River a Biosphere Reserve because of its remarkable, intact habitats: in 2002 there was still not a single road through it. The reserve is surrounded by Aboriginal lands—the name "Aborigine" means "one who has been there from earliest times." Killed in large numbers by European settlers, the Aboriginal population has recovered to stand at 265,000 people, of whom three-quarters are of mixed heritage. In Aboriginal culture, Mount Trafalgar symbolizes harmony between humans and the Earth, rocks, and other living things, all created by ancestral spirits.

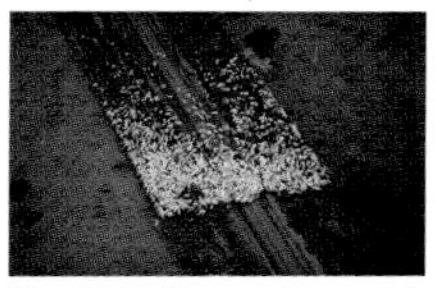

**PAGES 64–65**
HERD OF ZEBU ON A ROAD NEAR CÁCERES, MATO GROSSO DO NORTE, BRAZIL
(16°05′ S, 57°40′ W)

The Mato Grosso is one of Brazil's richest agricultural regions, where livestock and crops are raised on immense, extensive farms called *fazendas*. Almost two-thirds of the country's cultivable land is owned by less than 3 percent of the population; of those land holdings, half are not farmed at all. At the same time, more than 25 million landless peasants support themselves by itinerant farm labor. This situation has led to violent conflict, which has killed more than 1,000 people over the last ten years. The struggle is driven by the Movimento dos Sem Terra (Landless Movement), which is fighting for fairer distribution of farmland. Since 1985, direct occupation of land has forced the state to grant ownership to more than 250,000 families. However, only agricultural reform can improve matters—but no government has yet dared to commit itself to it, for fear of going against the interests of rich landowners and the multinationals active in Brazil.

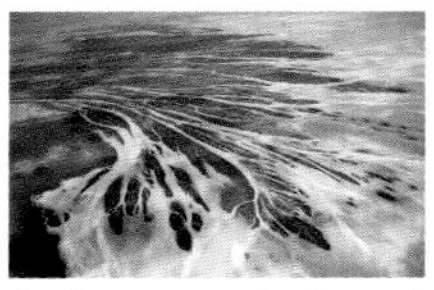

**PAGES 66–67**
SEBJET ARIDAL, NEAR BOUJDOUR, WESTERN SAHARA, MOROCCO
(26°12′ N, 14°05′ W)

As they evaporate, the waters that feed this *sebjet* or *sebkha* (temporary salt lake) carve channels in the sand and leave behind deposits of salt. The sebkha can be of great economic importance to regions such as this, at the heart of the Western Sahara, which extends some 1,500 miles (2,500 km) along the Atlantic, covering an area half the size of France. Once a Spanish colony, this region is rich in underground deposits of phosphate and coastal fishing grounds, and it was claimed by Morocco when the Spanish left in 1975, much against the will of the local people—the Saharawi nomads, who are represented by the Polisario Front. Although they have never been granted any kind of sovereignty, the Moroccans broke the resistance of the Saharawi and built 180 miles (300 km) of walls across the open desert, separating hundreds of families. Some 400 Moroccan soldiers are still engaged in fighting the Polisario Front, but this conflict is due to be resolved by a referendum in 2009. However, much has changed since 1975, and the number of Moroccans who have settled in the region is now greater than that of the native Saharawi.

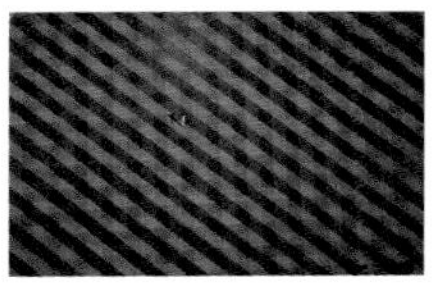

**PAGES 68–69**
YANKEE STADIUM, NEW YORK CITY, UNITED STATES
(40°50′ N, 73°56′ W)

Standing in the heart of the Bronx, in New York City, Yankee Stadium has a meticulously maintained grass lawn. This famous ballpark, home to the New York Yankees, holds 55,000 spectators at baseball games. The national pastime was born in the United States just before 1850 and was soon professionalized. Practiced by more than 150 million players worldwide, which makes it the second most practiced sport after volleyball (180 million players), baseball was first included in the Olympic Games in 1992. This universal sporting event took place in Athens, Greece, in 2004, with athletes from 202 countries participating in 37 disciplines. Although the Olympics brings together almost all the countries of the world, it does not erase the disparities between them: at the Athens Games 2,618 medals were awarded, of which 1,617 (62 percent) went to 37 industrialized nations and 1001 (38 percent) to 36 developing nations.

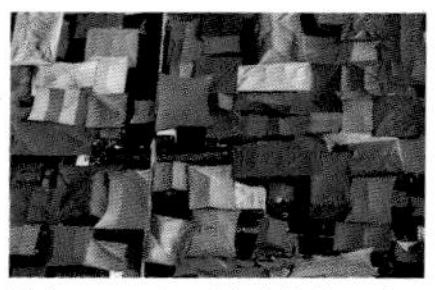

**PAGES 70–71**
MARKET NEAR XOCHIMILCO DISTRICT, MEXICO CITY, MEXICO
(19°20′ N, 99°05′ W)

This mosaic of brightly colored parasols hides a bustling, noisy market, set up for the day in a street of the capital. Shaded from the sun, stalls selling fruit and vegetables, herbal remedies, and spices sit side by side with others that sell cloth and craft artifacts. Mexico's flourishing markets are a national institution, held daily all over the country. Like their crafts, their traditional clothing, and the façades of buildings, the markets express Mexicans' love of vivid, bright colors, such as the brilliant pink known as "rosa Mexicana." Internationally, Mexico was a world champion of commercial growth between 1985 and 1999. Although the national GDP doubled during this period, it is only today that household consumption has begun to rise. This trend may benefit some of the wealthier urban population, but life has not improved for the majority of Mexicans, half of whom live below the poverty line. The social unrest that has troubled the state of Chiapas since 1994 is partly due to this.

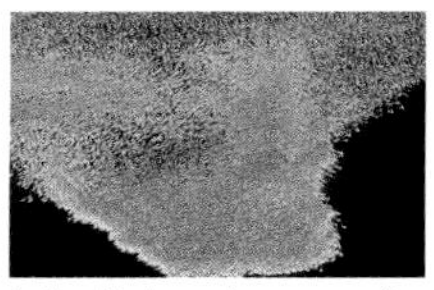

**PAGES 72–73**
GREATER FLAMINGOS ON LAKE NAKURU, KENYA
(0°17′ S, 36°04′ E)

Lake Nakuru has a surface area of 17 square miles (44 km²) and takes up one-third of the national park of the same name that was created in 1968. It shelters nearly 400 bird species, including the lesser flamingo (*Phoeniconaias minor*) and the greater flamingo (*Phoenicopterus ruber*), of which 1.4 million have been counted on the site. Like the other alkaline lakes scattered along the Rift Valley, its location on a rocky volcanic substrate, weak flow, intense evaporation, and average depth of 40 inches (1 m) give it a high soda content. These briny waters are favorable to the formation of blue-green algae, microorganisms, and small crustaceans, which provide the staple diet of flamingos. However, deforestation in the region, chemical products used in river farming and the water runoff from the nearby city of Nakuru have gradually polluted the lake waters, to the detriment of the local wildlife and people. Since 1990 Lake Nakuru has been classified as a Wetland of International Importance.

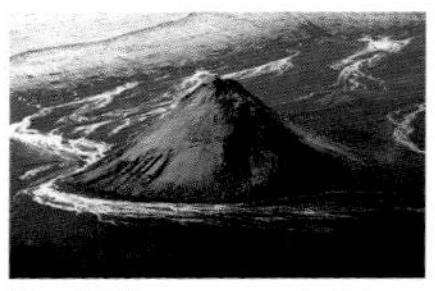

**PAGES 74–75**
MAELIFELL, BORDERING THE MYRDALSJÖKULL GLACIER, ICELAND
(63°47′ N, 18°56′ W)

Maelifell was created by one of the many eruptions under the Myrdalsjökull glacier in southern Iceland. It is a volcanic tuff, a cone made up of an accumulation of solidified ash and other volcanic material. Freed from the glacier about 10,000 years ago, Maelifell is now bathed by the rivers that flow from the glacier. Its perfect cone, rising to 650 feet (200 m) above the plain, is covered with grimmia, a moss that proliferates on cooled lava, which varies in color from silver-gray to luminous green, depending upon the soil's humidity. It is one of relatively few plants to have flourished in Iceland, which has fewer than 1,300 recorded plant species (including 500 mosses) and only 40 percent of its land covered with permanent vegetation. Geologically very young, only 23 million years old, Iceland has more than 200 active volcanoes and many glaciers, which comprise nearly one-eighth of the area of the island.

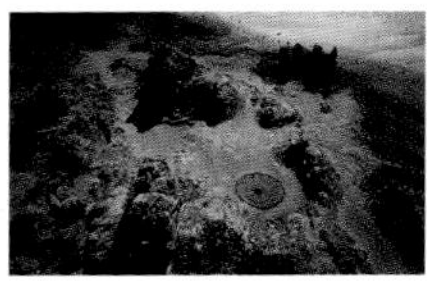

**PAGES 76–77**
ENCLOSED NEOLITHIC TOMB, SOUTH OF DJANET, TASSILI N'AJJER, ALGERIA
(24°26′ N, 9°34′ E)

In the Sahara there are a large number of tombs from the Neolithic period, which extended from the first appearance of agriculture some 10,000 years ago to the first forms of writing 5,000 to 4,000 years ago. Generally they are simple structures covered with a pile of similarly sized stones to form a tumulus. In Tassili N'Ajjer these enclosed sepulchers are particularly numerous, and the oldest of them date back some 5,500 years. Systematically dug into the hills, they are visible from far away. There is a first circle around the tumulus, beneath which lies the burial chamber, and a second circle surrounding the whole structure. Only men were buried there, laid on their side with their heads facing east. There are thousands of such painted or engraved relics in the Sahara going back thousands of years, and they make this desert into the world's largest open-air museum of the Neolithic period.

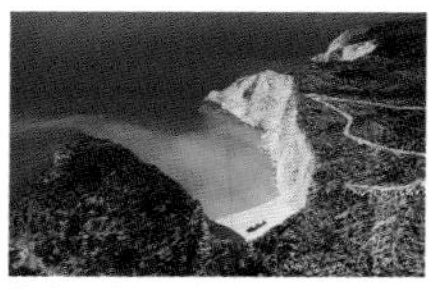

**PAGES 78–79**
BOAT RUN AGROUND, ZAKYNTHOS, IONIAN ISLANDS, GREECE
(37°54′ N, 20°39′ E)

Zakynthos, the southernmost of the Ionian islands and the second-largest in area, is situated 10 miles (16 km) off the shore of the Peloponnese. It takes its name from the abundant wild hyacinths that grow there. One part of the island features imposing chalky cliffs, lined with white gypsum, which have crumbled away—from the effects of erosion and several earthquakes, the most serious of which occurred in 1953—forming beaches of fine sand. These beaches are favorite egg-laying sites of loggerhead turtles (*Caretta caretta*). However, boat propellers, pollution, urbanization, and tourism have all affected the numbers of sea turtles that come to Zakynthos, which now range between 800 and 2,000 animals. Conservation measures and public awareness campaigns since 1981, reinforced by the creation of the Zakynthos National Marine Park in 2000, are now starting to bear fruit. A few of the best-known endangered species, including sea turtles, benefit from ambitious protection programs. Nevertheless, one-fourth of the Earth's mammal species, one-third of fish species, and one-eighth of bird species are still threatened with extinction today.

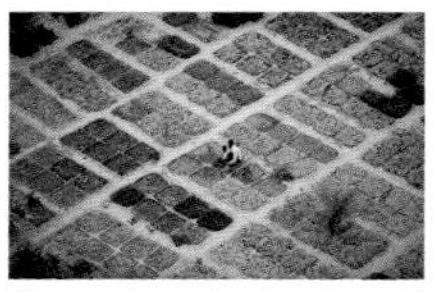

**PAGES 80–81**
MARKET GARDENING NEAR TIMBUKTU, MALI
(16°48′ N, 3°04′ W)

Situated on the borders of the Sahara and the Sahel, Timbuktu endures temperatures which during the day can rise to 122°F (50°C), while rainfall is never more than 150 mm a year and the soil is clay. In such conditions, agriculture poses an enormous challenge. The dunes are stabilized by belts of trees (often fruit trees) and protective barriers, so that the vegetation can sink its roots. The gardens are laid out in tiny plots about 3 ft (1 m) square, and water is used as sparingly as possible, enabling them to survive these extreme conditions. They produce vegetables (peas, fava beans, lentils, haricot beans, cabbages, lettuces) for a population that suffers from vitamin deficiencies and a lack of mineral salts. This market gardening is a way of combating the advance of the sands—driven by the *harmattan* wind blowing from the Sahara—which take over more and more land every year and are threatening to engulf Timbuktu and its ancient heritage.

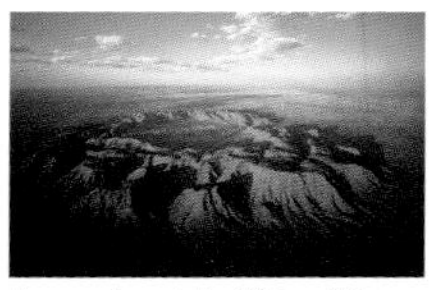

**PAGES 82–83**
GOSSE'S BLUFF METEOR CRATER, NORTHERN TERRITORY, AUSTRALIA
(23°49′ S, 132°19′ E)

Approximately 135 million years ago a meteorite fell on Australian soil, devastating more than 8 square miles (20 km²) in what is now the Northern Territory. Today a crater 3 miles (5 km) in diameter and 500 feet (150 m) deep remains, called Gosse's Bluff; it is known as *Tnorala* to the Aboriginal people. Thousands of meteorites fall to the Earth's surface each year, but they are usually less than 3 feet (1 m) in diameter and cause no damage because they fragment and burn on entering the atmosphere, reaching the ground as dust. Although it is rare, the arrival of meteorites or asteroids more than 30 feet (10 m) in diameter can cause serious damage, and even lead to the worldwide extinction of species. This is what is believed to have killed off the dinosaurs some 65 million years ago. Such wide-scale extinctions are not only a thing of the past and do not always originate from extraterrestrial sources, however. We are currently experiencing the sixth major wave of extinctions in the planet's history but, this time around, the human race itself is the cause.

Current and former Communist countries show certain shared traits. Fertility is declining rapidly in these countries: 1.25 children per woman in Russia, Ukraine, and Belarus; 1.3 in Romania, Bulgaria, Hungary, and Lithuania; 1.5 in Cuba; 1.7 in China. The mortality trend in these countries is even more striking. Throughout the world the death rate is declining, yet their rates have often increased in the past 20 or 30 years: from 70 years in 1970, Russia's life expectancy has fallen to 66 years today. All of Eastern Europe has lost one year of life expectancy in the course of each of the past three decades. The same trend is seen in the other Communist regimes, such as North Korea and ex-Soviet Central Asia. Despite their economic success, the Chinese have gained only 3.5 years of life expectancy in 20 years, while their neighbors in India, Pakistan, and Thailand have gained 10. These poor performances have no obvious connection with economic level, climate, or population density. They probably are the more general expression of a profound disturbance in relations with the environment resulting from an arrogant productivism and the idea that centralized technology can dominate nature. As for the declining fertility, aside from the imposed Chinese policy of only one child, it contradicts the notion of the proletariat (etymologically, the term comes from the Latin word for "progeny") and in ten years has caused (along with emigration) a reduction in the populations of Russia, Ukraine, and Belarus. These populations will have to deal with the severe consequences of a total contempt for ecological balances, including drying up the Aral Sea, the salination of the lands of Central Asia, and the creation of gigantic nuclear waste cans.

Subsaharan Africa seems to be confronted by a "curse" of underdevelopment. Here is a vast area less populous than the world average: the Democratic Republic of Congo has 56 inhabitants per square mile, Gabon and the Central African Republic have 5 inhabitants per square mile. The region enjoys a nature that is often luxuriant and rich in abundant mineral resources, and yet the standard of living is declining, and the death rate is rising. Over the past several years, life expectancy has dropped by 10 years in Zambia and 15 years in Zimbabwe, primarily because of Aids. At the same time, the birth rate in these same countries is declining slowly. These problems are the direct result of political troubles and the inability of governments to ensure the maintenance of services. In addition, the subcontinent has collided with the world economy, which after having upset its equilibrium twice, through the slave trade and then through colonization, has lost interest except to drain it of resources (large plantations and precious minerals). Left to their own devices and with a birth rate that is still growing at an elevated speed (2.3 percent a year in the west, east, and center of Africa, and 1.5 percent a year in the south), and without any economic progress, the farmers of these countries are forced to stretch the traditional modes of farming to the limit for the stationary population. The result is frequent ravages, such as the exhaustion and dispersal of fragile tropical soils because of the increased burnings of the land and the shortening of the periods during which the ground is left fallow and given time to recover.

The situation for the most developed countries, Europe, North America, and Japan, is obviously the opposite of those considered so far. Birth rates are low but stable (1.5 children per woman in Western Europe; 2 in North America; 1.35 in Japan) and the death rate, which has already fallen to levels considered impossible 30 years ago, continues to decline rapidly. The life expectancy in France rose from 72 to 80 years between 1975 and the present, in Japan it rose from 73.5 to 81.5 years, and in Germany from 71 to 79 years. This rise has meant 150,000 fewer deaths in France every year, which is a factor in demographic growth twice as great as immigration. Immigration from the southern hemisphere represents less than one-thousandth of the European population each year and, despite frequent public fears, should not increase as long as the demand for labor remains stagnant. The population of developed countries will thus continue to increase slowly, despite the low birth rate, and its impact on the global environment, which is already considerable, will grow, unless strict regulatory measures such as those proposed by the Kyoto agreement are put into practice. Eighty percent of greenhouse gas and chlorofluorocarbon emissions, responsible for the hole in the ozone layer, originate in developed countries.

Although their specific situations are very different, the majority of populations from developing countries have both a very rapid decline in birth rate and a rapid rise in life expectancy. This is where the real fate of our planet is played out. India, which has just passed the 1 billion population level, is an exemplary case among these emerging countries, which, despite great difficulties, are taking advantage of globalization. In thirty years India's birth rate declined from 5.7 to 3 children per woman, and life expectancy rose from 48 to 63 years. Mexico and Brazil (with a decline from 6 to 2.1 children per woman) and Indonesia (from 5.2 to 2.4 children) provide further examples of this extraordinary change. In the cities the birth rate is even lower; 1.8 children per woman in greater Cairo and in the federal district of Mexico City, which has a population of 22 million. But this success, the result of better education and women's rights as well as persistent economic development, has environmental risks as well. The rapidly growing middles classes are adopting a Western way of life—high meat consumption, intensive automobile usage—and cannot reduce the $CO_2$ and other greenhouse gas emissions that result. In addition, the availability of a skilled and low-cost workforce in developing nations attracts industries such as the treatment of toxic chemicals (which lead to the Bhopal catastrophe in India in 1984) and the relocalization of potentially dangerous industrial installations, which are banned from developing countries. This leads to increases in water, air, and land pollution.

From this summary we see how culture and global relationships affect a nation's relationship with the environment. Will Argentina, Venezuela, and Colombia join the group of former Communist countries in decline, or will they continue to grow as developing countries? These countries could be left behind by globalization, sharing the fate of Subsaharan Africa, or could become integrated into it—but at what price? Meanwhile, in Southeast Asia, is it possible to imagine China's population of 1.5 billion by the year 2050 and the similarly high population of India reaching the same standard of living, and thus of consumption, of North America today? And will this mean that India and China will create the same rate of $CO_2$ emissions and the same demand for meat (and thus for grains grown for dometic animals) as the North Americans and Europeans of today? This might appear to be a just outcome in social terms, but it would be absolutely catastrophic for the environment.

**MARATHON CROSSING THE VERRAZANO BRIDGE, NEW YORK CITY, UNITED STATES**
(40°36' N, 74°03' W)

Two centuries ago, the world's population was 1 billion; today it is 6.4 billion. The fear is that one day, like this crowd of marathon runners, it will be so dense that life on our planet will become impossible. It continues to increase at an alarming rate, by some 76 million people a year. But in contrast to the fears of just ten years ago, demographic growth has slowed down. By 2050 it should reach 8.9 billion, which is one billion less than forecast in 1990. The impact of Aids on Africa, which had been underestimated, and the quicker than expected flattening of the demographic curve in the developed countries are the main causes of this shift. The prime factor in population growth by 2050 will be greater life expectancy, with a ninefold increase in the number of people over 60 in developing countries. The real challenge is to combine this dynamic demographic expansion with sustainable forms of development.

## ⟩ THE EVOLUTION OF THE WORLD'S POPULATION

**IMBALANCE BETWEEN NORTH AND SOUTH**
**96%** of future demographic growth will take place in the developing countries.
By **2050**, **85%** of the world's population will be living in the developing countries.
Birth rate in the industrialized nations is currently **1.6** children per woman (below the rate required to maintain the present population, which is **2.1** per woman).
The populations of Europe and Japan are already shrinking, and the rate of reduction is likely to double between 2010 and 2015.

**CONTINUOUS GROWTH**
The current world population is **6.4 billion**.
Annual growth is now running at **76 million** people (**+1.18%**).
Between now and **2050**, the population will increase by **40%** to over **9 billion**.

**TOWARDS A PROGRESSIVE SLOWDOWN**
Demographic growth is slowing down after reaching its peak during the **1990s** at around **82 million** a year.
Since **1960**, the average number of children per woman has fallen from **6** to around **3**.
The world's population may begin to level off by the middle of the century, with the birth rate falling to the level of replacement or below.

## ⟩ THE ENVIRONMENT UNDER PRESSURE

**PRODUCTIVE LAND IS DISAPPEARING**
Concrete: more than **5,000 km²**—twice the area of Luxembourg—was built on every year between **1960** and **2000**.
During the last 50 years, degradation of the soil has reduced the amount of arable land by around **13%** and pasture land by around **4%**.
Deserts are increasing by **60,000 km²** a year.

**EXPLOITATION OF RESOURCES IS INCREASING FASTER THAN THE POPULATION**
Water: since the **1950s**, world demand for water has tripled.
Energy: since **1950**, world consumption of fossil fuels has increased sixfold.
Fishing: since **1960**, catches have quadrupled.

## ⟩ DEMOGRAPHIC GROWTH: THE REAL PROBLEMS

**SOCIAL SCHEMES AND INDIVIDUAL IMPACT**
Between **1970** and **2000**, with increased income, urbanization, and smaller families, the average number of people per household fell from **5.1** to **4.4** in developing countries, and from **3.2** to **2.5** in the industrialized nations.
Savings achieved through communal use of energy are being lost. In the United States, a single-person household uses **17%** more energy per head than a two-person household.

**DEBT AND POLITICAL GOVERNANCE OF POOR COUNTRIES**
The debts of the poor countries force them to overexploit their natural resources.

**ABUNDANCE AND CONSUMPTION OF PRODUCTS AND SERVICES**
One child born in the industrialized world adds more in his lifetime to levels of consumption and pollution than **30** to **50** children born in the developing nations.

## ⟩ INTERPRETING THE DOUBLE IMPACT OF THE POPULATION ON THE ENVIRONMENT

**POPULATION GROWTH INCREASES HUMAN DEMAND: ADDITIONAL EFFECTS**
Each individual needs a basic minimum to survive: **1.5 liters** of water and **2,000 calories** per day, together with energy, transport, and accommodation.
Since **1960**, the world's population has increased by **113%**.

**THE GROWTH OF INDIVIDUAL NEEDS INCREASES PRESSURE ON THE ENVIRONMENT: ACCUMULATIVE EFFECTS**
Since **1960**, the average worldwide ecological footprint of one person has increased by **30%**.

**INTERPRETING THE DOUBLE IMPACT**
Since **1960**, human impact on the environment has increased by **177%**.

## ⟩ WHO IS RESPONSIBLE FOR THE MOST DAMAGE?

**EXAMPLES OF INDIA AND THE UNITED STATES**
The population of the United States is one-fourth that of India, but its impact on the environment is **3** times greater. The United States discharges **15.7 million tons** of carbon dioxide into the atmosphere per year, compared to India's **4.9 million tons**.

An average North American town with a population of **650,000** needs **11,600 square miles (30,000 km²)** of land to provide for all its requirements. A similar town in India needs **1,080 square miles (2,800 km²)**.

The impact on the environment of the annual population growth of **3 million** in the USA is greater than that of **16 million** in India.

## ⟩ ENVIRONMENT AND POPULATION: HEADING FOR COMPULSORY CONTROLS?

**DESTRUCTION OF THE ENVIRONMENT HAS A DIRECT EFFECT ON THE POPULATION**
Air pollution kills nearly **3 million** people a year worldwide.

Desertification affects more than **800,000** people by causing the disappearance of farmland, loss of soil fertility, and increased poverty.

When the environment is destroyed, living creatures die in large numbers, as is currently the case with many species of plants and animals all over the world. The same thing may soon happen to the human species.

---

⟩ **GINSENG FARMING NORTH OF POCHON GUN, KYONGGI-DO PROVINCE, SOUTH KOREA** (38°10' N, 127°15' E)

Few medicinal plants have the reputation of ginseng; its Latin name *panax* even means "panacea," the universal remedy reputed to cure all illnesses. The earliest written references to the powers of ginseng date from the 1st century AD, but the Chinese have been using it for over 3,000 years. Two species of ginseng make up the majority of world production and trade: Asian ginseng (*Panax ginseng*) and American ginseng (*Panax quinquefolius*). Both varieties are undergrowth plants, which eat up nutrients and fear excess humidity and sunlight. While American ginseng is cultivated mainly in forests, Asian ginseng is grown in open fields, under large canopies that filter out almost 80 percent of the sun's rays. This means that growth conditions are optimized and the ginseng can be harvested after only three or four years (as opposed to eight to ten years in forests).

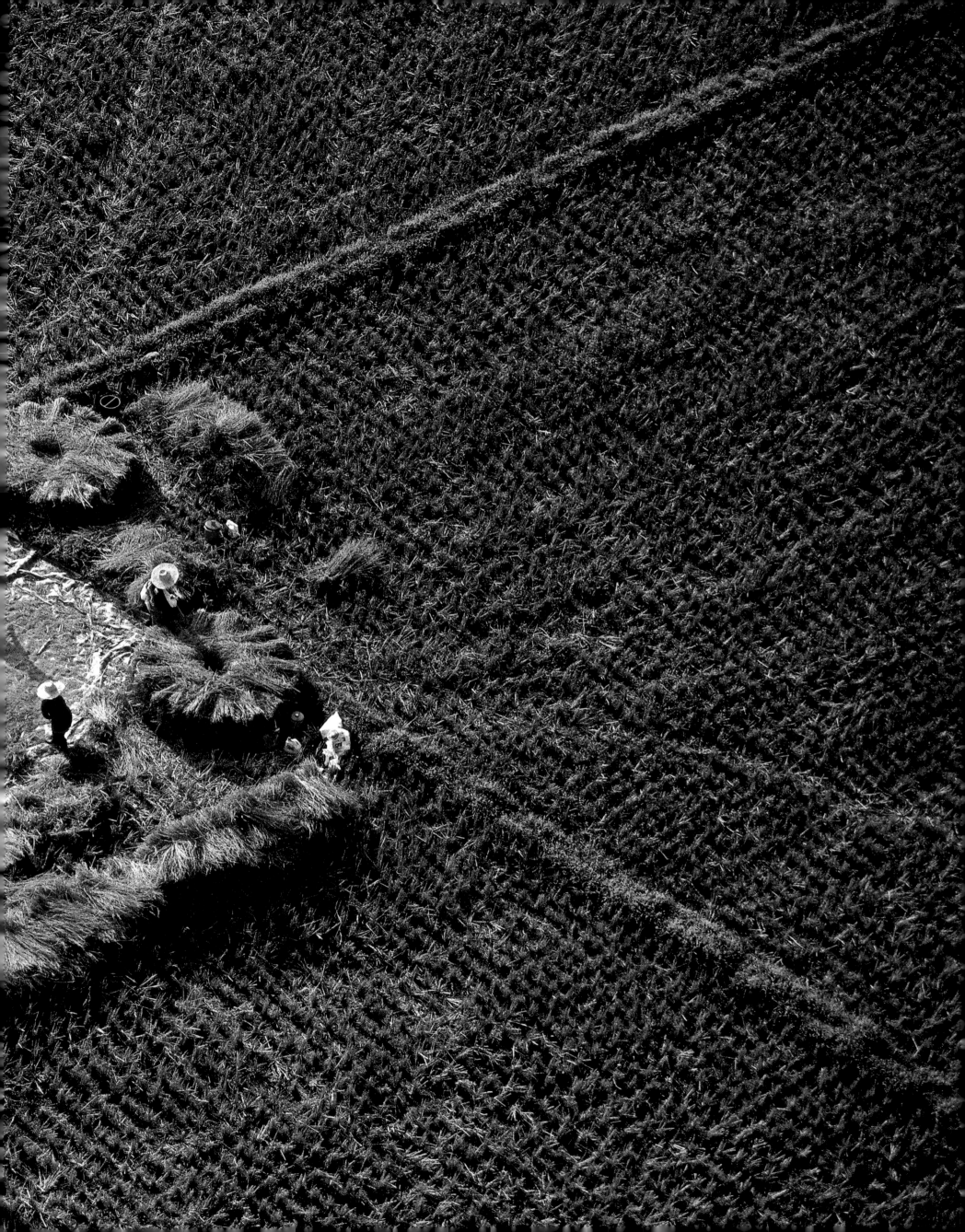

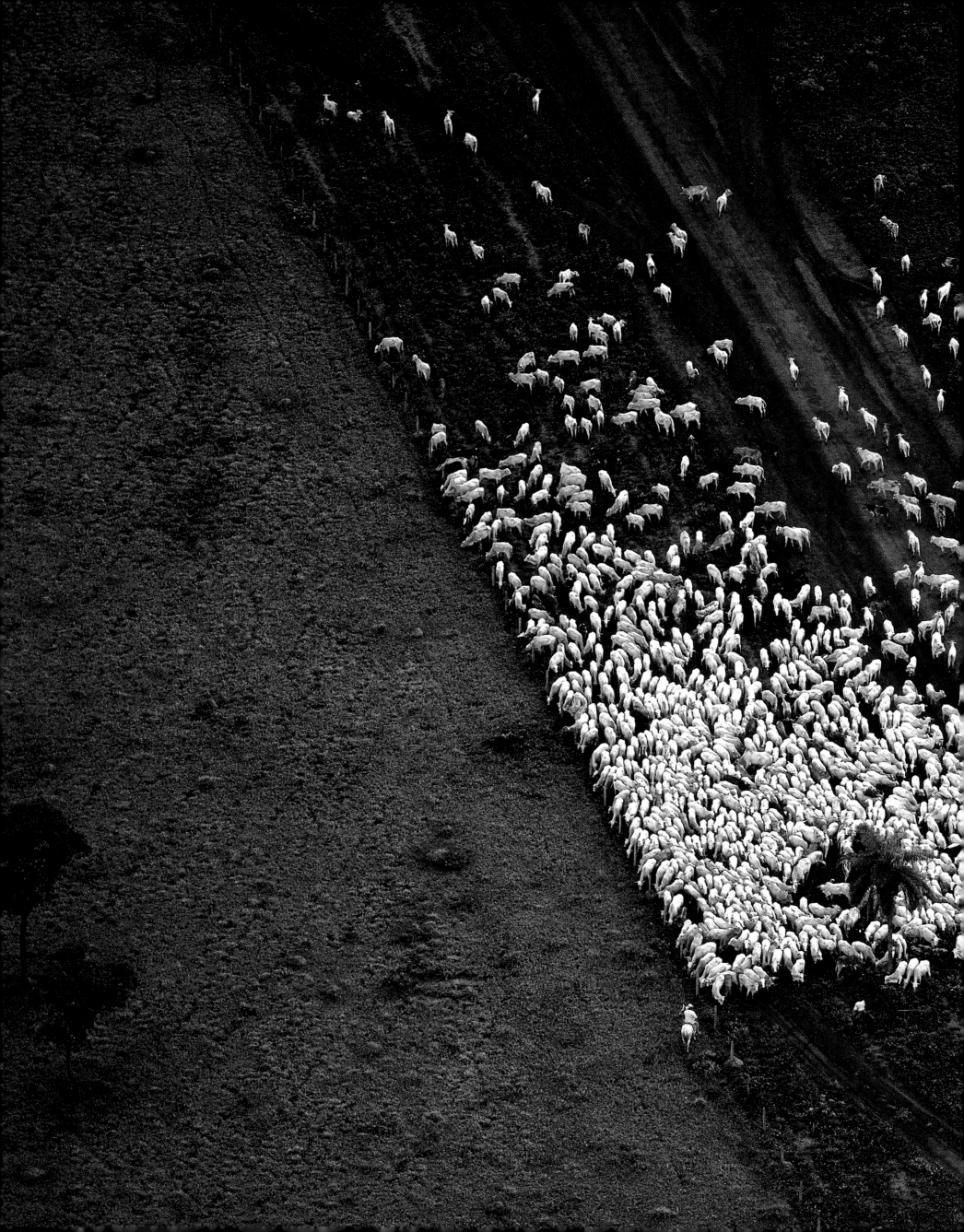

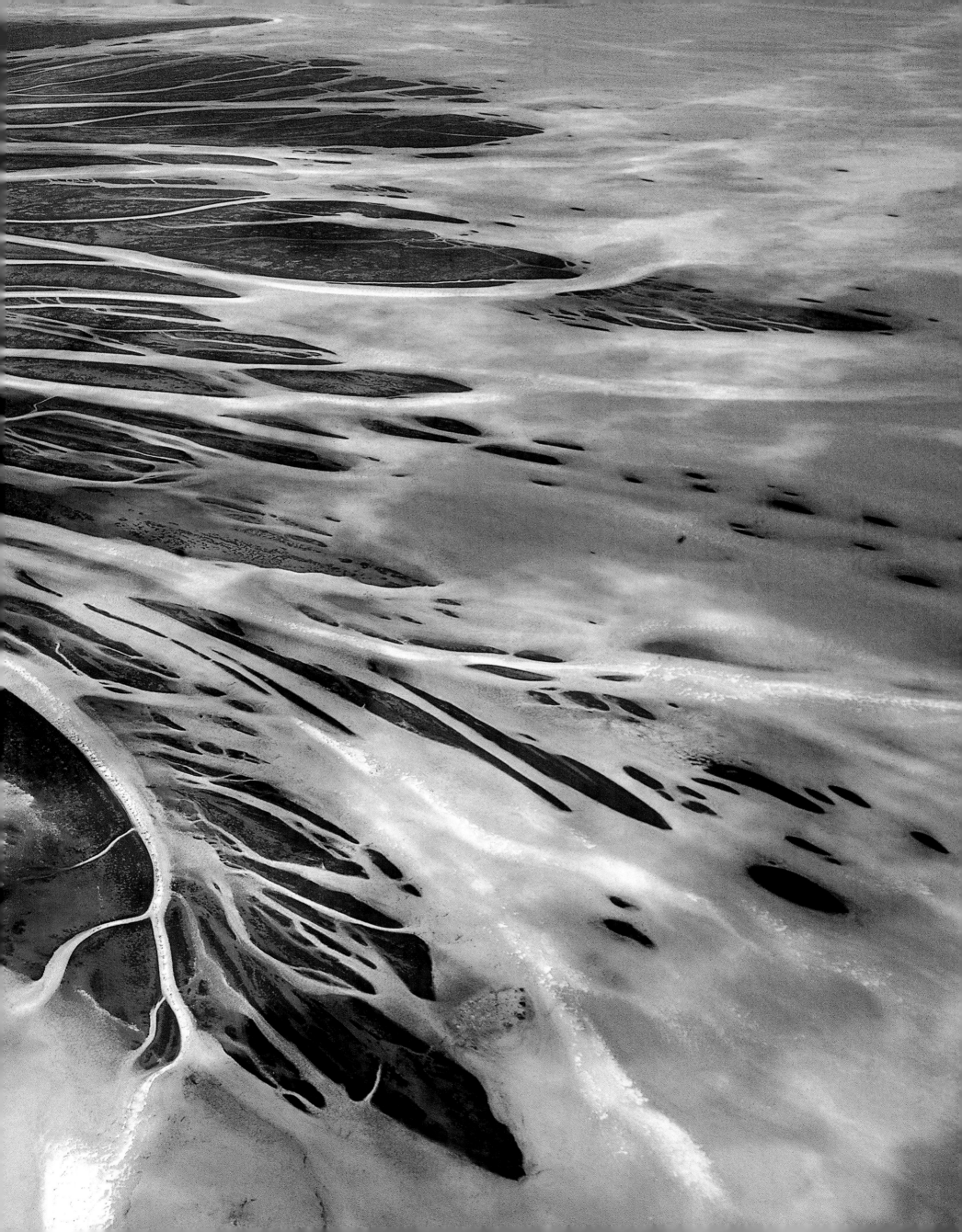

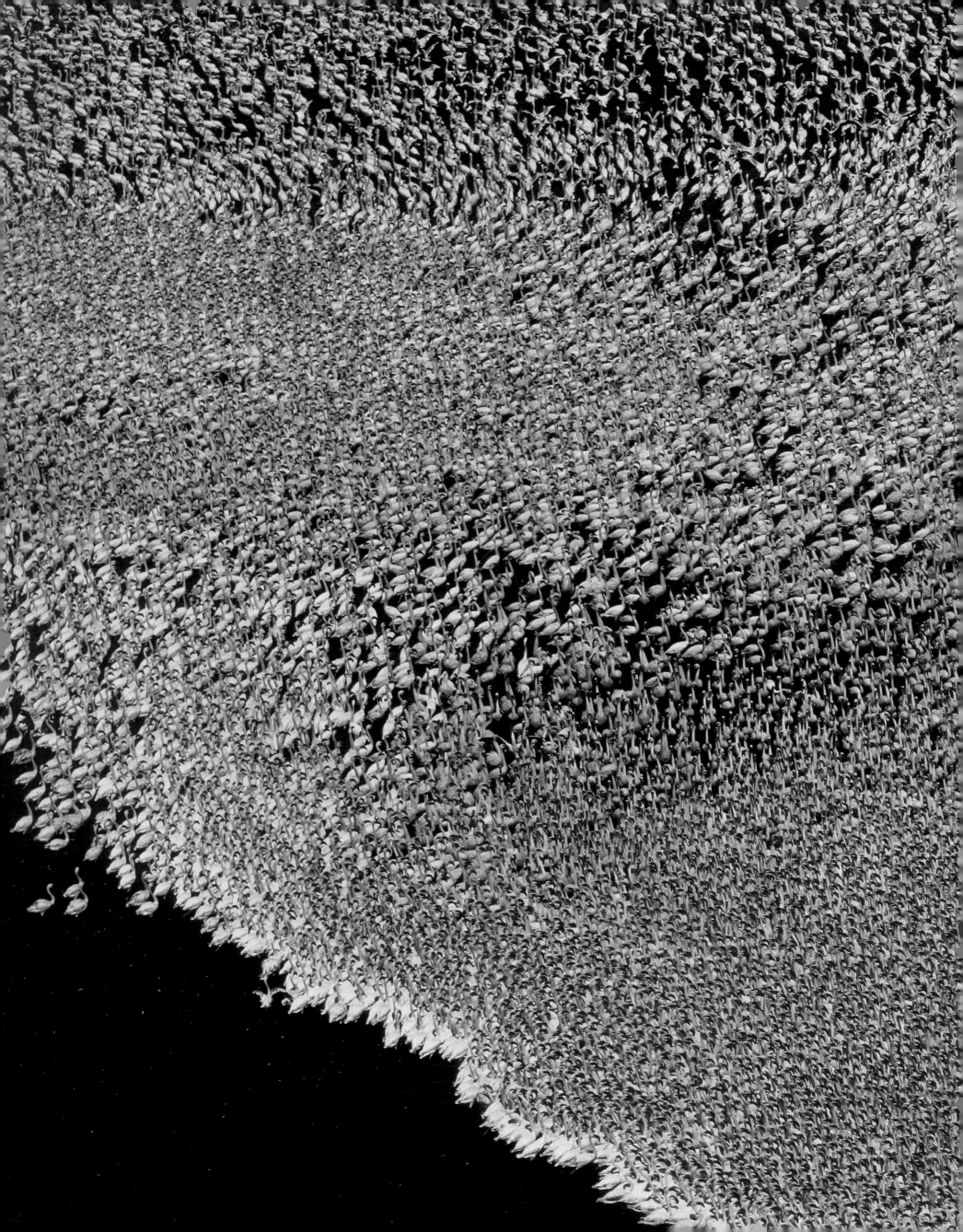

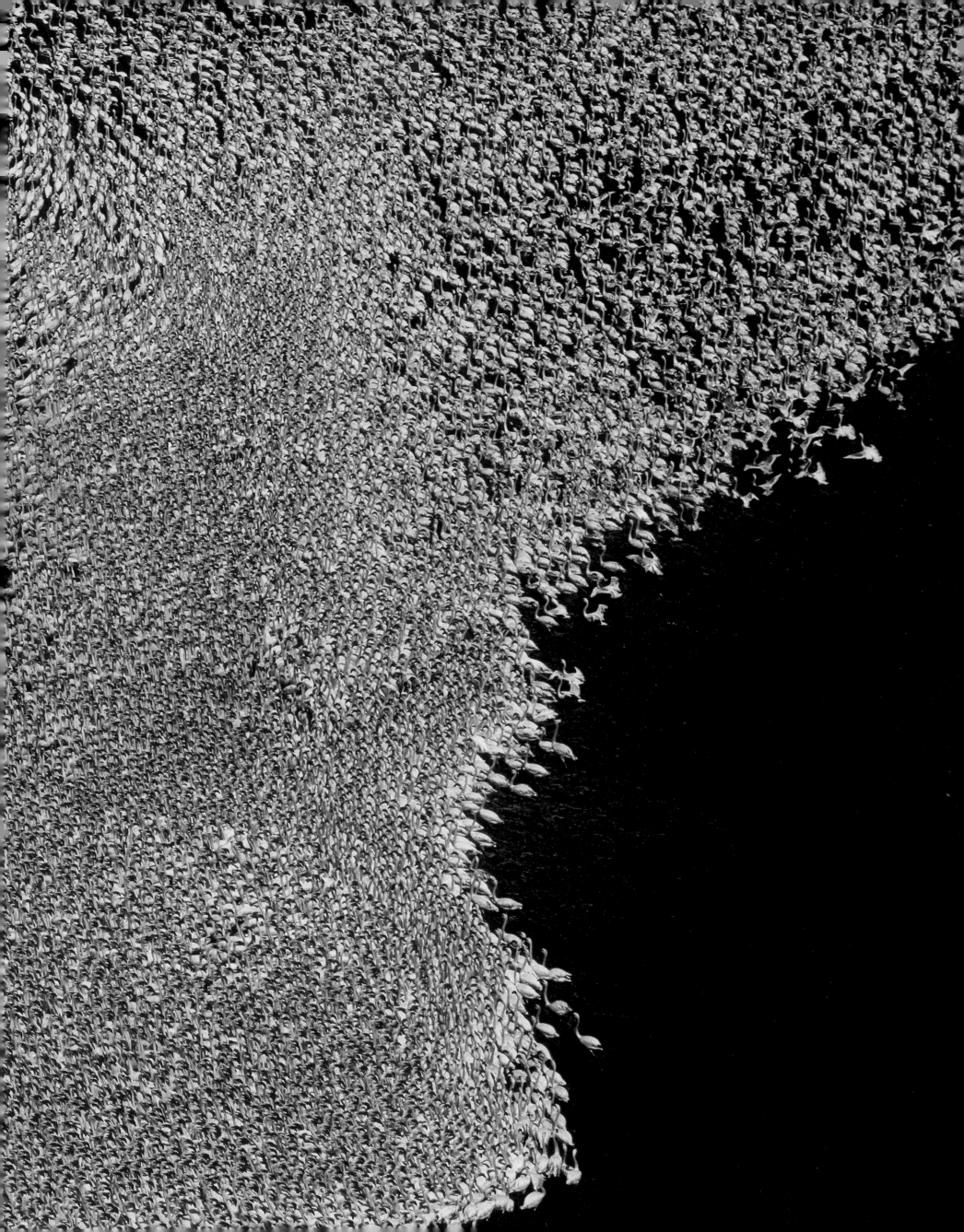

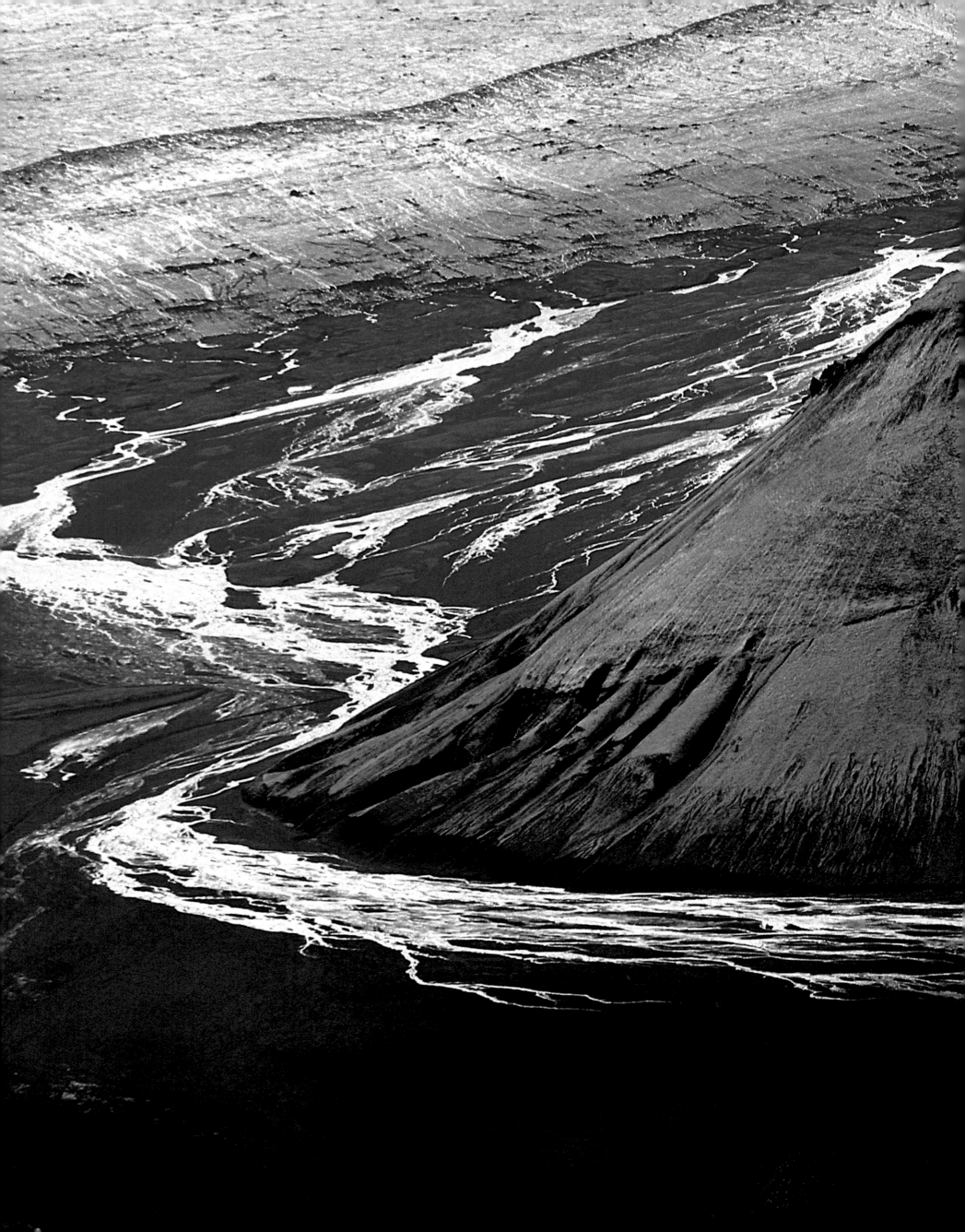

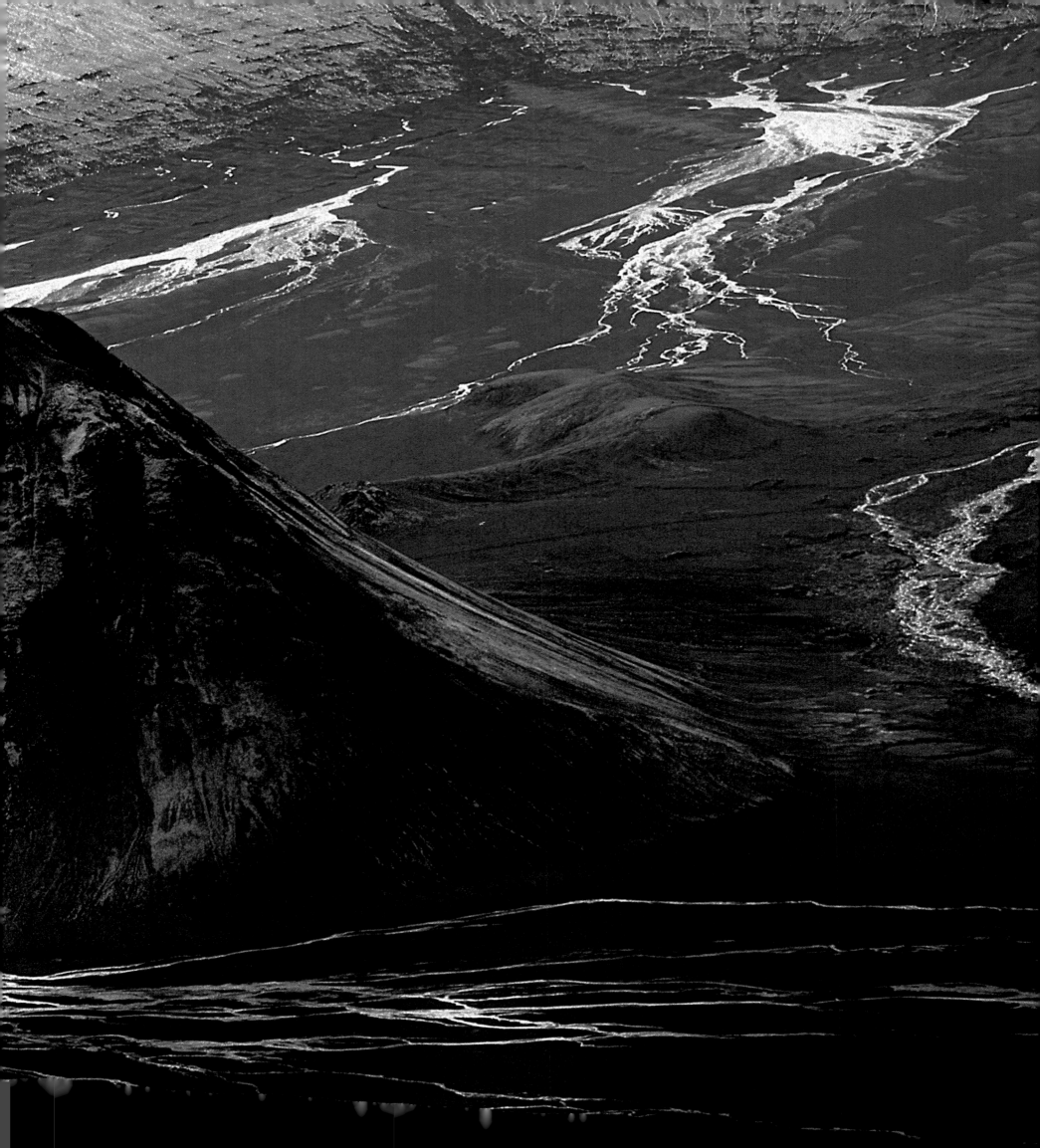

# URBAN LANDSCAPES,
# LANDSCAPES OF URBANISM

Cities are home to half of the Earth's 6 billion inhabitants.
They have become difficult to avoid, given the many advantages
they offer and the attractions they exert. But the city is also the victim
of its success. The shantytowns and slums that house workers
often have poor air and water quality, hygiene, and safety.
It is time for human beings to reclaim the urban space.

The twentieth century was marked by the greatest revolution our planet has known since the arrival of human beings: the concentration of half of its population in these unlikely areas called cities. Cities are indeed unlikely, because all of human history has consisted of a territorial expansion of societies in the search for vegetable and animal nourishment, even to the extremes of the cold, hot, dry, or wet frontiers of our continents. Suddenly, such needs seem not to govern us, and cities have swollen to levels no one could have imagined a few decades ago. Thirty million are crammed into greater Tokyo; 25 million in and around New York, the heart of the megalopolis of the northeastern United States; more than 15 million around Mexico City, São Paulo, Osaka, Jakarta, Los Angeles, Bombay, and Manila. Ten or more additional metropolitan areas are near or above the 10 million mark. Before the nineteenth century only ancient Rome and Edo (Tokyo) exceeded a million in population. Then came the explosion.

If cities have seen enormous success, it can only be because they have advantages. When the industrial revolution, and then the service revolution occurred, the countryside was gradually sidelined into a role as a center for agriculture and tourism. There are scattered exceptions, such as Germany, the Benelux countries, the northwest of Italy, Japan, eastern China, and a few other areas of the world, where major industrial centers are found in a rural environment, but the population densities of these regions are among the highest in the world and the rural environment should more properly be termed "rural-urban."

It may seem paradoxical that this evolution has affected poor and rich countries alike; this is because, among poorer countries, country life is often precarious. The rural population is at the mercy of climatic

irregularities that can destroy the chances for an adequate harvest. In the country, people are also subject to strong social pressures from families, ethnic groups, religious communities, and local leaders whether legitimate or criminal. In the city, despite its uncertainty, discomfort, and crowding, there is always some small deal to be made, some scraps from a wealthy table to be picked up. Even for those with minimal qualifications, work can be found, perhaps physically arduous work on a building site, or in health services, or temporary and illegal work if necessary, even degrading work at times, but bringing in a subsistence wage and a little something to send home to the family overseas or in the country. This was the growth process for London, Paris, and New York up to World War I and even beyond. The new arrivals, destitute, settled near train stations and ports, in the underdeveloped outskirts, in the slums. This is still happening in the gigantic, barely controlled urban sprawl of Mexico City, Rio de Janeiro, Calcutta, Manila, Lagos, and so many other cities in the southern hemisphere. Yet in times of peace and prosperity order seems to reign, and the city becomes welcoming, attractive, and intense.

Cities fascinate people. The ancient inhabitants of the fertile crescent and the great civilizations of the Mediterranean (Egypt, Israel, Greece, Rome), China and pre-Columbian America (Mexico, the Andes) established their gods in cities. In the shadow of the sacred, they developed politics, the art of government, as well as commerce, art, the exchange of ideas, and social life. The high places at the heart of such cities as Jerusalem, the Acropolis and Agora of Athens, the seven hills of Rome, and the Temple of the Sun in Mexico City embody the permanence of this sense of space and of the world, this vertical bond between earth and heaven, between the profane and the sacred. With the possible exception of Subsaharan Africa, which had scarcely any urban tradition before the colonial era, cities on all continents have preserved from ancient times their status as the center of the world. We need only think of the cathedrals, the forbidden cities of China and the Far East, the Imperial Palace of Tokyo where the emperor resides—with his modest constitutional title of "symbol" of Japan—or the model of the Plaza Mayor in Spain or Latin America. As soon as places take on meaning, speak to the heart and the mind, become enchanted, life there becomes possible. For as long as cities have been seen (through

Nations Center for Habitats, at least 500 million city-dwellers in the world are homeless or inadequately housed. The reasons are clear: between 1950 and 1990, industrialized countries have seen their population double and their per capita gross domestic product (GDP) triple. In the same period, the urban population of developing countries increased fivefold, while their per capita GDP grew by a factor of only 1.5. In the former Soviet Bloc countries and China, relative social discipline is still in force and the residents of the immense concrete districts favored by Communist regimes tolerate one another fairly well. When ethnic groups in a nation are poorly integrated, relations become tense, and violence can erupt at the slightest opportunity. This is now the rule in France in the approximately 200 large projects built in the 1960s and 1970s for the eternal happiness of their contemporaries, by architects who took Le Corbusier for a new Vitruvius and his *Map of Athens* for gospel. Sincerity and good intentions are no excuse; the road to hell is paved with them.

⌃ **EPISCOPAL CATHEDRAL OF SZÉKESFEHÉRVÁR SURROUNDED BY MODERN BUILDINGS, HUNGARY** (47°12' N, 18°25' E)

Between Budapest and Lake Balaton, Székesfehérvár and its contrasting architecture bear witness to the greatest eras of Hungarian history. A thousand years old, and capital of the Hungarian kingdom for five centuries, the city became a bishop's see in 1777 and was enriched by the ecclesiastical buildings in the purest Hungarian Baroque style. The Episcopal cathedral is one of the few buildings of the period that survive. Modern apartment blocks, built when Hungary was part of the Soviet bloc, stand where once there were ancient city walls. Since the fall of Communism, Hungary, like the rest of central Europe, has witnessed a strong resurgence of Christian faith, and people can now visit churches freely. The Christian church suffered 50 years of religious persecution in central Europe. During World War II, 3,000 priests were interned in the concentration camp at Dachau. Under Communism, the faith was not officially forbidden in all countries but nevertheless went underground. Some monks and nuns were imprisoned and even killed.

No city exists without people's desire to live together and thus to soften the sharp edges that invariably occur in any society. The larger the city, the more difficult this process becomes. The less competent and honest the politicians, the lower the likelihood of finding humane solutions. As Jean Bodin used to say, the only form of wealth is in people. All we can do is second that opinion. Provided, of course, that people are educated, refined, responsible, concerned for the common good—in a word civic-minded, attached to the civitas, the municipality for which our cities have served as a laboratory for thousands of years. This is a program for the urban policies of tomorrow. The human upheaval brought on by globalization is neither good nor bad in itself. It is unavoidable. Only human wisdom will make it a form of wealth and an opportunity, a means of exchange between different cultural experiences. If we accept this outlook, the city becomes an extraordinary experimental space.

We need to reinvent inviting neighborhoods and public spaces, like those once created by people all over the world. The Mediterranean street and town square have long been places of great social vibrancy. Why can't we invent contemporary versions of the same model, adapted to the different cultures of our planet, conducive to sharing and conviviality? The model for an ideal city does not exist; nor are there any ideal cities. Humans' living space is fragile. It is fragile in the countryside, in daily contact with the so-called natural environment. It is still more so in the city, where the environment consists of human material, the most sensitive but also the most difficult to sculpt.

JEAN-ROBERT PITTE

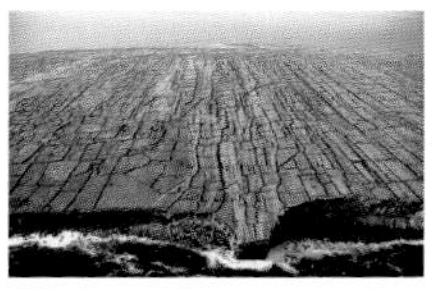

**PAGES 92–93**
CLIFFS OF INISHMORE, ARAN ISLANDS, COUNTY GALWAY, IRELAND
(53°07' N, 9°45' W)

Off the Irish coast, the Aran Islands—Inishmore, Inishmaan, and Inisheer—have cliffs that rise to heights of 300 feet (90 m) and guard Galway Bay from the rough winds and currents of the Atlantic Ocean. Inishmore, the largest of the islands (9 by 2.5 miles, or 14.5 by 4 km), is also the most populous, with nearly 1,000 inhabitants. For centuries the inhabitants helped to fertilize the rocky soil of these islands by regularly spreading a mixture of sand and algae on the ground, intended to provide the thin layer of humus necessary for farming. Rare ferns and flowers find this a welcoming environment. To protect their plots of land from wind erosion, the islanders built a great network of windbreaking walls, totaling some 7,000 miles (12,000 km) in length, which lend these lands the appearance of a gigantic mosaic. The Aran Islands derive most of their resources from fishing, farming, and herding, and they receive a growing number of tourists, particularly attracted to the majestic fortress of Dun Aonghasa that dominates the Atlantic coast, and the hermitages and churches that are traces of the early days of Christianity in Ireland.

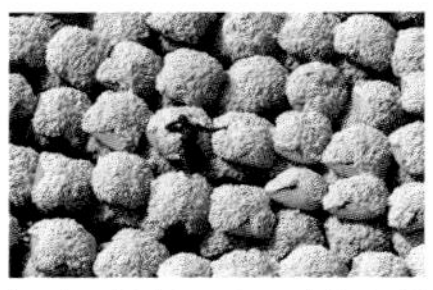

**PAGES 94–95**
WORKER RESTING ON BALES OF COTTON, THONAKAHA, KORHOGO, CÔTE D'IVOIRE
(9°28' N, 5°36' W)

In the 19th century West Africa received its first cotton seeds of the *Gossypium hirsutum* variety, which originated in Central America and remains the most widely cultivated variety of cotton in the world. At the beginning of the 20th century this raw material represented 80 percent of the world textile market (47 percent today, following the invention of synthetic fabrics). Cotton cultivation and manufacture still employs one billion people worldwide. But the fall in prices—which have halved since 1995—is having a serious effect on some countries, particularly in West and Central Africa. Faced with high input costs—cotton-growing alone uses one-quarter of the pesticides sold worldwide—and the casualization of labor, some governments are urging a reduction in the quantity of pesticides used. Fair-trade supply chains, which ensure a higher price for producers and working conditions that conform with international regulations, are also being set up.

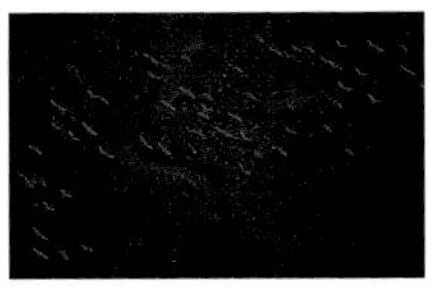

**PAGES 96–97**
FLOCK OF SCARLET IBIS, NEAR PEDERNALES, AMACURO DELTA, VENEZUELA
(9°57' N, 62°21' W)

From the Llanos region to the Amacuro delta at the mouth of the Orinoco River, more than one-third of the area of Venezuela is made up of humid zones, the habitat of choice of the scarlet ibis (*Eudocimus ruber*). These waders nest in large colonies in mangroves and move no farther than a few miles to seek food. Carotene derived from the shrimp, crabs, and other crustaceans they eat helps create the characteristic pigmentation of the species. The scarlet ibis's feathers, at one time used by the indigeneous population to make coats and finery, are now a component in the manufacture of artificial flowers. This bird, sought after for its meat as well as its feathers, is now endangered; fewer than 200,000 survive in Central and South America.

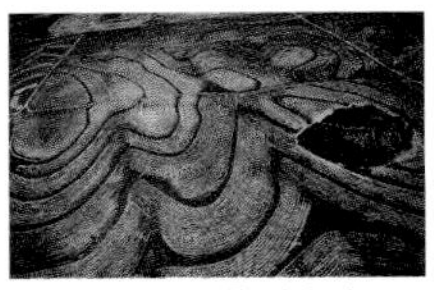

**PAGES 98–99**
FIELDS NEAR THE TOWN OF HAMMAMET, NABEUL GOVERNORATE, TUNISIA
(36°24' N, 10°37' E)

Northeastern Tunisia has a long tradition of irrigation and of planting crops so that they follow the contours of the land. Between 30 percent and 40 percent of the country's agricultural investment goes toward infrastructure for obtaining, transporting, and distributing water. In thirty years, the amount of irrigated land has quadrupled to total 380,000 hectares today, closely reflecting the growth in the country's population, which has doubled in twenty-five years. Agriculture uses 82 percent of Tunisia's water, but the exhaustion of water near the surface has led to a quest for supplies ever deeper underground. This increased pumping of groundwater is a threat to farmland because it causes seawater to penetrate the aquifers, especially near coasts. Faced with a water crisis, Tunisia drew up a national water and soil conservation strategy in 1991–2000.

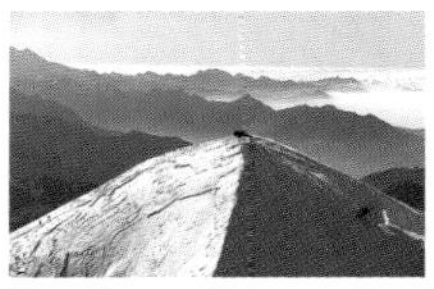

**PAGES 100–101**
ROPED PARTY OF MOUNTAINEERS CLIMBING MONT BLANC, HAUTE-SAVOIE, FRANCE
(45°50' N, 6°53' E)

The Alps, which are the largest mountain range in Europe, began forming about 65 million years ago. At 15,765 feet (4,807 m), Mont Blanc is their highest peak. Known in the 16th century as the *Montagne Maudite* (cursed mountain), it was seen by the inhabitants of the Chamonix Valley as a chaotic mound of rocks and glaciers until 1787, when the climbers Jacques Balmat, Gabriel Pacard, and Horace Bénédict de Saussure became the first to reach its summit. Many more ascents followed. Between 1787 and 1860, 115 people reached the summit. Then the scientific motivation of the Enlightenment gave way to the quest for physical achievement, then in more recent times to tourism. The summit receives up to 10,000 visitors a year. While it remains the major local economic resource, the site is fragile and is now deteriorating. When tourism becomes a major source of revenue for a region, it leads to increasing artificialization. For example, 80 percent of ski resorts are now equipped with snow cannons, but this widespread use damages landscapes and ecosystems: 4,000 $m^3$ of fresh water, stored in artificial reservoirs, are needed to produce 1 hectare of snow.

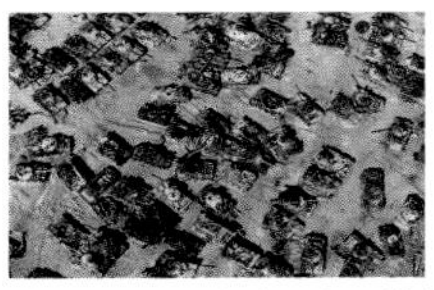

**PAGES 102–103**
IRAQI TANK GRAVEYARD IN THE DESERT NEAR AL-JAHRAH, KUWAIT
(29°26' N, 47°24' E)

This graveyard of tanks will bear witness for many years to the damage that war causes both to the environment and to human health. In 1991, during the Gulf War when Saddam Hussein invaded Kuwait, a million depleted uranium shells were fired at the Iraqi tanks, spreading toxic, radioactive dust for miles around. Such dust is known to have lasting effects on the environment and to cause various forms of cancer and other serious illnesses among humans. Depleted uranium ammunition is still being used in Chechnya and in Iraq, and was also used recently in Bosnia, Kosovo, and Afghanistan. The cost of such wars, borne almost exclusively by the ten richest nations, have risen by 18 percent over the last ten years. They amount to more than $956 billion, or the equivalent of 2.7 percent of the entire wealth of the world. The political desire for peace and international cooperation seems helpless when faced with the economic interests of the arms industry. Mankind's greatest challenge at the beginning of the third millennium, if economic development and international political stability are to be guaranteed, is to save the Earth's biosphere and reduce the inequality between north and south. Just 10 percent of the money spent on war over a period of ten years would be enough to achieve these objectives.

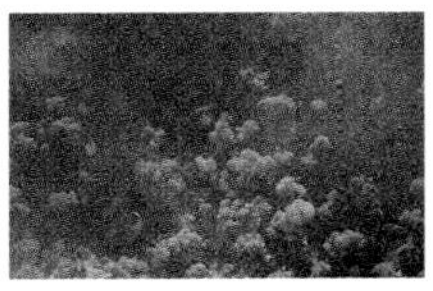

**PAGES 104–105**
LOCUST SWARM OUTSIDE RANOHIRA, NEAR FIANARANTSOA, MADAGASCAR
(22°27' S, 45°21' E)

Madagascar's cereal crops and pastures have been chronically destroyed for centuries by invasions of migratory locust (*Locusta migratoria*) or red locust (*Nomadacris septemfasciata*). Several miles long and numbering as many as 50 billion insects, the hordes move at a rate of 25 miles (40 km) per day, laying waste to all vegetation in their path. In summer 2004, a large region of Africa from Senegal to Egypt was invaded for several months by swarms of desert locust (*Schistocerca gregaria*), which ravaged crops and threatened some of the poorest people with famine. To eradicate this scourge, the massive spreading of insecticides by airplane or helicopter is required. However, the cost, the toxicity to humans and the environment, as well as the development of resistance in harmful insects, have shown the limits of this procedure. A recently discovered natural pesticide made from mushrooms might provide an organic method of eliminating these locust swarms.

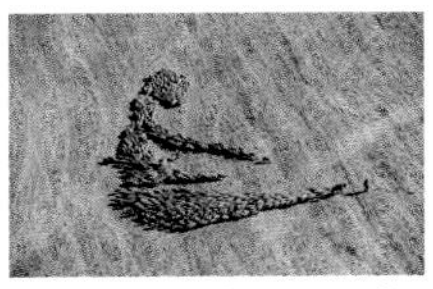

**PAGES 106–107**
FLOCK OF SHEEP NEAR KEFRAIYA, LEBANON
(33°39' N, 35°43' E)

These sheep form a curious arabesque design on the bare pastures of Mount Lebanon, the country's main mountain range. Once its slopes contained forests of centuries-old cedar, but these are now reduced to a few isolated shreds. Up to 60 percent of Lebanon's forests vanished between 1972 and 1994 as a result of civil war, urban expansion, and repeated forest fires. Deprived of vegetation, the ground became extremely vulnerable to erosion, especially from the heavy winter rains typical of the Mediterranean climate. Overgrazing has speeded up this process and made the land ever more barren—especially on Mount Lebanon, where the number of animals far exceeds the land's capacity to support them. Overexploitation of land is the chief cause of soil erosion in the world today: it is estimated that 20 percent of pasture and common land is no longer productive.

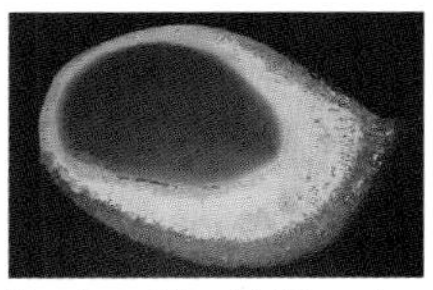

**PAGES 108–109**
THE EYE OF THE MALDIVES, ATOLL OF NORTH MALI, MALDIVES
(4°16' N, 73°28' E)

The Eye of the Maldives is a *faro*, a coral formation on a rocky base that has sunk, hiding all but a ring-shaped reef that encircles a shallow lagoon. Coral can only form in water of a relatively high temperature, and thus atolls develop principally in intertropical regions. The lowest country in the world, with a high point not exceeding 8.25 feet (2.5 m), the Maldive archipelago contains 26 large atolls, including 1,190 islands, nearly 300 of which are inhabited either permanently or seasonally by tourists. The archipelago was severely hit by the tsunami of December 26, 2004, which killed 83 and injured more than 2,000. The coastlines were altered, and some of the islands sank beneath the sea. The coral reefs were also partially destroyed by the gigantic wave and the debris it carried. As well as affecting the tourist trade, the Maldives' main economic resource, the damage to the coral food chain has harmed fishing and the livelihoods of the local people. Aware of the archipelago's fragility, the authorities and the international community had already set up containing measures to limit the rise of the water level, but the barriers around the capital, Male, did not stop the water from getting through.

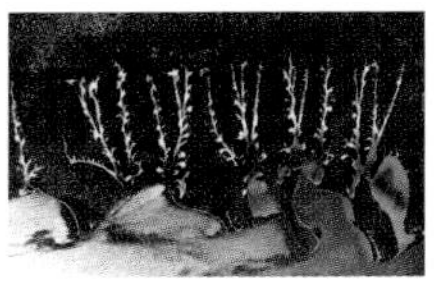

**PAGES 110–111**
LAKE SHORE IN ETOSHA NATIONAL PARK, NAMIBIA
(18°50' S, 15°32' E)

The salt deposits collected in the shoreline cavities of this lake in Namibia's Etosha National Park seem to form startling shapes of bizarre plants and animals when seen from the sky. Encompassing an area of 8,685 square miles (22,270 $km^2$), this park is Africa's largest protected space. It surrounds the Etosha Pan, a great basin of 2,160 square miles (5,600 $km^2$) covered with salt, which transforms into a lake for a few weeks out of each year during the rainy season, from November to April. Its water, although repellent to mammals, allows the growth of a blue-green algae, which attracts tens of thousands of flamingos. When the basin dries up, it is covered with grasses on which the park's great herbivores feed. Namibia's national parks make up one-fifth of its territory, and environmental conservation is among the chief objectives in its constitution. Today the world includes about 102,000 protected areas, covering more than 7.2 million square miles (18.8 million $km^2$), 12.5 percent of the Earth's land; this is almost quadruple the area protected thirty years ago. Some of these areas, however, are protected in name only and are still exploited: agriculture is practiced in nearly half of them.

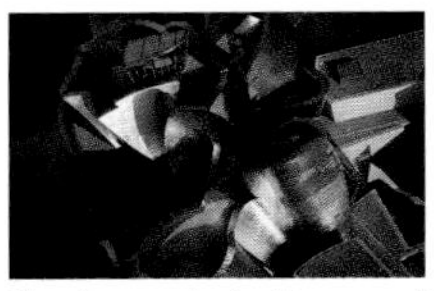

**PAGES 112–113**
GUGGENHEIM MUSEUM BILBAO, BILBAO, BASQUE REGION, SPAIN
(43°15' N, 2°58' W)

The Guggenheim Museum Bilbao, inaugurated in 1997, is part of a program of urban renewal in this industrial city. Built at a cost of $100 million, the structure was designed by the Californian architect Frank O. Gehry, with the help of a computer program used in aeronautics. Its glass, steel, and limestone construction, partially covered with titanium, echoes the city's shipbuilding tradition. Encompassing a total area of 250,000 square feet (24,000 $m^2$), the museum has 118,000 square feet (11,000 $m^2$) of exhibition space divided among nineteen halls, including one of the world's largest galleries (310 by 100 feet, or 130 by 30 m). This cultural attraction has raised the number of visitors to Bilbao from 260,000 to more than 1 million each year on average. By energizing the local economy (the gross industrial product of the Basque region grew fivefold), the museum has also brought new life to the city.

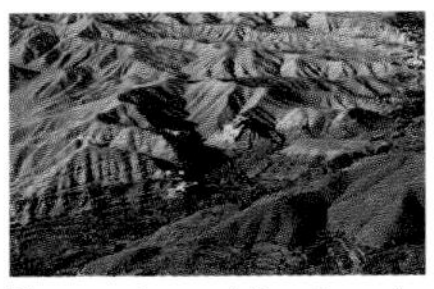

**PAGES 114–115**
MOUNTAINS AND DWELLINGS AROUND BAMIYAN, AFGHANISTAN
(34°50' N, 67°40' E)

The province of Bamiyan, in east central Afghanistan, is a poor and arid region, where the people earn their meager living from agriculture, like 80 percent of Afghans. Preserving the environment is a priority in a country so dependent on its natural resources. But droughts, massive deforestation, overgrazing, and a lack of consistent government policy as a result of twenty-five years of war—all of these have led to large-scale soil erosion that threatens all the country's agricultural resources. The forests have fallen victim to vast black-market operations, and are gradually disappearing while neighboring countries reap the profits from buying the wood. The primary victims of this trade and of the lack of regulation are the wild animals, including the Siberian crane, the snow leopard and the urial (wild goat), all of which are close to extinction if not already extinct. Their skin, horns, or meat yield more profit than the small harvests from the impoverished soil.

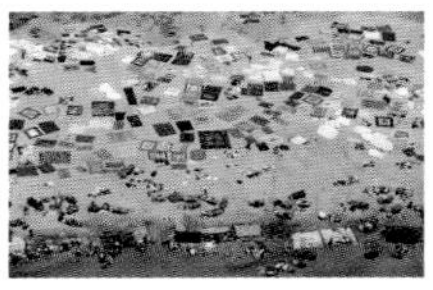

**PAGES 116–117**
LAUNDRY DRYING BY THE CHARI RIVER NEAR N'DJAMENA, CHAD
(12°07' N, 15°03' E)

Carpets, hangings, and other brightly colored materials brighten the many sandbanks of the Chari near Chad's capital, N'Djamena. The Chari river is the main tributary to Lake Chad, whose surface area has literally melted away in the last thirty years, shrinking from 9,650 to 965 square miles (25,000 to 2,500 $km^2$). The river's waters, which are used for laundry, personal hygiene, and kitchen use, may well suffer from these competing demands, and their quality could deteriorate. Sources of fresh water are rare in this part of the Sahel, which has suffered repeated droughts; only 27 percent of Chad's population has access to drinking water. This is the third most critical situation in the world, after Afghanistan and Ethiopia. Groundwater supplies are also threatened by the planned Chad–Cameroon oil pipeline, which is supported by the World Bank. Any oil leaks could contaminate rivers and wells. In 1990, thirteen African countries suffered water supply problems or shortages. By 2025, this number could double.

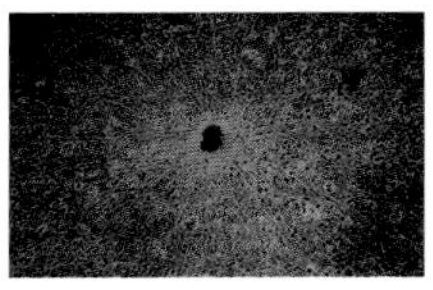

**PAGES 118–119**
"TREE OF LIFE," TSAVO NATIONAL PARK, KENYA
(2°11' S, 38°25' E)

This acacia is a symbol of life in vast expanses of thorny savanna, where wild animals come to take advantage of its leaves or its shade. Tsavo National Park in southeastern Kenya, crossed by the Nairobi–Mombasa road and railway axis, is the country's largest protected area (8,200 square miles, or 21,000 $km^2$) and was declared a national park in 1948. Tsavo was already famous for its many elephants when, in the 1970s, more animals fleeing drought entered the park. Consuming more than 440 pounds (200 kg) of vegetation daily, they seriously damaged the natural environment. Controversy surrounded the question of whether selective slaughter was necessary, but poachers put an end to the debate by exterminating more than 80 percent of the 36,000 elephants in the park. Tsavo's rhinoceroses, sought after for their horns (considered aphrodisiacs in Asia), suffered the same fate. The prohibition of international trading in ivory and rhino horns has enabled certain wild animal populations to increase in number. However, poaching and disappearing natural habitats remain disturbing threats. World trade in wild flora and fauna provides between $12 billion and $19 billion in revenues each year.

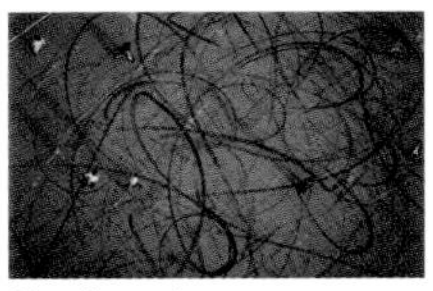

**PAGES 120–121**
RUBBER TRACKS ON A RECREATION GROUND NEAR DOHA, QATAR
(25°17' N, 51°32' E)

The tires of teenage motorcyclists have traced extraordinary arabesques over the surface of a recreation ground in the suburbs of Doha, the capital city of Qatar. With a population of barely 800,000, 80 percent of whom are from immigrant families, the little peninsula of Qatar is a complex mixture of indigenous Qataris, in a minority that jealously guards its traditions, living side by side with an immigrant Arab and Western elite who share with them the key positions in the economy, along with a huge army of Pakistanis, Indians, and Iranians who make up the principal workforce of the country. The latter, mainly men, constitute nearly half the population, and as a result Qatar finds itself in the unusual situation of having twice as many men as women.

geomancy) as the hub of the cosmos, they have been sought out, loved, and embellished.

One of the most intense emotions felt by city-dwellers is the give-and-take among all the members of the social body. A city that is livable and healthy lets rich mingle with poor, generation speak to generation, and all the professions collaborate. A city in equilibrium is a social elevator that offers an escape from the divisions of birth and inheritance and allows knowledge to spread as widely as possible. Rastignac, the ambitious young hero of Balzac's *Père Goriot*, shakes his fist at Paris, vowing to conquer or be conquered, summing up all the hopes ever inspired by cities. We find the same feeling in the Chinese peasant who arrives in Shanghai or Beijing after a grueling train journey, or the Indian from the *altiplano* who uses his last penny to get to Lima, or the African bushman who squeezes into, or hangs precariously onto, the ramshackle taxis and overfilled trucks, higher than they are long, to reach the Eldorado of his dreams, Dakar, Bamako, Nouakchott, Kinshasa, or Abidjan. Some take enormous risks to escape their country, Romania, Albania, Pakistan, or Turkey, and get to London, Paris, Dusseldorf, or Milan. They know it won't be easy, that they will have to put up with humiliation, indifference, or contempt on the part of those who have been there longer. They don't mind; they count on ethnic solidarity and will take advantage of humanitarian associations or official assistance. If necessary they work on the margins, even illegally, despite the known risk of passing a point of no return. Many succeed. The descendants of Italian *mafiosi* in Chicago have melted into American society. No one pays attention now to the family names of the children or grandchildren of Russians, Poles, Armenians, Spaniards, Italians, or Portuguese who arrived a century ago in Marseilles, Lyons, or Paris. A successful city is like a machine to integrate, not crush, personalities. Most cities still retain their eminent function as a place of welcome.

For anyone lacking regular or sufficient income, city life is hard, but humanitarian aids such as soup kitchens and shelters exist; in the countryside in poor countries they are not to be found. Despite the poverty, violence, and ignorance of shantytowns, *favelas*, camps of gypsy wagons in Western Europe, and nomad tents in the cities of the Sahel, these places are the scene of true solidarity, a complicity, a sense of community among their residents. For most residents, they provide a difficult transition; people leave them as soon as possible, or do their utmost in order that their children can achieve a better status. The bottom line is unmistakable: people live longer in the city than on the farm. Because, no matter what, the city is more effective at providing subsistence and ongoing care.

Whether prosperous or poverty-stricken, cities are usually powerful stimulants for their residents. There is a continuous intermingling of so many people, goods, services, and ideas. The open-minded, responsible city-dweller can find a wealth of intellectual and spiritual nourishment as well as economic ferment. The city-dweller is constantly challenged to give the best, and even when beset by despair, to bounce back and move on.

This explains why the supreme human creations have come about in cities. This is true in the fields of the visual arts, literature, the sciences, and philosophy. The social environment favors them; so does the architectural, urban environment. No one can remain indifferent to the Parthenon of Athens, St. Peter's in Rome, Piazza San Marco in Venice, the Place de la Concorde in Paris, the pyramids of Cairo, or the cupolas of the Kremlin. Living close to them, no one can despair. Preindustrial civilizations had a vague sense of this, and thus in ancient times, even in the poor quarters of cities, attention was paid to beauty in Hindu and Buddhist temples, in Christian churches, mosques, public buildings, and the urban landscape in general. Their aim was not to offer consolation but to diffuse strong doses of creative feeling, to dispense the energy required for the only progress that mattered—that of the human spirit.

As living beings, diverse and fantastical, cities also bring great hardship to their inhabitants, whether powerful or poverty-stricken, although the latter of course bear more of the pain. The sudden piling up of immense crowds in tight spaces that have not been properly developed causes pollution of air and water. In most cities of wealthy countries, there is an awareness of these problems and an effort to solve them. Except for a few days each year, you can breathe fairly well in the great European and North American cities, because heating and cooking with wood and coal have been replaced. These cities have faucets that dispense drinkable water, even if it is not always free of odor and taste. Such is not the case in Russia, China, and surrounding countries, much less in countries of the southern hemisphere, where cities are covered in a thick cloak of pollution and water is both scarce and undrinkable, because of dangerous germs—although this does not prevent it from being drunk and used for every imaginable purpose. The Ganges is probably the most utilized river in the world, believed to purify and carry its worshippers to the gods, while in fact it gives them thousands of harmful bacteria.

While the city leaves no opportunity for boredom, it is also a place where people can waste a great deal of time. Distances in cities are not always great, but travel is often impeded by congestion. In most of the world's megalopolises, many residents spend two or three hours each day in public conveyances or in their private automobiles, amid noise and discomfort, accumulating pollutants in their lungs and bad moods that can affect the people around them. In wealthy countries, reduced working hours for wage earners has made possible a better distribution of commuting and periods of leisure or vacation. Everyone gains by this. In poorer countries, time spent in factories, studios, and shops has hardly decreased. Working lives often begin before the age of ten and continue as long as health allows, because the concept of retirement has no meaning.

Space can also pose problems. Few of the world's city-dwellers have sufficient living space. Conditions are good in America and in northern Europe or in the wealthy urban areas of poor countries, which house a tiny minority of citizens. Elsewhere, whether in individual or collective residences, crowding is the rule. In cases where the social organization of the family, the street, and the neighborhood teaches a city-dweller, from an early age, to accept lack of privacy while respecting precise rules, order prevails. This is true of Japanese cities or Arab medinas with their low family homes; it applies as well to cities of Korea, China, or the northern Mediterranean, where multi-storied collective residences are the rule. Elsewhere, in the absence of habitual respect for one's neighbors, anxiety and insecurity predominate. For lack of anything better, many families occupy American or South African urban ghettos, the large French housing projects, or the shantytowns of cities in the southern hemisphere. According to the Report on the Situation of Human Habitats in the World, published in March 1996 by the United

**MURAL, MEXICO CITY, MEXICO** [19°20' N, 99°45' W]

The muralist movement sprang from the Mexican revolution in 1910, with roots in the country's history and its workers' movement. An expressionist and nationalist school, muralism promotes a typically Mexican art form that has astonished, even scandalized, the world. Muralists initially used walls to evade censorship, but they became almost official artists when, in 1921, the new government asked them to help launch a popular development campaign. Gigantic frescos appeared on the walls of government buildings. Bearing a message for the masses, muralism allowed Mexican art to assert itself. Today it is seen as a breeding ground for ideas and modes of expression. Its influence has been enormous throughout Latin America and in some U.S. cities, notably San Francisco.

## CITIES ARE THE DEMOGRAPHIC CENTERS OF THE FUTURE

**RECORD CONCENTRATION OF POPULATIONS**
In 1950, **2** cities had populations of over **10 million** (megalopolises). Today, **20** cities have passed that figure. By **2025**, the number of people living in cities will have doubled. It will reach **5 billion**, or **6** out of every **10** people.

**RAPID GROWTH OF THE URBAN POPULATION**
1800: **20 million** people,
    or 2% of the world's population.
1960: **1 billion** people,
    or 33% of the world's population.
2002: **3 billion** people,
    or 48% of the world's population.
By 2017, the figure could reach **4 billion**.

## DEVELOPING COUNTRIES AND URBANISM

**DEVELOPING COUNTRIES: THE URBAN CENTERS OF TOMORROW**
In recent years, towns in developing countries have grown at **4 times** the rate of those in the industrialized countries. It took London **130 years** to go from **1** to **8 million** people; It took Seoul **25 years** to make the same demographic leap. In 2015, **16** of the **22** megalopolises will be situated in developing countries.

**RURAL EXODUS AND ESCALATING URBANISM**
Worldwide, **1 million** people move to cities each week In China during the 1980s and 1990s, some **100 million** people moved from rural into urban areas.

## THE URBAN MYTH

**IN DEVELOPING COUNTRIES THE INFORMAL ECONOMY IS DOMINANT IN CITIES**
In Delhi (India), **61%** of jobs are part of the informal economy. The figure in Bombay (India) is **50%** and in Dhaka (Bangladesh) it is **63%**.

**IN RICH COUNTRIES THERE ARE STILL WIDE SOCIAL GAPS**
In the industrialized nations, **17%** of households live in poverty. In 2003, **3 million** people in European cities had no fixed abode, the highest level since 1950.

**URBAN POPULATION: A SIGN OF DEVELOPMENT?**
In the developed countries, urbanization coincided largely with economic growth and an improvement in the quality of life. In the most developed countries, the urban population is over **70%** of the total, whereas in less developed nations it is less than **30%**. In Africa, more than **70%** of the urban population live in shantytowns. Since 1990, the population of African shantytowns has increased at an annual rate of nearly **5%**.

**CITIES AS CENTERS OF WEALTH?**
Cities produce on average **60%** of the world's GDP and provide the bulk of formal employment (as opposed to the informal economy—undeclared earnings, black market, and other clandestine activities). Between one-quarter and one-third of urban households worldwide are thought to be living in absolute poverty, i.e. earning less than **$1** per person per day.

## THE SERIOUS RISKS OF UNCONTROLLED GROWTH

**POVERTY AND UNSANITARY LIVING CONDITIONS**
In 1995, a United Nations summit on housing estimated that **1 billion** people were without adequate accommodation, and more than **100 million** were homeless.

**NATURAL DISASTERS: UNCONTROLLED GROWTH IN DANGER ZONES**
According to the UNEP (United Nations Environment Program), between **30** and **60%** of the populations of southern megalopolises live in buildings that have been erected without planning permission, including those in areas subject to earthquakes and floods. Developing countries suffer **67%** of deaths linked to natural disasters.

**INEQUALITY AND CRIME**
In Rio de Janeiro, the number of murders in the *favelas* (shantytowns) is **37 times** greater than that in the tourist areas.

## URBAN CONCENTRATION AND POLLUTION

**POLLUTION OF THE ATMOSPHERE**
An inhabitant of Shanghai produces about **4 times** as much $CO_2$ as the average Chinese citizen. According to WHO, **1.5 billion** city-dwellers suffer from air pollution higher than the maximum recommended levels. Pollution linked to transport causes **500,000** a year and between **4** and **5 million** new cases of chronic bronchitis. In the United States, it is estimated that **1 out of 5** cases of lung cancer is caused by exhaust fumes.

**ACCUMULATED WASTE**
Municipal authorities spend up to **30%** of their budget on refuse disposal. In developing countries, disposing of solid waste can cost up to **50%** of the budget. In developing countries, between **30** and **60%** of solid urban waste is not collected, and less than **50%** of the population have their domestic garbage collected. In Buenos Aires, nearly **20,000** people live by sorting refuse.

**QUALITY OF WATER**
Dirty water and insufficient purification plants are a constant source of danger to the inhabitants of shantytowns. Diarrhea is the second most common cause of infant mortality, and is responsible for killing **12%** of children under 5 in the developing countries—some **1.3 million** deaths a year.

---

**ROAD BLOCKED BY A SAND DUNE, NILE VALLEY, EGYPT** (25°24' N, 30°26' E)

Grains of sand, deriving from ancient river or lake alluvial deposits accumulated in ground recesses and sifted by thousands of years of wind and storms, pile up in front of obstacles and thus create dunes. These cover nearly one-third of the Sahara, and the highest, in linear form, can attain a height of almost 1,000 feet (300 m). *Barchans* are mobile, crescent-shaped dunes that move in the direction of the prevailing wind at rates as high as 33 feet (10 m) per year, sometimes even covering infrastructures such as this road in the Nile Valley. Deserts have existed throughout the history of our planet, constantly evolving for hundreds of millions of years in response to climatic changes and continental drift. Twenty thousand years ago forest and prairie covered the mountains in the center of the Sahara; cave paintings have been discovered there that depict elephants, rhinoceros, and giraffes, testifying to their presence in this region about 8,000 years ago. Human activity, notably the overexploitation of the semi-arid area's vegetation bordering the deserts, also plays a role in desertification.

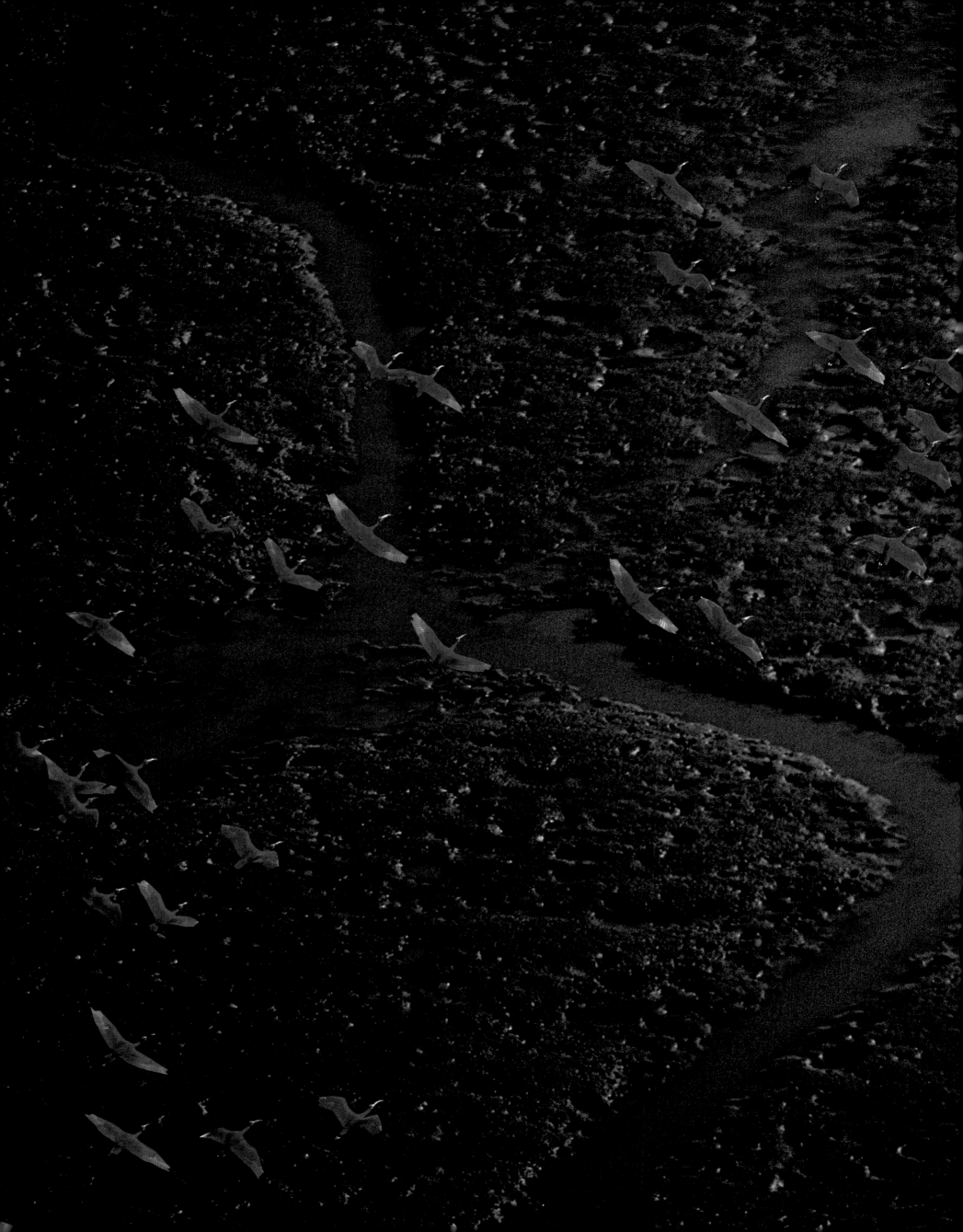

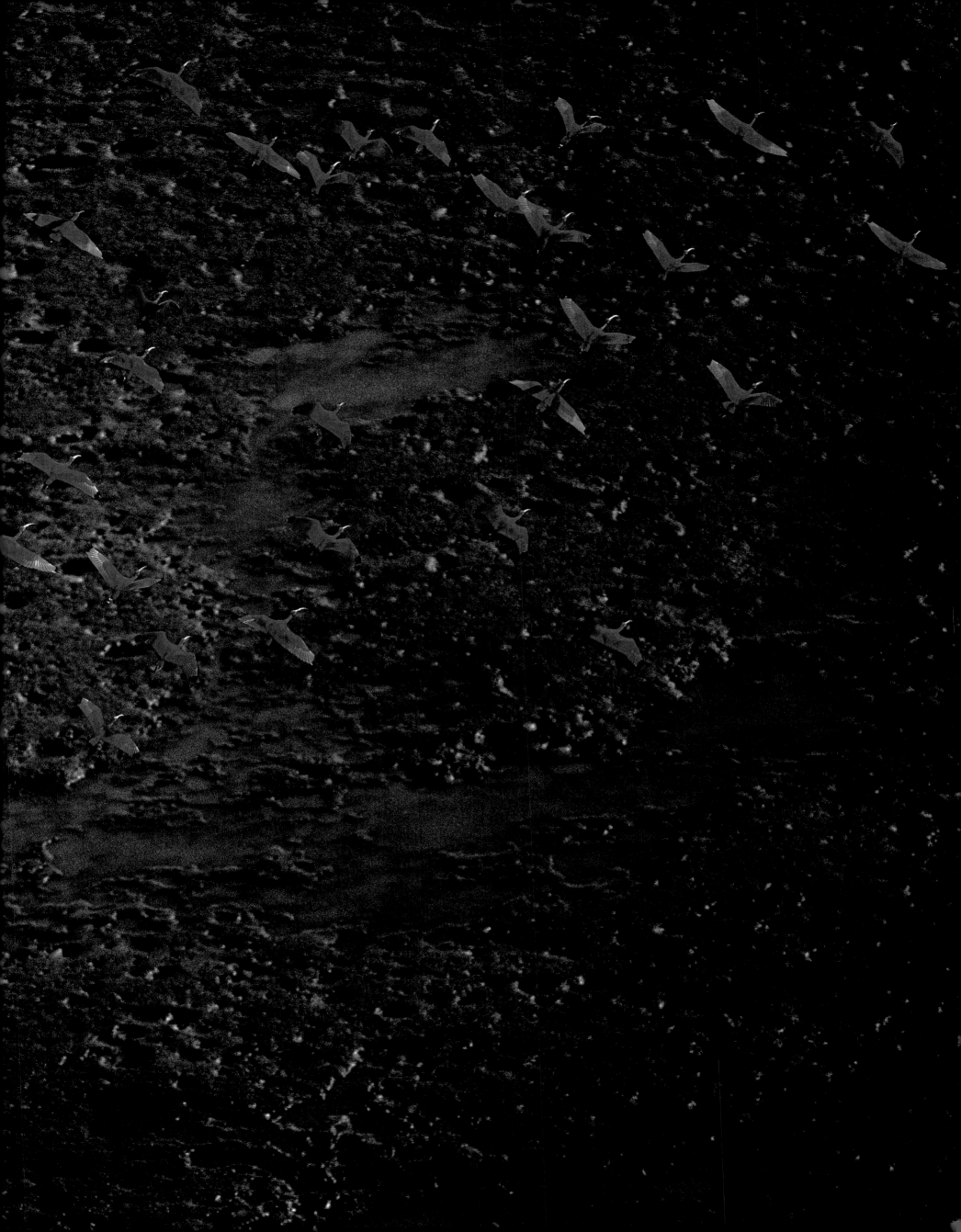

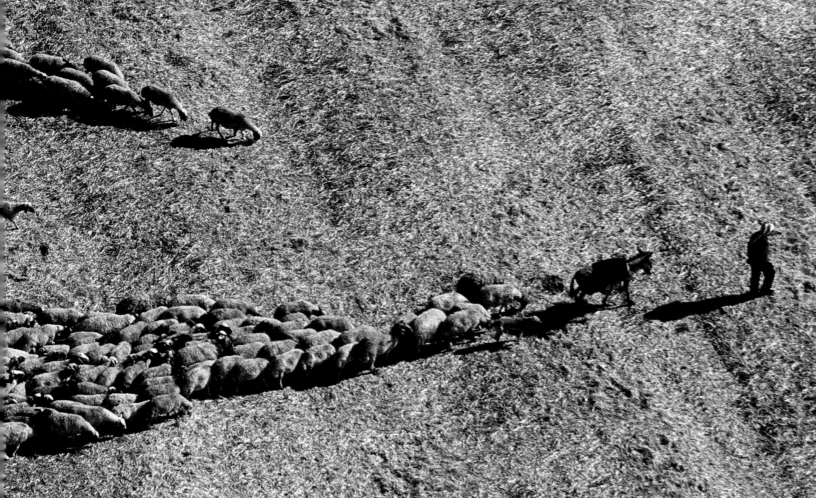

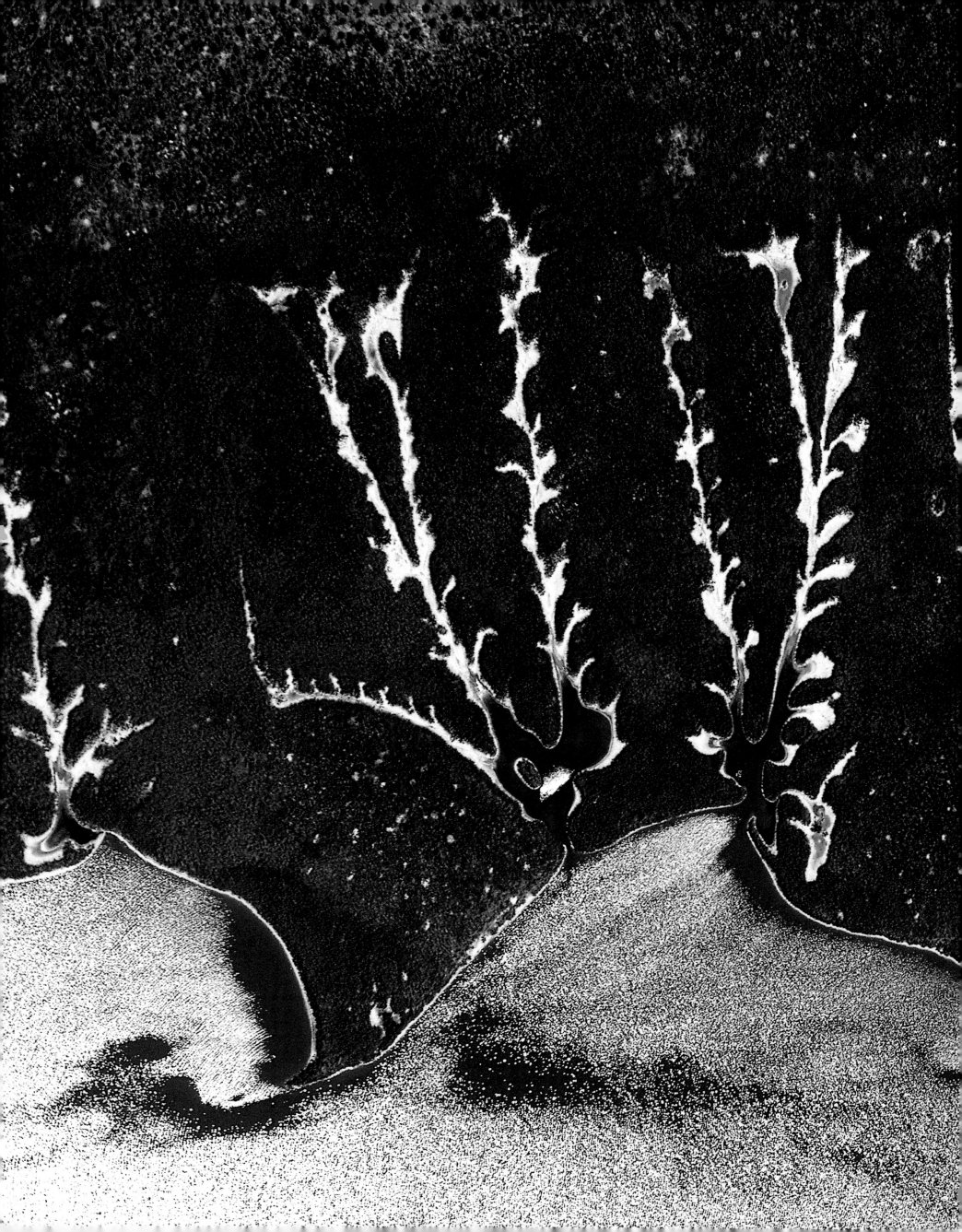

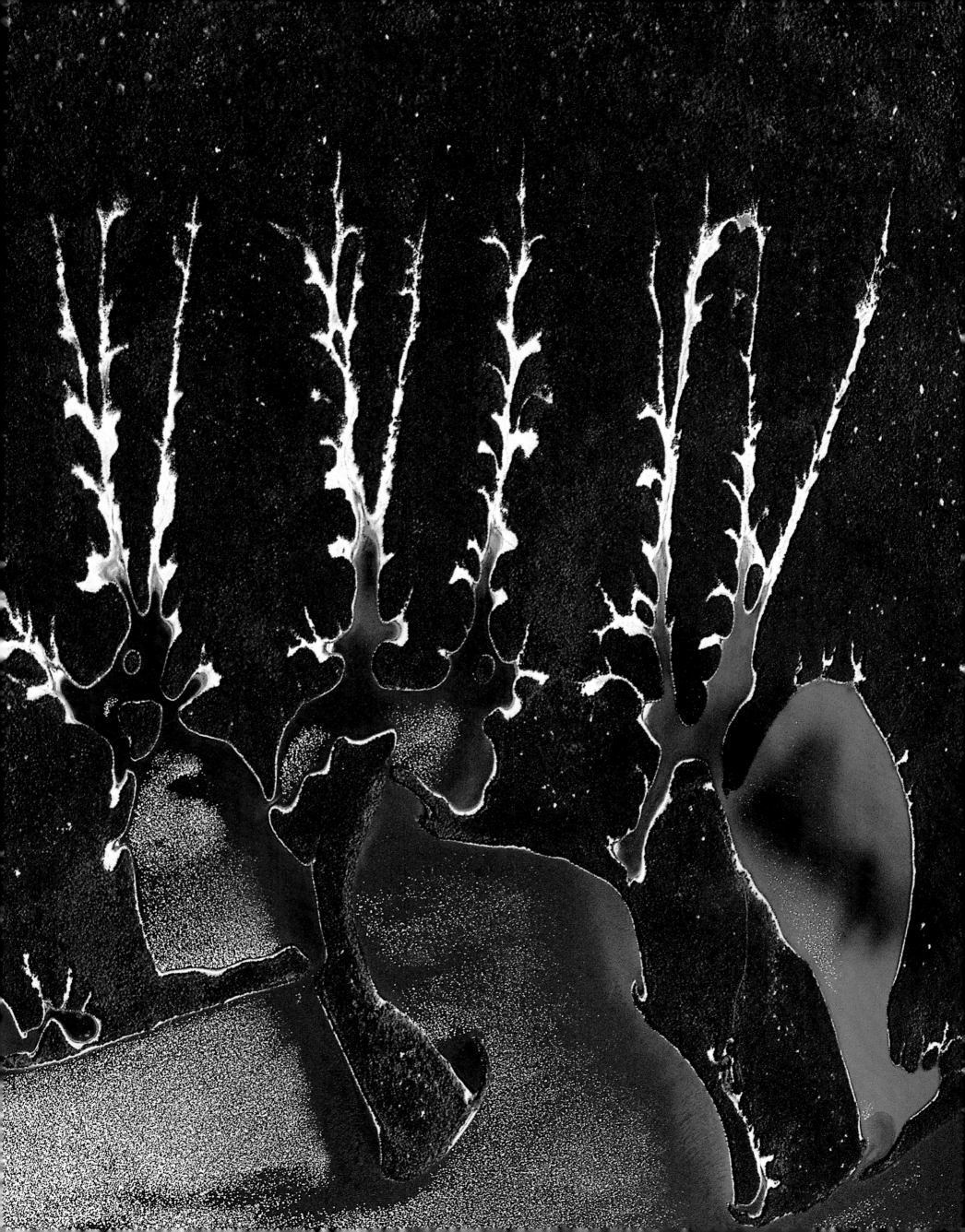

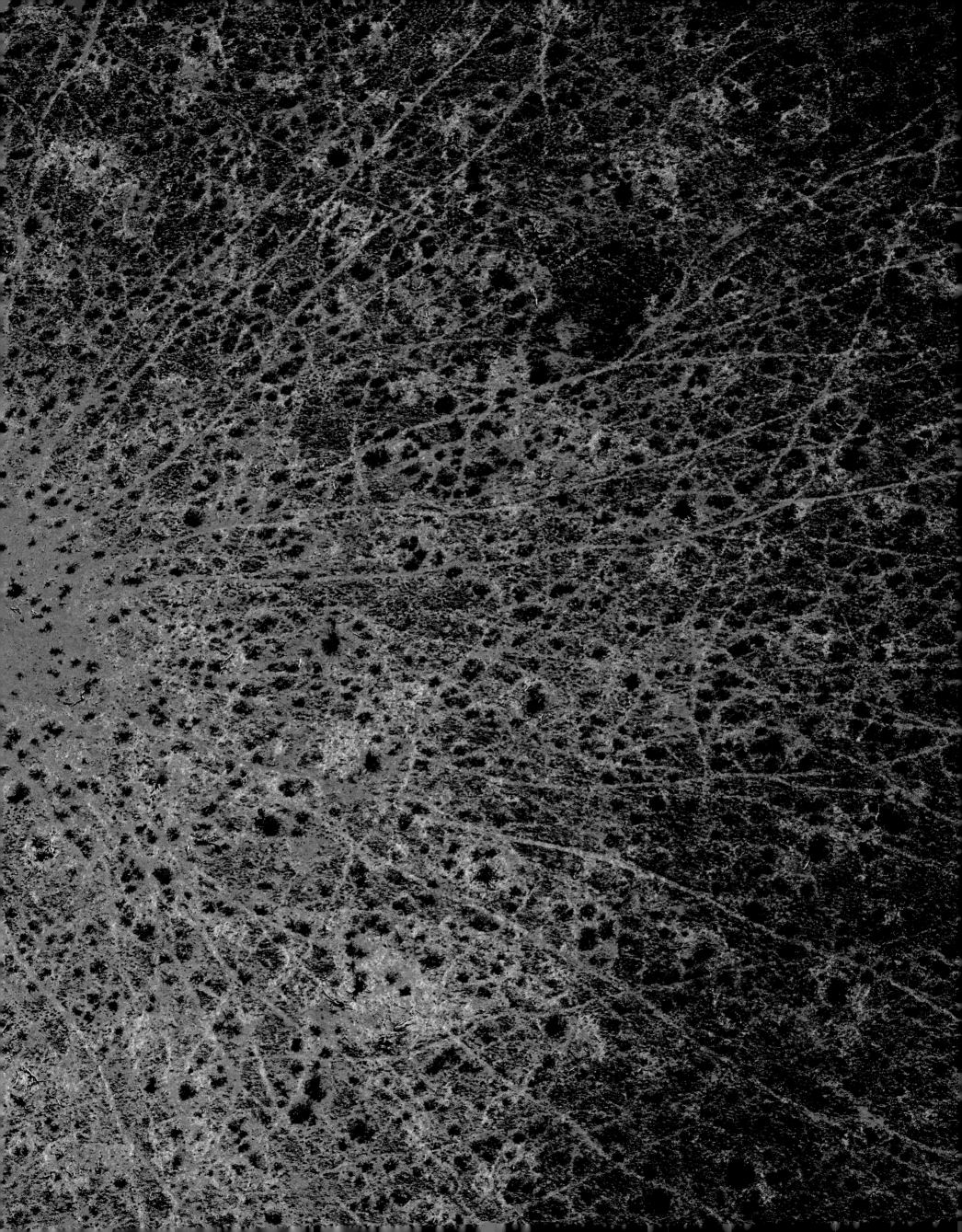

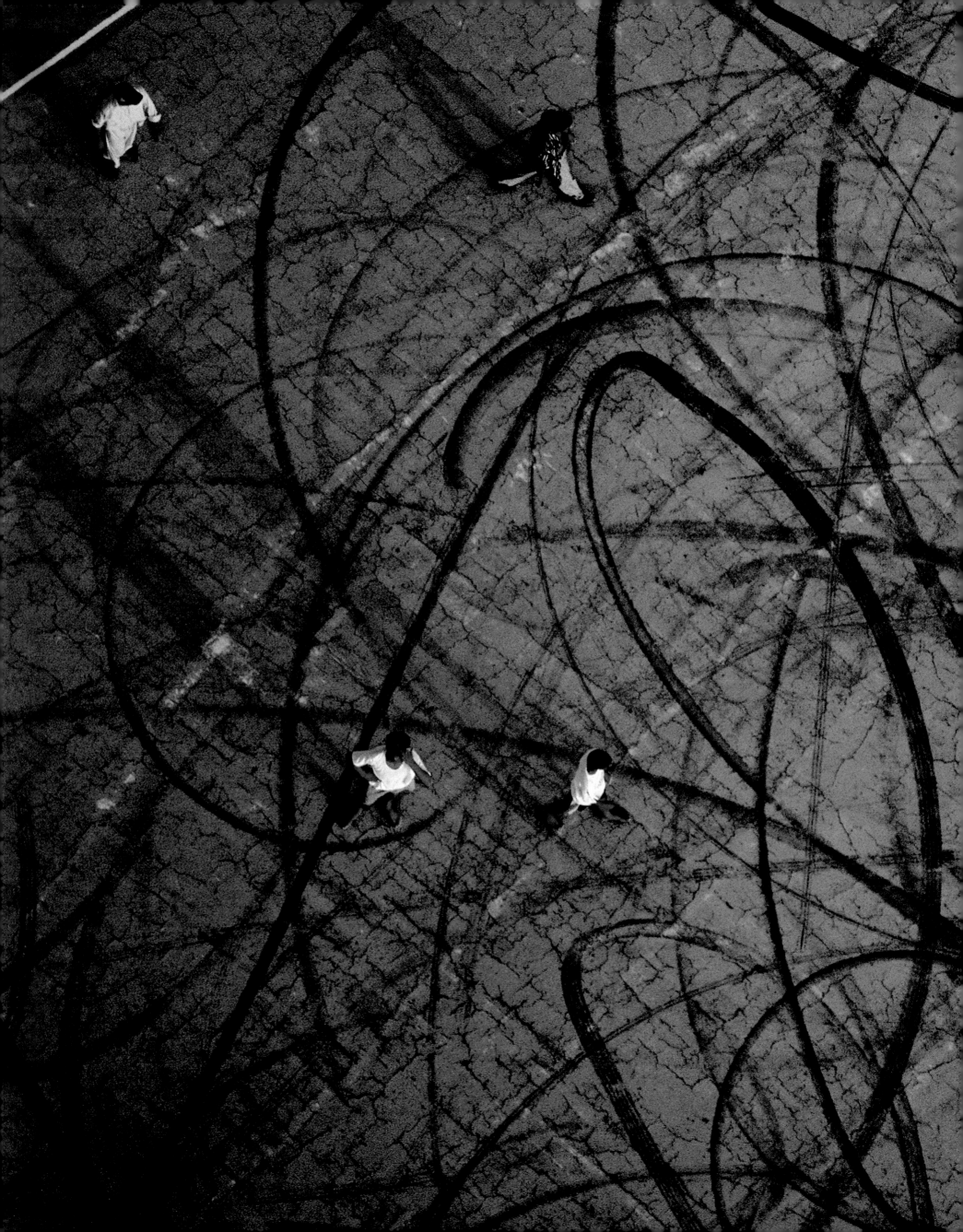

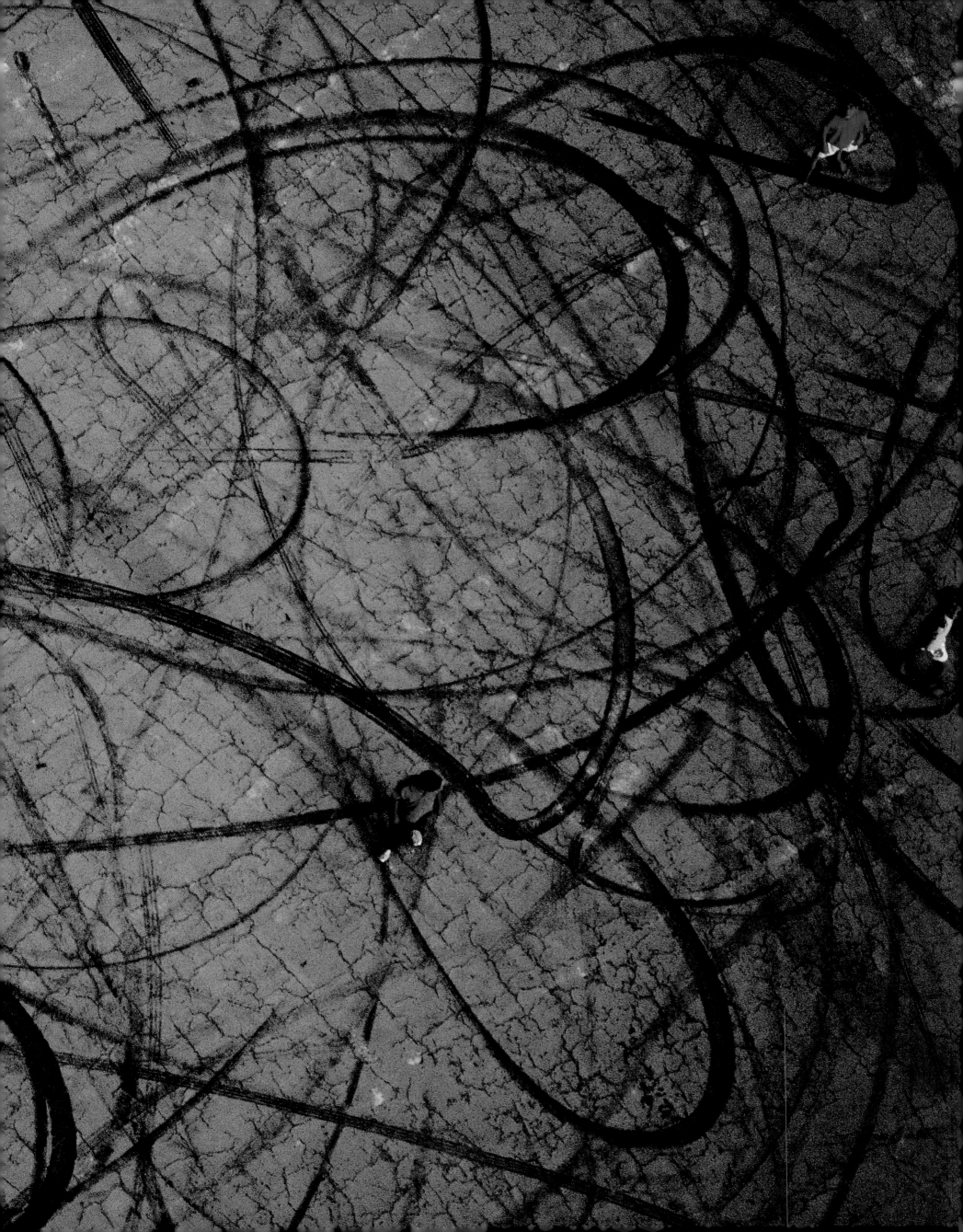

# FARMERS OF THE WORLD: THE PRICE OF OUR FUTURE

There have never been so many farmers on the planet, and the great majority of them work only with simple hand tools. Forced competition against highly equipped, far more productive agro-businesses leads to decades-long developmental deadlock and the impoverishment of the poorest people, even to the point of famine. However, to feed the approximately 9 billion people expected on Earth by 2050, all of the world's forms of agriculture must be mobilized.

Seen from the sky, the Earth is covered with water, swaddled in forests, lightly clad in savannas, veiled in steppes, or adorned with harlequin fields of a thousand or more crops: rice fields checker the valleys, climb the slopes, and ribbon the mountains; vegetable gardens nest in the hollow of tiny crevices; grains and legumes alternate their bright colors in a stream of patchwork fields; roots and tubers crowd together in profuse mounds. Planted terraced fields and close rows of grape vines, tea and coffee plants climb and follow jagged contours. Olive, almond, and apple plantings protect grain fields. Proud date trees, scattered or aligned, protected by a low wall or a small sand dune, open their wide palms on vast oases as they do on the least suspicion of moisture. Different livestock animals, roaming but guarded, enliven these calm landscapes.

On the whole, however, very little equipment can be seen, and practically no tractors or large agricultural machinery. Most poor farmers are so poorly equipped that it is hard to believe they were able, for centuries, to model and remodel this Earth, and constantly restructure these cultivated landscapes so filled with usefulness and elegance.

Yet these images do not lie. At the beginning of the twenty-first century, the active agricultural population numbers 1.3 billion people worldwide, yet there are only 28 million tractors, or barely more than two tractors per 100 people working the fields. Farmers who have great motorized, mechanized capabilities are thus a tiny minority. The best equipped among them use four-wheeled motorized tractors of more than 200 horsepower and other large machines, which are very expensive—costing an average of more than $300,000 per worker—and very effective, allowing a grain cultivator working alone to plant more than

500 acres (200 hectares). Those who use animals are more numerous: there are 250 million working animals in the world, or around one-fifth of the total number of agricultural workers. The best equipped use horses or cattle, to work plows or pull carts, equipment that can cost as much as $10,000, and which allows a grain cultivator working alone to cultivate about 25 acres (10 hectares).

The other four-fifths, approximately, of the world population working in agriculture and livestock, or 1 billion people today, only have manual tools such as hoes, spades, machetes, knives, sickles, baskets, or pestles for clearing, plowing, sowing, weeding, harvesting, winnowing, transporting, and piling up grain. The best tools cost less than $100 and scarcely enable the cultivation of 2.5 acres (1 hectare) per worker.

In addition to these enormous inequalities of equipment and arable area per worker, there are inequalities of access to the most productive crops, to fertilizers and treatment products, which cause great disparities in yield per acre. For instance, the most productive grain varieties, resulting from advanced selections, can bring yields greater than 10 metric tons per hectare, with an expenditure of $500 per hectare for mineral fertilizers and treatment products. On the other hand, so-called domestic grains, which have not been subjected to any systematic selection and are still cultivated without fertilizers or treatment products, rarely reach a yield of more than 0.4 tons per acre (1 metric ton per hectare).

Thus, the gross productivity of a peasant working with manual tools, without selected crops, fertilizers, or treatment products, can barely exceed 1 ton of equivalent grains (quantity of grain of the same caloric value) per worker per year, whereas the productivity of a farmer who is among those best supplied with mechanical, chemical, and biological resources exceeds 2,000 tons of equivalent grains per worker per year. The difference in productivity between the most productive and the least productive agriculture in the world today is therefore a ratio of 1 to 2,000!

Before World War II this proportion was only 1 to 10. In the past century, the "modern agricultural revolution" occurred in developed countries. Motorization and mechanization became more effective (and costly), plant varieties and animal races grew ever more productive, and fertilizer, treatment products, and concentrated foods for

◁ DWELLINGS ON AN ISLET IN THE RIVER NIGER, BETWEEN BOUREM AND GAO, MALI
(16°30' N, 0°12' W)

The river Niger takes its name from the Tuareg expression *egerou n-igereou*, which means "river of rivers." In giving it this name, the nomads meant to emphasize the inestimable value of this river, which flows through Mali's Saharan sands. Tracing a great loop through West Africa, this "Western Nile" floods every year, between July and December. But the local people are not alarmed, for they have adapted their lives to this seasonal fluctuation and are well aware of the floods' importance in fertilizing the soil and helping fish to breed. They do not attempt to build embankments along the river but are content instead to build their houses on land that is not prone to flooding. They prefer to live on *togué*, hillocks whose tops remain above water—like islets—when the river is in flood. What does worry them is drought, which has reduced the river's floods over the last 30 years.

can feed four people on 880 pounds (400 kg) of grain. In fact, at this price he can neither completely replace his tools, as cheap as they are, nor eat his fill and renew his strength to work; he is therefore condemned to debt and to emigration to the under-equipped, under-industrialized shantytowns.

In addition, in many former colonies (such as Latin America and southern Africa) and former Communist countries (Ukraine, Russia), which did not experience any recent agrarian reform, most of these poorly equipped peasants are more or less deprived of land by large farms. With an available area of land smaller than the area they could feasibly cultivate and which would be needed to make their own family self-sustaining, these "*minifundia*" farmers are obliged to seek day-to-day work on the huge "*latifundia*" farms, for wages of around $1 per day, or else move to the city slums.

Under these conditions, it is easy to understand why in developing countries, most of the 800 million people who are malnourished, going hungry almost every day, are the farmers who have the worst equip-

ment, the worst location, and the worst lodgings, or are salaried workers on under-funded farms. Most of the hungry people in the world, then, are not urban consumers who purchase their food but peasants who grow and sell agricultural produce. It is clear, therefore, that development policies that consist of pushing forward the agricultural revolution and the green revolution into the most disadvantaged regions, and food policies that consist in supplying cities with surplus food at constantly lower prices, are useless in combating hunger.

In the year 2050 our planet will have 9 billion people. To feed such a population adequately, without malnutrition or famine, the quantity of vegetal produce intended for feeding people and domestic animals must be more than doubled all over the world. It will have to be nearly tripled in developing countries, increased more than fivefold in Africa, and more than tenfold in several African countries.

To obtain such an enormous increase in production, some are looking toward new progress in the modern agricultural revolution and the green revolution. However, in regions and on farms where these are already well advanced, the potential rise in production that they offer will soon come up against many of the problems we have discussed. As for genetically modified organisms (GMO), the latest avatar of these two agricultural revolutions, they are no better equipped to bring about a miraculous restoration of the agricultural and food situation. The creation of GMOs is very expensive, and monitoring their ecological and digestive safety costs even more. It is so costly that research is basically oriented to suit the needs of the most prosperous producers and consumers. It is so expensive that the seeds of GMOs

⌃ **HARVESTING ALMONDS ON MAJORCA, THE BALEARIC ISLANDS, SPAIN**
(39°36' N, 3°02' E)

As in all Mediterranean countries, the ancient cultivation of almonds has remained traditional in the Spanish archipelago of the Balearic Islands. The almonds are generally gathered by shaking the tree branches over sheets spread out beneath. The low productivity of each almond tree (4.4 to 11 pounds, or 2 to 5 kg, of almonds per tree) is compensated for by the large area planted with trees; however, that area has diminished considerably because old trees have rarely been replaced. Spain nevertheless remains the second-greatest almond producer in the world (after the United States), accounting for about 274,000 tons per year, nearly 80 percent of which are consumed by European countries in various forms: in confectionery and pastry (dried sweet almonds), as an aromatic agent (essence of bitter almond), or in cosmetics (sweet almond oil).

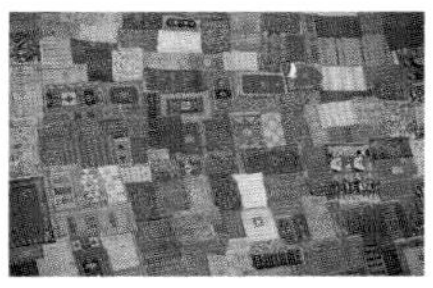

**PAGES 130–131**
PATCHWORK OF CARPETS IN MARRAKECH, MOROCCO
(31°32′ N, 8°03′ W)

Along with Algeria, Egypt, and Tunisia, Morocco is a major center of carpet production. The carpets are traditionally made of linen, a symbol of protection and happiness, and may incorporate silk, cotton, and sometimes camel or goat hair. The colors and designs are characteristic of the production regions, and the High Atlas Mountains, at the foot of which Marrakech lies, offer the warmest hues. The carpets are woven primarily by women workers, along with some children. Child labor has become a national issue in Morocco, where almost 600,000 children under the age of 14 are obliged to work and have no access to education. Worldwide there are 352 million child workers between the ages of 5 and 14, including more than 246 million who work illegally and almost 171 million in dangerous conditions. Asia accounts of 61 percent of child labor, Africa 30 percent, and Latin America 7 percent. Some products now include a label which guarantees to consumers that their purchase was made without child labor.

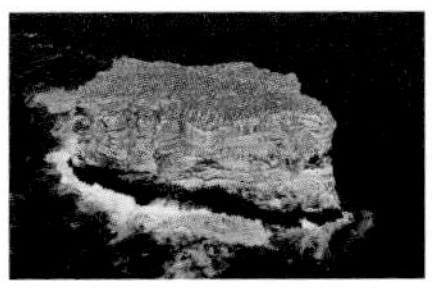

**PAGES 132–133**
NORTHERN GANNET COLONY, ELDEY ISLAND, ICELAND
(63°43′ N, 22°58′ W)

Iceland, at the crossroads of the Arctic, North America, and Europe, hosts a varied population of birds: 70 species regularly nest there, and 300 others arrive for shorter periods. Eldey Island, 9 miles (14 km) south of the Icelandic coast, is a rocky peak 224 feet (70 m) high that has been declared a nature reserve. Each year it attracts one of the world's largest colonies of northern gannets (*Morus bassanus*), which includes more than 40,000 birds. They arrive on the island in January and February for nesting, and each couple gives birth to only one offspring. In September the birds depart to spend the winter off the coast of Africa. Like nearly one-fourth of the bird species of the Palearctic region, northern gannets migrate toward Africa covering more than 180 miles (300 km) a day and braving natural perils (opposing winds, predators) as well as threats resulting from human activity (destruction of their habitats, pesticides, falling fish stocks). In 1844 on Eldey Island the last two specimens of the great auk (*Alca impennis*), a once common species, were exterminated.

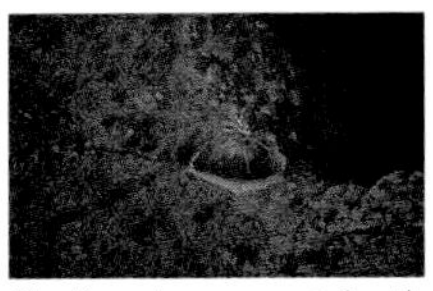

**PAGES 134–135**
PALM TREES IN THE MOUNTAINS OF THE MUSANDAM PENINSULA, OMAN
(26°06′ N, 56°16′ E)

The limestone mountains that dominate the Sultanate of Oman are actually sea floors that have emerged from the water as a result of contact between the Arabian Peninsula and the ocean during major tectonic movements. Isolated at the extreme north from the rest of the country and separated by the United Arab Emirates, the Musandam Peninsula juts out into the Strait of Hormuz, which connects the Persian Gulf and the Gulf of Oman. The desolate heights bear little if any vegetation; nevertheless, on these mountains, which rise 6,500 feet (2,000 m) above sea level, the Shihuh villagers graze their herds following the rainy season. Here they also plant date palms, encircling the land with small stone walls. The walls not only protect the crops from hungry goats; they also help to retain water and limit erosion, by trapping the fertile silt during the rare but violent rains in winter.

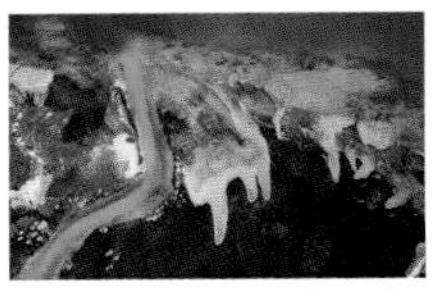

**PAGES 136–137**
VILLAGE NEAR PANDUCAN, PHILIPPINES
(6°15′ N, 120°36′ E)

The Panducan region, in the Pangutaran group of islands, is part of the Sulu archipelago. The islands are home to the Tausug, "people of the sea currents," who number 400,000. Formerly smugglers, the Tausug now live from trade and fishing. They live in small hamlets of bamboo houses on stilts, scattered along the coasts fringed with coral. The coral reefs of the Philippines make up 9 percent of the world's total, and are the most biologically diverse, with over half of tropical fish species. However, fishing with cyanide (used to capture aquarium fish) or with explosives—as is practiced by a minority of unscrupulous fishermen—has had a devastating effect on the reefs, nearly 70 percent of which are now badly damaged. The consequences are grave for the diet of the Filipinos themselves since the fish and mollusks are their main source of protein. In the neighboring Indonesian archipelago, increased surveillance of the national parks has reduced these local practices, and since 1998 fifteen villages have banned fishing in certain damaged reefs, thus creating the first natural marine reserves to be run by local communities.

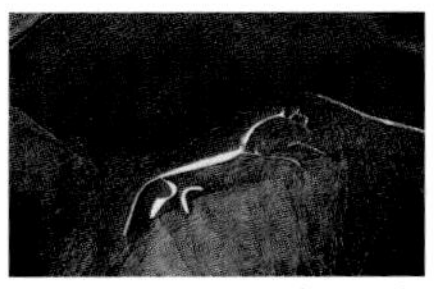

**PAGES 138–139**
WHITE HORSE OF UFFINGTON, OXFORDSHIRE, ENGLAND
(51°34′ N, 1°33′ W)

This 365-foot-long (111 m) silhouette of a horse carved into the chalky side of a hill in the county of Oxfordshire, west of London, stands out clearly downhill from the ruins of the castle of Uffington. Its similarity to the designs on ancient coins suggest that it is the work of Celts in the Iron Age, from around 100 BC. Local tradition maintains that this stylized depiction is the image of a dragon, drawn in homage to Saint George, who, according to legend, killed the monster on a neighboring hill. But the most likely hypothesis is that this engraving was dedicated to the cult of the Celtic goddess Epona, who was usually depicted in the form of a horse. A dozen other white horses, carefully preserved, decorate hills in this region and neighboring Wiltshire, illustrating the age-old human desire to trace onto the landscape images of power and dreams.

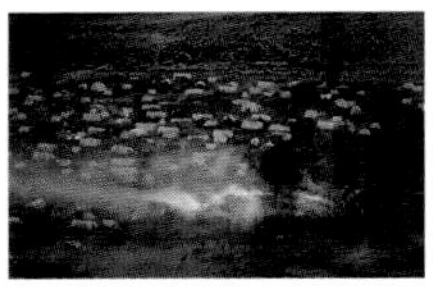

**PAGES 140–141**
SUDANESE REFUGEE CAMPS AT GOZ AMER NEAR THE SUDANESE BORDER, CHAD
(12°00′ N, 21°23′ E)

Sudan, an African giant with no less than nine borders, has experienced only eleven years of peace since it gained its independence in 1955. The origins of the civil war lie in the conflict between the dominant north, which is Arab and Muslim, and the black African south, with a Christian or animist majority. Since 2003, the war has intensified, and in the Darfur region in the southwest of the country it has changed and has now become a conflict between Muslims of Arab origin and those of black origin. The Arab Janjaweed militia are armed by the government, and in one year have driven out more than a million people. Nearly 200,000 of these have sought refuge in Chad. Nowadays, civil wars have become much more common than those between nations. Since 1990, 55 out of 59 recorded wars have resulted from internal conflicts, with a direct effect on civilian populations. Over two million children have been killed, and 20 million have lost their homes, with villages being burned down, looting, rape, murder, and the systematic destruction of all means of subsistence. People are helpless in the face of this violence since much of it stems from their own governments.

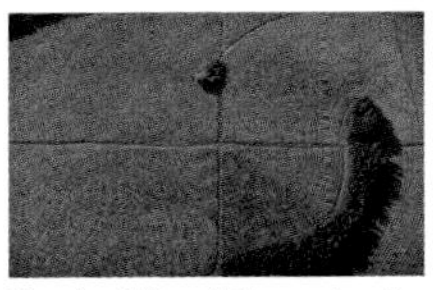

**PAGES 142–143**
TEA CULTIVATION IN CORRIENTES PROVINCE, ARGENTINA
(27°50′ S, 56°01′ W)

The fertility of the red soil and the regular rains of the Corrientes region create the ideal conditions for the cultivation of tea. In an effort to protect the soil against erosion, tea is planted along curved terraces and protected from the wind by hedges. Unlike Asian and African countries, where the young sprouts are hand-picked, in Argentina mechanical harvesting is the rule, done mainly with high-clearance tractors that are driven along the straight rows of tea bushes. The tea cultivated here, a hybrid of the Indian Assam variety, produces only a low yield (64,000 metric tons per year). Harvested in summer, it complements the large winter production of *maté* tea, a type of holly, also known as "Jesuit tea." Today tea is cultivated in forty-five countries; India, China, and Sri Lanka alone provide 70 percent of the world's tea production.

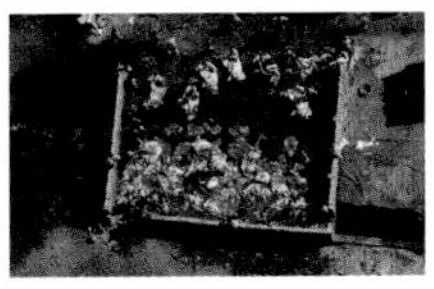

**PAGES 144–145**
SLAUGHTERHOUSE NEAR NEW DELHI, INDIA
(28°36′ N, 77°12′ E)

India's long tradition of vegetarianism is based on religious and philosophical principles, but the consumption of meat is on the increase. About two-thirds of the world's population are vegetarian and one-third carnivorous. The area of land and the amount of water and energy required to produce meat are considerably greater than those needed for plants, and the pressure exerted on the environment for a predominantly meat-eating diet is irreversible. Future generations will be deprived of vital resources if the modern world continues to consume such vast quantities of meat. Furthermore, nutritionists have demonstrated that excessive consumption of meat may lead to cardiovascular diseases and certain types of cancer. A rational movement towards a more balanced diet—richer in fruit and vegetables and less dependent on meat—would be beneficial both to the planet and to human beings.

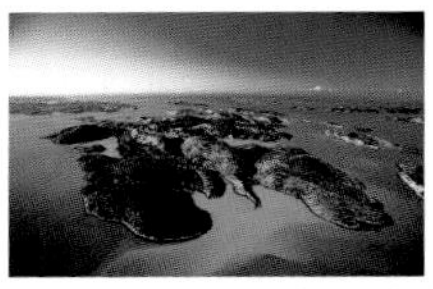

**PAGES 146–147**
BUCCANEER ARCHIPELAGO, WEST KIMBERLEY, AUSTRALIA
(16°17′ S, 123°20′ E)

Thousands of uncultivated islands, including Buccaneer Archipelago, emerge from the waters off the jagged, eroded coasts of northwestern Australia. The waters of the Timor Sea that surround these islands have remained relatively untouched by pollution, which has allowed fragile species such as the *Pinctada maxima* oyster to develop. Harvested in their natural setting, the sea floor, these mollusks are exploited for the production of cultured pearls. Australian pearls, 80 percent of which come from the west of the country, are twice as large (averaging a half-inch, or 12 mm, in diameter) and, according to experts, finer in appearance than those of Japan, which pioneered the pearl industry at the turn of the 20th century and remains the world's leading producer. Since 1992, the spectacular rise of the Australian pearl industry—from an average of one ton before 1993 to more than 8 tons a year in 1999—has led a major drop in prices. European and American imports doubled and quadrupled between 1995 and 2000. Today, pearl-farmers are debating whether it is worth increasing yields even further, at the risk of losing their reputation for quality.

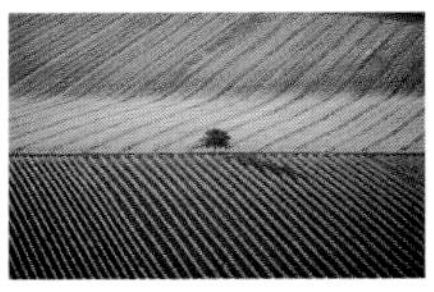

**PAGES 148–149**
AGRICULTURAL LANDSCAPE NEAR COGNAC, CHARENTE, FRANCE (45°42′ N, 0°17′ W)

In the 19th century phylloxera, an aphid-like insect, ravaged the vineyards of Charente along with nearly half of all French vines. A major part of the grape stocks of this region was replaced by cereal plantings, which still dominate the landscape. The vineyards were gradually restored around the city of Cognac, where the production of the liquor of the same name has steadily increased. Growing on chalky soil, the *ugni blanc* grape (known locally as Saint-Émilion) yields a wine that is distilled and aged in oak casks to produce cognac. The stock currently being aged exceeds the equivalent of 1 billion bottles, or six years worth of stock. The trade name Cognac is restricted to this area alone, limited by legal decree since 1909, and is divided into six vintages. Cognac takes up 11 percent of the agricultural land in its region and employs around 19,000 people: not just in vineyards and distilleries, but also in all the associated trades such as corkage, bottling, packaging, and marketing. Of the total production, 94.3 percent is exported, chiefly to the United States, the United Kingdom, and Singapore.

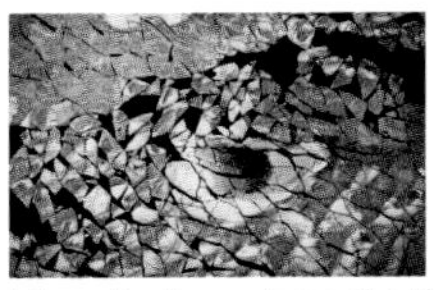

**PAGES 150–151**
FORMATION OF SEA ICE IN THE TURKÜ ARCHIPELAGO, FINLAND
(60°27′ N, 22°00′ E)

Like a broken mirror, the thin ice of the Baltic breaks into sharp fragments that reflect the feeble light of a Finnish winter. This fragile sheet breaks only to reform more solidly. Sea ice floats on the current and can break up, but the fragments then meet again and pile together, until they reach their maximum thickness (an average of 20 to 25 inches, or 50 to 65 centimeters) in early April. The ice then disappears rapidly in spring, leaving the islands of the Turkü archipelago ice-free. Finland has no permanent ice sheet. Although the country is at the same latitude as Alaska and Greenland, it has a relatively temperate climate thanks to the Gulf Stream. This great warm sea current, which crosses the Atlantic and warms Western Europe, may disappear as the climate changes and the Arctic ice cap melts. If this came about, Europe's climate would resemble that of Canada, which is at the same latitude.

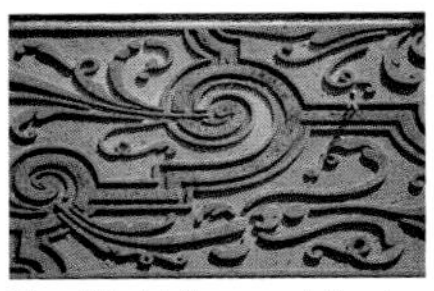

**PAGES 152–153**
GARDENS AT THE CHÂTEAU OF VAUX-LE-VICOMTE, MAINCY, SEINE-ET-MARNE, FRANCE (48°34′ N, 2°43′ E)

The "Turkish carpets"—decorative gardens of boxwood hedges—of the château of Vaux-le-Vicomte were designed by the landscape architect Achille Duchêne in the early 20th century. These were additions to the château buildings and grounds, which date from the 17th century. Built by Nicolas Fouquet, minister of finance to King Louis XIV, the château took five years and approximately 18,000 workers to complete. The garden, set off by several lakes and fountains, is 8,000 feet (2,500 m) long, which required the destruction of two hamlets. Fouquet invited the young Louis XIV to visit in 1661; offended by the splendor of his subject's abode, the king ordered an investigation of Fouquet and had him arrested. Le Nôtre, the architect of the gardens, was placed in charge of the royal parks and gardens. He designed other gardens in the classic French style for the châteaux of Saint-Germain-en-Laye, Saint-Cloud, and Fontainebleau, but his masterpiece was the gardens of Versailles, the palace of the Sun King himself.

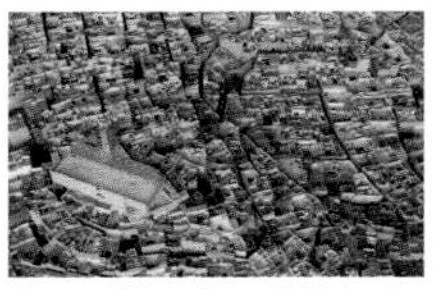

**PAGES 154–155**
EL ATEUF, M'ZAB VALLEY, ALGERIA
(32°27′ N, 3°44′ E)

Some 370 miles (600 km) south of Algiers, beyond the peaks of the Saharan Atlas Mountains, are towns of pink plaster, gentle light, and narrow covered lanes, extending along the M'Zab *wadi*, which winds through the first plateaus of the Great Western Erg. The climate here is rough, hot, and windy, and rain is extremely rare. But the towns built in the 11th century by the Mozabites are miracles of their kind which have never ceased to amaze such great architects as Le Corbusier, Ravereau, and Frank Lloyd Wright. With extraordinary uniformity, these towns in the M'Zab *wadi* are all built high up in order to avoid the rare but violent floods, and they all follow the same basic plan: the houses stretch from the mosque at the top of the town, down toward the lower levels where the city ramparts are, while palm groves provide fruit, vegetables and shade during periods of great heat. Each house is laid out around a main room whose ceiling is pierced by a large square opening, and this is the central patio where the family congregates. A flight of steps leads to the terrace, often artificially constructed and sometimes ringed with small rooms where people sleep in the winter.

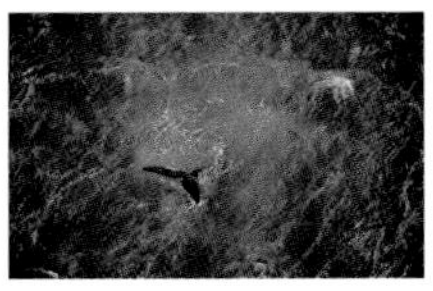

**PAGES 156–157**
WHALE OFF THE VALDÉS PENINSULA, ARGENTINA
(42°23′ S, 64°29′ W)

After summering in the Arctic, whales return to the southern seas each winter to reproduce. From July to November, whales mate and bear their young along the coasts of the Valdés Peninsula in Argentina. Until the 1950s, this migratory marine mammal was extensively hunted for its meat and the oil extracted from its fat, which brought it to the edge of extinction. Protective measures were adopted after international attention was focused on the problem in 1937. In 1982 a moratorium was declared on whale hunting for commercial purposes, and in 1994 the southern seas became a whale sanctuary; the Indian Ocean was established as a sanctuary fifteen years earlier. Despite these efforts it was estimated in 2001 that more than 21,000 whales have been killed since the moratorium came into force, mainly by Japan and Norway. After decades of protection, 7 of the 13 whale species, of which only a few thousand remain (10 to 60 times fewer than in the early 20th century), are still endangered.

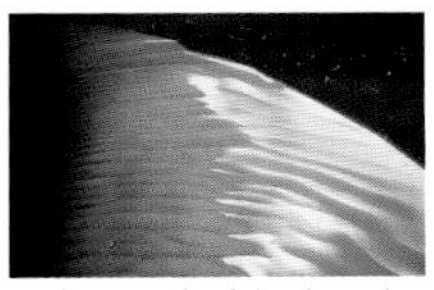

**PAGES 158–159**
NATURE RESERVE, ARGUIN BANK, GIRONDE, FRANCE
(44°39′ N, 1°15′ W)

At the mouth of the Arcachon basin, between Cap-Ferret and the Pilat dune (the highest in France, 350 feet, or 106 m, high), the Arguin bank shows through the waters of the Atlantic Ocean. The site is made up of a group of sandy islets that change form and position according to marine winds and currents on a relatively regular cycle of some eighty years, varying the area from 375 to 1,200 acres (150 to 500 hectares). It was declared a nature reserve in 1972 and became part of the Natura 2000 conservation network in January 2005. The Arguin bank serves as a place for short stops, hibernation, or nesting for many migratory bird species. It primarily hosts a colony of 4,000 to 5,000 pairs of sandwich terns (*Sterna sanvicensis*), one of the three largest in Europe. Despite its protected status, the nature reserve is threatened by growing crowds of tourists, the development of oyster farming on its periphery, and sea pollution. In January 2003 it suffered heavily from an oil spill from the tanker *Prestige*, but swift action from conservationists allowed the damage to be contained, and in May 2003 there were celebrations when a new generation of chicks was born.

livestock were used more intensely. These changes led to unprecedented levels of productivity. But the great majority of the peasants in developing countries were unable to profit from this revolution, because the monetary costs of doing so represented several hundred years of their labor.

As a result, the "green revolution," a variant of the agricultural revolution that does not include motorization and mechanization, spread much more widely in developing countries. This revolution consisted of the selection of highly productive varieties of rice, corn, wheat, soya, and a few large export crops, as well as wide use of fertilizers, treatment products, and, if appropriate, irrigation. Farmers capable of acquiring and profitably using these means of production were able to attain productivity levels of 10 tons of equivalent grains per worker per year for manual farming, or 50 tons for farming with draft animals. It should be emphasized that in most countries, both the modern agricultural revolution and the green revolution have been supported by public authorities.

At this time the modern agricultural revolution has aided only a few million farmers throughout the world, whereas the green revolution has helped almost two-thirds of farmers. The over one-third of world farm workers remaining, 500 million in number, representing more than a billion people to be fed, not only work with strictly manual tools but also without fertilizers or livestock feed, without product treatments or selected plant and animal varieties.

These two agricultural revolutions were heavily responsible for the very steep rise in world food production: it multiplied by 2.6 between 1950 and 2000, while the human population multiplied by 2.4. This meant an enrichment of the food ration of most residents of developed countries and of the wealthiest inhabitants of developing countries.

The modern agricultural revolution and the transportation revolution have led to the replacement of the former systems of vegetable and animal polyproduction with systems of production specialized in one or another type of agriculture or livestock. With the use of mineral fertilizers and tractors, farms were dispensed from maintaining livestock to produce manure and draw agricultural machinery; and because of the motorization of transport and the facilitation of exchange, farms have been freed from the obligation to provide all sorts of vegetable and animal products to supply the local market. In consequence, each farm was able to orient itself toward producing the simplified production combination that is most profitable to itself. This has meant a great deal of spatial redistribution and regional regrouping: grains here, weeded plants there, viticulture, fruit tree plantings, horticulture, timber, milk-producing cows or sheep, meat production in other places. Within these simplified ecosystems, wild flora and fauna are suppressed by artificial means and have therefore been considerably reduced. The utilization of strong doses of fertilizer and chemical-treatment products or the massive distribution of waste from great numbers of animals concentrated under one roof can cause, in some places, pollutions of surface and groundwaters and sometimes an alteration in food products themselves (excessive nitrates in vegetables, pesticides on fruits, hormones and antibiotics in meat).

All of these problems are seen as well, to various degrees, in the areas of the green revolution, which have also experienced salination of bodies of water, as well as irrigated and poorly drained soils.

In countries where these two revolutions have developed on a large scale, productivity gains have been so rapid and large that they have exceeded industry and services. The result has been a strong decline in real agricultural prices. Prices dropped by factors of three, four, or five, resulting in the impoverishment and then the elimination of a growing number of farms.

Moreover, some countries have been able to produce exportable surpluses at prices far below production costs of other countries. International exchanges of basic agricultural products only affect a small portion of world production and consumption (about 15 percent for grains, for example). On the corresponding markets, where solvent demand is relatively low, prices tend to be close to the most competitive export prices. The large agro-exporting businesses of Brazil and Argentina, South Africa and Zimbabwe, and Ukraine and Russia, are well equipped and have vast spaces at low cost as well as workforces that are among the least expensive in the world. At this kind of estate, an agricultural worker earning $1,000 per year (a hypothetically high sum) can produce more than 1,000 tons of grain; therefore the cost of labor per ton of grain is less than one dollar, and a ton of grain is exportable at about $70. But these prices are far below the cost prices of the great majority of the world's farmers. At those prices, even most of the farmers in the developed world would have no profit or negative profits. They therefore cannot resist the competition of international markets, nor can they stay in business for long periods, unless they come from countries with higher incomes, keen to protect their independence or their food production levels, and where, because of this, they receive large public subsidies. In a few poor countries (e.g. Thailand and Vietnam) gains in productivity due to the green revolution are combined with salaries and revenues that are so low that the countries export rice even though malnutrition is still a serious problem.

For the vast majority of the world's poor farmers, international prices for basic subsistence goods are too low to allow them to live off their work and to renew their means of production, let alone to invest and get ahead. Because of the decline in transport costs and the growing liberalization of international trade, agricultural prices within different countries tend to be close to international market prices. This obstructs development, impoverishes the ever-growing class of poor country people, and drives them to emigrate, thus increasing unemployment and serving to drive down wages.

To help explain this process of extreme impoverishment of the peasant class to the point of hunger, consider the example of a Sudanese, Andean, or Himalayan grain farmer who uses manual tools and produces 2,200 pounds (1,000 kg) of net grain (with seeds removed), without fertilizer or treatment products. Fifty years ago a grain farmer received the equivalent of $40 (in modern terms) for 220 pounds (100 kg) of grain; thus he had to sell 440 pounds (200 kg) to replace his equipment, clothing, and so on, leaving 1,760 pounds (800 kg) for the modest feeding of four people. By depriving himself a little, he could even sell 220 pounds (100 kg) more to buy some new, more efficient tool. Twenty years ago he received the equivalent of just $20 today for 220 pounds (100 kg); this meant he had to sell 880 pounds (400 kg) of grain to replace his equipment and would have only 1,320 pounds (600 kg) left to feed four people, inadequately in this case. Thus he could no longer buy new tools. Today he receives just $10 for 220 pounds (100 kg) of grain; he would have to sell more than 1,320 pounds (600 kg) to replace his equipment, a clear impossibility because no one and the means of production necessary for them will be no more accessible to the poor peasants of disadvantaged regions than those of the green revolution.

To allow all the farmers in the world, in particular the poorest of them, to construct and exploit cultivated ecosystems on a sustainable basis that can produce a maximum of high-quality foodstuffs without environmental harm, there must be a halt to the war of international agricultural prices. An end must be put to the liberalization of exchanges that tends to align agricultural prices everywhere with those of the lowest price of surplus exporters. As we have seen, such prices impoverish and starve millions of rural residents, which swell the ranks of the rural exodus, unemployment, and urban misery. Moreover, by excluding entire regions and millions of peasants from production, and by discouraging the production of those who remain, these prices keep agricultural production well below what would be possible with sustainable production techniques known to date. Such prices, which at the same time cause the underconsumption of foodstuffs and low levels of agricultural production, are thus doubly Malthusian. In addition, they impact negatively on the environment, health security, and the quality of produce.

On the contrary, it is necessary to ensure prices that are sufficiently high and stable to allow peasants to live in dignity from their work. For this purpose, it is necessary to organize international agricultural exchanges much more equitably and effectively than they are today; every large country (such as China and India) or every group of countries having fairly similar agricultural productivities (such as West Africa, Southeast Asia, Western Europe, Eastern Europe, North Africa, and the Near East) ought in fact to be able to levy a variable customs duty on every bargain-rate agricultural import, sufficient to allow all peasants not just to survive but also to make progress. In addition, equitable international agreements would determine, product by product, an average sales price for international markets, as well as the quantity and price of exports granted to each country or group of countries. Of course, such a reorganization of the international exchanges will have to be accompanied, in each country, by policies designed to promote agricultural development: access to land and security of tenure (agrarian reforms, farm tenancy statutes, conflict of interest legislation, set-up grants); access to credit and equipment; access to markets; transport and business infrastructures; access to knowledge; research and training, adapted to the needs and means of different regions and types of farms, beginning with those most in need. This is the price of a future for the farmers. And the price of our own future too.

LAURENCE ROUDART

MARCEL MAZOYER

127

**DEFORESTATION IN AMAZONIA, MATO GROSSO DO NORTE, BRAZIL** (12°38' S, 60°12' W)

Almost 2 million hectares of the Amazon rainforest are cleared every year. This deforestation, which is speeding up, brings little benefit to local people. Its main function is to free up land for growing cheap cereals—especially soya—to feed livestock in rich countries. These cash crops for export generate foreign currency; in their quest for growth, big farming concerns do not hesitate to clear areas of forest, when they are not driving small farmers off the land and forcing them to retreat to forested areas. Worldwide, the expansion of farmland, the wood industry, and road building destroy almost 15.2 million hectares of natural tropical forest per year—the equivalent of the Netherlands, Belgium, Switzerland, and Denmark put together, or the whole of Florida.

## ⟩ DEVELOPMENTS IN WORLD AGRICULTURE SINCE 1950

INCREASE IN
Yields: an average of **+145%**
Cultivated land: **+13%**
Irrigated land: **+237%**
Worldwide production: **+160%**

## ⟩ AGRICULTURE AND ECONOMICS

PROPORTION OF FARMWORKERS WITHIN WORKING POPULATION
**45%** worldwide (**1.3 billion**)
**5%** in Europe (**17 million**)
Less than **3%** in the US

CONCENTRATION OF TRADE AND OF FOOD PROCESSING
In the US, 4 companies control more than **61%** of the market in flour, **80%** of the market in soya, and **81%** of the market in meat.

MAJOR INEQUALITIES IN AGRICULTURE
Three-quarters of the world's farmworkers use only hand tools.
**1/3** use animal labor.
Only a tiny proportion of farms are mechanized: for **1.3 billion** farmworkers there are **28 million** tractors, or just over **2** tractors for every **100** workers.
In OECD (Organization for Economic Cooperation and Development) countries, **80%** of farm subsidies are paid to the richest **20%** of farmers.

A FAIR PRICE?
Reduction in the price of agricultural food products (rice, wheat, corn): between **−50** and **−60%** in dollars.

## ⟩ AGRICULTURE AND WORLD HUNGER

More than 60% of the 815 million people in the world who are suffering from food shortages work on the land.

AGRARIAN CAPITALISTS ARE NOT NECESSARILY WHERE YOU MIGHT EXPECT
Between 1990 and 2001, the USA sold rice at **80%** of its actual production costs, maize and soya at **70%**, wheat at **60%**, and cotton at **43%**.
The EU has **40%** of the world market in powdered whole milk, and **31%** in skimmed milk, but it exports these at **50%** of the actual production costs.

Today, the large farms of South America, South Africa, Ukraine, and Russia are selling on the world market products such as wheat, soya, chicken, and beef, at prices which would ruin farmers in the north if they did not receive heavy subsidies.

## ⟩ AGRICULTURE AND BIODIVERSITY

SHRINKING BIODIVERSITY IN THE MODERN WORLD
It is estimated that **75%** of the varieties of foodstuffs cultivated at the beginning of the 20th century have disappeared.
In the US, **86%** of the **7,098** varieties of potatoes grown between 1804 and 1904 are no longer sold or available from gene banks. **95%** of cabbage varieties, **91%** of field corn, **94%** of peas, and **81%** of tomatoes have also disappeared.
Every week, two breeds of domestic animal vanish from the face of the Earth.

HUMANITY HAS LONG BEEN AWARE OF THE EFFECTS OF REDUCED AGRICULTURAL BIODIVERSITY
1845–1848: Famine in Ireland: **1.5 million** dead as a result of the economic and social crisis caused by mildew in the two main varieties of potato cultivated there.
1980: **40%** of Cuba's sugarcane harvest was destroyed by rust disease.
Winter 1972: **15 million** hectares of a single variety of wheat (sensitive to cold) were ruined in Russia.

## ⟩ AGRICULTURE AND THE ENVIRONMENT

AGRICULTURE USES MORE WATER THAN ANY OTHER HUMAN ACTIVITY
Agriculture consumes almost **70%** of the world's fresh water, mainly for irrigation.
These massive quantities are not always drawn in synchronization with the climate's renewal of groundwater. Some countries use up more than **100%** of their annual, renewable water resources.

AGRICULTURE IS ONE OF THE MAIN CAUSES OF SOIL DEGRADATION
Bad practices in drainage and irrigation have led to the salination of about **10%** of irrigated land (i.e. 30 million hectares rendered infertile).
The amount of organic matter in the soil of countries with temperate climates has on average shrunk from **4** to **2%** which is the limit below which the process of desertification begins. With sustainable practices, agriculture can benefit the environment, notably by limiting soil erosion through plant cover.

AGRICULTURE AND TRANSPORT
In **1999** France imported more than **1 million** metric tons of milk, and exported the same quantity. Similarly, it imported **393,000** live pigs and exported **586,000**.
A team of researchers at the University of Essex (UK) concluded that if British farmers sold their produce within a **12 mile (20 km)** radius of their farms, they would do more for the environment than if they all switched to organic farming.

128

⟩ **WASTE FROM A WATER DESALINATION PLANT IN THE SEA OF AL-DOHA, JAHRA REGION, KUWAIT** (29°21' N, 47°48' E)

For a long time Kuwait depended upon imports from Iraq for its supply of drinking water, but today it has several seawater desalination plants that produce 75 percent of the country's water supply. These plants use the instant thermal distillation technique (also known as the "flash" system). After treatment, water unfit for consumption is rejected into the sea, where it mixes with the waters of the Persian Gulf, creating the shape of a tentacled monster. Thanks to 12,500 desalination plants in 120 countries, the Earth's oceans furnish almost 5,300 million gallons (20 million m³) of fresh water—around 1 percent of the fresh water consumed in the world. Two-thirds of this derives from seawater, and the remaining third from estuaries. Desalination plants require enormous amounts of energy and are expensive to operate and thus are available only to states that have considerable resources, particularly petroleum, such as those in the Persian Gulf, which produces half of the world's desalinated water. One ton of fuel is needed to produce around 26,400 gallons (100 m³) of fresh water. At a time when the need for fresh water is a concern in a growing number of countries, Europeans use 66 to 92 gallons (250 to 350 liters) of water per person each day (a single toilet flush uses 1.5 gallons, or 6 liters).

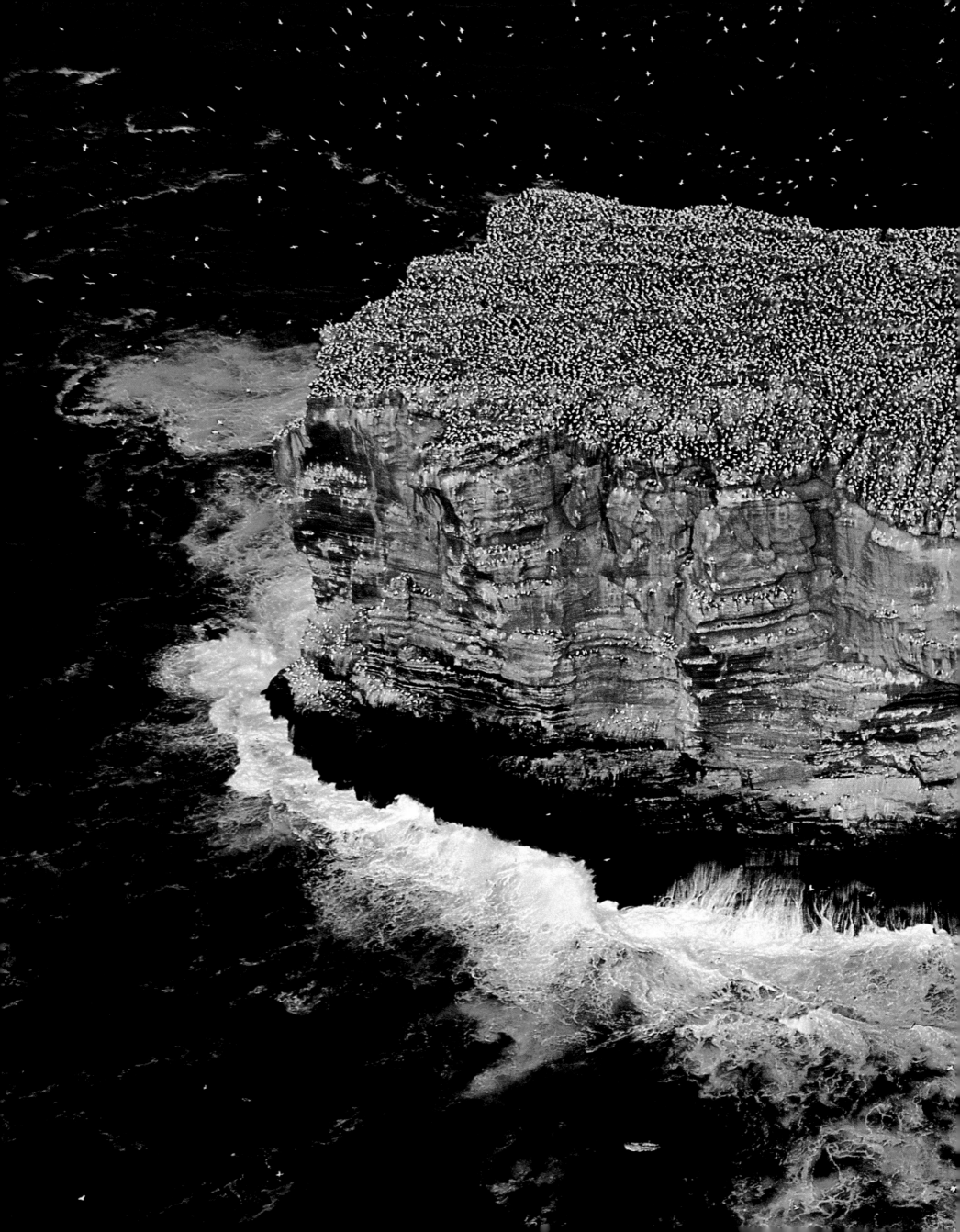

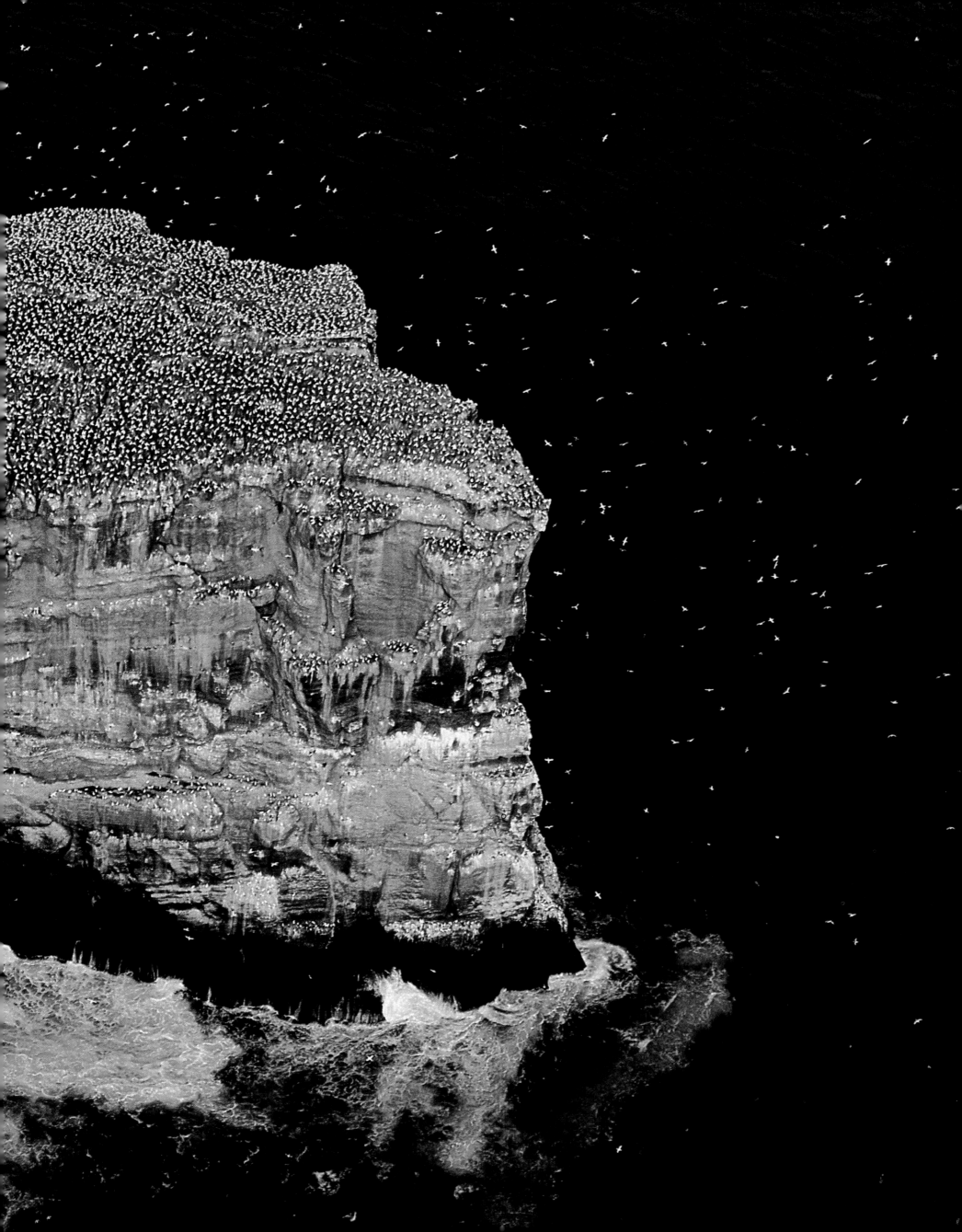

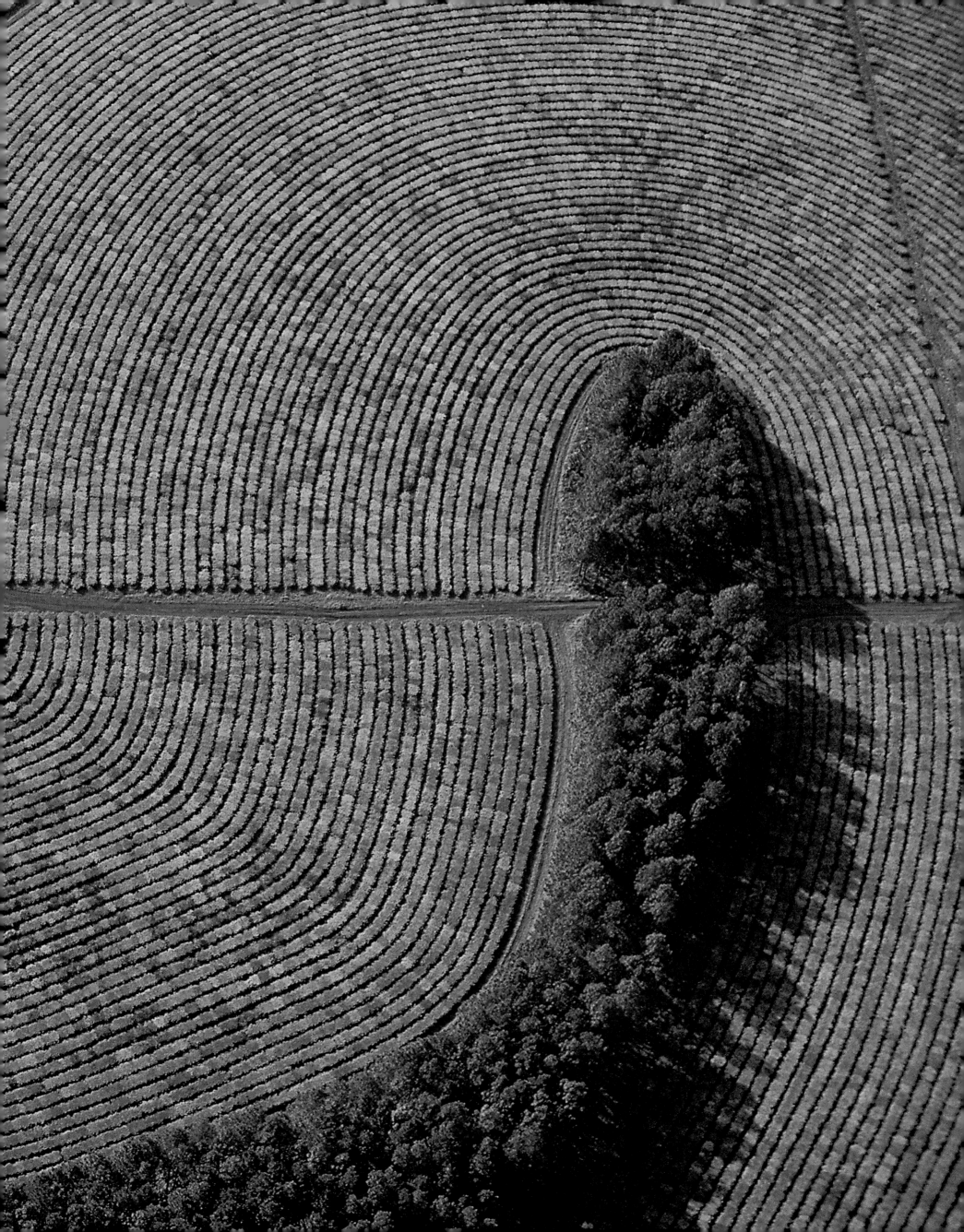

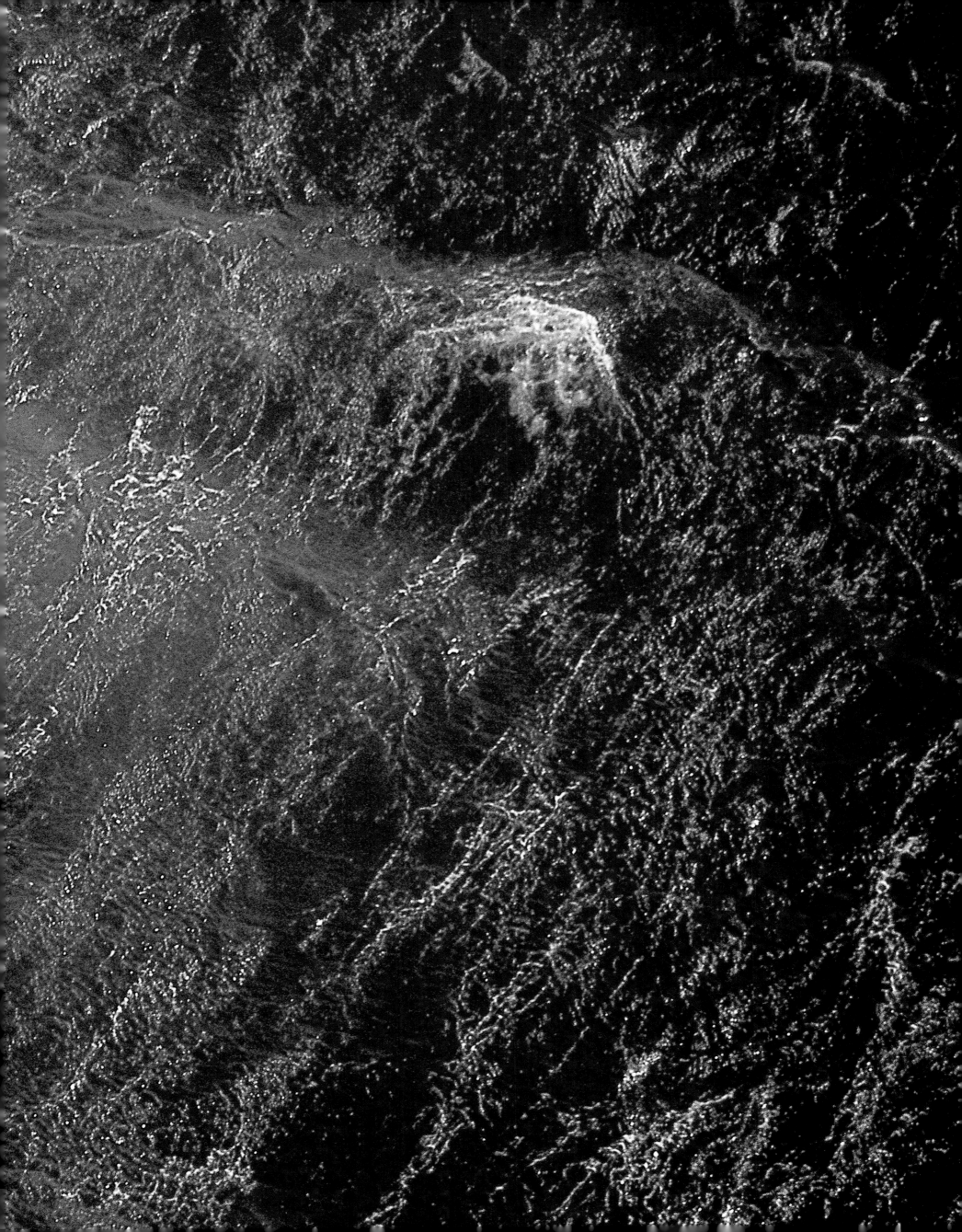

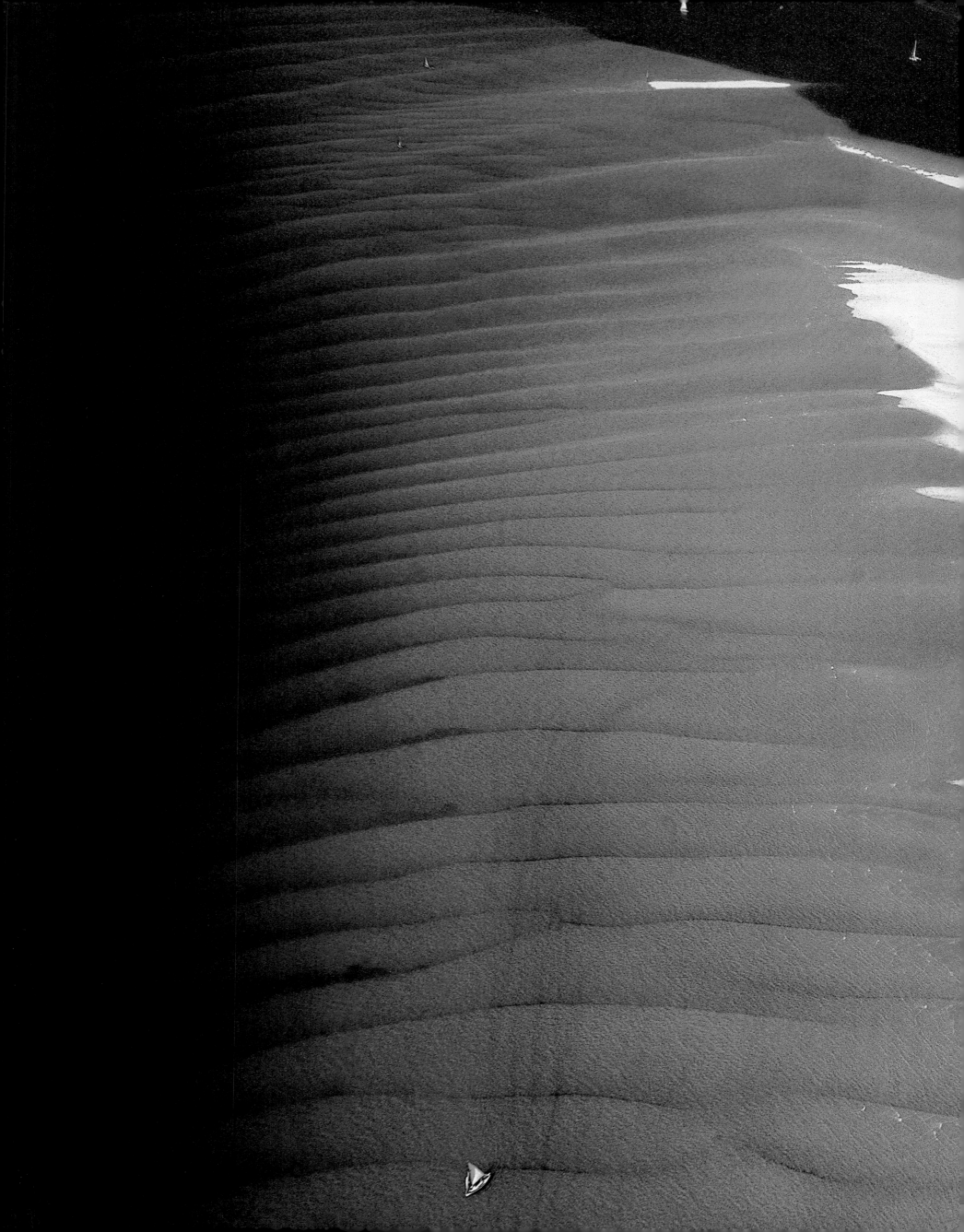

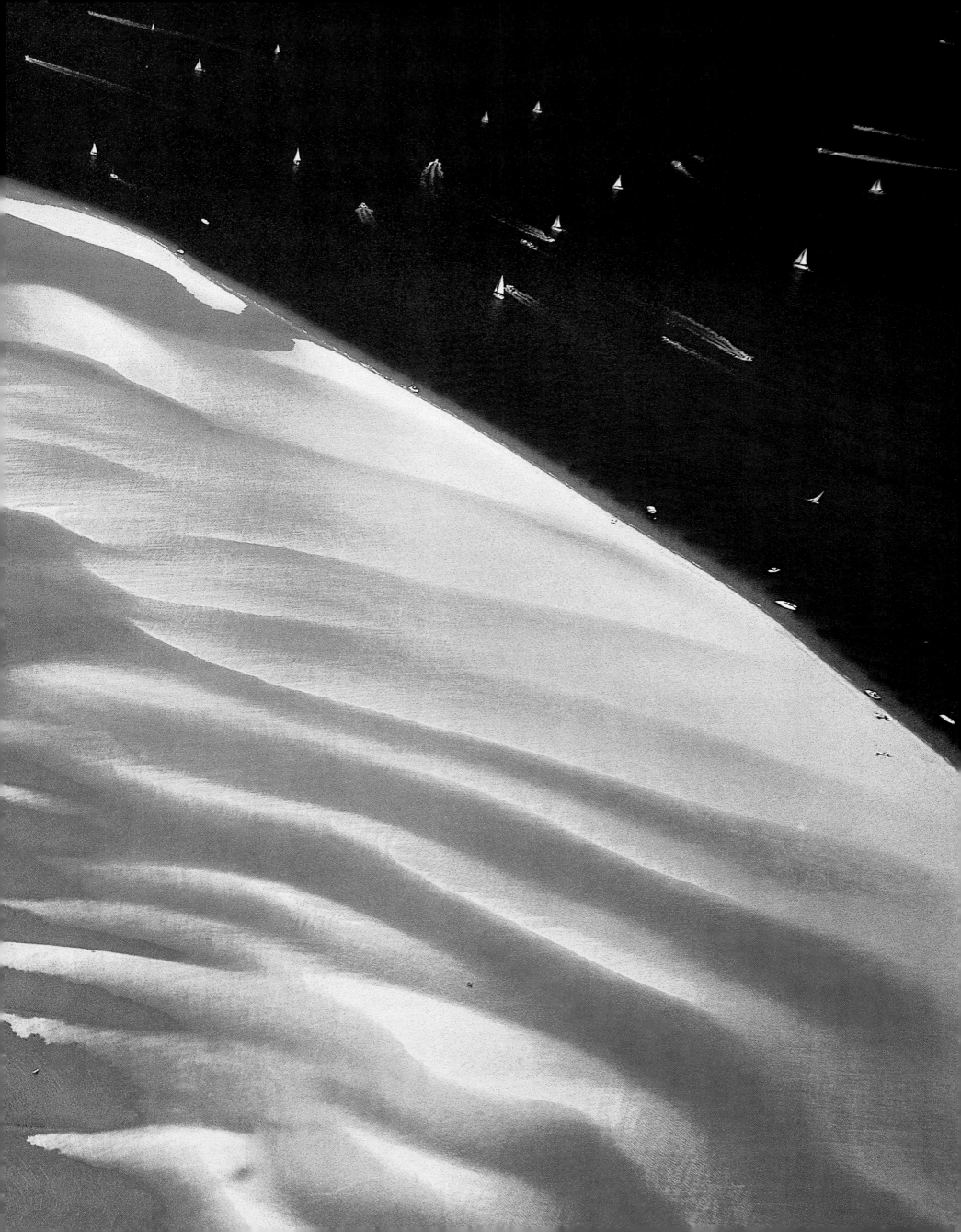

# WATER: HUMANITY'S HERITAGE

We drink water every day, yet this natural need could become a problem in the future. It already is for a large number of the Earth's inhabitants who suffer from illnesses carried by contaminated water or must travel miles to find this precious fluid. The water available for our use makes up less than one-thousandth of the planet's supply. The rest is contained in ice or seawater or is consumed by the Earth's forests. Water is not a never-ending resource: it needs to be preserved for the future.

Earth is a planet ruled by water. This water, which covers nearly three-quarters of its surface, was given to the Earth at birth by the accumulation of successive waves of debris from comets encased in frozen water washed from the depths of the cosmos. In a tumultuous clash of stones, ice, and water vaporized by incandescent masses from the entrails of the planet, the continents and the oceans took shape. A gas bubble, in which water vapor figured prominently, enveloped them in a kind of atmospheric pane of glass, 25 miles (40 km) thick, which protected the Earth from harmful rays and meteorites and which trapped solar radiation through the greenhouse effect. Without this layer the average temperature of the planet would not exceed about −0.4°F (−18°C), and all its water would be solid ice.

A mighty storm gave rise to the water cycle, which for billions of years has been putting water molecules through an endless spiral. The sun is the machine that lavishes its energy on this mighty steam engine, whose boiler consists of the oceans and earth masses, while the cooler layers of the atmosphere provide the condensation system. Every year approximately 120,000 cubic miles (500,000 km³) of ocean water is changed to vapor. Most of this vapor, condensed at high altitudes, falls back on the oceans in the form of precipitation. The remainder, approximately 10,000 cubic miles (40,000 km³), is added to the exhalation from the rivers and lakes and from living beings. Trees, in particular, act almost like living wicks and vaporize 200 to 400 times their weight in water each year of vegetation. All this atmospheric water, about 27,000 cubic miles (111,000 km³), falls as precipitation onto the land masses. Two-thirds of it evaporates as soon as it falls; the balance is filtered into the soil or feeds the free waters, and finally every year the rivers return some 10,000 cubic miles (40,000 km³) of fresh water to the oceans. This is like the functioning of a purification and distillation plant working

nonstop on a planetary scale, propelling water from the earliest ages of the Earth, through billions of lives who cannot survive without it. This is because the quantity of groundwater has remained about level since the beginning: 339 million cubic miles (1.4 billion km³). It is a figure that defies the imagination, and yet if the Earth were reduced to the size of an orange, this world water would amount to just a drop.

Two atoms of hydrogen, the primordial element present at the birth of the universe, linked to one atom of oxygen, a speck from inside a star—the water molecule is simple and minuscule, and yet its properties are exceptional, so that the most common liquid is also the most disconcerting. Water needs considerable quantities of energy in order to change its state. Before becoming vapor, it stores up a great deal of heat, which it frees upon condensation, and each molecule of water vapor in a cloud is a tiny aerial packet of energy. Because every evaporation releases cold, and every condensation gives off heat, water contributes to a permanent redistribution of solar energy on the globe, which it organizes and uses to regulate the climates. Water has a long "memory": oceans and earth engorged with water play the role of thermal regulators by storing up solar energy for years, even millennia. Unlike other substances, water expands when it solidifies. This fact has enormous consequences for our environment, explaining the oceans, the lakes, the shattering of rocks, and our landscapes. Before it freezes, water achieves a maximum density at 39°F (4°C), and this strange trait makes cold waters sink. This fact, combined with the floating of ice, makes a body of water freeze on the surface and not down below. Otherwise all of the Earth's waters would have long since turned to ice. The phenomenon is also at the origin of ocean currents, water turbulence, and its oxygenation.

Seen from the sky, water creates characteristic patterns of erosion. At the four corners of the Earth we find, on every scale, the same organization and branching of streams and tributaries, the same meanders, the same deltas, the same glacial valleys and alluvial plains. The hardest rock cannot resist the pressure that results from the freezing of water that has infiltrated it. Night after night, ice-filled crannies shatter the mountains and sculpt landscapes, which liquid water erodes and dissolves, because its corrosive power makes it a universal solvent. Each year the rivers carry toward the oceans 15 to 30 billion tons of muds and sediments: the flesh of continents. Fluid,

increase by 4 to 8 percent per year if our usage does not change. Modern megalopolises, always thirsty, will fetch water from farther and farther away and drain the deep underground water resources. The agricultural demand for water in developing countries could double every twenty years. Water is one of the most poorly distributed natural resources, and the immutable sequence of its cycle, ignoring frontiers, masks cruel inequities. Fifteen percent of global fresh water resources is located in the Amazonian basin, which contains only 0.3 percent of the population, whereas 60 percent of the world land masses are in a situation of chronic water scarcity. While the privileged 9 percent of the world population consume nearly three-fourths of the available fresh water, half a billion people live in a state of deprivation in countries where water is used at a rate far ahead of its replenishment. It is predicted that in 2025, 1.5 billion people will lack an adequate water

⌂ **CENTER-PIVOT IRRIGATION, MA'AN, JORDAN** (29°43' N, 35°33' E)

This self-propelled, center-pivot irrigation machine, invented by the American Frank Zybach in 1948 and patented in 1952, drills for water in the deep strata 100 to 1,200 feet (30 to 400 m) below the surface. A pivoting pipeline with sprinklers, extending about 550 yards (500 m) is mounted on tractor wheels, and irrigates 195 acres (78 hectares) of land. Production of 1 ton of grain requires about 1,000 tons of water, and because of their growing need for food supplies, the countries of the Middle East have begun to use modern agricultural methods that endanger their water reserves. The water tables in the region are being quickly drained. Techniques such as microirrigation make savings on water of up to 50 percent, but because they are very labor-intensive, their use has slowly declined in recent decades. Making the desert bloom may look like a miracle, but a high price is paid in water rationing and the salination of the soil and of subterranean water reserves: the mineral salts that are naturally present in the soil become concentrated and make it sterile. The Food and Agriculture Organization estimates that 125,000 hectares of land are lost worldwide every year through salination.

supply. More than 2 billion people lack sanitary facilities, and illnesses carried by water kill more than 25 million per year in developing countries. Half of these victims are children. This squandering of water, these pollutions, and this runaway demand generate awesome tensions between countries—the wars of tomorrow might well be fought over water. Egypt is aware that eight African nations control the upper Nile Valley; Iraq and Syria know that Turkey can dam up the Tigris and Euphrates; and India is in constant discord with Bangladesh about the use of the Brahmaputra and the Ganges. Water has been decreed, justly, a world heritage. Humans, like all living beings, are the children of water, and water is their most precious commodity, one that they must now distribute and use better, wasting and polluting less. It is a matter of survival. Technology is already giving hope in the areas of seawater desalination; the mining of fresh water from submarine springs; the trapping of water from fog in desert countries; and new methods of irrigation by spraying and by drip, techniques supported by computer that can economize as much as 70 percent of our water. Biologists are currently determining which food plants require the least amount of water.

To reduce the waste of water in industrial and domestic life, northern European countries are setting up chains of businesses that exchange their refuse, which can become raw material, and Japan puts laundry water through a simple treatment process for reuse in toilet tanks. Following the example of space shuttles, we are learning to recycle water on Earth. It is also possible to improve the purification

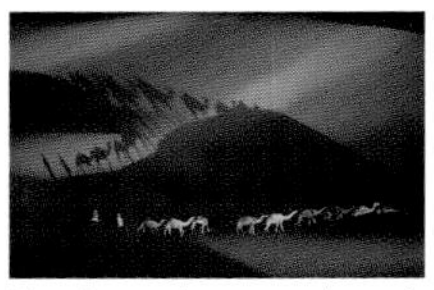

**PAGES 168–169**
DROMEDARY CARAVANS NEAR NOUAKCHOTT, MAURITANIA
(18°09' N, 15°29' W)

The dromedary camel, perfectly adapted to the aridity, is an important livestock animal in Mauritania and all of the other lands bordering the Sahara. Its domestication several thousand years ago enabled humans to conquer the desert and develop trans-Saharan trade routes. The camel eats 22 to 44 pounds (10 to 20 kg) of vegetables a day and can survive without water for many months in the winter. In the summer, because of the heat and expended effort, the camel can last only a few days without drinking; by comparison, a human would die of dehydration within twenty-four hours. The reserve fat contained in its single hump helps in thermal regulation, allowing the camel to withstand the heating of its body without needing to perspire to cool down. The Maurs, the ethnic majority in Mauritania, raise the camel for its milk and meat as well as its skin and wool. In 2001 the country numbered over 1 million camels.

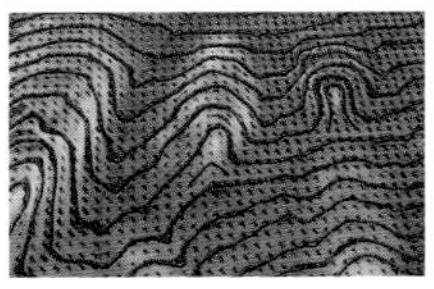

**PAGES 170–171**
NEWLY PLANTED OLIVE GROVES, ZAGHOUAN, TUNISIA
(36°24' N, 10°23' E)

These olive groves at the foot of the 4,250-foot-high (1,295 m) Jebel Zaghouan in northeastern Tunisia are planted in curved embankments to retain water and limit erosion, which viewed from above look like the lines on a relief map. A symbol of peace, the tree is native to the Mediterranean basin, where 90 percent of the planet's olive trees grow. An olive tree can live as long as 1,000 years, producing 11 to 65 pounds (5 to 30 kg) of olives yearly. In the past its oil was used in small clay lamps, but it has been replaced by petroleum. Today we consume both table olives and olive oil, which is renowned for its dietary and medicinal properties and also used in cosmetics. The lands of the Mediterranean are the greatest olive producers and also the greatest consumers. The Greeks consume 4.7 gallons (18 liters) of olive oil per person per year, and the Italians and the Spaniards 3.4 gallons (13 liters), compared to 0.4 gallons (1.6 liters) a year in France and 0.2 gallons (0.7 liters) in the United States.

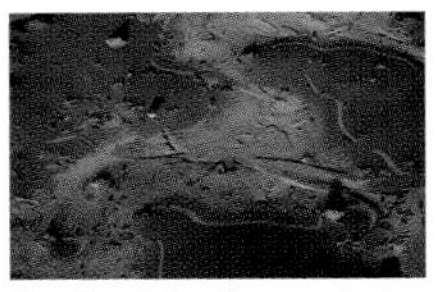

**PAGES 172–173**
ORYX IN THE NAMIB DESERT, SWAKOPMUND, NAMIBIA
(24°39' S, 15°07' E)

On the Atlantic coast of southern Africa, the Namib Desert covers the entire 800 miles (1,300 km) of the Namibian shoreline and extends inland to a width of 62 miles (100 km), comprising one-fifth of the country's territory. Although its name, in the Nama language, means "place where there is nothing," its biological richness makes it a site unique in the world. The Namib has a secret: the humid air masses coming from the Atlantic condense on contact with the desert surface, which cools at night, enveloping the area in a thick morning fog nearly 100 days each year. This fog adds up to 1.2 inches (30 mm) of annual precipitation and constitutes the desert's main source of water and thus of life. When the orange-red sand is moistened, it allows many plant and animal species to subsist in the Namib Desert, such as an insect that specializes in capturing the water vapor. Only species that have evolved characteristics adapted to the extreme conditions of desert locations (aridity, harsh temperatures, scarce food resources) can survive here, including this gemsbok (*Oryx gazella*), a type of oryx, a large African antelope.

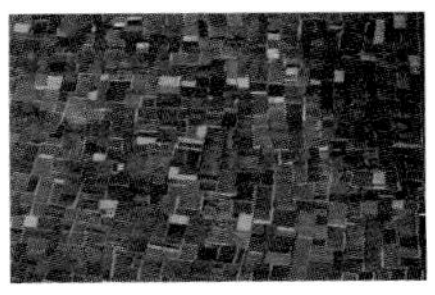

**PAGES 174–175**
ALGAE CULTIVATION IN BALI, INDONESIA
(8°43' S, 115°26' E)

Algae was used exclusively as a fertilizer in antiquity and was incorporated in the form of ash into glass manufacture in the 20th century. Today 97 percent of algae production serves the food industry. Out of approximately 30,000 algae species known throughout the world, only a few dozen are exploited. They include carrageen (*Chondrus crispus*), also called Irish moss, from which is extracted a colloid used as a jelling, thickening, or stabilizing agent by the food, pharmaceutical, and cosmetic industries. In the Far East, the cultivation of this kind of red algae is an important source of revenue for coastal populations. Cuttings of algae are attached on submerged ropes, held taut between stakes, following the main current. Indonesia is the fourth-largest producer of red algae, a market dominated by the Philippines, which produced over 600,000 tons in 2002 (32 percent of global production). If all of the species of algae are combined, however, China is the leading producer and consumer.

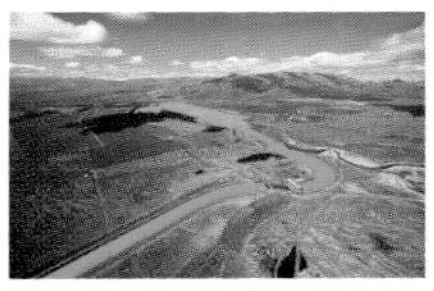

**PAGES 176–177**
OHAU A POWER STATION, SOUTH ISLAND, NEW ZEALAND
(40°40' S, 175°15' E)

New Zealand's South Island is a land of contrasting scenery, dominated by the New Zealand Alps which rise to a height of nearly 12,500 feet (3,800 m), from where a number of rivers flow. Several of these, like the Ohau, have been harnessed to provide for the country's energy requirements. The hydroelectric Ohau A Power Station is a huge complex of dams and canals. Its construction began in 1971, and some two million cubic meters of rock had to be excavated from the banks of the river Ohau, plus another half a million cubic meters for the pipelines. Such gigantic dams put enormous pressure on the ecosystem, and are denounced by environmental organizations: some rivers die, others gradually lose their salmon stocks, and species disappear. These threats to biodiversity, combined with soil erosion and deforestation, are a source of great anxiety in a country which depends partly on its income from tourism.

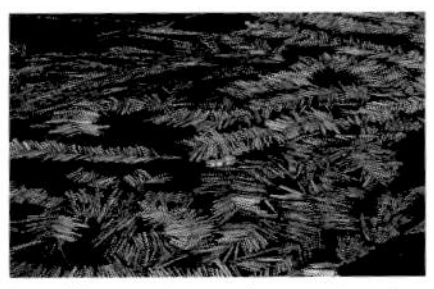

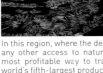

**PAGES 178–179**
FLOATING WOOD DOWN THE AMAZON, NEAR THE CITY OF MANAUS, AMAZONAS, BRAZIL
(3°03' S, 60°06' W)

In this region, where the density of vegetation precludes any other access to natural resources, rafting is the most profitable way to transport wood. Brazil is the world's fifth-largest producer of industrial wood and the number-one producer of tropical woods, but this major economic resource comes at a cost of almost 92,000 square miles (24 million hectares) of deforestation each year. The Amazonian forest has already lost more than 16 percent of its original area. Although some of those who exploit the rainforest are beginning to promote the benefits of a protected forest over a devastated one, the process of deforestation still tends to increase. Conflicts of interest can be bloody: in February 2005, a series of murders carried out by *pistoleiros*, financed by unscrupulous businesses, led the government to turn an area of some 5 million hectares into a protected zone that cannot be exploited. But the timber trade is not the only cause. Deforestation in the Amazon is also linked to the rise in soya crops, which are exported to industrialized countries for use as feed in intensive meat farming.

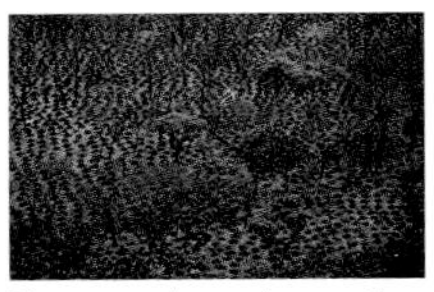

**PAGES 180–181**
YAMS GROWING IN NORTHERN TAGADI, BONDOUKOU REGION, CÔTE D'IVOIRE
(8°43' N, 2°39' W)

The yam, planted according to traditional farming techniques under mounds of earth, as in this field near Bondoukou in eastern Côte d'Ivoire, is grown for local consumption in most of the world's tropical countries. This starch- and protein-rich tuber is especially common in the northernmost part of Africa's forest regions, from Côte d'Ivoire to Cameroon. As the basic ingredient of one of the main Ivorian dishes, *foufou* or *foutou* (a kind of thick puree), this starch is a staple in the diet of both rural people and city-dwellers. Côte d'Ivoire remains the third-largest African producer of yams (after Nigeria, which alone accounts for 70 percent of African production, and Ghana). In Africa as a whole, agriculture occupies almost 55 percent of the active population, but because of major population movement toward cities, this figure is falling fast.

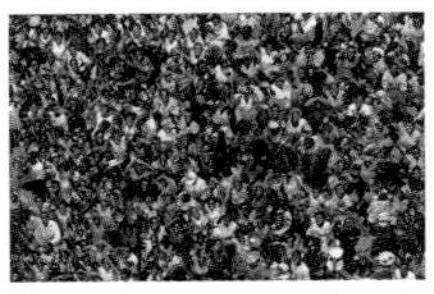

**PAGES 182–183**
CROWD IN ABENGOUROU, CÔTE D'IVOIRE
(6°44' N, 3°29' W)

Africa has a population of 800 million, making up 13 percent of the human race. This colorful crowd, enthusiastically waving to the photographer, was photographed in Abengourou, in eastern Côte d'Ivoire. These children and adolescents remind us of the country's youthfulness; as in most of the African continent, 40 percent of the population is under 15 years of age. The country's birth rate in 2003 was 4.7 children per woman, which is representative of the average for the continent (the world average is 2.7). Modernization and cultural and socio-economic influences have gradually lowered the birth rate. The ravages of the Aids epidemic in Subsaharan Africa (home to 70 percent of the total 39.4 million people infected in the world) will have a severe impact on the region's demography: every day in Africa 6,300 people die of the Aids virus and another 11,000 become infected.

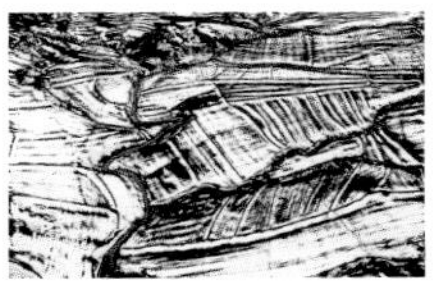

**PAGES 184–185**
THE HODNA MOUNTAINS COVERED WITH SNOW, NEAR EL HAMMADIA, ALGERIA (35°55' N, 4°47 E)

Situated in the northeast of Algeria, the Hodna mountains form a line parallel to the coast, and rise to a height of 6,200 feet (1,900 m). This region is basically used for agriculture and sheep-rearing. Market gardening, fruit trees, wheat, grapes, and olives are all to be found in the little plots of land. Once these peaks towered over mountainsides covered with forests of olive trees, cedars, and oaks, but today they have been cleared, leaving behind soil that is impoverished by erosion and overgrazing. In 150 years Algeria has lost almost 40 percent of its forests. The continental, semi-arid climate of this mountainous region alternates between hot, dry summers and harsh winters. Rainfall varies between 27 and 39 inches (700 mm and 1,000 mm) per year, but at the beginning of 2005 the region experienced the rare phenomenon of heavy snow. It was the worst for sixty years according to the local people—something of a paradox at a time when global warming is at the center of world attention. Meteorologists, however, confirm that such extreme phenomena in no way contradict the fact of global warming. In the long term, they predict a rapid thaw of snow in the high mountains, and a drastic reduction of snow at mid-mountain level.

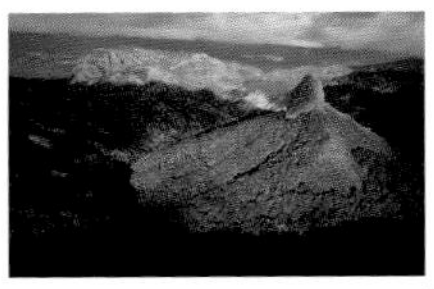

**PAGES 186–187**
BEECHES IN THE MOUNTAINS OF VILLA TRAFUL, NEUQUÉN PROVINCE, ARGENTINA
(40°40' S, 71°16' W)

In the midst of Nahuel Huapí National Park in the southwestern Neuquén province, Argentina, many high-lying glacial lakes of brilliant blue water—at average altitudes of 2,300 feet, or 700 m—can be seen at the foot of mountains and rocky peaks of the Andes range. The region's humid climate favors the growth of southern beech trees (of the *Nothofagus pumilio* and *antarctica* varieties), which have spread over the mountainsides, enlivening them with flamboyant hues in autumn. Farther south, at steadily declining altitudes, the beech forests thin out, giving way to the grasslands of Patagonia. The stretch of the Andes chain between Argentina and Chile, stretching approximately 3,100 miles (5,000 km), is the longest natural land border on the planet. It includes the mountain Aconcagua, the highest peak in the western hemisphere at 22,800 feet (6,960 m), which dominates the entire continent of South America.

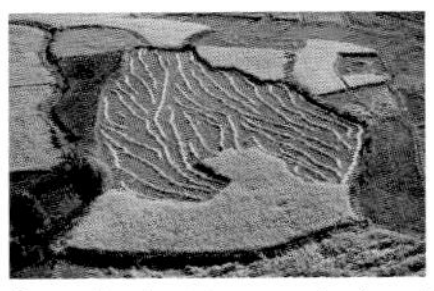

**PAGES 188–189**
RICE PADDIES ON THE SHORES OF LAKE ITASY, ANTANANARIVO REGION, MADAGASCAR
(18°55' S, 47°31' E)

Over the last two centuries, the region around Lake Itasy has been given over to rice cultivation, which is controlled by big landowners. The transition from mixed farming to irrigated monoculture has caused malaria to spread in Madagascar's high plateaus. Rice's growing season coincides with the breeding season of *Anopheles funestus*, a species of mosquito that is an efficient carrier of the disease. Malaria kills at least 1 million people every year, most of them in poor countries. Since the 1950s, the World Health Organization (WHO) has endeavored to eradicate the disease, but it has not been able to secure enough funds for research and treatment. To try to correct this imbalance, WHO created a world health fund in 2001. In 1992, more than 90 percent of world spending on medical research was devoted to just 10 percent of the illnesses that affect the planet.

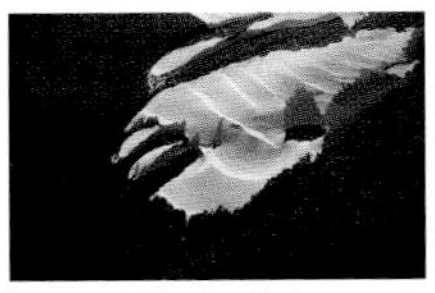

**PAGES 190–191**
SAND DUNE IN THE HEART OF VEGETATION ON FRASER ISLAND, QUEENSLAND, AUSTRALIA
(25°15' S, 153°10' E)

Fraser Island, off the coast of Queensland, Australia, is named after Eliza Fraser, who was shipwrecked on the island in 1836. At a length of 75 miles (120 km) and a width of 10 miles (15 km), it is the world's largest sand island. Yet on top of this rather infertile substratum, a humid tropical forest has developed in the midst of which wide dunes intrude, moving with the wind. Fraser Island has important water resources, including nearly 200 freshwater dune lakes, and has varied fauna such as marsupials, birds, and reptiles. Exploited for its wood since 1860, used for the construction of the Suez Canal, and for its valuable mineral deposits, the island was later coveted by sand companies during the 1970s. Now the tourist industry is beginning to grow here. Welcoming 200,000 visitors a year without damaging the local fauna and flora is a real challenge to sustainable development on the island, which was declared a World Heritage site by UNESCO in 1992.

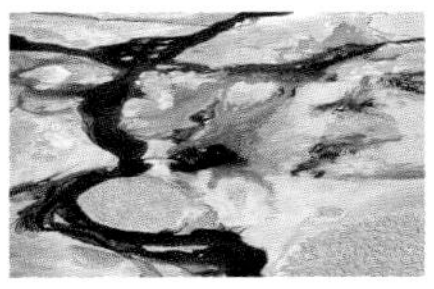

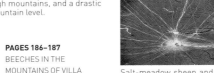

**PAGES 192–193**
SALAR DE ATACAMA, CHILE
(23°30' S, 68°15' W)

A scattering of pink flamingos is all that breaks this uniformly mineral scene in the Salar de Atacama. The birds take advantage of the water of the San Pedro river before it vanishes into the landscape, evaporating into the dry air or soaking into the surface of this vast salt plain that covers 1,158 square miles (3,000 km²). The Salar is part of the world's most arid region, after Antarctica: the Atacama Desert, an enormous strip of land 1,677 miles (2,700 km) long in Peru and Chile. Its hostile climate is due to the dual action of the cold Humboldt Current, which flows along Chile's Pacific coast and prevents evaporation, and a warm anticyclone, which traps dry air at ground level. Only a grimy drizzle, the *chamanchaca*, falls here and there. The El Niño phenomenon, which occurs every seven years, may bring more abundant rainfall, but this is often too much, as was the case with the disastrous floods of 1983 and 1997.

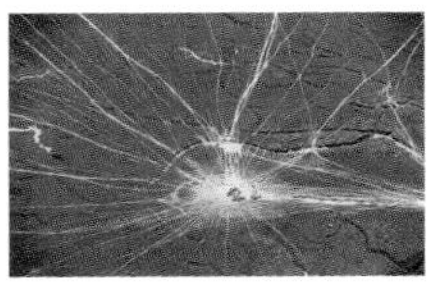

**PAGES 194–195**
SALT-MEADOW SHEEP DRINKING IN THE BAY OF MONT ST MICHEL, FRANCE
(48°40' N, 1°35' W)

Salt-meadow sheep and their lambs come together in the field and gather round a watering place. Raised principally in the bays of Mont St Michel and Somme, they feed on marine plants that are rich in iodine and salt, giving the meat a flavor that is highly prized by gastronomes. 2,200 salt-meadow lambs are consumed every year in this region, and such products meet the strict requirements of consumers preoccupied with the safety and quality of their food. Above all, sheep farming plays a vital role in the survival of local agriculture at a time when every twenty-five minutes a French farm closes down for good. European policies on food quality have opened up new areas of development to those farmers who want to escape from the standardization of food production. Labeling, AOC (*appellation d'origine contrôlée*—a quality control system indicating the place of origin), and organic farming are all subject to increasingly strict controls. 120,000 French farms are involved in AOC production, and in total their various products generated a turnover of some 19 billion euros (around $19 billion) in 2003.

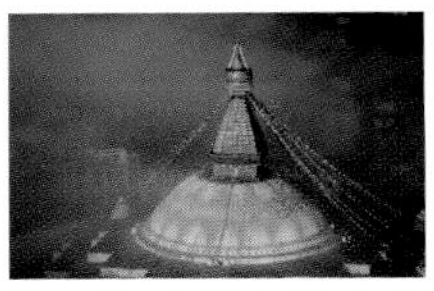

**PAGES 196–197**
THE STUPA OF BODNATH, BUDDHIST TEMPLE, KATHMANDU, NEPAL
(27°43' N, 85°22' E)

The city of Bodnath is home to one of the holiest Buddhist temples in Nepal, especially venerated by the thousand Tibetan exiles who now live in this neighboring country. The stupa, which is a reliquary in the form of a tumulus topped by a tower, holds a bone fragment of Buddha. At a height and width of 132 feet (40 m), the temple is one of the largest in Nepal. Everything in the architecture of this sanctuary is allegorical, representing the universe and the elements (earth, air, fire, and water). The Buddha's eyes are fixed on the four cardinal points, while the stages in the acquisition of supreme knowledge, Nirvana, are represented by the thirteen steps of the tower. On religious holidays the monument is decorated with yellow clay and hung with votive flags. It is estimated that Buddhism today has between 150 million and 300 million followers worldwide but more precise figures are difficult. Asian religions are rarely exclusive and the influence of Buddhism in Communist countries such as China is hard to evaluate.

capable of rising by capillary action into the slender sap conduits, is omnipresent, infiltrating everywhere, making the rain and fair weather, endlessly dissolving and carrying a thousand substances that it precipitates and distributes at will—ranging from the scale of a cell to the scale of a continent. Water is the great unifier of the planet, the bond that connects all living beings, even beyond the barrier of time. Dinosaurs drank this same water that we today put into bottles or use to cook our food.

Life was born from and in water. When life crawled out of the sea onto land, each terrestrial organism preserved in itself, in the form of sap, serum, or blood, a small internal ocean as proof of a common origin in the seas.

Water determines the distribution of living beings on Earth, who have evolved to economize water and fight off dehydration: from the camel's hump to the human kidney that cleans thousands of liters of blood daily. Every life form on land is confronted with the challenge of preserving this ancestral link with the liquid that no living cell can do without. From our birth to our death, water flows in the human body and constantly renews itself. Two-thirds water, a human being dies if more than 15 percent of it is lost. No one survives more than a week without drinking, and the loss of water is still more serious in hot climates. Thus, the history of humanity was determined by the quest for and conquest of water. The great civilizations were born from water and near water, and its mastery determined their grandeur, its mismanagement brought their decline and sometimes disappearance. Humankind grafted itself onto the water cycle and gradually put water to work, to its benefit. To water their plantings, people established the first canals and the first dams, then a multitude of hydraulic apparatuses each more ingenious than the last. Then they used water as a communication path and for transport, by channeling it. Well before Egyptian civilization, the Mesopotamians had already elaborated an astonishing system of dikes, canals, reservoirs, and dams, and six centuries before the birth of Christ, the Chinese had linked Beijing to Hangchu by a canal 1,000 miles (1,600 km) long.

We can read the history of a society's links with water in the landscape. Ditches testify to the ancient strategic importance of water; a canal bears witness to trade relations between the rivers, or to an ancient chain of crafts related to living water; an aqueduct tells of supplying a city with spring water. And all religions have always maintained complex relationships with water, a fundamental symbol that conveyed powerful myths.

Some countries with sufficient water resources have been able to develop impressive technologies based around water. Having known the age of moving water, whose energy drove the mills, then the age of stagnant water, whose humidity allowed the fermentation of the fibers required for the textile industry, they put water to work in steam engines. A decisive step was taken one day in 1880, when the mill wheel became an alternator and water power was converted into electric current. At that point water became fire and sun, providing heat and light. This water, whose turbulence fed electric power stations yesterday, serves to cool nuclear stations today.

It was only late in the game that cities cleaned themselves, installed gutters to evacuate soiled water and distribution networks to convey it, purified, to a faucet. The Europeans did not achieve running water and the bathroom until the nineteenth century. And it was only after

Pasteur had demonstrated that we were drinking 90 percent of our illnesses that people committed themselves to real programs of decontamination and control of water. But while humans were becoming cleaner, they dirtied enormous quantities of water, and, making it their handmaid to drench, rinse, dissolve, dilute, heat, cool, transport, evacuate, or irrigate, they began to consume it in prodigious quantities. The sweat of an industrious civilization, water is sick and dirtied in countless ways.

Driven by the demands of growth and by demographic explosion, humanity has indulged in an orgy of water wastage. Wholesale deforestation and poor development practices, which defy natural filtration, have led directly to floods that each year cause 100,000 deaths all over the world, as well as to poor replenishment of running waters and groundwater. Indirectly, this action contributes to the degradation of the climate. Each year the desert gains 15 million acres, while one-third of exposed land is already unsuitable for agriculture. The rivers in many places have been reduced to the size of streams; the 38,000 large dams that encumber them have changed their natural flow by more than 16 percent. These constructions can bring prosperity, but they can also generate serious problems by modifying the water equilibrium of entire regions.

In the past century the total area under irrigation throughout the world increased sevenfold, and it continues to grow. This area alone consumes 70 percent of fresh water used in the world, because of agriculture's enormous need for water; it takes 1,500 tons of water to bring one ton of wheat to maturity, and three times that for a ton of rice. In developing countries, where irrigation is vital, watered surfaces use almost all the water consumed. This is because agricultural irrigation is often poorly managed; three-fourths of the water evaporates and some gets lost in leaks. Irrigation is the principal cause of soil salination; ultimately, some 100 million acres are said to have been sterilized by excessive salt.

Since the 1960s water pollution has reached global proportions, becoming one of the most disturbing aspects of our civilization. Every year about 20 billion tons of various types of refuse ends up in the oceans—we are turning our rivers and oceans into garbage dumps. No one is spared; at Varanasi, the Ganges is transformed into a sewer, while the Great Lakes of North America are acidified by air pollution. The nature of the pollutants is as diverse as their sources: heavy metals emitted by industry, which build up inside the bodies of living beings; pesticides and nitrate fertilizers escaping from tilled fields to poison and asphyxiate sea and river life; illegal dumping or leaks of hydrocarbons—every year brings more sophisticated and more harmful pollutants, requiring purification processes that grow more costly and elaborate all the time. We cannot continue to waste and soil fresh water without courting disaster; our habits must be changed, because water is no longer an inexhaustible resource. It is a legacy as rare as it is fragile, as indispensable as it is unevenly distributed.

It is illusory to believe that fresh water is abundant, because the Earth's water is 97 percent salt water, and of the remainder, three-quarters is immobilized in the form of ice or buried deep. The only available portion, a tiny fraction, represents less than one-thousandth of the Earth's water. What we use up today represents one-tenth of the total annual flow of our rivers. From 1940 to 1990 global consumption increased fivefold while the Earth's population doubled; it should

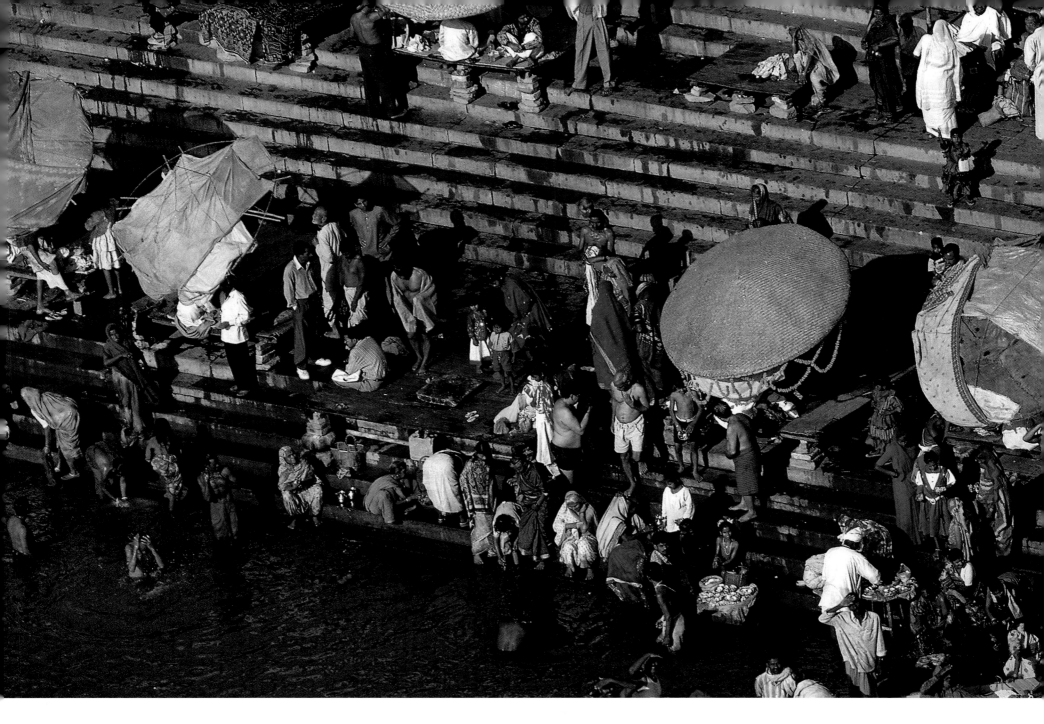

of our effluents and reduce pollution more effectively, starting at the product-manufacturing stage.

The water problem has to be addressed globally; on the level of everyday life, it concerns every one of us. On a planet that, seen from space, is blue and white, the colors of ocean and cloud, water has become the symbol of life. In the transparency of one perfect drop, it embodies in equal measure the concern for an uncertain future and the fragile gleam of hope that, at last, we may use it wisely.

MARIE-FRANCE DUPUIS-TATE
BERNARD FISCHESSER

**VARANASI, THE GHATS: RITUAL BATHING IN THE GANGES, UTTAR PRADESH, INDIA**
(25°20' N, 83°00' E)

The word *ghats* refers both to the vast plateaus that stretch from the Himalayas to the river Ganges and to the steps on the banks of the river itself. The ghats of the holy city of Varanasi are visited by Hindu pilgrims for purification, worship, or cremation of their dead. Leading a virtuous life and carrying out their *dharma* (duty) increases their chances of being reincarnated in a higher caste. India's 2,000-year-old caste system uses the accident of birth to dictate the place an individual occupies in society. Almost 170 million Indians— or one in six—are "untouchables," or *dalits*, who are excluded from the four main castes: Brahmins (priests and teachers); Ksatriyas (warriors and rulers); Vaisyas (farmers, merchants, artisans); and Sudras (servants and laborers). Although India's constitution forbids discrimination based on caste, these *dalits* have no access to land, live in separate districts, and are forced to accept the most menial jobs and violations of their basic rights. In 2001, UNESCO estimated that two-thirds of *dalits* were illiterate, and that only 7 percent had access to clean drinking water, electricity, and sanitation.

## WATER: A TREASURE ESSENTIAL TO LIFE

The amount of water needed for survival:
1.5 liters a day. Without water, a human
being can survive for four days.

## A LIMITED RESOURCE

**FRESH WATER IS NOT ABUNDANT**
**97%** of the Earth's water is saline, and of the remaining **3%**,
the main bulk is unusable because it is either in the form of ice
or is buried deep underground.

Only **0.3%** of the Earth's water makes up our reserves of usable
fresh water.

## AN UNEVENLY DISTRIBUTED RESOURCE

**RESERVES (AVAILABLE QUANTITIES)**
Fewer than **10** countries share **60%** of the world's supply
of fresh water.
The average amount available to each person varies in a ratio
of **1** to **20,000** between the United Arab Emirates and Iceland.

**15%** of the world's supply of fresh water is situated in
the Amazon basin, which houses only **0.3%** of the world's
population, whereas **60%** of the emerging nations suffer
from a chronic shortage of water.

## THE QUALITY OF WATER

**DRINKING WATER AND PURIFICATION**
**1.3 billion** people have no access to drinking water
of consistent quality.
**4 billion** are not connected to any industrial water
purification network.

**DIRTY WATER AND HEALTH**
**2 billion** people are without proper sanitation.
Contaminated water (through organic or chemical pollutants)
kills **5 million** people a year.

## WHAT WATER IS USED AND NEEDED FOR

**HOW THE WORLD USES ITS FRESH WATER**
**70%** for agriculture (irrigation, three-quarters of which
evaporates)
**22%** for industry
**8%** for domestic use (50% of which is lost through leaks in the
network)
**1.5 tons** of water are needed to grow **1 kg** of wheat, three times
that quantity for **1 kg** of rice, and **500 liters** to build
a car.

**INCREASED CONSUMPTION**
In the 20th century, the human population multiplied by **3**,
and world consumption of fresh water increased by **6**.
Consumption of water has **doubled** in the last **20 years**,
mainly to meet the demands of agricultural irrigation.

World consumption of fresh water may increase by **4** to **8%**
a year if the present rate continues.
Agricultural demands in developing countries may double every
**20 years**.

## A DISAPPEARING RESOURCE

**INDIVIDUAL CONSUMPTION OF WATER**
According to the World Health Organization (WHO), basic
requirements (drink, hygiene, cooking) amount to **50 liters** per
person per day.
The average American consumes **630 liters** of water per
day—more than **12 times** more than necessary.
By contrast, some people in less developed countries have access
to only **20 liters** per person per day, which is not enough for
their basic needs.

**DIMINISHING SUPPLIES OF WATER**
The amount of water available to each individual has shrunk by
more than **50%** since 1950.
In 1950, the amount of water available to each individual was
**17,000 m³** per year.
In 2001, it was only **7,800 m³**.
The minimum annual requirement per person is **1,000 m³**
of water.

**DRAMATIC CONSEQUENCES IF CURRENT TRENDS CONTINUE**
Shortages: by **2025**, **1.5 billion** people will not have enough
water to live on.
Disappearance of natural resources: in 1963, Lake Chad was the
fourth-largest lake in Africa; since then it has shrunk by **95%**,
mainly because of exploitation for irrigation. This decrease affects
the lives of **20 million** people.

Since the **1960s**, irrigation work downstream from the
Aral Sea has reduced its area by **50%** and its volume of water
by **75%**, and its salt content has doubled. Today there is no longer
any fishing in the Aral Sea, which may disappear altogether
by **2020**.
Exploitation and shortages also create geopolitical tensions such
as those between Turkey, Syria, and Iraq over the Euphrates.

> **FISH MARKET NEAR DAKAR, SENEGAL** (14°43' N, 17°26' W)

Senegal's 435 miles (700 km) of coasts teem with marine life, thanks to the seasonal alternation of mineral-rich cold
currents from the Canary Islands with warm currents from the equator. This local wealth supports coastal fishing, 80 percent
of which is done on a small scale, using lines or nets from dugout canoes made out of baobab or kapok logs. But it also
attracts European trawlers. Once they have the required permits, these boats can catch fish in far greater quantities and fish
intensively, depriving the countries of the region of this resource. Fishing is still Senegal's main industry, producing over
400,000 tons a year, chiefly destined for the local market. Tuna, sardines, and hake are mostly sold on the beaches where the
canoes come in to land. For the Senegalese, as for 3.5 billion others in the world, the ocean is the primary source of food.

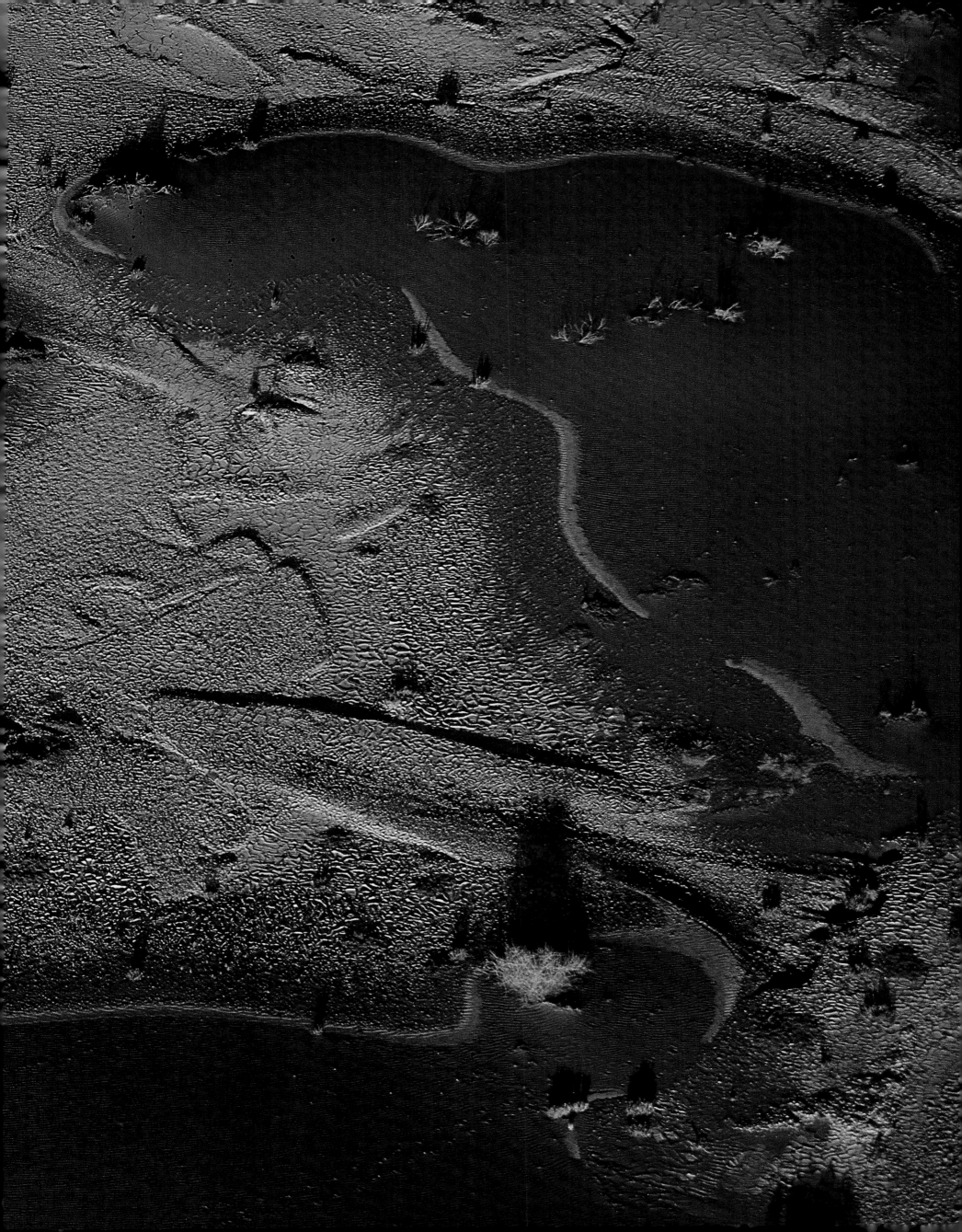

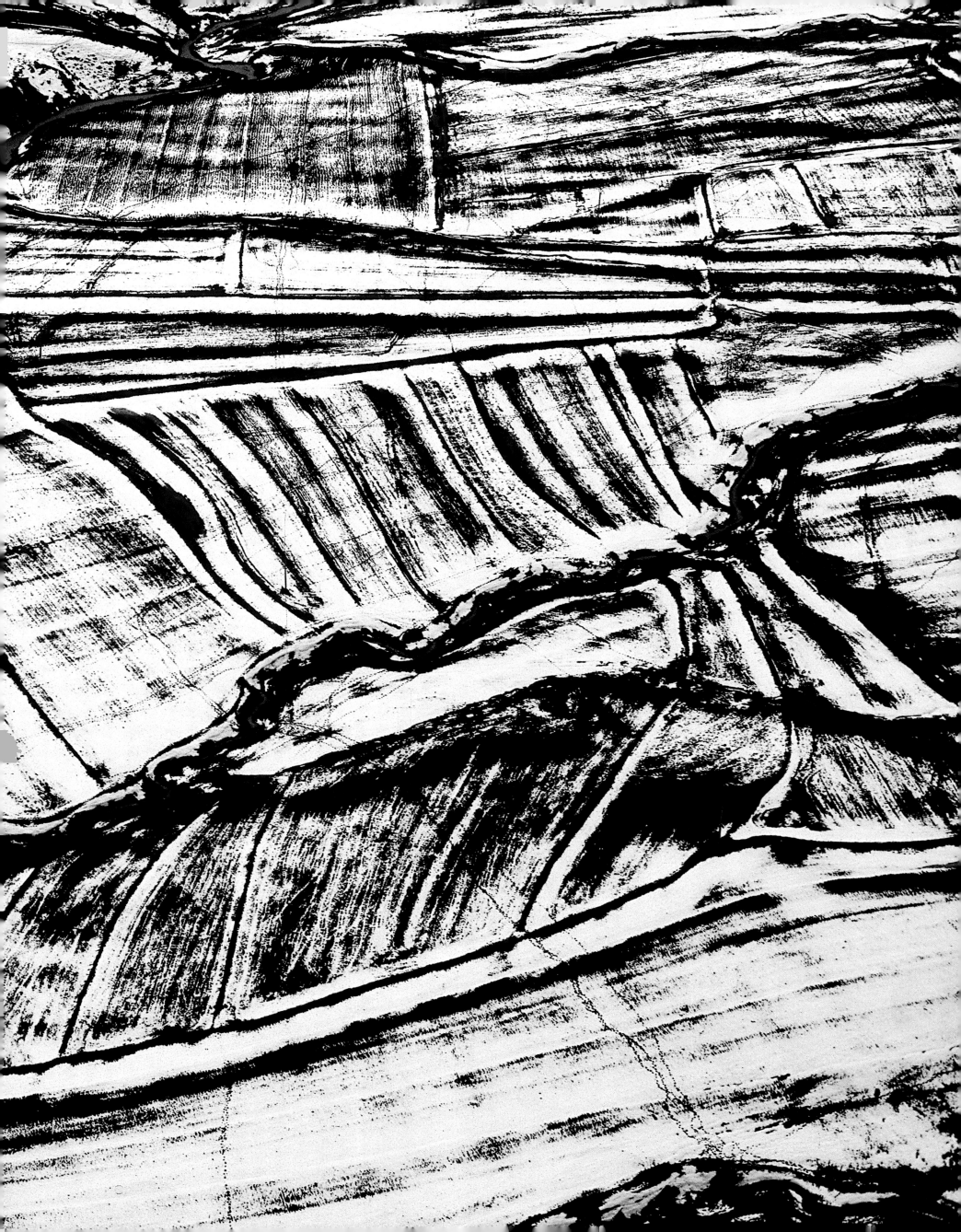

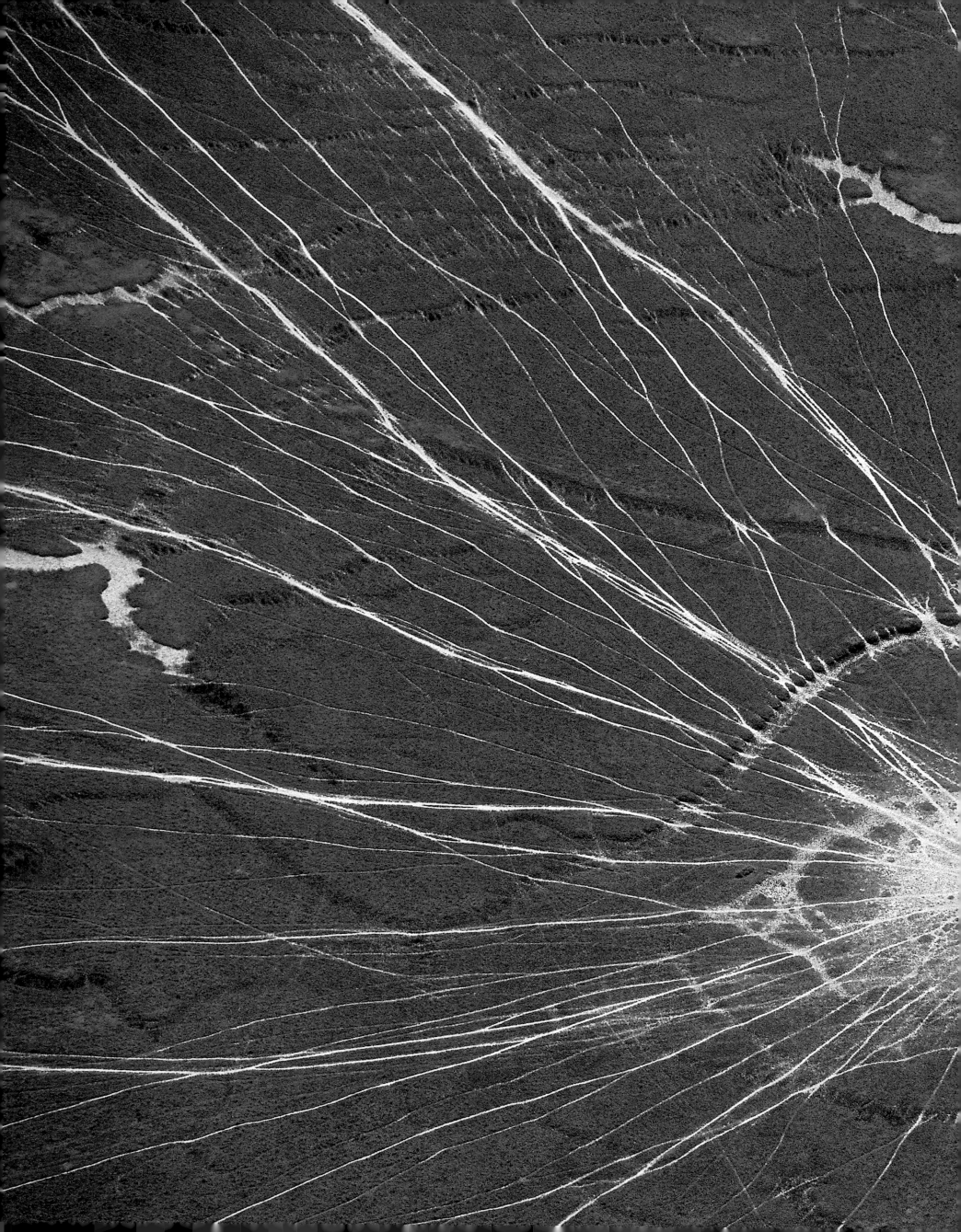

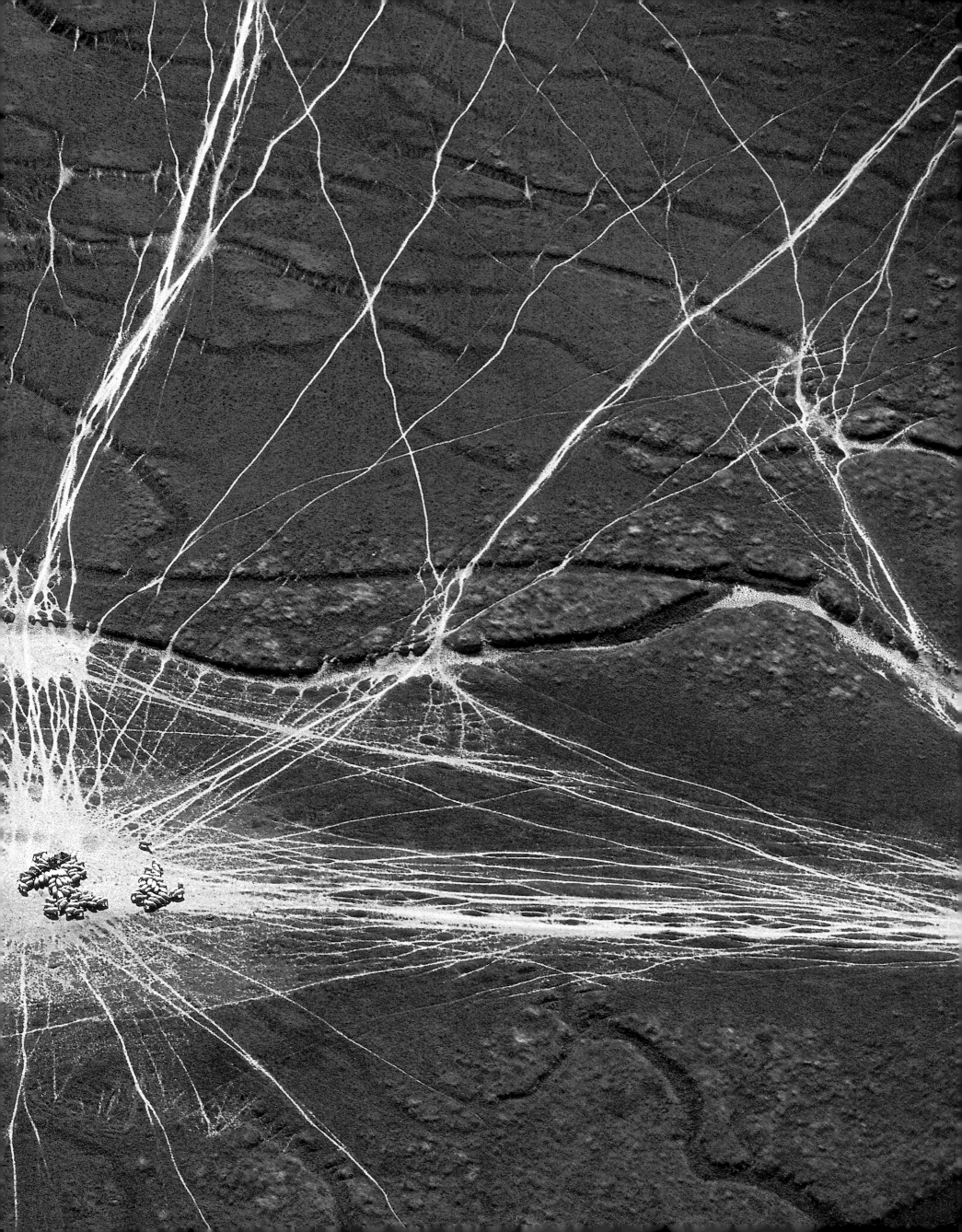

# BIODIVERSITY:
# A QUESTION OF SURVIVAL

Viewed alongside other living species, the human race stands apart.
We have managed to take advantage of the earthly environment to reduce
our death rate and increase our birth rate, and thus our numbers constantly rise.
Yet this mastery and exploitation of the environment has caused entire species
to perish, and others are in the process of disappearing. Will we ever learn to
stop destroying life? Every species plays its role in the global equilibrium of
the environment to which we belong, and we ignore this at our peril.

Encased in the huge Russian taiga, Lake Baikal, the greatest freshwater reservoir in the world, resembles a long comma drawn through the heart of Asia. At Irkutsk, the closest city, naturalists strive to count and identify the plant and animal species that inhabit the lake. No fewer than 2,600 species have been inventoried, three-quarters of which are specific to Lake Baikal and exist nowhere else on Earth. Why so many entirely different species, when the lake might just as well contain only one—or none? But then we would no longer be on Planet Earth, where for nearly 4 billion years species have constantly diversified, feeding one another. We could imagine Lake Baikal functioning with one type of seal, which would feed on one species of fish, and this fish would subsist on a single crustacean species, which in turn would live at the expense of an algae produced by photosynthesis, occupying the base of this four-story ecological pyramid. The pyramid is purely theoretical, however, because in reality on each level below seals (only one freshwater seal exists, the nerpa) we can count numerous species of fish, shellfish, and algae. During the 60 million years of the lake's formation, biological evolution has constantly diversified and increased the numbers of species, in the process of creating life.

There is not an environment in existence, whether natural or artificial, forest or garden, steppe or cultivated field, where different species cannot be found, to every one of which scientists have given a name. The diversity of life is the guise in which nature appears to us, and the same applies within each species, including our own. In a crowd, no two faces are identical, except twins who share the same hereditary substance. In the same way, no two spotted cows, no two cats or oak trees are absolutely identical, even if these often minuscule differences appear more clearly within our own species. We can identify a face, but our eye is not practiced enough to distinguish between two spruce trees or two violets of the same species.

To recognize the species, describe their characteristics, and classify them—this is the job of natural scientists, who are unfortunately too rare; today they are replaced in our universities and research institutes by molecular biologists or geneticists, whose influence now rules biology. What a strange paradox, just when there is so much talk of preserving spaces and species. How can we protect them if we do not even know them?

In the fishermen's nets at Lake Baikal it is easy to identify the famous *golomyanka*, a strange carnivorous fish that feeds 50 percent on crustaceans and 50 percent on its own young. Stranger yet, these fish do not lay eggs in water as all other members of their genus do but give birth to larvae and then die. In addition to these oddities, they are perfectly transparent, to the extent that one could, it is claimed, read a newspaper through their bodies. But the fishers on Lake Baikal also eat plentifully of sculpin, omul, and many other fish, and they also eat seals. Birds, humans and seals, and fish are part of three large groups of vertebrates known on the planet today: 9,950 species of birds, 4,360 of mammal, and 25,000 of fish; in addition to the 7,400 species of reptile and 4,950 of amphibians (the last group is the most endangered). Yet these figures are modest when compared to the 270,000 species of flowering plants—including more than 50,000 species of trees—and the 950,000 insect species. Altogether, today some 1.75 million species have been identified. Our extremely approximate estimate of the total number of species in nature varies from the most modest figure of 10 million up to much higher figures posited by others. After all, innumerable worms, arachnids, mollusks, algae, insects, and mushrooms are still entirely unknown to us.

This diversity is particularly great in intertropical forests, which alone contain a good half of all species on the planet. A northern forest of conifers has scarcely more than two species of tree per square kilometer, whereas a temperate zone forest of the eastern United States has as many as twenty, and an Amazonian forest has several hundred. Thus, it is no surprise that Brazil holds the record for the number of vertebrate species (6,100) and the number of higher plants (56,200).

**OPEN-AIR WASTE DUMP, SANTO DOMINGO, DOMINICAN REPUBLIC**
(18°28' N, 69°53' W)

In this open-air dump, the poorest people sort through the garbage and recover anything that might be sold unofficially for reuse or recycling. In the Dominican Republic the amount of refuse doubled between 1994 and 2000, and the country has no infrastructure for dealing with such volumes of waste. Less than 25 percent of solid materials are recycled, and such open dumps pollute the coast and approaches to Santo Domingo. Garbage collected from the city is unloaded onto these sites without any form of control. The spread of disease, the ruination of the countryside, the stench, and the emission of toxic gases—all of these have contributed to the escalating level of pollution. Sporadic incineration of the garbage causes 20 percent of the air pollution here and—a matter of the utmost concern—toxic waste from hospitals is not treated separately. In a region that is right at the heart of a cyclone belt and is regularly subject to violent storms, the consequences to the health of the people, to tourism, and to the environment are extremely grave.

of industrial countries and the developing countries, where genetic resources are found, in accordance with the decisions of the Rio de Janeiro Earth Summit of 1992. One aim of these agreements is to compensate the countries that provide these resources whenever they lead to a new form of medication, for example.

This prodigious "gene bank" of diverse species throughout the world ensures that the needs of human populations will be met. Protecting nature means recognizing our own links and membership in this environment that feeds, heals, and dazzles us. All of our technological devices, even the most sophisticated, could vanish in an instant without decisively compromising the survival of humanity, because the first of all of nature's resources is the Earth and its fruits. We are obliged to protect and love nature. In his 1968 book on condor protection, *Man and the California Condor*, the naturalist Ian McMillan explained his belief that the true importance of preservation was "as a cultural practice which developed and strengthened the human attributes needed in working out a new program for the welfare and survival of our own species."

JEAN-MARIE PELT

⌃ **VOLCANO ON THE WEST COAST OF THE ISLAND OF SAN SALVADOR, GALAPAGOS ISLANDS, ECUADOR** (0°22' S, 90°35' W)

The nineteen islands that form the Galapagos Archipelago are of volcanic origin and rose from the waves of the Pacific Ocean 3 to 5 million years ago. Despite their lunar appearance, they offer exceptional biological diversity and are home to the richest colony of sea iguanas in the world and to the giant tortoise which gave its name, *galápago*, to the archipelago. Visitors have always responded to the magical charm of the place, and Darwin found inspiration here for his theory of the evolution of species. The Galapagos Islands were recognized as a national park in 1959 and a world marine reserve in 2001, and joined the UNESCO list of World Heritage sites in 1978, allowing almost all of their exceptional biodiversity to be preserved. However, the islands are affected by demographic growth, the rise of tourism and illegal fishing along their coasts. In addition, falling prices on the world agricultural market have favored the importation of foodstuffs to the detriment of local agriculture. The species that have been introduced in this way now threaten this natural evolutionary laboratory.

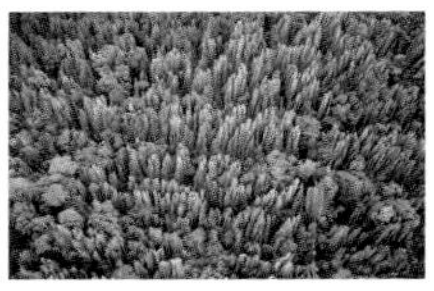

**PAGES 206–207**
TSINGY OF BEMARAHA, MORONDAVA REGION, MADAGASCAR
(18°47' S, 45°03' E)

The strange mineral forest of Tsingy of Bemaraha stands on the western coast of Madagascar. This geological formation, called karst, is the result of erosion, as acid rains have gradually dissolved the stone of the chalky plateau and carved out sharp ridges that can rise to heights of 100 feet (30 m). This nearly impenetrable labyrinth (*tsingy* is the Malagasy term for "walking on tiptoe") shelters its own unique flora and fauna, which have not yet been completely recorded. The site was declared a nature reserve in 1927 and a UNESCO World Heritage site in 1990. Madagascar is a 230,000-square-mile (587,000 km²) land mass created by continental drift; isolated for 165 million years in the Indian Ocean off the coast of southern Africa, it has developed distinctive and diverse animal and plant species, sometimes with archaic characteristics. It has an exceptional rate of endemism: more than 90 percent of the approximately 12,000 plant species and 80 percent of the animal species recorded are unique to the island. Nonetheless, many Madagascan species are now at risk of extinction.

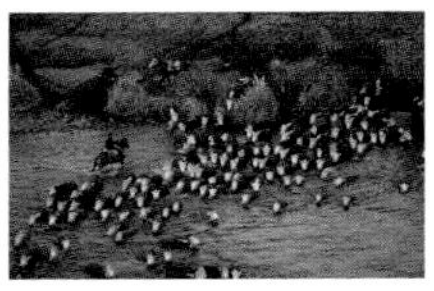

**PAGES 208–209**
CATTLE CROSSING THE CHIMEHUIN RIVER, NEUQUÉN PROVINCE, ARGENTINA
(40°03' S, 71°04' W)

Patrolled by *gauchos*, this herd of Hereford cows crossing the Chimehuin River is returning to its home in the fields after seasonal migration to the high-lying pasturelands of the Andes cordillera. Partly covered by thorny grasslands, Neuquén is better suited for raising sheep than cattle, which remain a minority in the Patagonian region. Most of the country's bovine livestock live farther north, in the vast grassy plains of the pampas. These nearly 51 million cows consist primarily of breeds that originated in Great Britain. The world's fifth-largest producer, Argentina exports its beef products, famed for their fine flavor, throughout the world. Argentinians are the world's leading consumers of beef: nearly 137 pounds (62 kg) per person per year. Yearly per capita consumption is 95 pounds (43 kg) in the United States, and 86 pounds (39 kg) in Australia, as opposed to 10 pounds (4.6 kg) in the Philippines and in China (double the consumption five years ago), and 5.5 pounds (2.5 kg) in India.

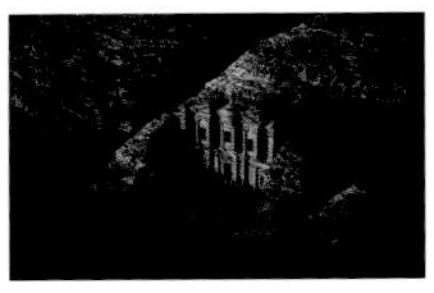

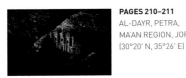

**PAGES 210–211**
AL-DAYR, PETRA, MA'AN REGION, JORDAN
(30°20' N, 35°26' E)

Jordan occupies a strategic position between the Mediterranean and the Red Sea. In the 7th century BC the Nabataeans, a people of merchant nomads, settled here. They carved a city out of the pink and yellow sandstone of the cliffs in the southern part of the country and made it their capital. They called it Petra, the Greek word for "rock." Through the trade of rare products (incense from Arabia, spices from India, gold from Egypt, silk from China, and ivory from Nubia) and taxation of caravan routes, Nabataean civilization extended its influence far beyond the Transjordan region before it fell to the Romans in AD 106. Like most of the city's buildings, Al-Dayr was made between the 1st century BC and the 2nd century AD, when the Nabataean culture was at its height. Because of its height (42 meters, or 138 feet), it dominates the 800 monuments of Petra. After the fall of the Nabataean civilization, it was used by Byzantine Christians, hence its name of *Al-Dayr*, "the monastery." Petra was declared a UNESCO World Heritage site in 1985, but a new threat to the cliffs has emerged in recent years: mineral salts dissolved in groundwater that reaches the base of the monuments become encrusted on the stone and make it fragile. Wind also adds to the gradual erosion of the monuments.

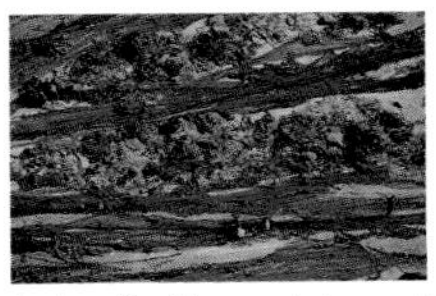

**PAGES 212–213**
FISHING NETS IN THE PORT OF AGADIR, MOROCCO
(30°26' N, 9°36' W)

At Agadir, Morocco's largest fishing port and the world's leading sardine port, nets measuring several hundred feet in length are stretched out on the ground for repairs to be made before the next sea outing. The Moroccan waters, with 2,135 miles (3,500 km) of sea coast, are home to nearly 250 species of fish, particularly sardines, which swim along the shore to feed from the upwelling of the nutrient-rich lower waters. Employing trawlers and small motorboats, 75 percent of Moroccan fishing remains a small-scale activity. Since 1970 the world fishing output has doubled, reaching 133 million tons in 2002. The increase in captive fishing, made possible by a sixfold increase in the world fleet since 1970, has now led to a drop in resources: over 70 percent of fisheries are exhausted or exploited to capacity. Large fish such as cod, halibut, and tuna are on the brink of extinction: 90 percent of the stocks have gone and the fish that are caught are decreasing in size.

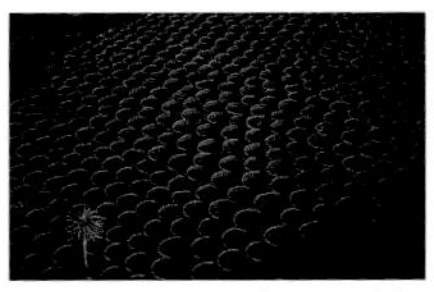

**PAGES 214–215**
VINEYARDS, REGION OF GERIA, LANZAROTE, CANARY ISLANDS, SPAIN
(28°48' N, 13°41' W)

Lanzarote, one of seven islands in the Spanish archipelago known as the Canaries, lies closest to the African continent. Agriculture is difficult because of the island's desert climate and the total absence of streams and rivers on its territory of 313 square miles (813 km²). Its volcanic origins, however, have provided the island with a fertile black soil made up of ash and lapilli over a substratum of fairly impermeable clay. Residents have developed a distinctive viticultural technique to adapt to these original natural conditions. Vine stocks are planted individually in the center of holes dug in the lapilli in order to draw on the accumulated moisture, shielded from the dry winds from the northeast and Saharan regions by low, semicircular stone walls. In 2001 Spain's total wine production represented around 9 percent of the approximately 7.5 billion gallons (28.2 billion liters) of wine produced worldwide each year, ranking third among wine-producing countries after France and Italy.

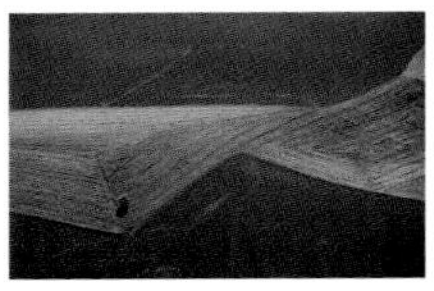

**PAGES 216–217**
AGRICULTURAL LANDSCAPE BETWEEN ANKARA AND HATTOUSA, ANATOLIA, TURKEY
(40°00' N, 33°35' E)

The great plateaus and arid steppes of Anatolia are the cradle of Turkish civilization and were inhabited by nomads for centuries. Since 1977, this region, through which the Tigris and Euphrates rivers flow, has been the site of the Southeastern Anatolia Project (GAP), which entails the construction of 22 dams and 19 hydroelectric power stations by 2010. This project would increase the area of irrigated land in Turkey by 50 percent, and the country's output of electricity would double. The diversion of the waters of these two rivers is causing serious tension between Turkey and its neighbors in the Mesopotamian basin: Syria, Iran, and Iraq. In 2001, the United Nations Environment Program raised the alarm for this internationally important ecosystem, in which hundreds of miles of mountain valleys are to be flooded, while the lower regions are parched by huge drainage projects, reduced river flows, and damage caused by war. We are therefore seeing the disappearance of one of the world's great wetlands systems—the Mesopotamian marshes, which straddle Iraq and Iran.

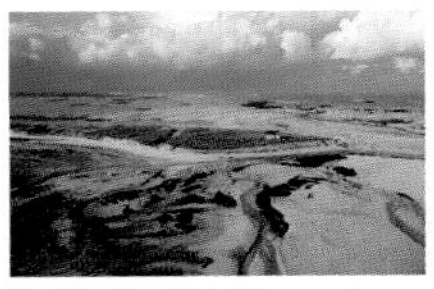

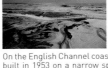

**PAGES 218–219**
HOUSE IN KEREMMA, ON THE KERNIC COVE AT LOW TIDE, FINISTÈRE, FRANCE
(48°39' N, 4°13' W)

On the English Channel coast of Brittany, this house was built in 1953 on a narrow spit of granite sediment that extends the dunes of Keremma and closes the Kernic cove almost entirely, leaving the boats only a narrow passageway into the bay. Looking out on great expanses of sand at low tide, this thin arrow of a dune is almost totally surrounded by water when the sea rises again. Rough ocean winds and the daily rise and fall of the tides (about 26 feet, or 8 m) gradually eroded the fragile support for this isolated home. The house, which in 1983 stood nearly 150 feet (45 m) inland, by 1999 was just 6 feet (2 m) from the cliff edge overhanging the sea. It disappeared from the landscape in March 2000, when the inevitable erosion of the dune forced the owner to have it demolished before it could collapse. Installations by the shore conservation agency are trying to protect the Keremma dunes against the erosive action of the surf. Tides, daily shifts in the height of the coastal waters resulting from lunar and solar attraction, are typical of all the Earth's seas, creating differences varying from just a few inches in the Mediterranean Sea, to more than 52 feet (16 m) in the Atlantic (in the Bay of Fundy, Canada).

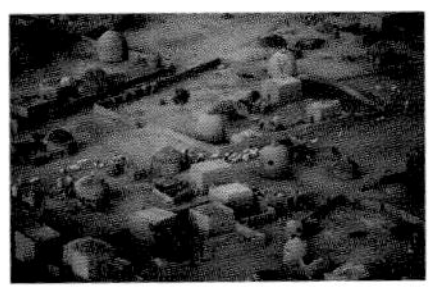

**PAGES 220–221**
DETAIL OF A VILLAGE NEAR TAHOUA, NIGER
(15°03' N, 5°12' E)

This village near Tahoua, in southwestern Niger, shows typical Hausa architecture: cubelike houses of *banco* (a mixture of earth and plant fibers), alongside imposing egg-shaped grain storehouses. The Hausa people, who make up 54 percent of the country's population, are farmers, but they are most renowned for their craftwork and trade. The Hausa city-states in northern Nigeria have had commerce with numerous African countries for several centuries. Today the region of Tahoua is crossed by a road that leads northward, commonly called the "uranium route." A vein of uranium was discovered in 1965 in the ground below the Air Massif, and mines in the northern town of Arlit yield nearly 4,000 tons of uranium each year, or about 10 percent of the world output, making Niger the third world producer.

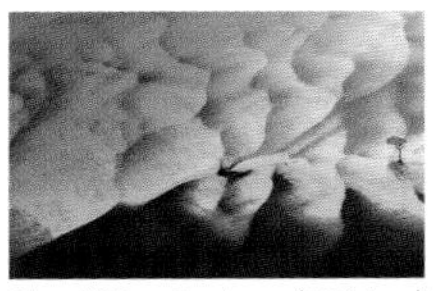

**PAGES 222–223**
SAND BANK OF THE RÍO CARONI, BOLÍVAR STATE, VENEZUELA
(6°00' N, 62°52' W)

The 425-mile-long (690 km) Río Caroni flows northward through the Venezuelan state of Bolívar (commonly called Guayana), descending in a series of falls and meeting vast sandbanks on its way. The Caroni, along with the other waterways that cross Guayana, is rich in alkaloids and tannins from the degradation of dense forest vegetation. They are therefore grouped together under the general category of "black" rivers, as opposed to the "white" rivers that descend from the heights of the Andes carrying mud and silt; the waters of the black rivers are dark but clear, whereas the white rivers are murky. Before ending its course in the Orinoco River, the Caroni powers the hydroelectric Guri Dam (in service since 1986), which is one of the most powerful in the world. However, the major drought in Venezuela between 2001 and 2004 has considerably affected the use of dams. Hydroelectric dams produce 16 percent of electricity worldwide.

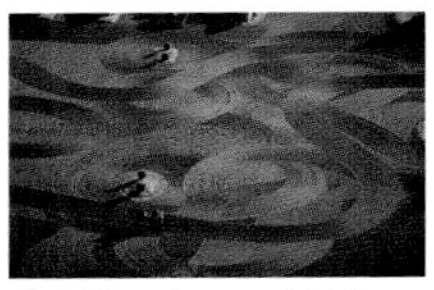

**PAGES 224–225**
TRAINING ARENA IN THE HIPPODROME OF MAISONS-LAFFITTE, YVELINES, FRANCE
(48°57' N, 2°09' E)

The hippodrome of Maisons-Laffitte, near Paris, is one of the largest equestrian training centers in France, with tracks and stables that accommodate close to 800 horses. In the training arenas—shown here is the Adam arena—the grooms exercise the young horses and prepare them for jumping obstacles before allowing them to run on the practice ground and racetracks. The hippodrome of Maisons-Laffitte hosts more than 250 races each year, featuring a total of over 3,000 competitors. Horse races account for a considerable portion of the gambling industry: more than $100 billion is bet on racehorses throughout the world each year.

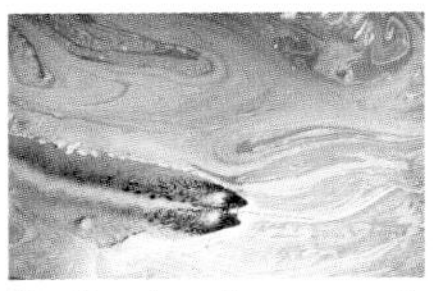

**PAGES 226–227**
AERATOR IN A SHRIMP FARM, TUNGKANG LAGOON, TAIWAN
(22°26' N, 120°28' E)

The Tungkang lagoon, southwest of the island of Taiwan, is checkered with brackish pools devoted to farming seafood, particularly shrimp, which is highly profitable. Parting the white froth produced by the shrimp's waste, this aerator oxygenates the tanks where they are raised. Over the last twenty years, world production of shrimp has risen sharply, reaching 814,000 tons in 1999—more than sixteen times the figure for 1980, which was 50,000 tons. Asia, where the tiger shrimp is the predominant species, produces 80 percent of the world's output. Since shrimp need warm water to grow, shrimp farms are established in coastal regions in the tropics. Here, they often replace mangrove swamps—unique, fragile ecosystems that are a refuge and breeding ground for fish and crustaceans. Moreover, large amounts of waste from these intensive farms, as well as the antibiotics widely used, pollute the surrounding area. It is estimated that in some areas, for every pound of farmed shrimp, nearly half a pound of wild fish and shrimp disappear. This is harmful to local people for whom shrimp farming, aimed at export markets, brings no benefits.

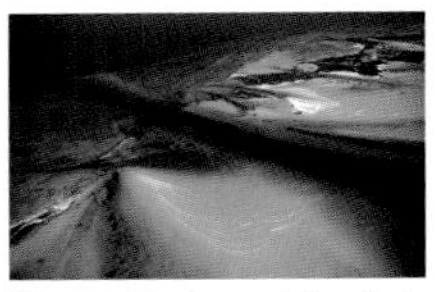

**PAGES 228–229**
ISLET AND SEA BED, EXUMA CAYS, BAHAMAS
(24°00' N, 76°10' W)

The archipelago of the Bahamas, which takes its name from the Spanish term *baja mar* ("shallows"), spreads out in an arc in the Atlantic Ocean, running 750 miles (1,200 km) with 5,405 square miles (14,000 km²) of land above water level from Florida to Santo Domingo. It consists of more than 700 islands (29 of which are permanently inhabited), plus a few thousand rocky coral islands called cays. It was on these islands, specifically on Samana Cay, that Christopher Columbus first set foot on October 12, 1492, during his first voyage. During the 16th and 17th centuries the Bahamas were a center of piracy. They became a British colony in 1783, which they remained until their independence in 1973. They derive most of their resources from tourism (60 percent of the GNP), which employs two out of three Bahamians but which suffered from the damage caused by Hurricane Jeanne in September 2004. The country's second major source of revenue is banking (15 percent of the GNP): it is a haven with no income tax. The Bahamas have also become one of the centers for drug traffic (marijuana and cocaine) and illegal immigrants bound for the United States.

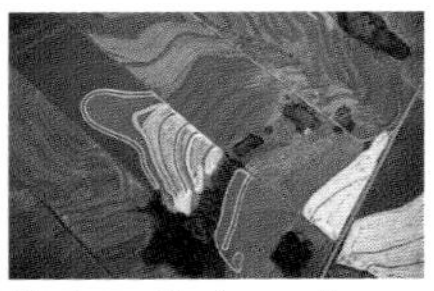

**PAGES 230–231**
FIELDS IN MISIONES PROVINCE, ARGENTINA
(27°00' S, 55°00' W)

At Argentina's northernmost tip, the province of Misiones is the cradle of *maté*, the ubiquitous drink of Argentina. The *maté* herb originated in this region, where the local Guarani people drank it as an infusion long before the Jesuit missions arrived in the 16th century. Today, plantations of this crop, whose leaves have tonic properties, follow the contours of the land. This mode of cultivation was made compulsory in 1953 to protect crops from erosion caused by the often torrential rains. Rural areas have been severely hit by the country's present economic crisis: 90 percent of small *maté* producers are particularly badly affected. By contrast, cultivation of GMOs has increased sharply, with the area under such crops rising thirtyfold between 1996 and 2001. Argentina now has 22 percent of the world's transgenic crops, which puts it in second place behind the United States.

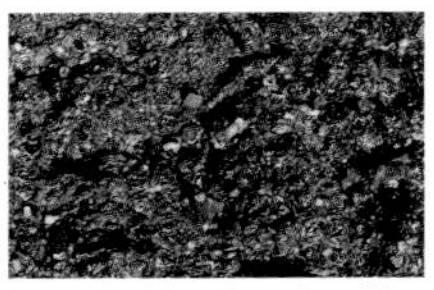

**PAGES 232–233**
REFUSE DUMP IN MEXICO CITY, MEXICO
(19°24' N, 99°01' W)

Household refuse is piling up on all continents and poses a critical problem for major urban centers, like the problem of air pollution resulting from vehicular traffic and industrial pollutants. With some 21 million residents, Mexico City produces nearly 20,000 tons of household refuse a day. As in many countries, half of this debris is sent to open dumps. The volume of refuse is increasing on our planet along with population growth and, in particular, economic growth. Thus, an American produces more than 1,500 pounds (700 kg) of domestic refuse each year, about four times more than a resident of a developing country and twice as much as a Mexican. The volume of debris per capita in industrialized nations has tripled in the past twenty years. Recycling, reuse, and reduction of packaging materials are potential solutions to the pollution problems caused by dumping and incineration, which still account for 41 percent and 44 percent, respectively, of the annual volume of household garbage in France.

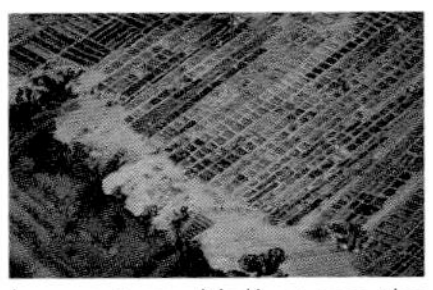

**PAGES 234–235**
MARKET GARDENS ON THE SENEGAL RIVER NEAR KAYES, MALI
(14°34' N, 11°46' W)

In western Mali, near the frontiers of Senegal and Mauritania, the city of Kayes is a major ethnic and commercial crossroads. The Senegal River passes through the entire region, and many market gardens lie along its banks. The river is an important resource in this zone of the Sahel, and the waters are transported in containers by local women to allow the manual watering of tiny plots of land to produce fruit and vegetables intended for the local market. The Senegal River, which begins at the confluence of the Bafing ("black river") and the Bakoy ("white river") rivers slightly upstream from Kayes, runs for 1,000 miles (1,600 km) across four countries. The hydraulic stations along its course allow the irrigation of only 234 square miles (600 km²) of farmland, but its basin measures 136,500 square miles (350,000 km²) and provides water for nearly 10 million people.

These records are nearly matched by the tropical forests of America and Southeast Asia, although the African forests have fewer species. It is important, however, not to confuse the notion of species with that of population, which indicates in a given area the number of individuals that belong to each of the known species. The human species today has more than 6 billion individuals, but we are far from being able to compute this number for each of the known animal or vegetable species. The most we can say is that by adding up all of the trees on the planet, we can count 500 trees per inhabitant.

This biological heritage, this biodiversity, is subject to continuous erosion, because of the constantly accelerating pace of human activity. In the tropical forests, we cut, burn, and flood hundreds of thousands of square miles each year to obtain timber and arable land, to build roads, to exploit petroleum concessions, or to create huge retaining basins for dams. The land lost in this manner each year is equal to the area of Belgium or the state of Maryland.

Scorched-earth farming, carried out by poor peasants on lands cleared by fire in order to exploit new arable surfaces, is not, as is sometimes claimed, the only predatory practice at the expense of forests. The big landowners often practice unacceptable timber exploitation, bulldozing hundreds of trees in order to find a few that are "valuable"; this ravages the forests, marginalizes native populations, and leaves the ground skeletal, disfigured, and unsuitable for farming. At the current rate all tropical forests could disappear within a half-century, along with the innumerable species they shelter.

Yet forests protect the soil, preventing water from rushing unrestrained into rivers, taking fertile silts with it and destroying fish resources. The underlayer of earth that is exposed as a result quickly becomes desertified, proving the truth of the maxim that the forest precedes humans and the desert follows them. The floods of the Ganges in Bangladesh and the Yangtze in China are the fatal consequence of the enormous deforestations in the hillside valleys of the Himalayas, particularly in Nepal, and in western China.

Now that we know the devastating cost, we can no longer massacre the forest. It is time to replenish it, to consider the planet a garden entrusted to humans to be managed with wisdom and care. In short, it is time to rebuild the garden of Eden, still alive and fresh as a memory and a hope in our collective unconscious. This is a worthy project for future generations.

The respectful treatment of nature can only be of benefit to humanity. In the United States, for instance, agricultural techniques that were too intensive and used too many chemicals profoundly changed the ecology of the water for New York City. Proposals were made to build large treatment plants, until experts decided it would be better to restore the biodiversity that had originally been present in the environment, by radically changing agricultural practices. This was done, to the great benefit of greater New York, whose waters were purified by a simple biological process. Intensely farmed land, full of chemicals from fertilizers and pesticides, takes a heavy toll on diversity: first insects are killed, next butterflies, then wild herbs, and then perhaps tomorrow bees. When the hives disappear, the victims of pesticides, what will happen to the pollination process, on which the fertility of our fields and fruit trees depend? In India and Latin America more than one hundred species of wild plants are used as food or medicine; what will

be left of these resources and knowledge if these plants are destroyed by the thoughtless use of chemicals or by competition from some genetically altered variety?

In a strange paradox, it is the Earth's cities, less subject to the spread of chemicals, which are becoming true havens of biodiversity. In Germany, cities such as Berlin or Munich, with areas of 340 square miles (880 km²) and 115 square miles (300 km²), respectively, are larger than any of their country's nature reserves. Some 260 species of butterfly have been counted in a public park of 1.5 acres (6,000 m²) in the center of Munich, which paradoxically means that these cities, with their open-air urbanism without excessive density, are actually richer in species than most of the rest of the country. This fact is very telling about the damaging effects caused by chemical agriculture, and pleads in favor of a form of farming that is closer to nature, particularly organic agriculture.

Biodiversity is also a guarantee of endurance and of the good health of natural and cultivated areas. If disease strikes a forest devoted to the monoculture of a specific spruce, the entire forest will disappear. This occurred in nineteenth-century Ireland, which had devoted itself solely to the potato crop. Between 1845 and 1849 disease struck the potato fields and totally ravaged them; famine followed, decimating entire families. In just a few years the Irish population fell by 1.5 million: 1 million perished, and 500,000 emigrated to the United States. A similar catastrophe nearly occurred in Africa in the 1970s, when cassava crops were stricken with two serious cryptogamic diseases. The salvation in this case came from the hybridization of the cultivated cassava with a wild cassava species that was immune to the pathogenic fungus and had become rare in nature. The new variety proved resistant, and the specter of hardship and famine was dispelled.

Respect for biodiversity also means preservation of these many useful species, both nutritional and medicinal. Today an estimated 3,000 edible wild species are known; each of them, improved by selection and hybridization, could become a new food source tomorrow. The task of selecting the best, of achieving judicious combinations—this is basically the way master chefs create recipes, incorporating foods that are carefully selected and harmoniously combined: fruits and vegetables, meats and game, spices and condiments, great vintage wines. Luckily, monoculture has not yet taken over our delicate palates, so eager for fine, rich flavors. Europe's firm resistance to genetically modified plants is explained largely by this desire to preserve diversified foods that reflect biodiversity itself.

Protecting nature means protecting this very diversity. Consider the example of a plant that is increasingly consumed to combat rheumatism, devil's claw (*Harpagophytum procumbens*); it is native to Namibia, and its natural environment is overexploited today. In recent years there has been a push to buy products that are harvested organically, respecting the volume of the resource and the quantities that can be harvested without exhausting the natural habitat, allowing the *Harpagophytum* plants to renew themselves from year to year. This can be applied to all harvests.

The creation of parks, reserves, conservation areas, and international agreements is a multifaceted strategy for the necessary protection of nature as well as agriculture and culture in general. Every culture has its own nutritional and medicinal traditions, which must be preserved. This need has led today to agreements between the major laboratories

◠ **VACATIONERS SWIMMING WITH DOLPHINS, PUERTO VALLARTA, JALISCO STATE, MEXICO** [20°37' N, 105°15' W]

On the western Pacific coast, facing the Bay of Banderas, the town of Puerto Vallarta has been a mecca of Mexican tourism for decades. Here, in the city's amusement park, vacationers can swim with dolphins. Though this might seem a tempting idea, it is severely condemned by many groups, especially those concerned with protecting the dolphins themselves. The large number of visitors, and the close contact with the animals, increase the chances of diseases being transmitted between people and dolphins. In a more general sense, dolphins in parks where people can feed or touch them are stressed, often obese, and frequently injured. The visitors are not always safe, and they risk being bitten or hit inadvertently. Nature conservation organizations are constantly demanding the closure of such "petting pools."

## BIODIVERSITY: A BOON FOR MANKIND

In the long term, the most essential resources will not be fossil fuels but renewable materials, mainly from biomass.

The diversity of products and needs that can be fulfilled in the future will depend on the biodiversity of the future and our efforts to protect and conserve the biodiversity of today.

The biodiversity of the planet Earth is estimated to be about **14 million** species.
Only **12%** of these, some **1.7 million**, have actually been identified and recorded.

## SPECIES DISAPPEARING AT AN UNPRECEDENTED RATE

**REDUCTION IN THE NUMBER OF SPECIES**
More than **11,000** species of plants and animals are endangered in the short term.
According to the IUCN (World Conservation Union), **2** or **3** species are disappearing every hour. At this rate, half the world's species will have become extinct by the end of this century.

**SHRINKING POPULATIONS**
The Living Planet Index, which measures the population trends of vertebrates living in the ecosystems, fell by nearly **40%** between **1970** and **2000**.

**AN INCREDIBLE RATE**
Although it is natural for species to disappear, the current rate of extinction is anything but natural, and is caused by human activity. It is **1,000** to **10,000 times** faster than it should be.

## EXTINCTION AT THE HEART OF THE RICHEST ECOSYSTEMS IN THE WORLD

**RAINFORESTS, NATURAL RESERVES OF WATER AND BIODIVERSITY**
Rainforests are the ecosystems with the greatest abundance of species. They cover less than **10%** of the Earth's surface, but contain around **90%** of the species that live on our planet. They are being subjected to rapid and continuous deforestation, amounting to **15.2 million** hectares per year (an area equivalent to the size of Florida, or to the combined area of the Netherlands, Belgium, Switzerland, and Denmark).

**CORAL REEFS THAT PROTECT AGRICULTURAL LAND**
More than **50%** of the world's coral reefs are under threat. **27%** of the world's coral reefs have already disappeared.

**WETLANDS PURIFY AND STORE WATER**
Half the world's wetlands have been destroyed since **1848**.

**MANGROVES, NURSERIES OF THE SEA**
Half the world's mangrove forests—essential to **75%** of commercial species of marine life—have disappeared.

## HUMAN RESPONSIBILITY

**A NEW KIND OF EXTINCTION**
The five previous instances of mass extinction were caused by geological or astronomical catastrophes, exacerbated by climatic and ecological upheavals.
One of these catastrophes, **65 million** years ago, wiped out **75%** of species, including the dinosaurs.
The latest catastrophe is happening now and is unique, because its sole cause is human action.

**INCREASING CONSUMPTION OF NATURAL RESOURCES**
World consumption of forest products such as paper has tripled in the last 30 years.
Consumption of fish has increased **240%** since **1960**.

**THE DISAPPEARANCE OF NATURAL HABITATS**
According to the IUCN, the disappearance of natural habitats is the prime threat to the survival of **91%** of the plants, **83%** of the mammals, and **89%** of the birds regarded as endangered.

**CONTINUED DESTRUCTION OF THE FORESTS**
Between **1990** and **2000**, worldwide deforestation accelerated. In **10 years**, an area about **3 times** the size of France (or the combined area of California, Texas, Florida, and Washington) was lost.

**OVERFISHING THREATENS THE WORLD'S FOOD SUPPLY**
**70%** of commercial species are now below the level of renewal, owing to bad management of marine resources.

**POLLUTION OF THE ENVIRONMENT**
More than **3 million** metric tons of DDT (insecticide) have been dispersed into the biosphere since its discovery. Appreciable amounts remain in contaminated environments, and will continue to be active for over a century after it was banned.

## THE PROBLEM OF REGULATING LIVING THINGS

On an international level, there is no accepted definition of biodiversity as a common property of mankind, and there are no laws governing conditions of its exploitation. This absence of legislation has opened the way to abuse by states and by businesses.

**RIGHTS OVER LIVING THINGS**
More than **50,000** patents on genetic sequences have been granted or requested worldwide since **1990**.
**8,000** biotech patents are granted every year by the USPTO (United States Patent and Trademark Office).
In **2001**, its Japanese equivalent registered more than **1,200** patents related to DNA.

**BIOPIRACY: THE BIODIVERSITY OF POOR COUNTRIES IS EXPLOITED FOR PROFIT BY LARGE COMPANIES IN THE NORTHERN HEMISPHERE**
Nations are robbed of their resources and are no longer allowed to use their own plants or medicines which have been patented. These nations have no benefit from the commercial exploitation of their plants or medicines: a United Nations report estimates that biopiracy of local plants by the major international pharmaceutical companies costs developing countries **$5.4 billion** a year.

---

**JEWISH MUSEUM, BERLIN, GERMANY** (52°30' N, 13°25' E)

A façade covered with zinc—a material typical of Berlin, which oxidizes in bad weather—and a symbolic design—based on the Star of David—composed of a connecting line that is twisted and endless and a straight but fragmented line representing the void: this striking building by the architect Daniel Libeskind is an invitation to reflect. This expression of the void is carried even further by the fact that some rooms have been left empty, symbolizing the absence of the victims and of those who will never be born. The Jewish Museum in Berlin traces 1,700 years of Jewish history in Germany, culminating in the Holocaust during World War II, when 6 million Jews were slaughtered in the 20th century's most appalling act of genocide. More than 700,000 people a year have visited the museum since 2001, and with its educational and publishing program, its mission is to teach and to commemorate. Since 1948 genocide has been a crime under international law. Nevertheless, other genocides took place during the 20th century, including the mass killing of Armenians by the Turks from 1915 to 1916, of Cambodians by the Khmer Rouge regime between 1975 and 1979, and of Hutus by the Tutsis in Rwanda in 1994.

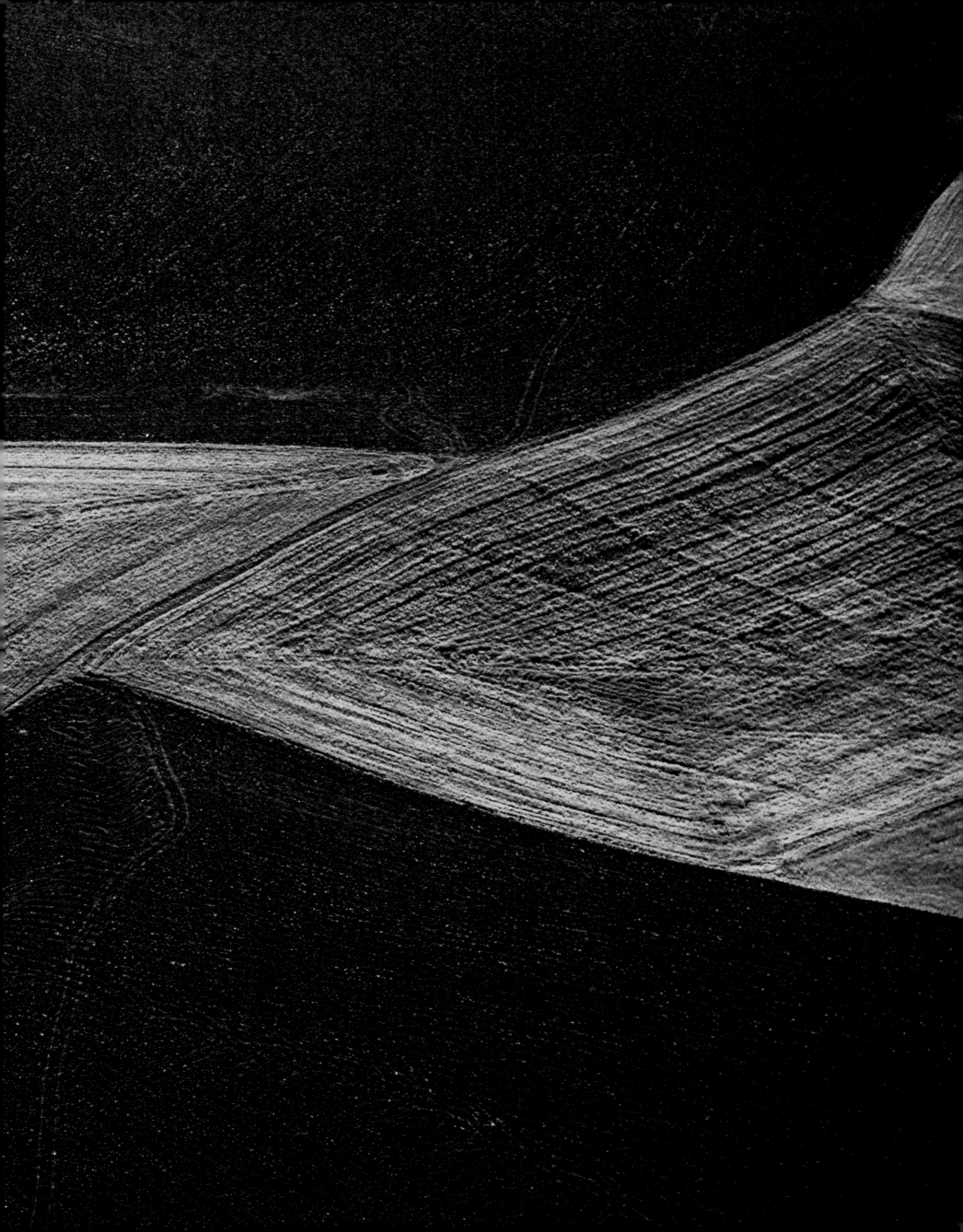

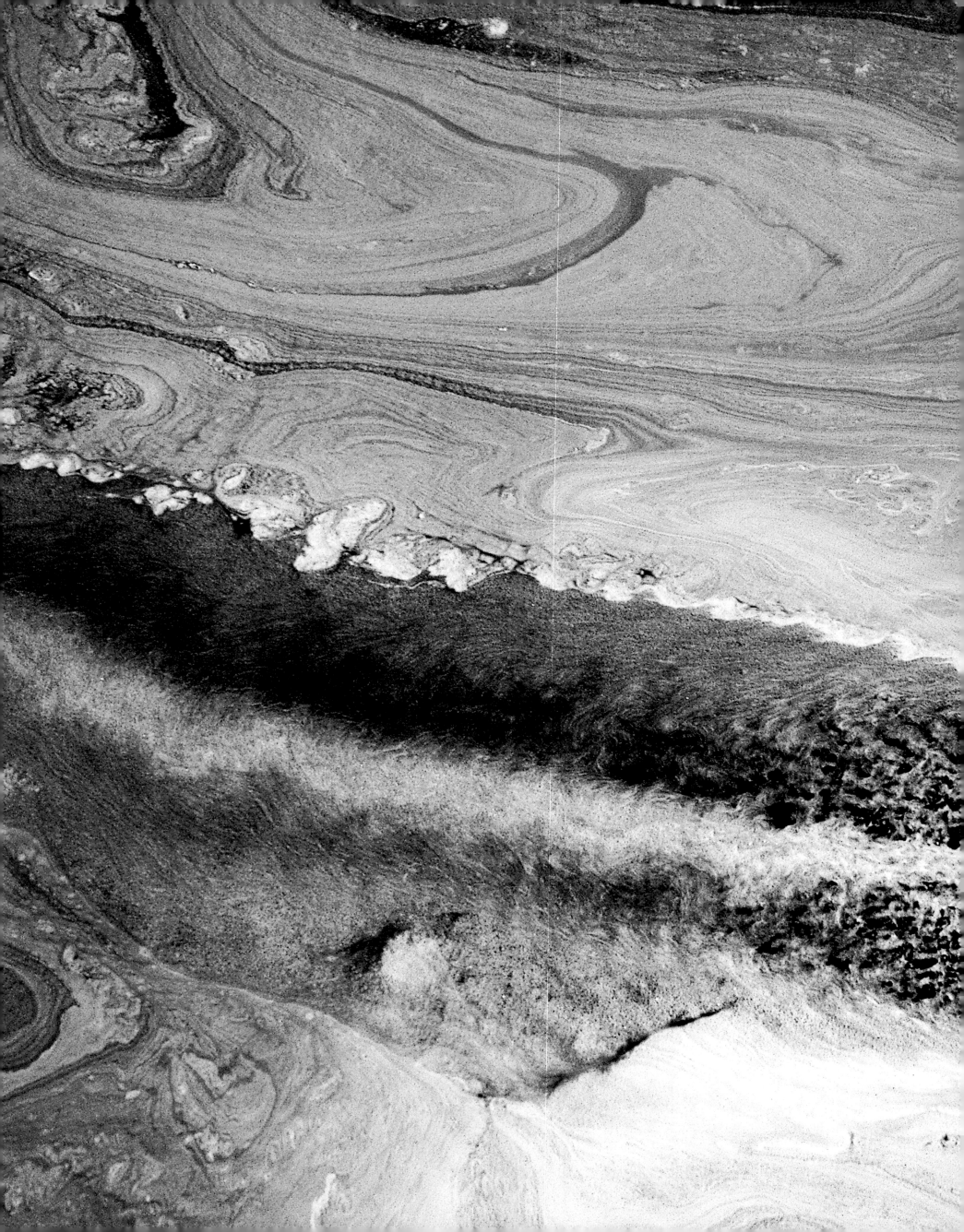

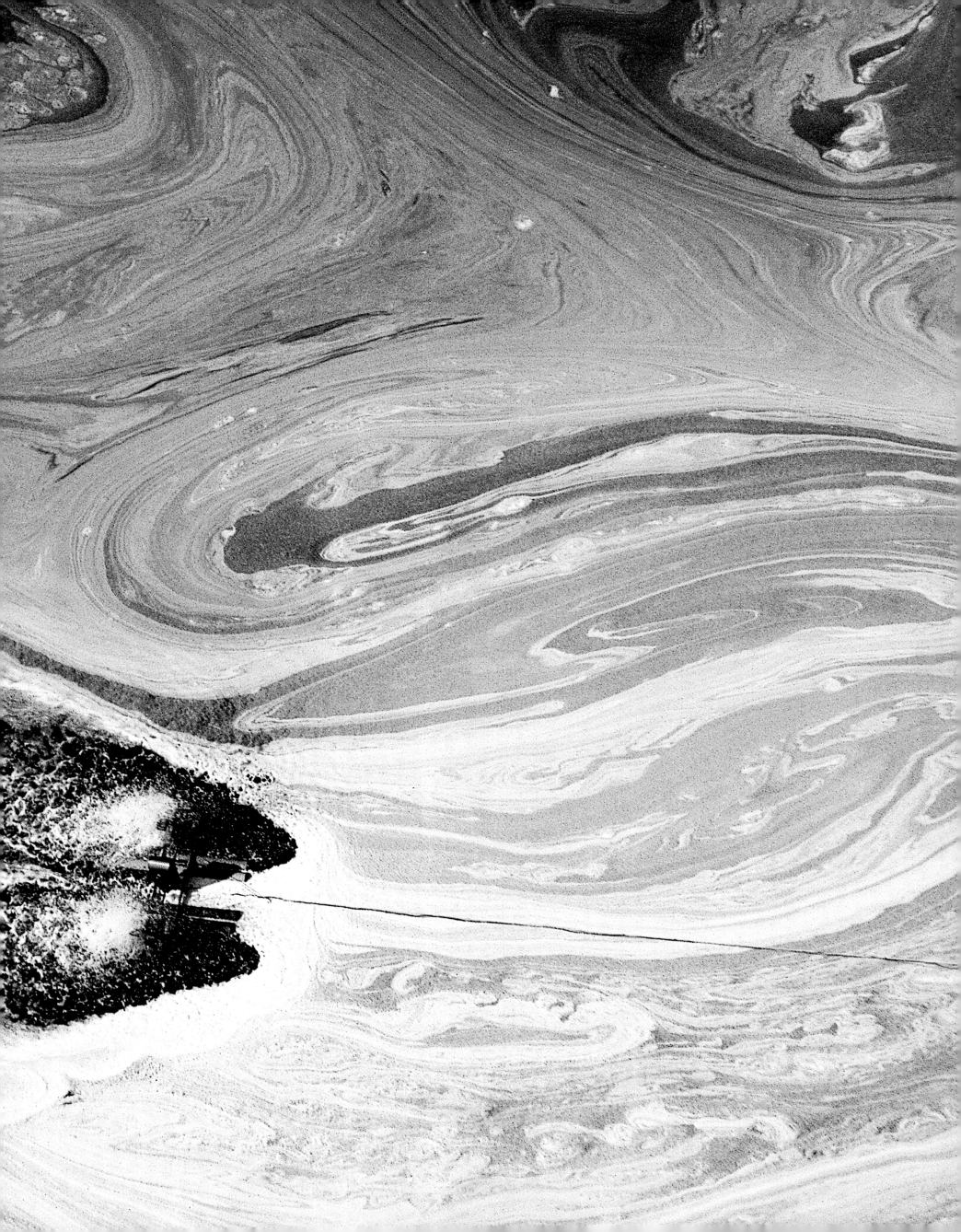

# SEAS AND OCEANS:
# RED ALERT

For a long time, the immense oceans seemed to be an inexhaustible source of food.
In the last few decades, that myth has been shattered. The oceans are in crisis,
and fish stocks are running out. Overfishing, bad practices, and ever-growing
demand for the sea's products has led to devastastion of the ocean depths,
destruction of coral reefs, and damage to the balance between marine species.
In the face of this wanton havoc, it is now time to react.

Mankind has always profited from the ocean's treasures, probably starting in prehistory by collecting the fish washed up on the beach. Such harmless activities were followed by many other kinds of more active intervention, and in due course there were whale hunts, seal hunts, aquaculture, nets, seines, longlines, trawling, dynamite, and a host of other techniques designed to rob the sea of its live contents. Mankind killed the animals for their fat, their bones, their fur, and above all for their meat, and this justified the massacre. While the need for food appeared to give ample reason for the slaughter, the immensity of the oceans and their vast stocks of food suggested infinite reserves. If a population of whales, seals, or shark happened to disappear, all the fishermen had to do was move to another area to find some more, or alternatively choose another species to attack. For a long time, many of these species seemed to be so abundant that human intervention appeared to pose no threat to them. Today, however, their vulnerability is clear and has put them in grave danger. In the course of time, the apparently inexhaustible treasure trove of the seas has revealed itself to be a human illusion.

With its vast area and depth, the marine ecosystem always seemed to be impervious to human despoliation. In the face of such vastness, and such abundance and diversity of living creatures, human actions appeared insignificant. In his inaugural speech to the International Fisheries Exhibition in London in June 1883, Thomas Henry Huxley talked about the issue of overfishing. While he believed that it was in theory possible to exhaust the supply of salmon in a river, this would never actually happen because the law would inevitably limit the catch. He went on to say: "At the great cod-fishery of the Lofoden Islands [off the Norwegian coast], the fish approach the shore in the form of what the natives call 'cod mountains'—vast shoals of densely-packed fish, 120 to 180 feet in vertical thickness. ...And these shoals keep coming in one after another for two months, all along the coast." In the light of these observations, Huxley believed that the supply of these types of fish—cod, herring, sardine, mackerel—was inexhaustible.

In 1961, Hawthorne Daniel and Francis Minot published *The Inexhaustible Sea*, a work described on its jacket as "an exciting book on the sea and its endless resources." Evidently the authors had not taken the trouble to read the newspapers, because at the very time when they were writing their book, journalists were noting the decline in the numbers of anchovies off the Peruvian coasts. Anchovies (genus *Engraulis*) and sardines (genera *Sardina* and *Sardinops*) are among the most commercially sought after species. After a record 750,000 tons in 1936, the Californian sardine industry—to which John Steinbeck pays tribute in his novel *Cannery Row* (1945)—had disappeared completely by 1962. Peruvian anchovies were so abundant at one time that they figured at the very top of industrial catches—more than 11 million tons in 1967. But the industry folded in 1973, as a result partly of overfishing and partly of the effects of El Niño that year. Anchovies, once the most common fish on the planet, are now one of the endangered species. As for cod—the starting point of the discovery and economic development of New England—it has now disappeared from there, and the "inexhaustible" fishing industry has closed forever.

Every day of the year, the Tsukiji fish market in Tokyo opens at 4 a.m., and in an area of more than two hectares it offers a vast array of seafoods of all kinds: fish, squid, octopus, sea urchin, shrimp, lobster, sea cucumber, seaweed, and some it is even impossible to name. By 10 a.m. there is nothing left, the market is closed, and the cleaners are washing the floors amid great pools of water.

Intensive fishing off the Japanese coasts and the disappearance of the Californian sardine and the Peruvian anchovy are just three major instances of a destructive industry that has been expanding faster and faster over the last few decades. Today there are a million fishing boats patrolling the world's oceans—twice as many as twenty-five years ago. However, the fish themselves are not reproducing at anything like the same rate.

◁ **BYZANTINE CHURCH IN VILNIUS, LITHUANIA** (54°41' N, 25°17' E)

Vilnius is the capital of the Republic of Lithuania, which was born in March 1990 after the break-up of the Soviet Union. It is situated in the southwest of the country, and was founded in around 1320 on a hill at the confluence of the Neris and Vilnia rivers. Generally regarded as one of the most beautiful cities in the Baltic states, Vilnius has a very rich architectural heritage, typified by a number of baroque churches built by the Jesuits during the period of Polish rule (14th–18th century) and by the Orthodox churches built after the city passed to Russia in 1795. Since independence and the return to democracy, religious freedom has been guaranteed by the constitution. There are nine recognized faiths: Catholic, with Latin and Byzantine rites, Lutheran, Reform, Orthodox, Old Believers, Judaism, Karaite Judaism, and Sunni Islam. Roman Catholicism is the dominant religion (75 percent of believers), but its influence is currently declining as new, dynamic Protestant faiths gain ground (Pentecostalism, the Reform Church, and the Lutherans).

consider the life cycle of the cod. Every female lays millions of eggs, which rise slowly to the surface to form plankton. The young fish are provided with a bag of vitellin on which they feed, as do all the other creatures that gobble up these tiny larvae. At this stage, the cod itself is already a predator, although it can only eat plankton organisms smaller than itself, such as the larvae of barnacles, shrimp, crabs, and small worms. A cod one inch long can apparently collect tiny parasites from the tentacles of the jellyfish *Cyanea* without being stung. At the age of two, the young cod begins to look like a miniature adult, and it swims into the deeper waters where it will spend the rest of its life. Along the way, it is threatened by all kinds of predators that prowl the middle waters, such as sharks, pollack, and even adult cod (predators and their prey may be of the same species, as the difference in size is all that matters). If it survives such dangers, the cod will reach maturity some 6 feet (2 m) from the seabed, feeding mainly on shellfish, but ready to pounce on anything that moves—or even that does not move—

as it passes by. The cod has an extraordinary ability to swallow inanimate and even inedible objects, such as tin cans, shoes, pieces of wood, nails, and even false teeth. At the age of two, the cod may have grown to 1 foot (30 cm) in length, and at three to nearly 2 feet (60 cm). The average age of a 5-foot (1.5-m) specimen is about forty. But there are no longer any left of this size, and even those of 3 feet long have become rare. The majority have been devoured by the most ruthless predator of all.

Overfishing of cod in the Atlantic has wrecked the entire ecosystem as well as the fabric of the food chain. The prey, whose numbers would have been kept in check by traditional predators, has now proliferated through the extinction of the latter. If the disappearance of the cod has proved a disaster for the fishing industry, it is also an ecological disaster for the system of which it was such an integral part. We are only just beginning to understand how these natural systems interlock. Overfishing in the sea, the slaughter of sea otters, the displacement and extinction of sea cows, the annihilation of seals, the hunting of whales, the drowning of albatross, the destruction of coral reefs—all these human interventions constitute acts of violence against the seas of the Earth which gave us life, and which for so long have provided so generously for the continuance of that life.

RICHARD ELLIS

---

CLEANING UP FUEL OIL LEAKED FROM THE TANKER PRESTIGE, BIARRITZ, FRANCE
(43°40' N, 1°35' E)

On November 19, 2002, the *Prestige*, a 26-year-old oil tanker, sank off the west coast of Spain, spilling 77,000 tons of crude oil. The most effective tools for cleaning up such spills are scoops, modified dragnets, and drift nets. The victims of such ecological disasters must turn to the International Oil Pollution Compensation Fund (IOPCF–FIPOL). Until 2004, this intergovernmental organization, financed by the oil industry, had provided up to 180 million euros ($204 million) for each such accident—a sum that is woefully inadequate in view of the total cost of such catastrophes, which runs into billions, and is even more laughable given the income that oil generates. In 2003, the French government levied over 24 billion euros (about $27.6 billion) in oil taxes. Fortunately, under pressure from the states of the European Union, the IMO (International Maritime Organization) has raised FIPOL's contribution to 1 billion euros ($1.13 billion), a fivefold increase of the original figure.

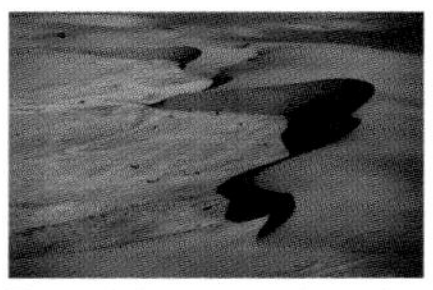

**PAGES 244–245**
DAIRY COWS PASSING BETWEEN DUNES, MAULE PROVINCE, CHILE
(35°16' S, 73°20' W)

The wind sweeps the volcanic dust before it. Here, an oceanic climate showers the land with abundant moisture, allowing grass to grow rapidly and favoring livestock farming. Chile is known for its remarkable geography. It measures 2,608 miles (4,200 km) from north to south, stretching over 35 degrees of latitude, but is only 62 miles (100 km) wide at its narrowest point—and 250 miles (450 km) at its widest. This means that the north is extremely arid; the Chilean economy here is dominated by copper, iron ore, and sulphur mining. The center has a more Mediterranean climate and contains the biggest cities and associated industry, as well as farming—chiefly fruit and vineyards. In the south, with its oceanic climate, fields give way to pasture, vast forests, and lakes until, gradually, the great glaciers of Patagonia take over. Chile finally comes to an end at the far southern tip of South America, not far from the Antarctic circle.

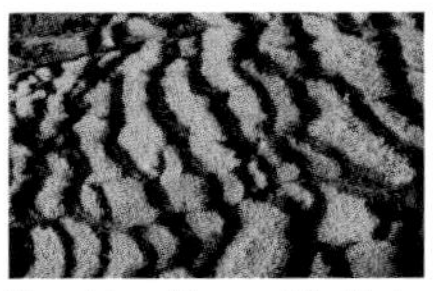

**PAGES 246–247**
TERRACED FIELDS NORTH OF KATHMANDU, BAGMATI REGION, NEPAL
(28°20' N, 85°55' E)

Nepal has the world's highest mountains and one of its highest rates of population growth, at 2.6 percent per year. Of Nepal's inhabitants, 80 percent are farmers who are obliged to cultivate hillside after hillside to grow enough food. However, even these ingenious irrigation networks, control of erosion, and intensive methods that allow up to four harvests per year—at a risk of exhausting the soil's fertility—are not enough to feed this growing population. Feeding humans and preserving the land is a problem that stretches well beyond Nepal's borders. Today, 23 percent of the planet's usable land is suffering degradation. Overgrazing, deforestation, poor irrigation, pollution by chemicals, and urban expansion are reducing its productivity. And yet it will have to feed 8 billion people by 2025.

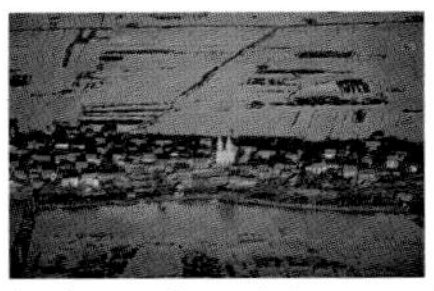

**PAGES 248–249**
VILLAGE IN THE HEART OF RICE FIELDS NEAR ANTANANARIVO, MADAGASCAR
(18° 57' S, 47°31' E)

In the region of Antananarivo, the Merina people, a Malayo-Indonesian ethnic group, use traditional methods to cultivate their rice paddies in the plains surrounding the villages. Rice paddies now take up two-thirds of the country's cultivated area. Two types of rice-growing are practiced on the island: wet cultivation on flooded terraces along the rivers, in the valleys; and dry cultivation on scorched earth on the steep slopes. Madagascar is the second-leading consumer of rice in the world (about 246 pounds, or 112 kg, per capita per year, behind Myanmar at 462 pounds, or 210 kg), but it is not a major producer (producing 2.8 million tons, it ranks approximately twentieth in the world). For a long time the country has imported rice of average quality while exporting a luxury variety. Rice, wheat, and corn are the three most consumed grains in the world.

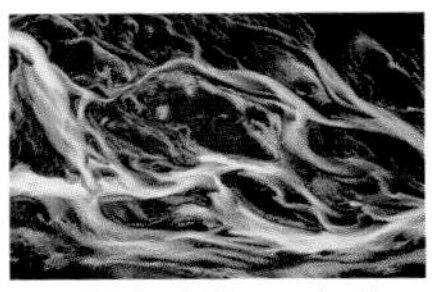

**PAGES 250–251**
DETAIL OF THE THJÓRSÁ RIVER, ICELAND
(63° 56' N, 20°57' W)

The Thjórsá River, the longest river in Iceland, travels 143 miles (230 km) through terrain covered with lava. The river carries a good deal of organic and mineral refuse to the ocean, lending the Thjórsá its characteristic color. The island is covered with a vast network of unnavigable rivers, most of which derive from subglacial torrents, whose variable, tortuous routes make the construction of bridges and dams difficult. However, hydroelectric energy makes it possible to satisfy more than 80 percent of the country's electricity needs, and its capabilities remain considerable, because only one-fourth of the hydroelectric potential is being exploited. Iceland is also planning to use its sources of renewable energy (hydroelectric and geothermal) to produce hydrogen, having made the pioneering decision to convert its entire economy to this new, nonpolluting fuel by the year 2040.

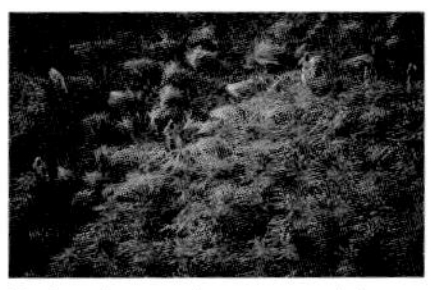

**PAGES 252–253**
WORKING THE FIELDS NORTH OF JODHPUR, RAJASTHAN, INDIA
(26°22' N, 73°02' E)

Rajasthan, the second-largest state in India in terms of area (133,500 square miles, or 342,240 km²), lies in the northwest region of the country. Two-thirds of the state is covered by sandy desert, and the scarcity of surface water is largely responsible for the low productivity of its soil. However, irrigation systems, which benefit 40 percent of arable lands in India, have allowed agriculture to develop. Millet, sorghum, wheat, and barley are cultivated here. The harvesting of these grains at the end of the dry season is a task that normally falls to women, who, even while working in the fields, wear the traditional *orhni*, a long, brightly colored shawl that is typical of the region. More than half of India's territory is devoted to farming, which produces one-fourth of the domestic national product and employs 60 percent of the population. Each year the country harvests about 210 million tons of grains, making it one of the largest cereal producers n the world. But the old conflict between production increase and demographic growth is now also affected by declining subterranean water reserves; a severe drought in April 2000 affected 20 million people in Rajasthan.

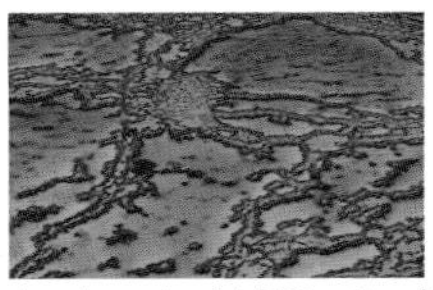

**PAGES 254–255**
GREAT BARRIER REEF, QUEENSLAND, AUSTRALIA
(16°55' S, 146°03' E)

At a length of 1,550 miles (2,500 km) along the northeastern coast of Australia, with more than 400 types of coral, the Great Barrier Reef is the largest coral formation in the world. This rich, silent sanctuary of submarine life was declared a marine park in 1979 (comprising 15 percent of the world's protected sea surface) and a UNESCO World Heritage site in 1981. The Great Barrier Reef harbors more than 1,500 species of fish and 4,000 mollusks, as well as such animals as the endangered dugong (sea cow) and six of the seven species of sea turtle. In total there are more than 800 coral species in the world, providing habitats for 4,000 different species of fish. Essential for the protection of coastlines and ocean fauna, the reefs supply a wide range of products and services to coastal populations: food, building materials, tourist revenue. It is now estimated that the monetary value of coral ecosystems is over $375 billion. This means that the protection of coral reefs is of vital economic as well as ethical importance.

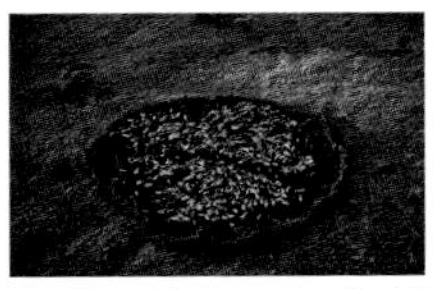

**PAGES 256–257**
MASAI CATTLE PEN, NEAR KICHWA TEMBO CAMP, KENYA
(1°13' S, 35°00' E)

The Masai believe that God (Enkai) made them owners of all the cattle in the world. The wealth of a Masai family is calculated according to the number of head of cattle, whereas the ownership of land is of no importance. They protect their stock against wild animals by keeping them in enclosures with thorns that are even more of a deterrent than barbed wire. This is where the cows spend the night after being attended to by the women. The land is 75 percent agricultural, and the Masai now tend to settle—particularly after the droughts of 1999 and 2000, which decimated their herds. This change in their way of life has created enormous pressure on the land, which cannot sustain such permanent overgrazing. The Masai rarely vaccinate their cattle, partly because they are so poor but also for cultural reasons. They prefer to use natural remedies. Their native medicines have been closely studied by the FAO (Food and Agriculture Organization), which hopes to popularize these traditional methods, so they will not be totally supplanted by modern veterinary techniques.

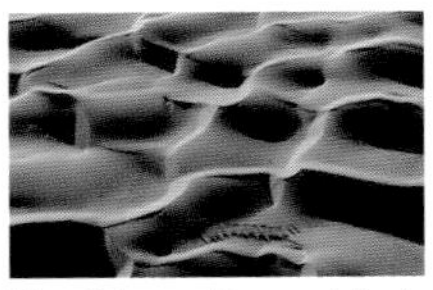

**PAGES 258–259**
DROMEDARY CARAVAN IN THE DUNES, NEAR NOUAKCHOTT, MAURITANIA
(18°09' N, 15°29' W)

The Sahara, the world's largest sandy desert, covers 3.5 million square miles (9 million km²)—equivalent to the area of the United States—spread over eleven countries. Mauritania, which lies on its western border, is three-quarters desert and is thus particularly vulnerable to the phenomenon of desertification. Excessive grazing, harvesting of firewood, and agricultural expansion are gradually destroying soil-retaining vegetation on the perimeters of the great dune ranges. This facilitates the advance of sand, which today endangers cities, including the capital, Nouakchott. In 1960 the town lay on a grassy plain, several days walk from the Sahara, but it now has the desert on its doorstep. In arid and semi-arid zones (which make up two-thirds of the continent of Africa), fragile arable lands deteriorate rapidly if farming and other exploitation become too intensive. In the past half-century, 65 percent of arable lands in Africa have suffered degradation, resulting in a drop in agricultural yield. In this vicious cycle, so difficult to break, poverty is both a cause and a consequence of the depletion of arable soil and the decline in agricultural productivity.

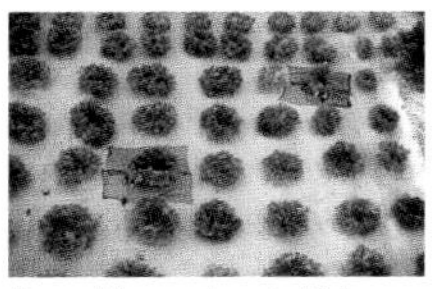

**PAGES 260–261**
OLIVE HARVEST NEAR LES BAUX-DE-PROVENCE, CÔTE D'AZUR, FRANCE
(43°44' N, 4°47' E)

From November to February, the Mediterranean's olive harvest is in full swing. Careful harvesting provides work, protects soil from compaction by heavy machinery, and produces extremely high-quality oil. Olive oil is popular all over the world for its nutritional and culinary properties, and it plays a part in many cuisines. Consumption has risen by 50 percent since 1990, rising from 1.6 million tons to 2.4 million in 1999. With its 840 million olive trees, olive cultivation in the Mediterranean has a bright future. Nonirrigated olive cultivation, which gets the best out of dry soils in a region where managing fresh water supplies is crucially important and soil degradation is a serious problem—is an example of sustainable use of soil, preservation of landscape, and support of populations living in economically marginal rural areas. It should retain its role in a region where tourism is eating up space and increasing pressure on land. The Mediterranean receives 30 percent of the world's tourists.

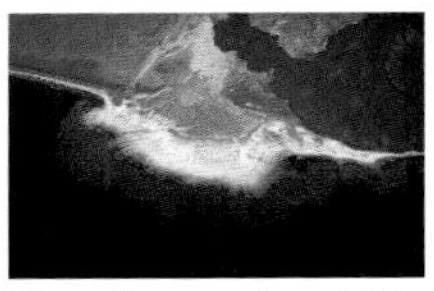

**PAGES 262–263**
GREATER FLAMINGOS ON THE EDGE OF LAKE LOGIPI, SUGUTA VALLEY, KENYA
(0°17' S, 36°04' E)

The whiteness of crystallized natron (a sodium carbonate) on the black volcanic shore of Lake Logipi contrasts with the blue-green algae that proliferates in the alkaline, brackish water. Seen from the sky, this part of the shore suggests the shape of a giant oyster. The tiny pearl dots that surround it are flamingos, congregating where the fresh water re-emerges. These birds seek nourishment in shallow lake waters rich in algae and small crustaceans, which give flamingos their characteristic color. Immense colonies of flamingos travel from lake to lake in the Rift Valley, guided by annual rain patterns that modify the concentration of soda and thus affect food supply. The Rift Valley is now home to almost 3 million greater flamingos, more than half of their entire world population.

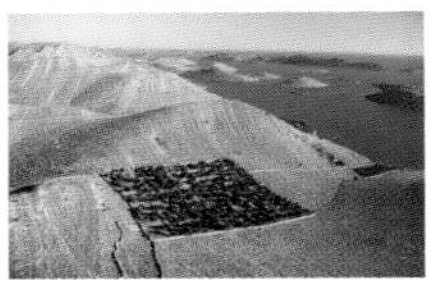

**PAGES 264–265**
ISLAND OF KORNAT, KORNATI NATIONAL PARK, DALMATIA, CROATIA
(43°50' N, 15°16' E)

The eastern edge of the Adriatic washes the shores of the 150 islands and islets that make up the Kornati archipelago. The largest island, Kornati, is 12.5 square miles (32.5 km²) in area and accounts for two-thirds of the archipelago's land surface. The fold in the Earth's crust that formed the Kornati mountain range was produced by the collision of the Adriatic and European tectonic plates. The melting of glaciers and rise in sea levels after the last Ice Age, 20,000 years ago, made the mountains into an archipelago which was then eroded by the sea and the wind, exposing fine striae in the limestone. A century ago, the inhabitants of the nearby islands used these rocks to build dry-stone walls to pen in their sheep and keep them from their olive groves and vineyards. Overgrazing has done considerable damage to wildlife and to the thin vegetation. This desertification contrasts with the richness of the waters around the archipelago, where most of the Mediterranean's fish and mollusk species can be found. Nevertheless, these too are threatened by fishing, which sometimes uses illegal methods. Almost 30 percent of the world's fish species are either extinct or facing extinction.

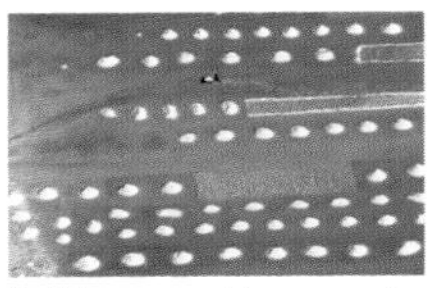

**PAGES 266–267**
DRYING SEA SALT IN THE SALTWORKS AT PUNTA VIGIA, OCOA BAY, DOMINICAN REPUBLIC
(18°20' N, 70°44' W)

Salt is present in sea water, at a ratio of 30 grams per liter, and in deposits of rock salt originating from the sea, and it is found all over the world. It can be mined (rock salt) or, as in this photo, obtained through the natural evaporation of sea water (sea salt). Like many of the Caribbean islands, the Dominican Republic produces salt, which is an inexpensive industry to run and is simple to operate in coastal areas. The salt crystals are harvested for six months of the year, and this comparatively unskilled labor is often carried out by women. Salt production is a major international industry, producing some 225 million metric tons a year, 20 percent of which comes from the United States, 15 percent from China, while other major producers are Germany, Canada, and India. The chemical industry uses 60 percent of worldwide salt production, and 10 percent is used for de-icing roads. The rest is used in the fishing (for preservation) and food industries, and for filling the salt cellars on our dining tables.

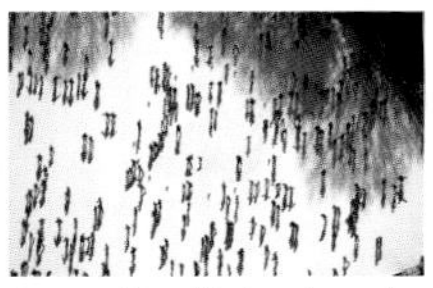

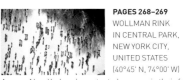

**PAGES 268–269**
WOLLMAN RINK IN CENTRAL PARK, NEW YORK CITY, UNITED STATES
(40°45' N, 74°00' W)

Among New Yorkers' greatest pleasures is their freedom to escape the city simply by stepping into Central Park. This green space, which covers more than 842 acres (341 hectares) between 59th and 101th Streets, has been at New York's disposal ever since 1859, when the city spent more than $5 million on what was then just a stretch of wild, muddy marshland. In summer it is a relaxing haven for roller-skaters and cyclists; in winter, ice-skaters can use the rink in the park's heart. Central Park is so much a part of Manhattan that few people realize it is entirely manmade. The park's architects, Frederick Law Olmsted and Calvert Vaux, could hardly have imagined when they were planning it how important the park would become to New York's identity—no more than they could have envisioned the flood of more than 250,000 people who would wander through its paths on spring weekends. At the time, Olmsted and Vaux were launching a plan to make leisure more democratic and to bring it within reach of all regardless of social barriers.

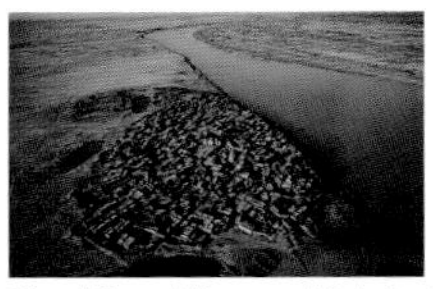

**PAGES 270–271**
VILLAGE ON THE BANKS OF AN ARM OF THE RIVER NIGER, MOPTI REGION, MALI (14°28' N, 4°12' W)

The River Niger, which is the third-longest in Africa (2,600 miles, or 4,200 km), has its source in the heights of the Fouta Djalon in Guinea. It crosses nine countries until it reaches a vast delta in Nigeria, where it flows into the Atlantic Ocean. More than 100 million people live on its banks, trading on the river, fishing, raising cattle, and farming to the rhythm of the rise and fall of the waters between August and January. But the drop in rainfall recorded since 1970 has resulted in increased silting: waste matter and plant debris is accumulating, and the waterflow is decreasing. In order to save the Niger and prevent an ecological and economic disaster, the governments of the nine countries have formed an association, the ABN (Niger Basin Authority), which will jointly oversee the restoration and use of the river. This is a positive initiative at a time when transnational sharing of river waters is still a major source of tension between many countries.

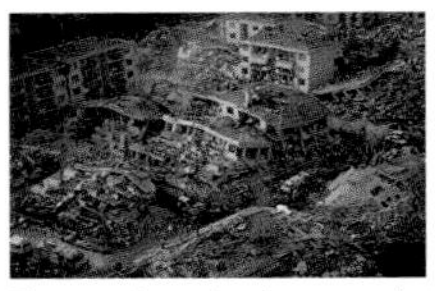

**PAGES 272–273**
EARTHQUAKE AT GÖLCÜK, ON THE COAST OF THE SEA OF MARMARA, TURKEY
(40°43' N, 29°48' E)

The earthquake that struck the region of Izmit on August 17, 1999, at 3:02 a.m., registered 7.4 on the Richter scale (9 is the maximum). Its epicenter was at Gölcük, an industrial city with a population of 65,000. The quake had an official death toll of at least 20,000 people, many buried in rubble while they slept. The partial or total collapse of 50,000 buildings led to enormous public outrage against building contractors, who were accused of disregarding earthquake-proof construction codes. Southern and northern Turkey are sliding along the North Anatolian fault at an average relative speed of 1 inch (2.5 cm) per year, but the movement actually occurs quite abruptly, in the form of earthquakes—the Earth moved nearly 10 feet (3 m) in less than a minute during the Izmit earthquake. Regions bordering tectonic plates, such as the trans-Asian zone running from the Azores to Indonesia by way of Turkey, Afghanistan, and Iran, are particularly exposed to the risk of seismic activity. Inhabitants of this zone account for 90 percent of earthquake-related deaths since 1990. The tsunami caused by an earthquake off the coast of Sumatra in December 2004 was responsible for the deaths of 295,000 people in Southeast Asia, more than the earthquake death toll worldwide over the previous decade.

Before the advent of industrialized fishing, the distance or depth of some oceanic regions made them inaccessible to fishermen, thereby safeguarding the species that lived there. But with the development of more and more sophisticated techniques, none can now escape the human predator. "Nowadays, every kind of seabed—silt, sand, clay, gravel, cobble, boulder, rock reef, worm reef, mussel bed, seagrass flat, sponge bottom, or coral reef—is vulnerable to trawling," said Carl Safina in 1998. "For fishing rough terrain or areas with coral heads, trawlers have since the mid-1980s employed 'rockhopper' nets equipped with heavy wheels that roll over obstructions." Fishermen can catch species that develop just 6 feet (2 m) from the seabed. They are able to locate shoals of fish whose presence—or even existence— had hitherto been unsuspected. They stay at sea for months on end, and process their catch on huge factory ships. They can detect seabeds almost a mile in depth, and they drag their immense nets over them, completely destroying whole ecosystems and wrecking the very fabric of the food chain.

"Bycatch" is the name given to those fish that are inadvertently caught up in the nets: species that are not large enough to be exploited commercially—for example young fish that have not yet reached the age of reproduction, or will not grow any bigger, or will not reproduce. The term is also used for creatures other than fish: marine birds, dolphins, whales, turtles. Between June and December 1990, American observers from the NOAA (National Ocean and Atmosphere Administration) were on board some Japanese ships in the North Pacific, and analysed 4 percent of the catch made by the fleet. In addition to 7.9 million squid (the species targeted), the bycatch made by the 74 ships included 82,000 blue shark, 253,000 tuna, nearly 10,000 salmon, 30,000 birds, 52 eared seal, 22 turtles, 141 porpoises and 914 dolphins. Most of these creatures need to be above the surface to breathe, and so they died by drowning after being caught in the nets. In 1990, in the Bering Sea, fishermen threw away 16 million Moluccas crabs because they were the wrong size—five times the number of those they took back to sell.

Undoubtedly the most high-profile bycatch was the hundreds of thousands of dolphins that were trapped and killed in the nets of tuna fishermen in the Pacific between 1960 and 1970—though this was unfortunately by no means the worst case. "For every pound of shrimp caught in the Gulf of Mexico," wrote Sylvia Earle in 1995, "eight to nine pounds of bycatch—ray, eel, flounder, gonelles, rockfish, batfish, including young specimens—were mutilated and thrown away, not to mention tons of plants and creatures not listed as 'bycatch', and whatever else constitutes the sea-floor communities that are in the path of the nets."

With a range of over 75 miles (120 km), longlines are equipped with thousands of hooks baited to catch tuna, swordfish, and other species. But they also kill young tuna, swordfish, and marlin, thus preventing them from maturing and reproducing, and the same is also happening on a disturbing scale with shark, birds, and other marine creatures. Swordfish can be caught with harpoons, and tuna with rods, but these are old-fashioned, laborious methods that are nowhere near as profitable. If there was ever an industry geared to profit and loss, it is modern fishing. Highly mechanized fisheries, often running at a loss, are striving to squeeze every last dollar, yen, or kopek out of the sea before fish stocks disappear, or before the legislators force them to obey laws devised to protect the reserves.

Fine mesh nets are still being used—these are submerged nets whose mesh traps the head and body of the fish. They cover a wide area, in medium or deep waters, and can be fixed or allowed to drift— hence the name driftnets. When in around 1975 the Japanese began to use unbreakable monofilament fibers for these nets, they invented the most destructive fishing technique of all time. The enormous bycatch earned these nets the nickname of "walls of death." Ships could deploy them over a distance of some 40 miles (60 km), and some 40,000 miles (60,000 km) of net could be deployed in a single night—or one and a half times the circumference of the Earth.

Many ecological organizations, most notably Earthtrust and Greenpeace, have launched intensive campaigns against this extremely destructive method of fishing, but only after years of scandals and protests have steps been taken to put an end to the carnage. In 1989, a cameraman named Sam LaBudde was employed as a cook on a Panamanian fishing boat; he secretly filmed the nets being brought on board with dead baby dolphins trapped in the mesh. The film became a vital weapon in the arsenal deployed to stop the use of driftnets. In April 1990, the FAO (Food and Agriculture Organization) announced that these had even more devastating effects than had previously been supposed: between 315,000 and one million dolphins were being killed every year, not counting the 20,000 that perished in the seines used for catching tuna. But despite a resolution signed jointly by the USA and Japan in 1991 banning the use of driftnets, Taiwan continued to defy the law and construct ships that used them off the African coasts. It was only under pressure from the international community that Taiwan finally agreed in 1994 to abandon the method.

The development of aquaculture (marine farming) in recent years seemed to offer a possible solution to the urgent issue of overfishing. However, this too has created problems which may exacerbate those of overfishing rather than solve them. Numerous species are now being reared intensively all over the world: carp, salmon, trout, shrimp, tilapia, milkfish (Chanos chanos), catfish, lobster, oysters, sea bass, giant clams, and other shellfish. Aquaculture production, 10 million tons ten years ago, had almost tripled by 2000 and constituted more than one-quarter of world fish consumption. But carnivorous species, like salmon and shrimp (which total only 5 percent of aquaculture products by weight but make up almost one-fifth of their total market value), need to be fed, and this is usually done in the form of ground fish powder. In this way, fishfarming actually contributes to overfishing, because small fish—such as Peruvian anchovies—are caught almost exclusively for the purpose of making fish powder. In other words, the fishermen are catching fish in order to feed the carnivorous fish that are being farmed.

Living matter is present throughout the Earth's oceans, which cover a total of some 510 million square miles (1,322 million km$^3$). This model of biodiversity brings together a vast multitude of organisms ranging from the most microscopic, such as diatoms, to the largest animals ever to have inhabited the Earth, the whales. Every living creature in the ocean is directly linked to others in a complex network of feeding processes. At the heart of this food chain, it is not necessarily the biggest that eat the smallest. Apart from pure predators like sharks and killer whales, all marine creatures are under threat from others at one time or another in their lives. The chain is often oversimplified, with a few large species being shown as devouring the many smaller species, whereas in reality it is far more complicated. One need only

238

**SALMON FARMING NEAR MECHUQUE, CHAUQUES ISLANDS, CHILE** (42°17' S, 73°34' W)

The cold and unpolluted waters of the Chauques Islands are well suited to salmon farming. This region is the second-biggest producer after Norway, and it has benefited from the world boom in fish farming since the 1970s. Although this industry is an alternative to reducing stocks of wild fish, it still remains poorly regulated. Most producer countries have no controls to limit the impact of fish farms on the environment. The high concentration of fish, and thus of their waste products and the food that is put in their cages, overenriches the surrounding water and deprives it of oxygen—a process known as eutrophication. On top of this, the use of medicines and antibiotics, which are poorly tolerated by the salmon themselves, threatens species living near the cages. Although pressure from ecologists and consumers has led to an improvement in the conditions of animals farmed on land, there has been little research on their marine counterparts.

## AN IRREPLACEABLE ENVIRONMENT

### MATCHLESS BIOLOGICAL WEALTH
Of all the taxonomic divisions of currently recorded animal and vegetable species (e.g. mollusks and vertebrates), **33** are found in the ocean, while only half are to be found on land. **15** are exclusively marine.

### A BASIC FOOD RESOURCE
For more than **2.6 billion** people, fish accounts for at least **20%** of the daily intake of animal protein.
In some island countries, fish accounts for about **50%**, and sometimes more, of the total intake of animal protein. The same is also true in Bangladesh, Cambodia, the Congo, Indonesia, Japan, and Sri Lanka.

### AN ENVIRONMENT ESSENTIAL TO MANKIND
Over one-third of the world's population live less than **40 miles (60 km)** from a coast.

## A POLLUTED HERITAGE

**6 million** metric tons of pollutants (hydrocarbons, pesticides, heavy metals, detritus) are legally discharged into the oceans every year.

### LAND-BASED ACTIVITIES
Some **80%** of all sea pollution is caused by land-based activities. Every year, between **400** and **4,000 kg** of waste pollutes each kilometer of coast, and **60%** of this waste is plastics.

### OIL DUMPING
When tankers clean out their tanks and holds to get rid of residual hydrocarbons, they cause **10 times** more pollution than an oil spill.
Oil dumping by tankers releases **2 million** tons of hydrocarbons every year.

### OIL SPILLS
Almost **10 times** the volume of oil that escaped from the tanker *Erika* was dispersed over the oceans in 1999.
Since **1960**, **65** accidents have occurred, each discharging over **35,000** tons of crude oil, creating total pollution of **6.3 million** tons of crude oil.

## UNSUSTAINABLE EXPLOITATION

### INCREASINGLY INTENSIVE FISHING
Since the **1950s**, the catch has increased **6 times**.
In all fishing zones, **76%** of the catch is regarded as overexploitation of the marine environment: **52%** of stocks are fished to their full capacity, **16%** are overfished, **7%** are exhausted, and **1%** are on the increase after being exhausted, as opposed to **21%** which are moderately fished and **3%** underfished.
The European Commission estimates that **40%** of European fishing fleets should be scrapped to allow stocks to regenerate.

### DESTRUCTIVE PRACTICES
Worldwide, the weight of fish caught and rejected is around **27 million** metric tons, or **25%** of the total catch.
Fishing with cyanide, used especially to catch tropical fish for aquaria, destroys algae and coral. For every fish caught alive with cyanide, **1 m²** of coral reef is destroyed.
Fishing with explosives: in Indonesia, this destroys **3.75%** of live coral per year, over 60% more than fishing with cyanide.
Aquaculture: up to **50%** of the mangroves destroyed in recent years have been sacrificed to make way for shrimp farms.

## ATTACKS FROM ALL DIRECTIONS

### DEAD ZONES
As a result of excessive nutriments, especially hydrogen, from agricultural fertilizers and industrial waste, nearly **150** ocean zones have been deprived of oxygen, thus killing fish, oysters, and other marine species, as well as their habitats, including marine plant life.

### STOCKS IN DANGER
Populations of marine species have fallen by around **30%** since **1970**.
Over the last **50 years**, populations of cod, tuna, grouper, and shark—the most valuable sea fish—have fallen by around **90%**.

### COASTAL RESOURCES UNDER THREAT
**50%** of the world's coastlines are threatened by activities linked to demographic growth and economic development.

## WHAT DOES THE FUTURE HAVE IN STORE FOR THE SEA?

### RISING SEA LEVELS
Because of global warming, sea levels may rise by about **34 inches (88 cm)** by **2100**.
This rise will threaten many coasts and millions of people. More than **2 billion** people live less than **40 miles (60 km)** from a coast.

### A CLIMATE OUT OF CONTROL?
Oceanic currents regulate the climate. Warmer waters and melting ice may alter existing cycles and cause large-scale changes to the climate. A slowing of the Gulf Stream, for example, could reduce temperatures in Europe by several degrees, as happened around **8,000** years ago.

### INCREASED GREENHOUSE EFFECT?
The oceans contain the largest store of carbon dioxide on Earth: **50 times** more than the atmosphere.
This store depends especially on the temperature. If the latter rises, $CO_2$ will become less soluble and will accumulate in the atmosphere, thus increasing the greenhouse effect and accelerating climate change.

### SLOW POISONING?
Pollution of the seas is affecting our food, particularly through heavy metals that find their way into marine life.
Mercury: the amount of mercury found in fish is several thousand times greater than that found in water. It is concentrated in the most toxic form for human beings: methylmercury.

---

> ENCAMPMENT NEAR THE AIGUILLE DU GOÛTER MOUNTAIN REFUGE ON MONT BLANC, HAUTE-SAVOIE, FRANCE
(45°49' N, 6°51' E)

Mont Blanc, Europe's highest mountain, attracts 3,000 climbers every year. They make their approach via the Mont Blanc du Tacul and Mont Maudit route of 13,110-foot (4,000-m) summits, or they climb via the Dôme du Goûter. Every day during the high season, 300 to 400 people crowd this glamorous peak. This heavy traffic, which is the chief economic resource of the valley below, threatens the site itself. A cleanup operation that lasted from 1999 to 2003 removed almost 12 tons of trash from the mountain. The high number of visitors also means an increase in health problems: half of those who attempt to reach the peak fail, and one-third return with frostbite, injuries, or serious illnesses.

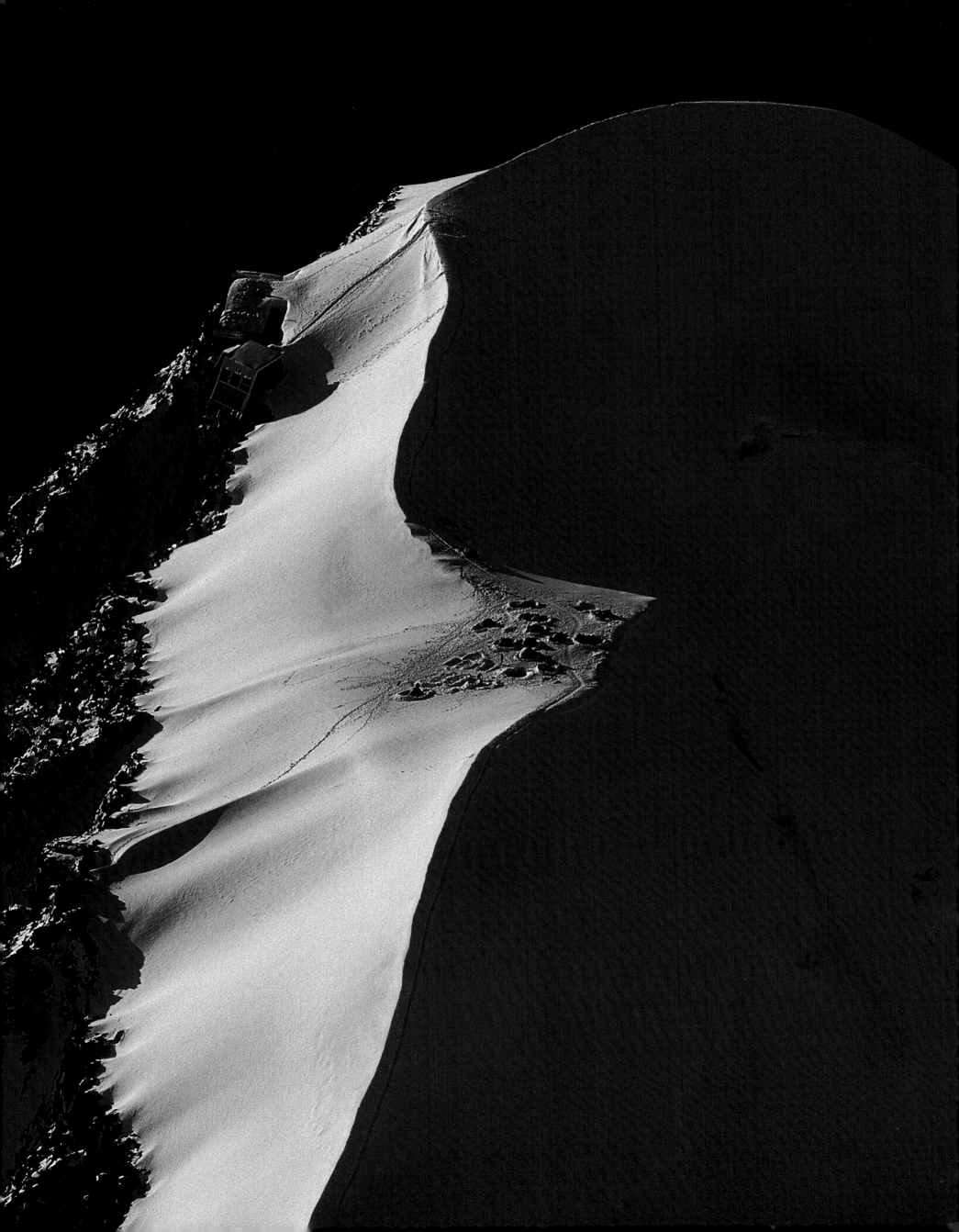

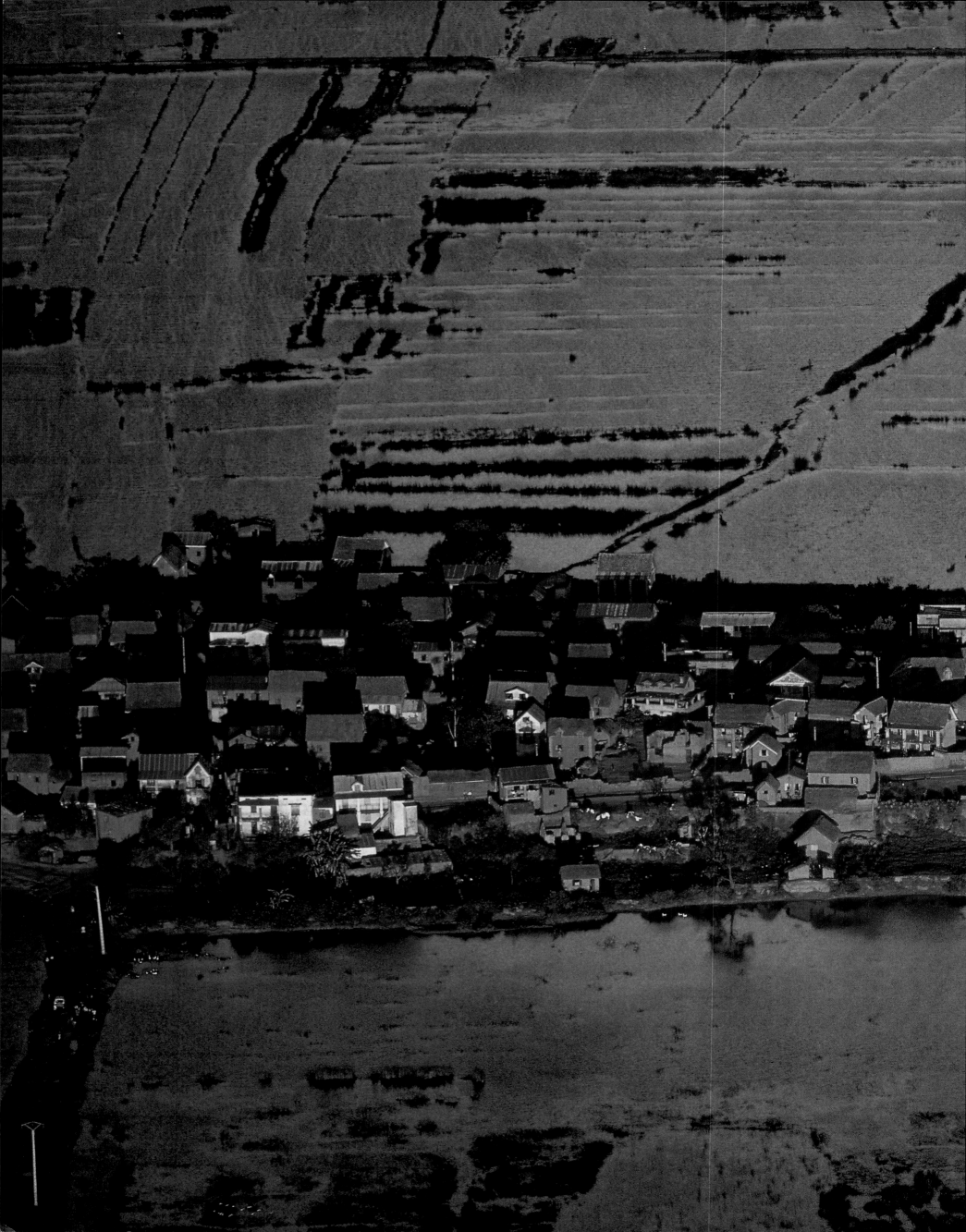

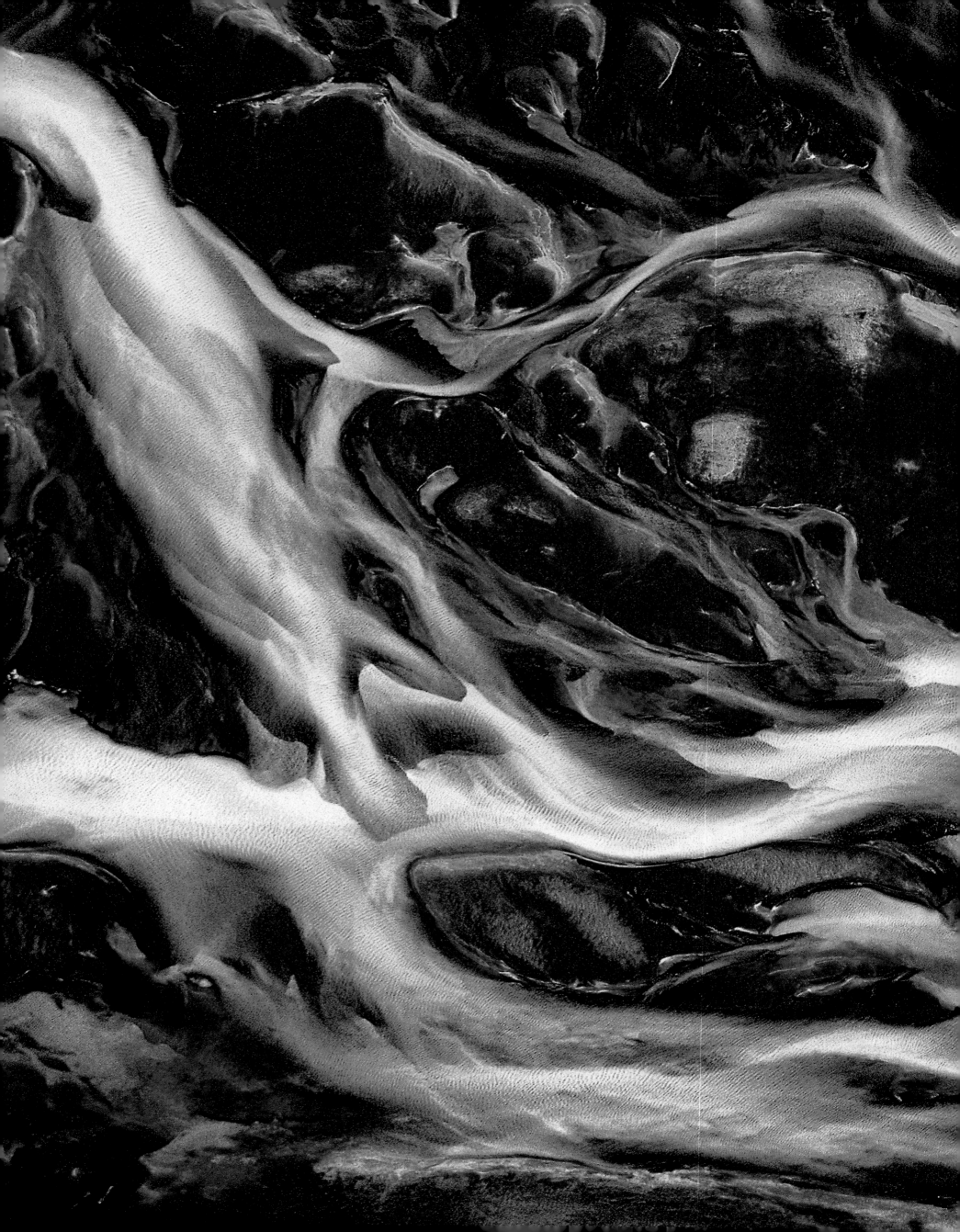

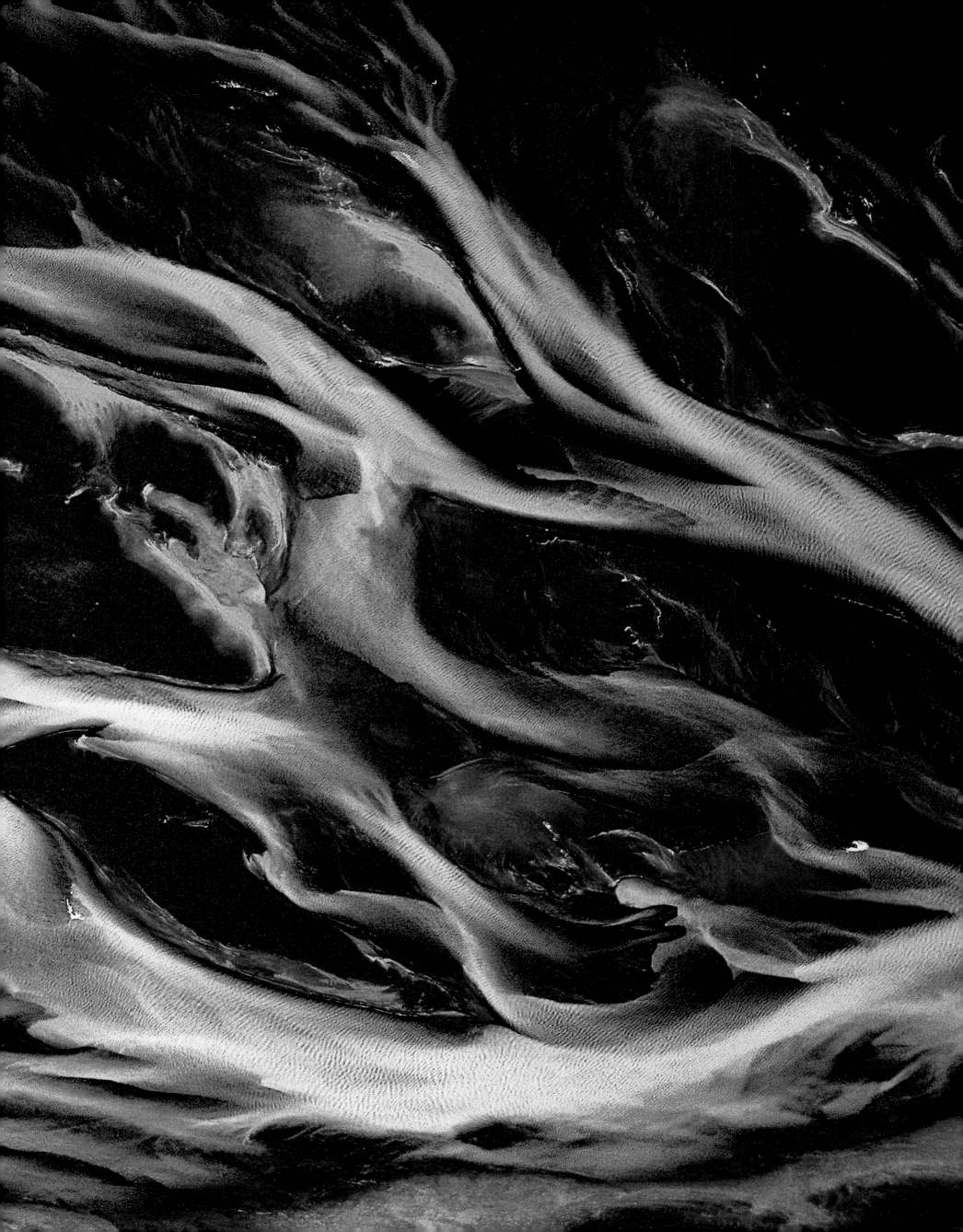

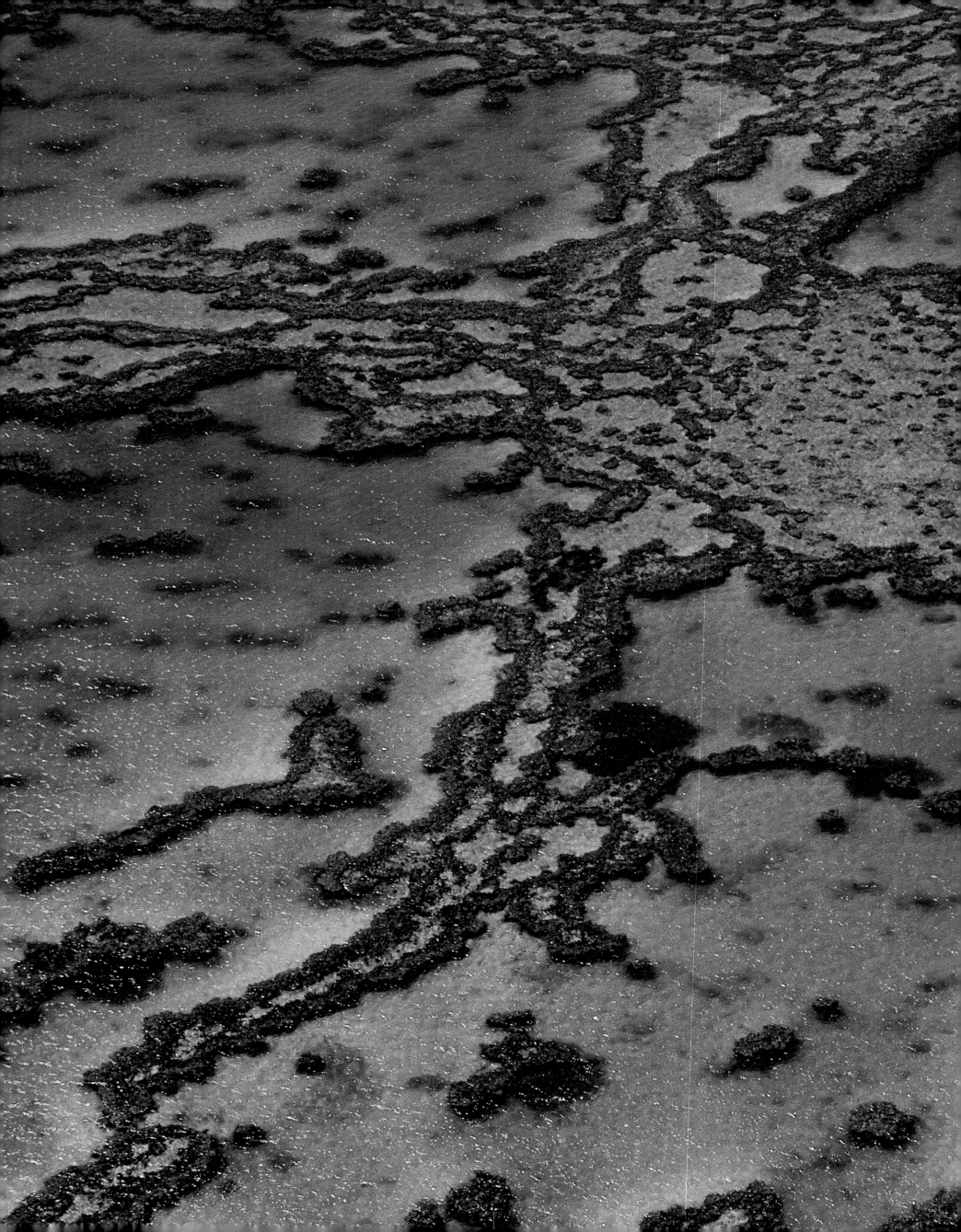

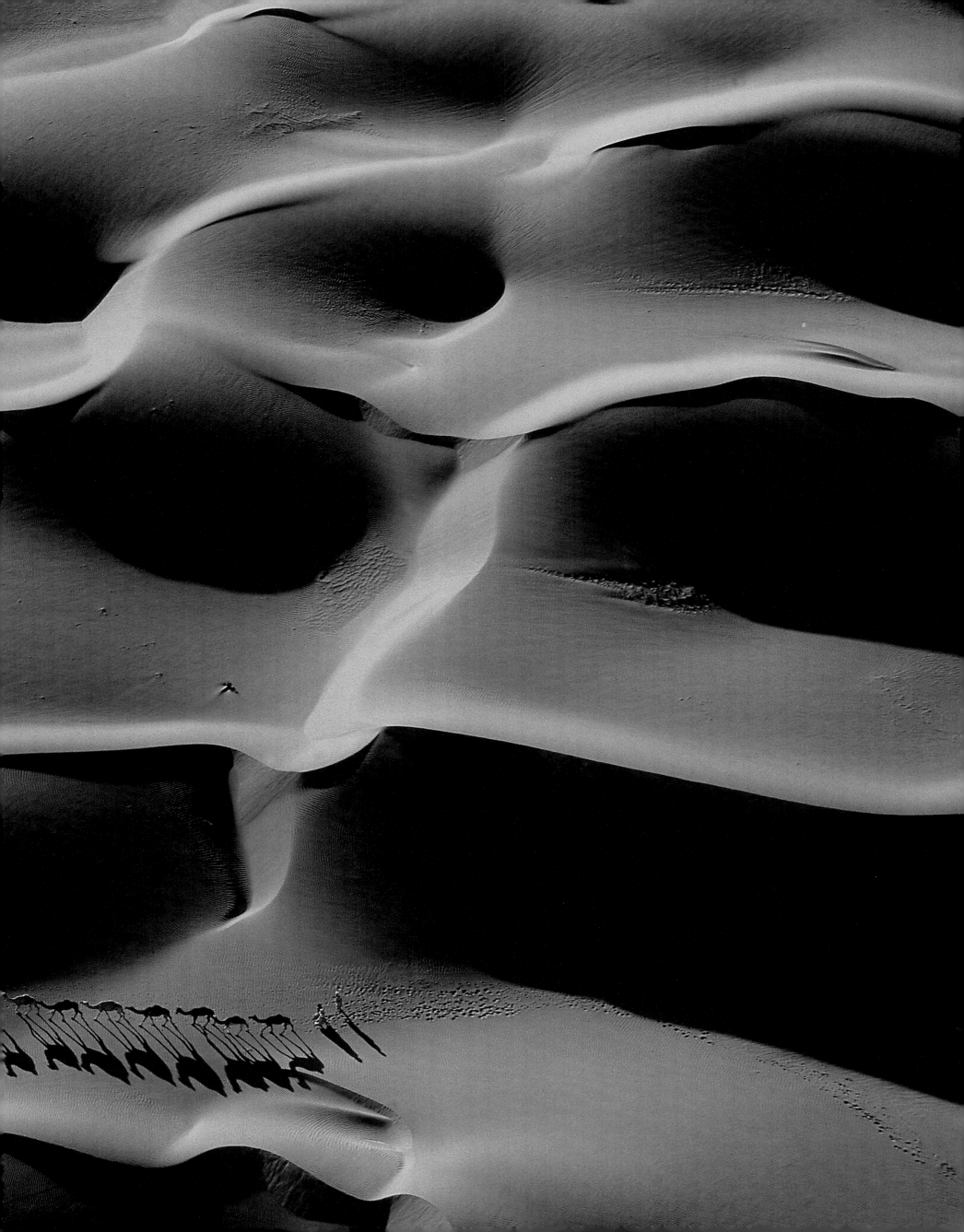

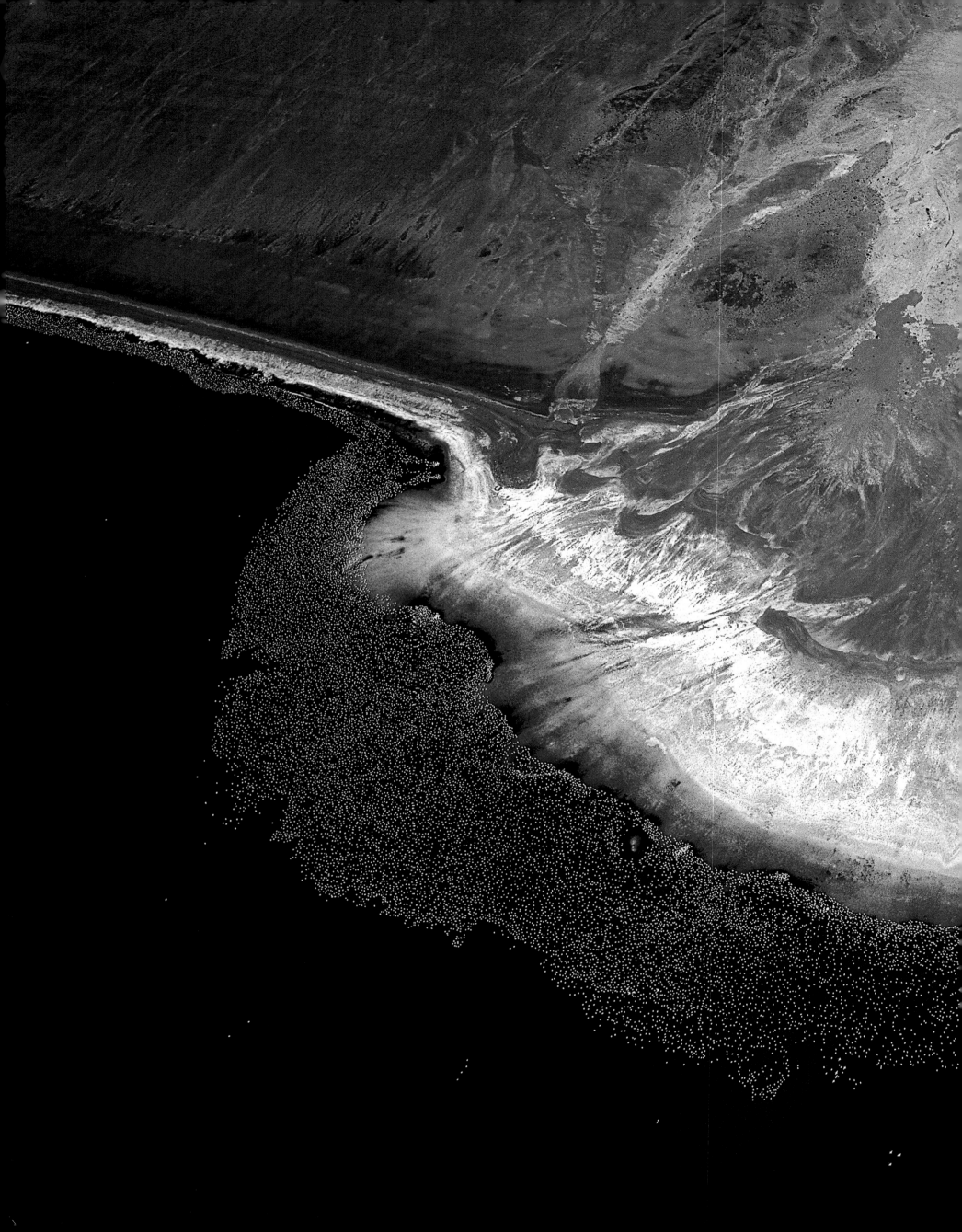

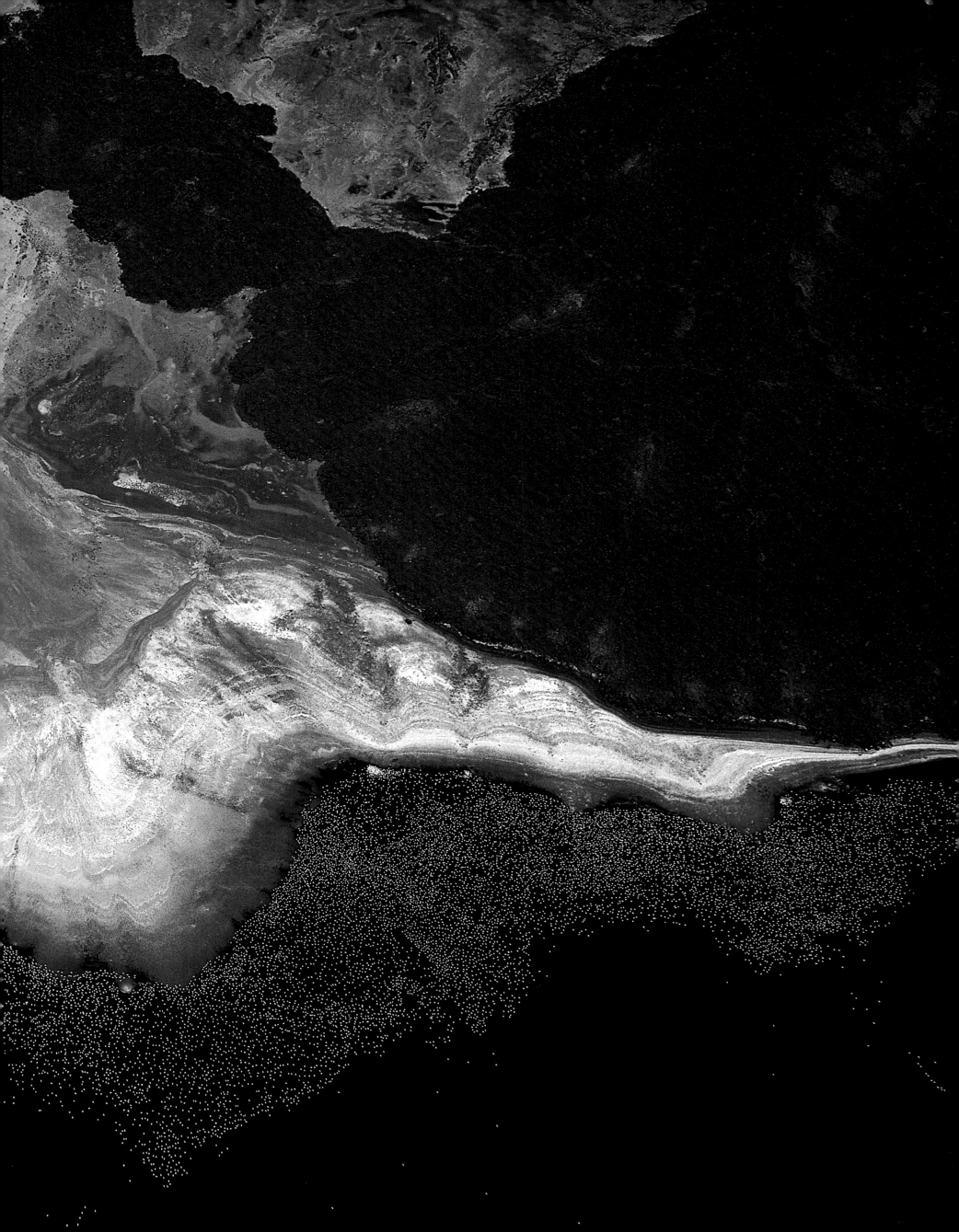

# CLIMATE CHANGE:
# DOUBTS AND CERTAINTIES

At the dawn of the third millennium, our mastery of space and time
have developed on a massive scale: today we can travel right around the globe
in only a few hours. However, our minds remain hostile to change, and our
awareness of the now inexorable alterations to the climate is in danger of
coming too late—with brutal consequences. It is imperative that
we act now, while there is still time.

The average temperature of the Earth's surface warmed by the sun would only be -0.4°F (–18°C), but because of the greenhouse effect, all the conditions are present to ensure life on our planet. Gases such as carbon dioxide ($CO_2$) and water in the atmosphere trap some of the Earth's radiation—solar radiation reflected back by the surface—and raise the temperature of our environment by several degrees. The average temperature of 59°F (15°C) therefore allows water to exist on the surface of the globe in solid, liquid, and gaseous form. However, the combustion of fossil fuels emits a surplus of $CO_2$ into the atmosphere, and this increases the amount of radiation trapped higher up. Ever since humans arrived on the planet, we have changed our environment through farming and animal-rearing, but the most drastic changes have come with the introduction of fossil fuels as a source of energy.

In just a few decades, climate conditions have reached values far in excess of those that had prevailed for hundreds of thousands of years, and the resulting upheavals are far from under control.

Study of the air bubbles trapped in polar ice have shown fluctuations in the concentration of $CO_2$ over the last few hundreds of thousands of years: it rose from 180 ppm (parts per million—a unit for measuring gas) some 20,000 years ago, at the peak of the last glaciation, to 280 at the beginning of the industrial revolution in the mid-19th century. Currently it stands at over 360 ppm. We are able to measure atmospheric $CO_2$ with great precision, and this is being carried out at several points of the globe, but it is not so easy to estimate the exchanges of carbon or the speed of these exchanges between the three great reservoirs—the sea, the atmosphere and the continental biomass (living organisms both animal and vegetable). Over a given period of time, the

same quantity of carbon atoms emitted in the form of $CO_2$ by the burning of fossil fuels ought to be trapped in the atmosphere, dissolved in the water, and absorbed by organic matter and the carbonated sediments that are created at the same time. In fact, however, more carbon is emitted than is stored. This shows that not all the processes involved in trapping have yet been identified. What we do know for certain is that if today every country was willing to abide by the Kyoto Treaty and to limit or even reduce its consumption of fossil fuels, the increase in $CO_2$ would not slow down straight away but would actually continue for some time. Carbon dioxide that has been stored in the oceans for several hundred years could be released—a phenomenon exacerbated by increased temperatures. In effect, natural and manmade processes operate on different, overlapping time scales, and these somewhat blur our vision of the future. The most widely used sources of energy are wood, coal, and oil—materials that have taken thousands if not millions of years to form. It has taken the human race just a few decades to drain a large proportion of these resources. Only the forests are a source of energy that might be renewed on a scale commensurate with human requirements, whereas reserves of coal, oil, and gas are limited and will probably be exhausted during the first half of the 21st century. It must also be pointed out that there are other factors that contribute to the greenhouse effect: water vapor, methane, nitrous oxides, and other gases.

There are some skeptics who still question the reality of future climate change, but the evidence is overwhelming. Glaciers are continuously shrinking. The snows of Kilimanjaro will soon be little more than a folk memory: they have already dwindled in volume, and it will not be long before they disappear completely, as will most of the tropical glaciers in the Andes. Ice in the Himalayas is in the process of melting, and it is to be expected that there will be considerable changes in the water network in Asia. Ice in the Arctic is also diminishing rapidly, and even that of the Antarctic, which had seemed to be intact, is now showing worrying signs of shrinkage. There are also other, more indirect clues that should sound warning signals: some migratory birds have shortened their journeys, because they have found sufficiently mild conditions in the south of Europe to make it unnecessary for them to fly all the way to Africa. From the poles down to the equator, there are

activity, as witnessed in the dark spots that are more or less visible on the sun's surface, are not enough to explain the variations in temperature in terms of the degree of heat. In particular, the eleven-year cycle that is known to be typical of the sun can also be seen in a number of climatic variations, but these are even manifest in caves, which proves that they cannot have been caused by direct radiation. It was long supposed that climatic changes on a small time scale were negligible. But it now appears that these variations (in temperature and rainfall) have occurred over the last few decades with remarkable regularity. Unfortunately, meteorological records have only been kept systematically and precisely for a relatively short period of time, and so it is difficult to build up a consistent overall picture of climate variations to cover the last few centuries. It is only by studying these, however, that we can decipher the slight variations that have occurred in recent times, which are of great importance since they are the ones that may have been caused by humans. What is needed is a back-up through which chronology can easily be established—for example, the growth rings of trees. We also need signs that are sensitive to climatic conditions: the thickness and density of tree rings vary according to local

temperature and rainfall. By comparing the information provided by a number of trees (and obtained without necessarily having to sacrifice those trees) or wooden beams, and by carefully distinguishing effects inherent to the physiology of the vegetable matter itself, scientists have been able to put together precise local reconstructions on all the continents. Similar studies have been carried out on coral reefs, revealing fluctuations of temperature and salinity in tropical seas.

It is also necessary to take into account the complete chain of reactions which can be self-canceling as well as accumulative. When the effects are cumulative, we speak of positive retroaction: an increase in temperature entails ice melting, and the exposed soil then absorbs solar radiation (this is the albedo effect—the ability to reflect the sun's rays. Snow has a stronger albedo than soil); this in turn reinforces the greenhouse effect. On the other hand, a rise in temperature may also transform a field covered in vegetation into a desert, whose albedo will help to increase radiation, thereby bringing about a lowering of temperature in what is known as negative retroaction. One of the major disadvantages of predictions obtained in this way remains the lack of spatial precision: the climatic system reproduced covers the whole globe, which is divided into very crude units. The more regional predictions are based on "new generation" models that use a reduced grid. Climatologists are realists, and one thing they are certain of is the fact that not all of the mechanisms that create climate change have been identified as yet. For example, no one fully understands the complex role of clouds, which can provide heat by absorbing and emitting long-wave radiation, and can also take heat away by absorbing solar radiation. Nevertheless, if we compare the different temperature estimates predicted by the different models for the coming century, all of

**STORM OVER THE AMAZON RAINFOREST, AMAZONAS STATE, BRAZIL** (2°00' S, 64°00' W)

There are 50,000 storms a day on the planet. They are caused by damp, unstable air that rises rapidly, cooling as it does so. Condensation occurs when the water-vapor saturation point is reached, forming a huge cumulonimbus cloud that can be 15.5 miles (25 km) across and 10 miles (16 km) high in the lower latitudes. Within this cloud, electrical charges produce lightning, followed by thunder and heavy rain. All over the world, storms cause serious damage to crops and buildings, disrupt air and land transport, interfere with communication systems, and kill hundreds of people and thousands of animals. Global warming is expected to cause an increase in the average amount of water vapor in the atmosphere and in the amount of rainfall. It is also expected to lead to more frequent extreme weather events such as storms, tornados, and cyclones.

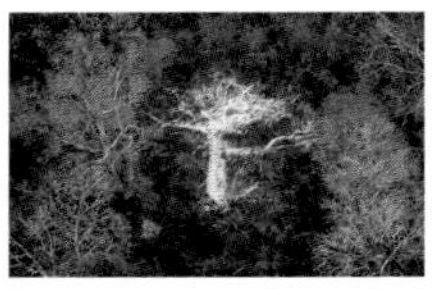

**PAGES 282–283**
ASHES OF A TREE NEAR THE GOROHOUI KONGOLI MOUNTAINS, BOUNA, CÔTE D'IVOIRE
(8°49' N, 4°07' W)

In northwestern Côte d'Ivoire, in a region covered with shrub savanna and sparse forests, this tree—downed by wind or lightning—was slowly consumed in a bush fire. Started by the local population, these fires can spread through as much as 30 percent of the savanna each year. When the fire has died out, the ashes act as a natural, organic fertilizer, stimulating the quick regeneration of fodder and pasture. In addition, with taller grasses eliminated, the stalking and hunting of game are made easier. Such fires do not cause deforestation in the country—the highest rate in Africa, with 3.1 percent of the forest destroyed each year—unless they are started too late in the dry season. It is then that they can grow into full-blown forest fires and cause severe damage to the tree layer.

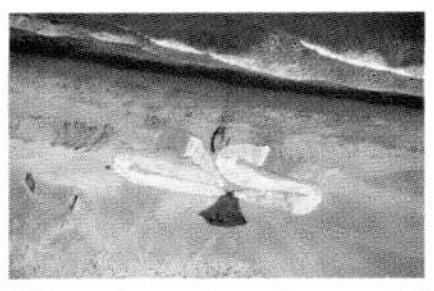

**PAGES 284–285**
FISHING NETS ON THE BEACH AT SAHAM, OMAN
(63°00' N, 24°20' E)

This seine net—a long net that is dragged over a sandy sea bottom—is ready to be used once again. The fishermen have patiently folded it up and laid it alongside their boats, and they now need only pull at the net's two ends to harvest their catch. More than 80 percent of Oman's fish are caught by such traditional methods, but the sultanate would like to modernize this sector. The country is well aware of the limits to its oil reserves (700,000 tons of crude) and would like to diversify its economy. Training fishermen is one of its priorities. With the help of young, qualified staff, it hopes to increase national output while still managing fish stocks sustainably; for while the Gulf of Oman is rich in fish, certain species there are threatened. Overfishing is a worldwide problem, and catches are falling—in the North Atlantic, for example, they have dropped by 25 percent since 1970.

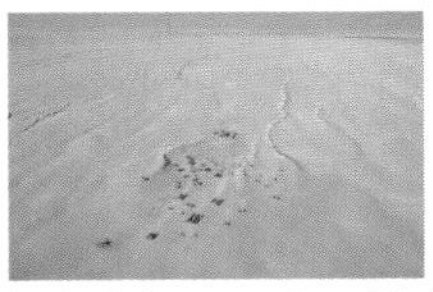

**PAGES 286–287**
VILLAGE OF ARAOUANE, NORTH OF TIMBUKTU, MALI (18°54' N, 3°33' W)

In the Saharan region of Mali, 168 miles (270 km) north of Timbuktu, the village of Araouane stands on the great caravan route, once heavily traveled, linking the north of the country with Mauritania. Today it is best known for its collections of ancient manuscripts written in Arabic and local languages. Araouane's numerous wells, which contributed to its ancient prosperity, still attract nomad campers to its periphery. Little by little, however, its fort-like houses are being swallowed up by the *harmattan*, the desert wind, which is threatening to wipe out the village completely. The only defense against the advancing sands is the plantations all around the wells, and this is a method that is beginning to reap rewards in a region for which the situation is serious and urgent. Desertification is a worldwide problem, which affects one-third of the land belonging to emerging nations. We are witnessing a disturbing acceleration of this phenomenon in its most acute form: between 1995 and 2000, 1,326 square miles (3,436 km²) of land turned into desert every year, compared to 602 square miles (1,560 km²) during the 1970s.

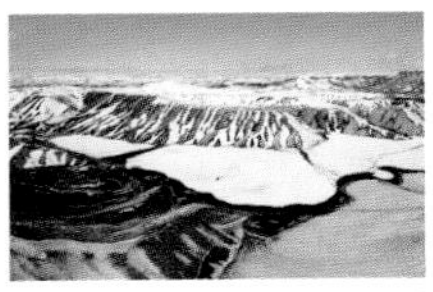

**PAGES 288–289**
SNOW-COVERED MOUNTAINS OF BAND E AMIR, AFGHANISTAN
(34°25' N, 69°20' E)

As Afghanistan's first national park, situated in the province of Bamiyan, Band E Amir is a spectacular sight. Covering an area of 158 square miles (41,000 hectares), it contains five lakes whose crystalline water is a vivid, bright blue, encased in red rocks that are separated by natural dikes of travertine. Popular belief credits this miracle of nature to Ali, cousin and son-in-law of the prophet Mohammed and founder of Shia Islam. Many pilgrims come here, attracted by the reputed healing powers of the waters in which they bathe on Fridays, the day of prayer. A jewel for the country's tourist industry, this natural park might once again bring back the foreigners who flocked here during the 1970s. The Afghan authorities intend to ask for it to be included in UNESCO's World Heritage list. Local people, who live on agriculture and fishing—in particular for the large yellow fish known as *chush*—would certainly benefit from such a move.

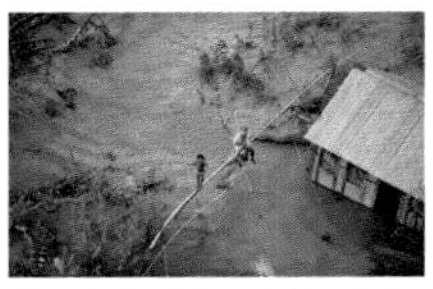

**PAGES 290–291**
FLOODED HOUSES SOUTH OF DHAKA, BANGLADESH
(23°21' N, 90°31' E)

Bangladesh is a delta plain covered by a vast network of three hundred waterways. From June to September, heavy monsoon rains cause the rivers to overflow their banks and flood nearly half of the country. Accustomed to this natural cycle, part of the country's population lives permanently on *chars*, ephemeral river islands made of sand and silt deposited by the rivers. In 1998, however, two-thirds of the country remained under water for several months following the worst flood of the 20th century, which claimed 1,300 lives and left 31 million Bangladeshis homeless. An effect of global warming, natural disasters of this kind are becoming increasingly common, and six years later Bangladesh was once again hit by devastating floods. It is one of the most heavily populated countries on Earth, and also one of the poorest and the most at threat from climate change. Before 2020, 20 million Bangladeshis may be forced to leave their country because of the gradual disappearance of their land under the rising waters.

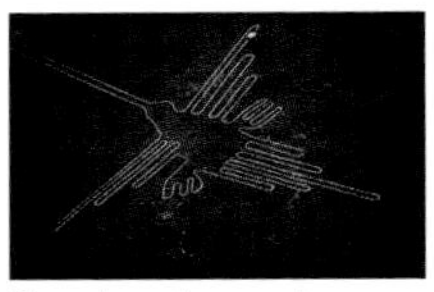

**PAGES 292–293**
OUTLINE OF A HUMMINGBIRD IN NAZCA, PERU
(14°41' S, 75°08' W)

Over two thousand years ago the Nazca people dug grooves in the desert earth of the Peruvian pampas, tracing impressive geometric figures and stylized depictions of plants or animals. This hummingbird, measuring about 320 feet (98 m), is among eighteen different silhouettes of birds in the area, which was declared a World Heritage site by UNESCO in 1994. Beginning in the 1940s until her death in 1998, the German mathematician Maria Reiche was tirelessly involved in the recovery, maintenance, and study of these lines. Thanks in large part to her efforts, we can still admire what is thought to have constituted an astronomical calendar. The Nazca Lines, the nearby burial complex, and other important archaeological finds are threatened today by *huaqueros*, tomb robbers, as well as by the influx of tourists, erosion, and industrial pollution.

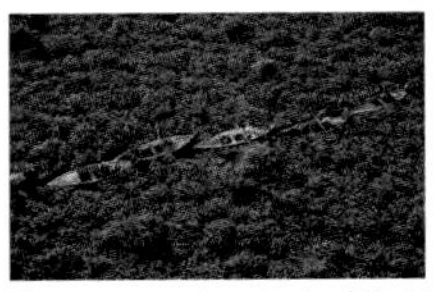

**PAGES 294–295**
SMALL BOATS CAUGHT IN WATER HYACINTHS ON THE NILE, EGYPT
(29°43' N, 31°17' E)

The water hyacinth (*Eichhornia crassipes*) was first reported at the beginning of the 20th century in the Nile delta in Egypt and in the province of Natal, South Africa. It is an invasive aquatic plant that originated in Brazil, where it grows at a moderate rate in its natural habitat. Introduced to Africa as an ornamental plant, in less than a century it spread to more than 50 countries around the world. An obstruction to navigation, this species can block agricultural irrigation canals and turbines in hydroelectric dams. It forms a thick vegetal carpet, which can double in area in twelve days and causes eutrophication—this is a fall in the oxygen content of deep waters, which leads to the asphyxiation of underwater life. No effective means of destroying this invader has been found to date, but organic defense methods could serve to limit its proliferation. Only 1 percent of introduced species cause major ecological and economic losses, but their presence remains the second cause, after the destruction of natural habitats, of the disappearance of species in the world.

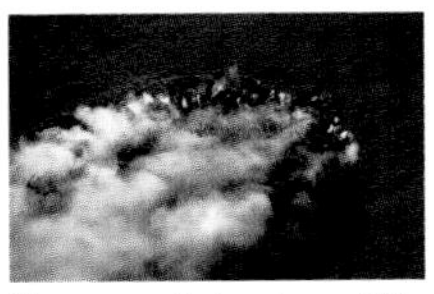

**PAGES 296–297**
NOMAD ENCAMPMENT, LAKE CHAD REGION, CHAD
(13°15' N, 15°12' E)

The nomadic herders of the Kanembu, Peul, and Fulbe peoples graze their livestock on Lake Chad's marshlands and fertile alluvial soils, as do the Buduma, who live on islands in the lake itself. At dusk, the herders light fires, as at this encampment on the lake's northeast shore. The livestock take cover of their own accord amid the thick smoke, avoiding the mosquitoes that infest the region and spread deadly diseases. But there is another threat to the survival of the Kuri breed of cattle, which now number 400,000 head. Endowed with impressive horns, which act as buoyancy aids, the breed is confined to the islands of Lake Chad, and its fate is closely dependent on that of the lake's waters, which unfortunately have shrunk by 95 percent over the past forty years, through the combined effects of human interference and climate change; in addition, half of the lake's surface has been taken over by plants. To save the lake from drying up completely, Chad, Niger, Nigeria, and Cameroon, which share its waters, plan to divert a tributary of the Congo River toward it, but the decision-making process is taking a long time.

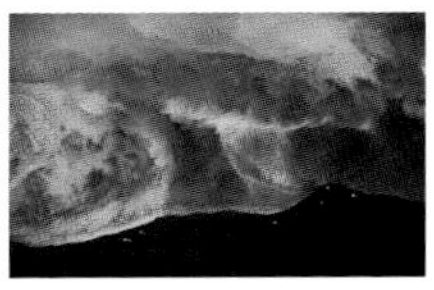

**PAGES 298–299**
DISCHARGE FROM THE GOLD MINE ON THE SHORE OF MINDANAO, PHILIPPINES
(6°52' N, 126°03' E)

The islands of the Philippines are rich in mineral deposits of chrome, copper, nickel, silver, and gold, which is mined here on the island of Mindanao in the southern Philippines. Although production is constantly falling, gold-mining still provides an important economic resource for the country, which produced 7 tons of gold in 2001. However, the refuse and sediments from the washing and sorting operations are discharged daily into the rivers and ocean. These discharges darken the waters and endanger marine flora and fauna both along the shore and out at sea, particularly the coral polyps that depend upon light for survival. In addition, heavy metals such as mercury, which is highly toxic, are used for cleaning and refining the gold particles. Discharged into the water, this mercury enters the food chain and damages the nervous systems of both animals and humans. In the gold mines of Mindanao, 70 percent of the workers display symptoms of mercury poisoning.

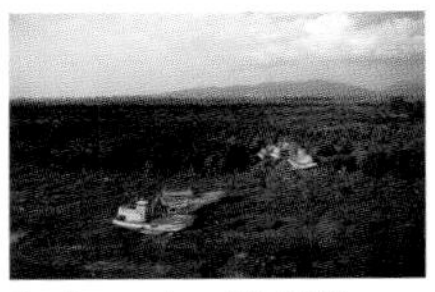

**PAGES 300–301**
BOATS WRECKED BY THE TSUNAMI OF DECEMBER 26, 2004, ACEH PROVINCE, SUMATRA, INDONESIA
(4°25' N, 95°50' E)

On December 26, 2004, an earthquake and subsequent tsunami caused the death of over 295,000 people in twelve countries around the Indian Ocean, and affected the livelihoods of more than 5 million people, who live mainly from farming and fishing. In Aceh province, two-thirds of the fishing fleet was destroyed within a few minutes, and half of the fishermen were carried away by the terrible waves that swept the coast. On an agricultural level, some 99,000 acres (44,000 hectares) of irrigated land was devasted in Indonesia alone. Five months after the disaster, with well-managed emergency aid, the 600,000 people affected on the island had shelter, food, and care, but reconstruction had not yet begun. Some boats have gone back to sea, and some farmers were able to desalinate their land and begin growing crops again. But for many other families, starting their normal lives again is not yet possible.

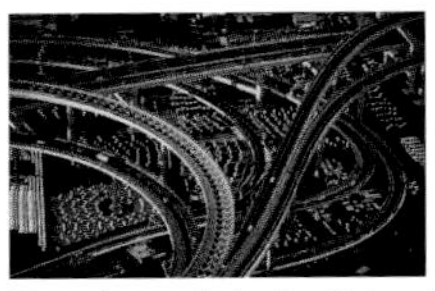

**PAGES 302–303**
FREEWAY INTERCHANGE NEAR THE PORT OF YOKOHAMA, HONSHU, JAPAN (35°42' N, 139°46' E)

Since it was linked to Tokyo by a railway line in 1872, the small fishing port of Yokohama has been growing continuously; today it is Japan's main international port and second-biggest city after the capital. The freeways that encircle it symbolize a type of economic development largely built around road transport, as in many industrialized countries. This dominant model has led to an increase in freeways all over the world. The number of vehicles has risen to almost 800 million, most of these in developed countries: 29 percent are in the United States alone, and just 2.4 percent in Africa. The level of ownership is also unequal: there are 790 vehicles per 1,000 inhabitants in the United States, but just eight in India. Despite the pollution and congestion in cities, the number of cars continues to grow relentlessly. Transport is the chief emitter of greenhouse gases, and the sheer number of users renders the measures for controlling it complex. Although emissions from industry have fallen since the Rio Earth Summit in 1992, emissions from transport have risen by 75 percent.

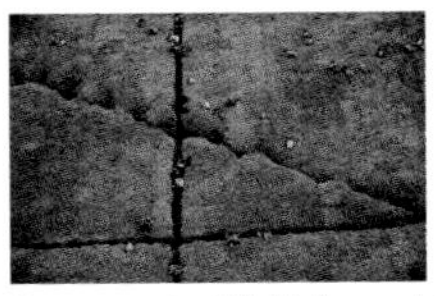

**PAGES 304–305**
TEA PLANTING, KERICHO REGION, KENYA (0°24' S, 37°00' E)

Between the Rift Valley and Lake Victoria, the region of Kericho lies at an altitude of 7,200 feet (2,200 meters); its soil has been impoverished by erosion, but its daily abundance of rain and sunshine makes it suitable for tea planting. During the harvest, only the top leaves are picked. Every plant has its own unique color, and the different shades of green indicate the quality of the tea produced. Narrow paths divide up the plots of land belonging to the small farmers who are responsible for 60 percent of Kenya's tea production. The rest comes from large plantations run by multinational companies, which employ large numbers of people. Standardization through cloning would allow mechanization, but the profits resulting from a reduction in labor costs would be offset by a reduction in the quality of the tea that would then come on the market. Furthermore, the social involvement of the multinationals is considerable; they have taken over whole communities and have invested in hospitals and schools in surrounding towns.

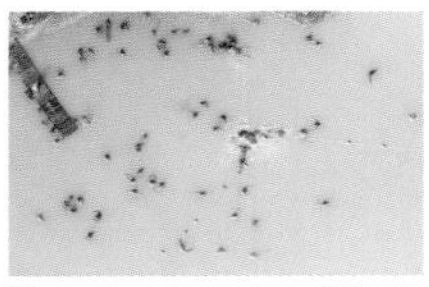

**PAGES 306–307**
THE BLUE LAGOON, NEAR GRINDAVÍK, REYKJANES PENINSULA, ICELAND
(63°54' N, 22°25' W)

The volcanic region of Reykjanes Peninsula, Iceland, has many natural hot springs. The Blue Lagoon (*Bláa Lónid*, in the Icelandic language) is an artificial lake fed by the surplus water drawn from the geothermic power station at Svartsengi. Captured at 6,560 feet (2,000 m) below ground, the water is raised to 464°F (240°C) by the molten magma and reaches the surface at a temperature of 158°F (70°C), at which point it is used to heat neighboring cities. The color of the lagoon results from the mineral mixture of silica and chalk from the basin combined with the presence of decomposing algae. Rich in mineral salts and organic matter, the hot waters (about 104°F, or 40°C) of the Blue Lagoon are known for their curative properties, particularly for skin ailments. The use of geothermic energy, a renewable, clean, and inexpensive energy source, is relatively recent, but it is being used with growing frequency. In Iceland, in 1960 less than 25 percent of the population benefited from this source of heat, whereas today it meets the needs of 85 percent of Icelanders. By using geothermic energy to produce hydrogen fuel cells, Iceland plans to make its economy oil-free by 2040.

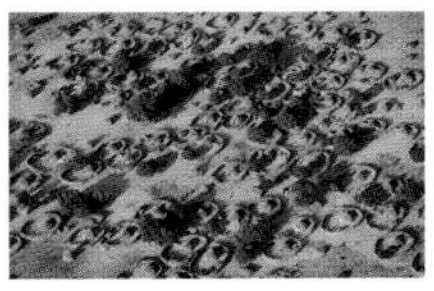

**PAGES 308–309**
VILLAGE ON LAKE CHAD, CHAD
(13°23' N, 14°05' E)

On the islands in Lake Chad, the fishermen depend on the waters around them, catching and drying their perch, catfish, and carp, and smoking them in traditional ovens. Chad is a mixture of some 200 ethnic groups who speak more than one hundred languages. The fact that it is an ancient settlement is proved by rock carvings that date from earlier than 2000 BC and show that regions which are now desert country once enjoyed an abundance of water and wildlife. In former times the lake spanned the frontiers of Chad, Cameroon, Nigeria, and Niger, but in the last forty years it has shrunk by 95 percent and is now confined to Chad and Cameroon. Although there have certainly been climate changes, this catastrophe is mainly due to human activity—overgrazing, deforestation, and unregulated irrigation which has siphoned off water from the rivers that feed the lake. Farmers, cattle breeders, and fishermen are all victims of the water shortage, with poor harvests, dying cattle, dwindling stocks of fish, salination of the soil, and, as a result of all this, grinding poverty. The situation is potentially explosive, for it affects some 20 million people in the four neighboring countries.

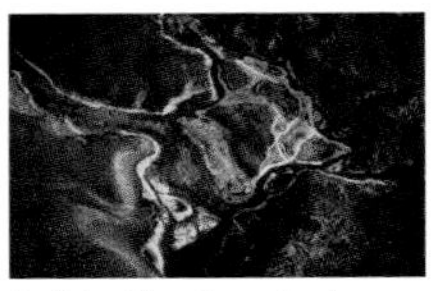

**PAGES 310–311**
RIVER NEAR MAELIFELLSSANDUR, MYRDALSJÖKULL REGION, ICELAND
(63°43' N, 20°10' W)

Fed by thawing glaciers and an annual rainfall of 47 inches (1.2 m), the rivers of Iceland all follow a glacial pattern: low water levels in winter and maximum volumes in summer when the big thaws occur. The rivers are interrupted by waterfalls and rapids, as the recent volcanic land formations have not yet been softened by erosion. A common phenomenon in this region is the *jökulhlaups*, a sudden and powerful flood made up of water, mud, and ash from the base of a glacier, caused by heat from a nearby volcano. The largest of the 20th century, in 1918, released a flood of water in one day that was three times greater than the Amazon river. These phenomena have a major effect on the surrounding landscape. The rivers are popular with fishermen, who come from all over the world to catch salmon and trout; the visitors often pay large sums for daily permits to the landowners whose farms they run through. The deep-sea fishing industry in Iceland, the source of 70 percent of the country's exports and employing 12 percent of its workforce, is now in decline due to falling Atlantic fish stocks.

many people whose way of life has been directly affected. The fishermen of Alaska have been appalled to see the soil of their villages become soft and unstable through the melting of the pergelisol (permanently frozen ground); inhabitants of some Pacific islands that are just a few feet above sea level—such as Tuvalu—have been constrained to seek refuge on neighboring islands; within barely one month last year, people living on the coast of Florida were forced to go inland on several occasions in order to escape from hurricanes whose force was directly related to the temperatures of the waters of the Atlantic, heated throughout the southern summer.

Five of the last ten years have been among the hottest of the last thousand years. Scientists are now certain that the increase in temperature, estimated globally to be around 0.6 percent since the beginning of the 20th century, is largely due to human activity. Nevertheless, there is a wide gap between the scientific approach and that of the industrial lobby. The former are constantly questioning their own conclusions with a degree of caution that might be taken for self-censorship, whereas the latter have no doubts about the validity of their economic arguments. For all that, it is essential that we evaluate the dangers of

climate change, and in due course take those measures which even now can only limit the damage.

In order to do this, we can use computer simulations which, based on current data, can reproduce weather patterns on a global scale. In this way changes in temperature, rainfall, atmospheric pressure, and other factors can be reconstructed for the future. Climatic mechanisms, such as the return of solar radiation trapped in the atmosphere close to the Earth, are translated into equations based on the physics and chemistry of the processes observed. The quality of information provided by these models depends on several things: changes in the composition of the atmosphere must be taken into account, and the climatic phenomena that bring about interaction between atmosphere, sea, and biosphere must be understood and mathematically transposed. Several of these digital models have been developed to take into account data from an identical starting point, with each involving its own specific set of calculations, ending in a different set of predictions. The validity of these calculations is tested by the model's ability to reproduce past variations known over the last few decades, ranging from the poles to the equator. As science progresses, so climate modeling becomes more precise and more realistic, and the predictions that are emerging from these different models are following increasingly similar patterns. One example is the sulphate products of industrial origin that are dispersed into the atmosphere. Their presence in the air causes a lowering of ground temperature, and by incorporating this into the models of the 1990s, it has been possible to reproduce more accurately the current rise in temperature.

For a long time now, the scientific community has been trying to identify the many different influences affecting variations in solar radiation on the surface of the Earth. Fluctuations due to violent solar

**⌃ GLACIER FLOWING INTO THE SAN RAFAEL LAGOON, CHILE** (46°38' S, 73°60' W).

In the soft twilight, the ice takes on a bluish tinge. More than 30,000 years old, it cascades into the San Rafael lagoon, filling this marine lake that is linked by icebergs to the Pacific Ocean. This is the only glacier at this distance from the poles that reaches the sea. It flows slowly, with much cracking and creaking, from the mountains of Campo de Hielo Norte, where ice fields covering 1,620 square miles (4,200 km²) are fed by the region's abundant rains (138 inches, or 350 cm, per year—six times that of London, England, and ninety-five times that of Riyadh, Saudi Arabia). Such an expanse is a considerable freshwater resource, but it is inaccessible: trapped in the form of ice, it is only drip-fed into the surrounding rivers and lakes. Glaciers and permanent snows contain 70 percent of the world's fresh water. Most of the remaining 30 percent is polluted or inaccessible, which is why, although water might seem to be plentiful, one-third of the world's population has only limited access to it.

the results point in the same direction, converging on a figure of between +1.8°F and +3.6°F (+1°C and +2°C).

In order to predict the climate that awaits future generations, we must also take into account the various possibilities that relate to social evolution—such as fluctuations in the size of the population and, above all, economic development, with special emphasis on sources of energy. It is to be noted that the alterations (from 2.7°F to 8.1°F, or 1.5°C to 4.5°C) created by different forms of energy entail far greater uncertainty than

those connected with climatic factors themselves. In recent times, we have used our intelligence and creativity in the name of progress and profit, to construct a new world without paying heed to the fact that we are actually threatening our own survival. The question now is whether we will be able to reinvent a working, viable society that will have more respect for the world around it.

ANNE JUILLET-LECLERC

**BEACH AT SAINT-RAPHAËL, CÔTE D'AZUR, FRANCE** (43°25' N, 6°46' E)

In the early 20th century, Saint-Raphaël was still a little fishing village, but it is now a fashionable resort town where eager sun-worshipers crowd every corner of the beach. But the price of a glowing tan can be a heavy one: skin cancer is on the rise in most areas of the world, and in France alone, the number of cases doubles every ten years. In countries at higher latitudes, the situation is made even more serious by the thinning of the ozone layer. In the spring, the quantity of ozone present in the higher atmosphere is reduced by between 30 and 50 percent and UVB rays become between three and twenty times stronger. Thus we find skin cancer is most common in Canada; in the south of Chile, seven minutes of exposure is enough to cause sunburn in the most dangerous seasons; and in Australia, the rising UVB rays pose even greater risks for a predominantly pale-skinned population with a taste for outdoor sports. Today it is estimated that one in every two Australians will develop skin cancer at some point in their lives.

## THE STATE OF THE WORLD

**THE TEMPERATURE IS RISING**
The average temperature on the Earth's surface rose by about **1°F (0.6°C)** during the 20th century.

**THE SEA LEVEL IS RISING**
The sea level rose on average some **4–8 inches (10–20 cm)** during the 20th century.

**THE ATMOSPHERE IS CHANGING**
The amount of carbon dioxide ($CO_2$) in the atmosphere has risen more than **30%** since **1750**; that of methane ($CH_4$) has risen over **100%** and that of nitrous oxide ($N_2O$) has risen **15%**.

## GREENHOUSE GASES

**ESSENTIAL GASES**
Without the greenhouse gases, which make up **1%** of the atmosphere, the average global temperature would be **–0.4°F (–18°C)**, instead of **59°F (15°C)**.

**DESTRUCTIVE HUMAN ACTIVITIES**
Just over **100 years** ago, industrial complexes in the richest countries began to discharge $CO_2$ into the atmosphere millions of times faster than it could be stored underground.

**THE SECTORS RESPONSIBLE**
Around three-quarters of manmade $CO_2$ emissions during the last 20 years have come from the burning of fossil fuels in all sectors: energy, industry, transport, construction.
Deforestation causes **15%** of worldwide emissions of $CO_2$.

**GEOGRAPHICAL DIVISION OF RESPONSIBILITY**
In **2002**, the annual $CO_2$ emission per inhabitant of India was **1.2 tons**, compared to **6.2 tons** per inhabitant of France, and **20.1 tons** per US citizen.

**THE FUTURE**
If the consumption of energy in the OECD countries continues to increase at the same rate, world demand for energy will have gone up by **65%** between 1995 and 2020, which will entail a **70%** increase in emissions of $CO_2$.

## THE CONSEQUENCES OF CLIMATE CHANGE

**MELTING GLACIERS AND REDUCED SNOW COVER**
Snow cover has fallen by **10%** since the late **1960s**.

**RISING TEMPERATURES**
Temperatures could rise by **10.8°F (6°C)** by 2100.
Only **9°F (5°C)** separates us from the last Ice Age **18,000** years ago, when almost the whole of Europe was covered with ice hundreds of meters thick.

**BIODIVERSITY UNDER THREAT**
A total of **1 million** animal and plant species could become extinct by **2050**.
The IPCC (Intergovernmental Panel on Climate Change), whose findings are validated by member countries of the OECD before being published, predicts the extinction of between **21** and **52%** of species.

**RISING SEA LEVELS**
Melting glaciers and expanding oceans will cause sea levels to rise between **9** and **88 cm** by **2100**.

**CLIMATE REFUGEES**
Coastal regions, where **50%** of the world's population live, and especially estuaries risk being overrun by the sea, and there is a greater danger of floods caused by storms and other phenomena. **7%** of Bangladesh is threatened with submersion, which will result in **15 million** refugees. **30 million** Chinese, **30 million** Indians, and **14 million** Egyptians could be exposed to the same risk.
The first "climate refugees" are on the verge of exceeding the present number of political refugees: more than **50 million** since **1950**.

**MOVEMENT OF ARABLE AREAS**
The average temperature rise of **+1.6°F (+0.9°C)** in France during the last 100 years is the equivalent of agricultural areas being shifted some **110 miles (180 km)**.

**THE INCREASING COST OF CLIMATE CATASTROPHES**
The environmental and social cost of catastrophes attributed to climate change has been estimated at **$300 billion** a year, equivalent to **25%** of the GDP of France.

## TOWARDS WORLD REGULATION

**ABSOLUTE OBJECTIVES**
According to the IPCC, in order to limit the catastrophic consequences of climate change, emissions of $CO_2$ must be reduced by **50** to **70%** (i.e. halved in relation to its 1990 level).
The maximum level of greenhouse gas emissions to stop them accumulating in the atmosphere is the equivalent of **1,000 lb (500 kg)** of carbon per person per year, which equals a **900-mile (1,500-km)** journey in a four-door saloon or a flight from Paris to New York.

To achieve this level, many countries will have to reduce their emissions: Americans must divide by **13**, Germans by **7**, and Mexicans by **2**.
According to UNEP (United Nations Environment Program), the rich countries need to reduce their energy consumption by **90%** to limit the number of disasters.

**THE KYOTO TREATY**
The Kyoto Treaty signed by **180** countries in **1997** came into force on February 16, 2005.
According to this agreement, the richest countries must reduce their emissions by **5.4%** compared to the level in **1990**.
The Kyoto Treaty is only the first step in an inevitable process of compulsory and increasingly radical reduction of greenhouse gas emissions on an international scale.

**RIVER ON THE AUYÁN TEPUI, GRAN SABANA REGION, VENEZUELA** (5°55′ N, 62°32′ W)

The Gran Sabana region in southeastern Venezuela is a wide plain covered with savannas and dense forest, interrupted by imposing mesas of sandy rock known as tepuyes. The mesa of Auyán Tepui, or "devil's mountain," covers 275 square miles (700 km²) and rises to a height of 9,675 feet (2,950 m). The Rio Carrao zigzags across Auyán Tepui and, at its edge, plunges in a steep waterfall. The Salto Angel waterfall is the world's highest free-falling waterway, at a height of 3,210 feet (978 m). Rich in gold and diamond ore, the Gran Sabana region and its many waterways have attracted prospectors since 1930—towns such as Icabaru, which was made famous by the discovery in 1942 of a diamond of 154 carats, or El Dorado, whose name alone conjures up the age of the conquistadors.

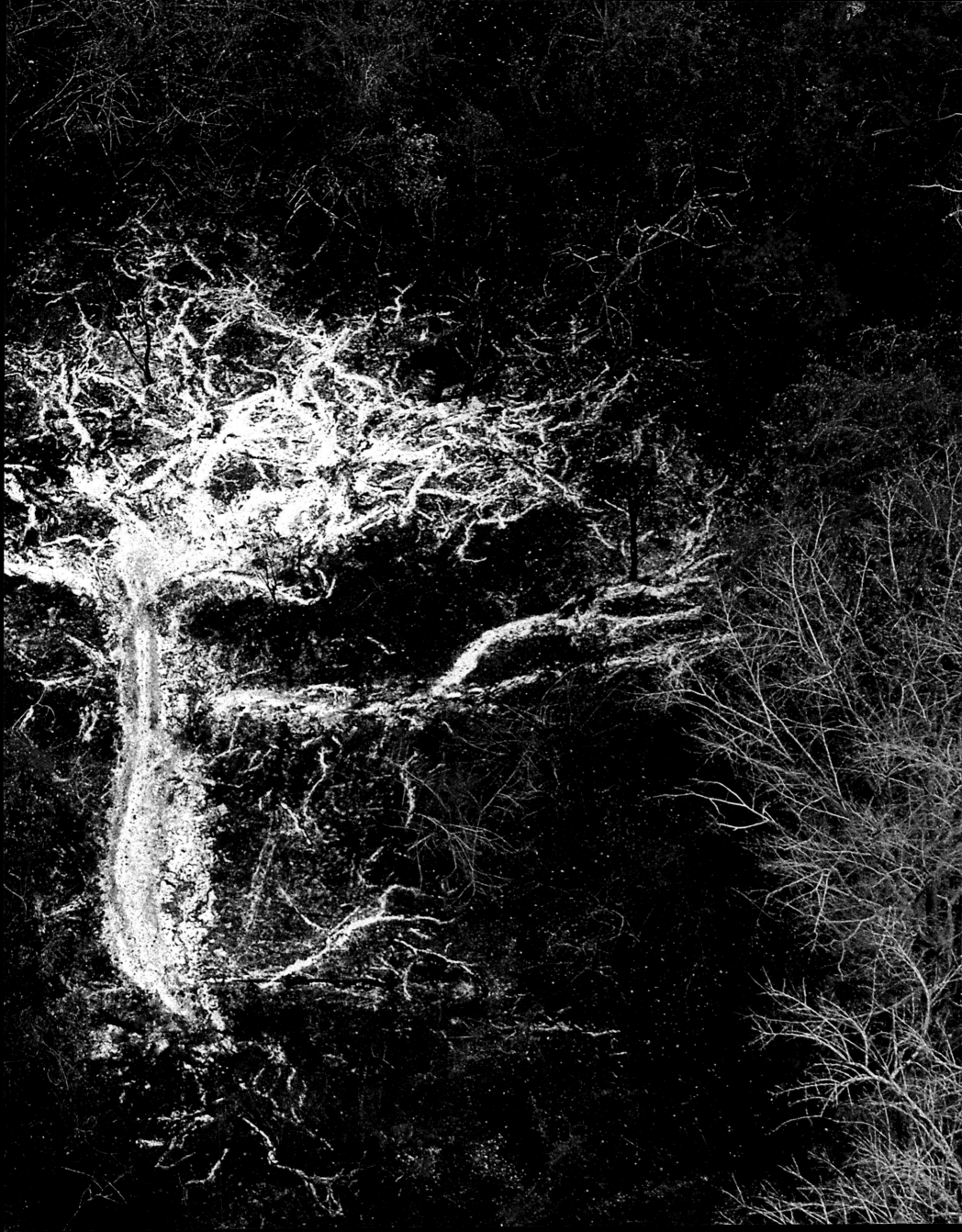

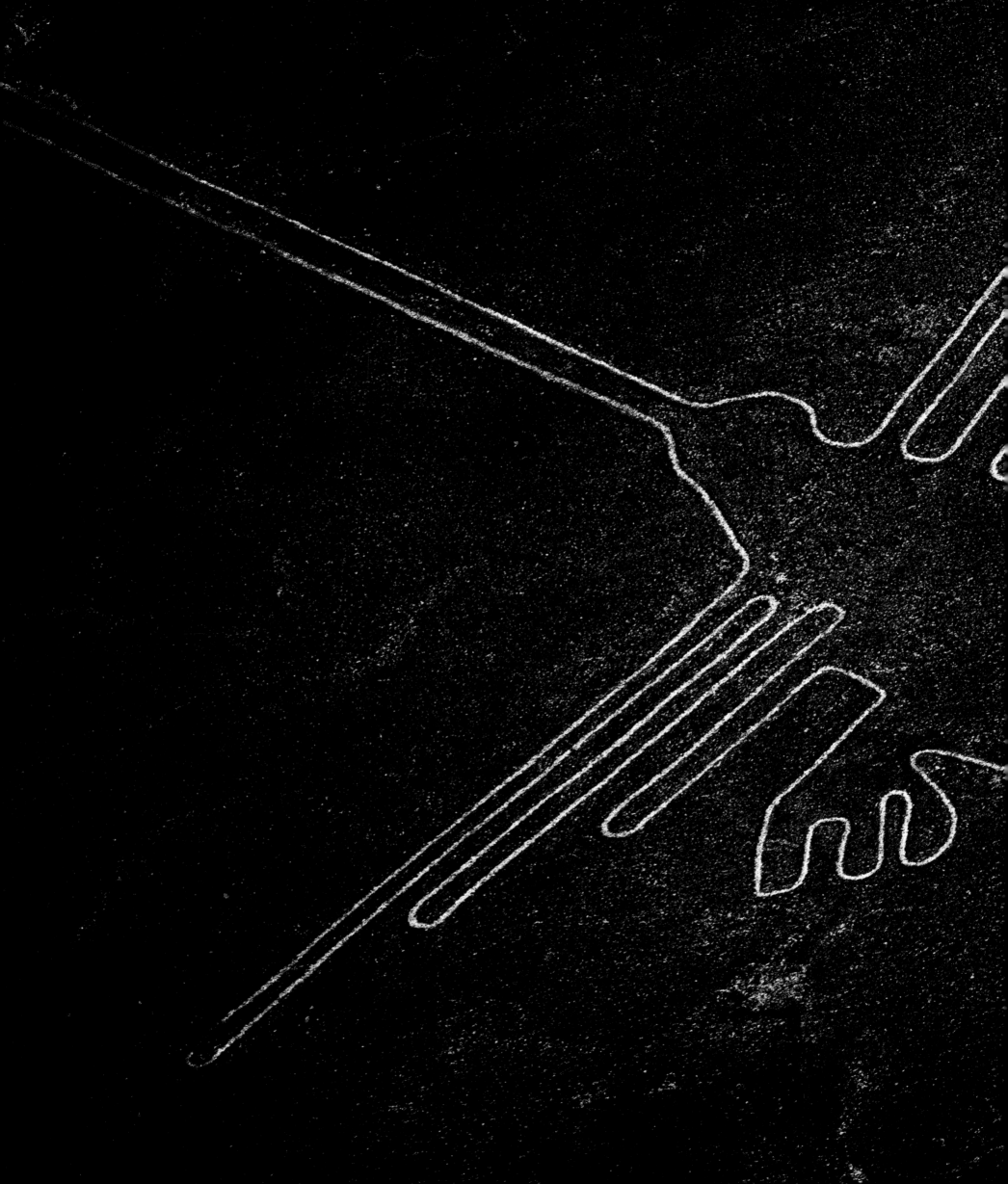

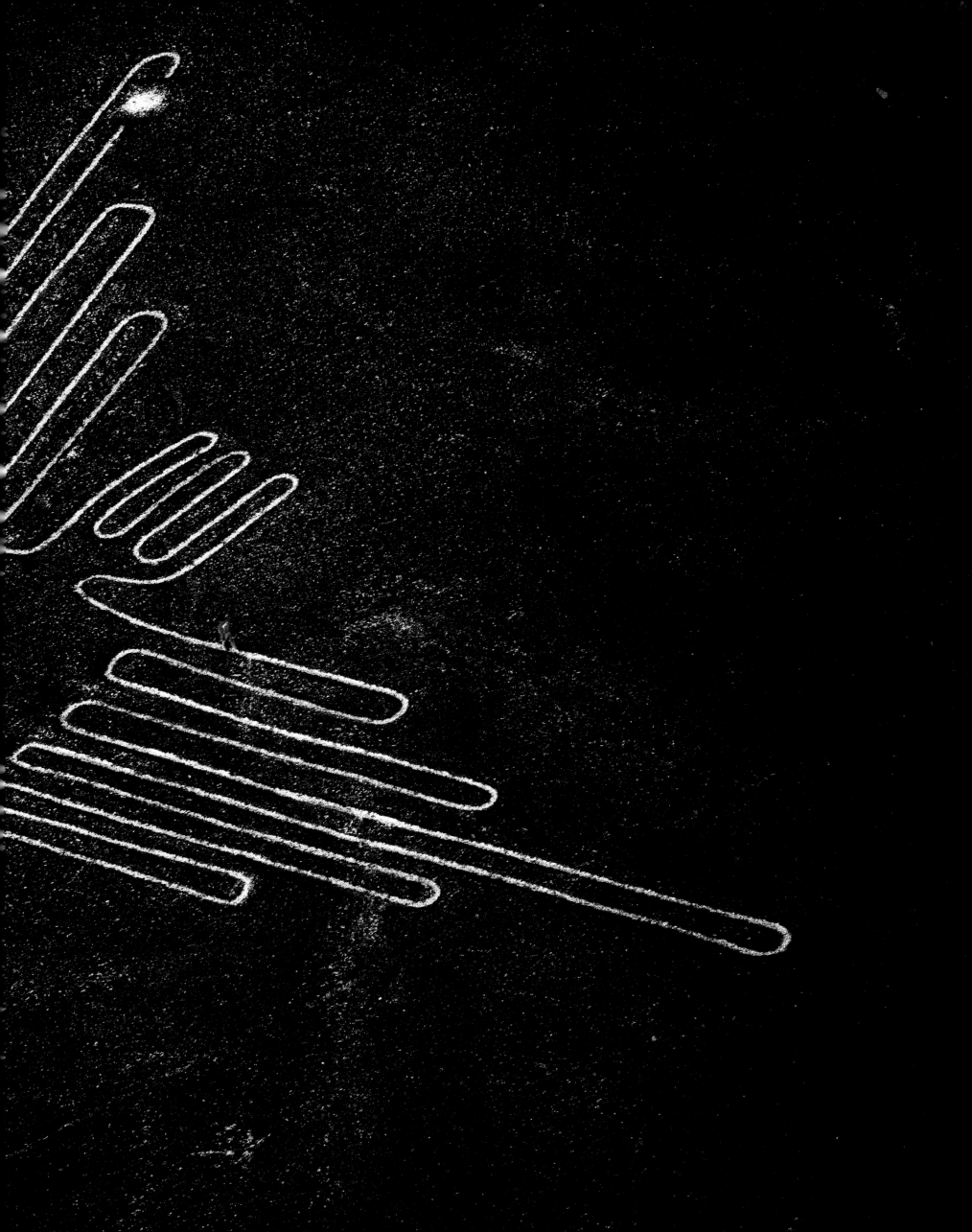

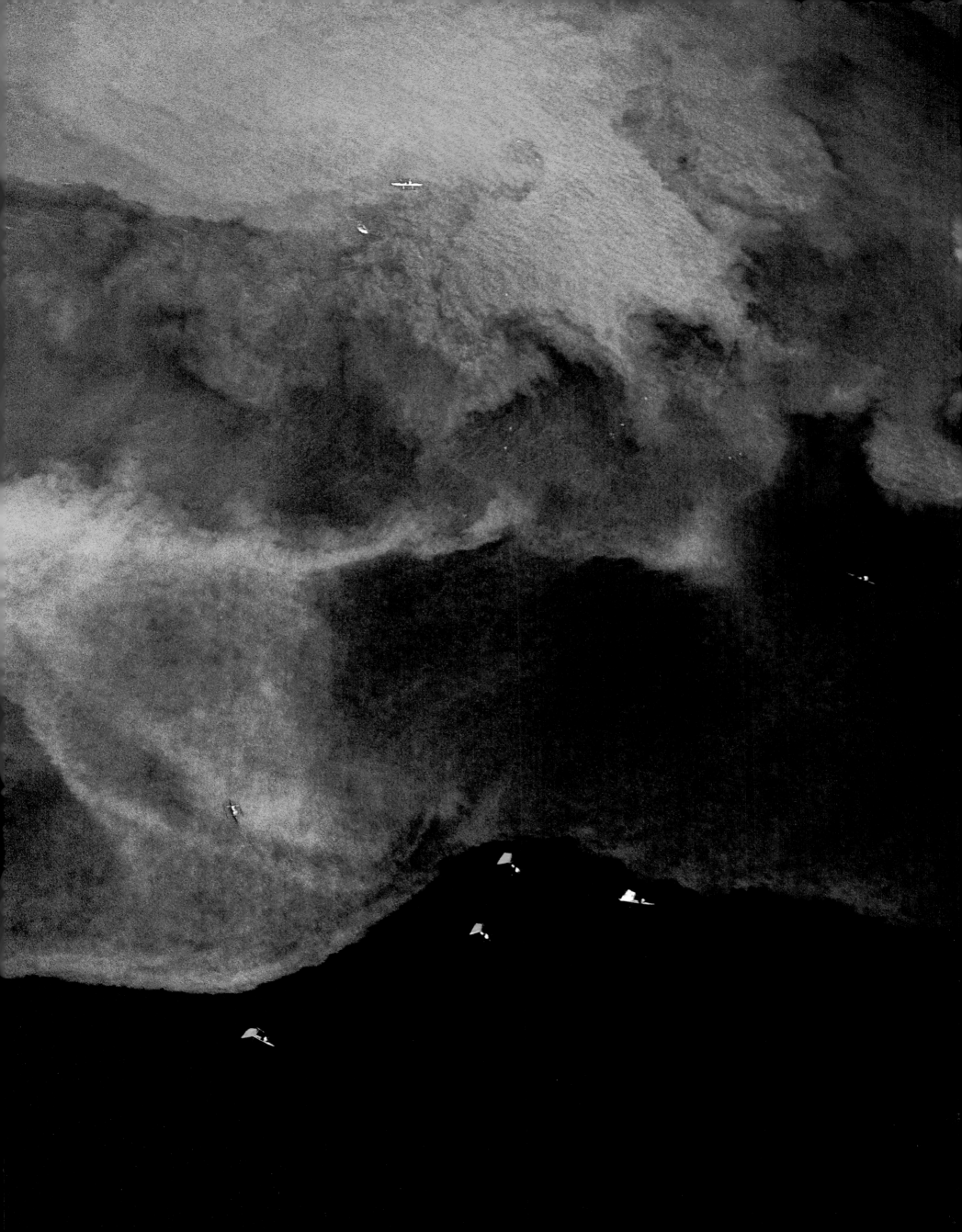

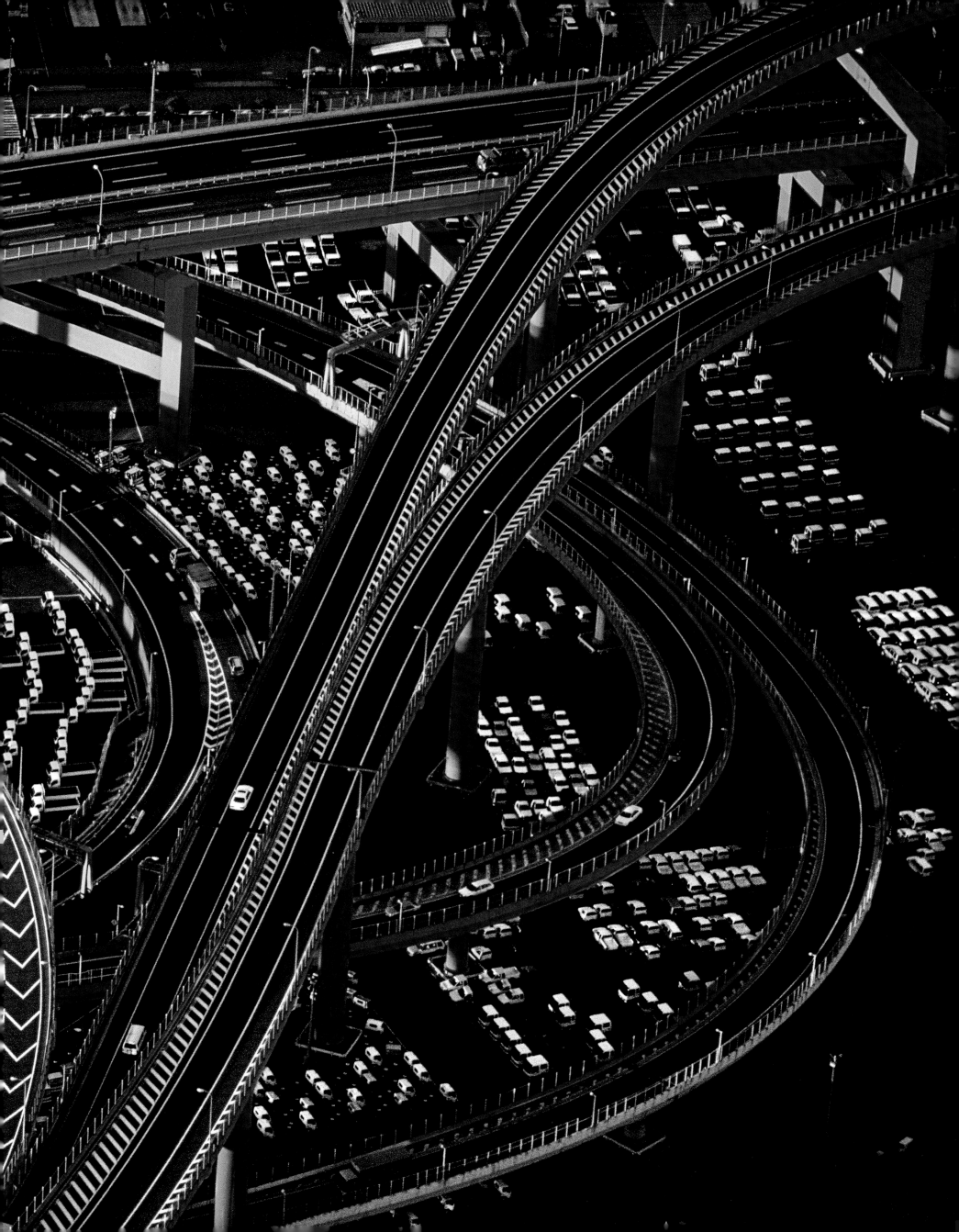

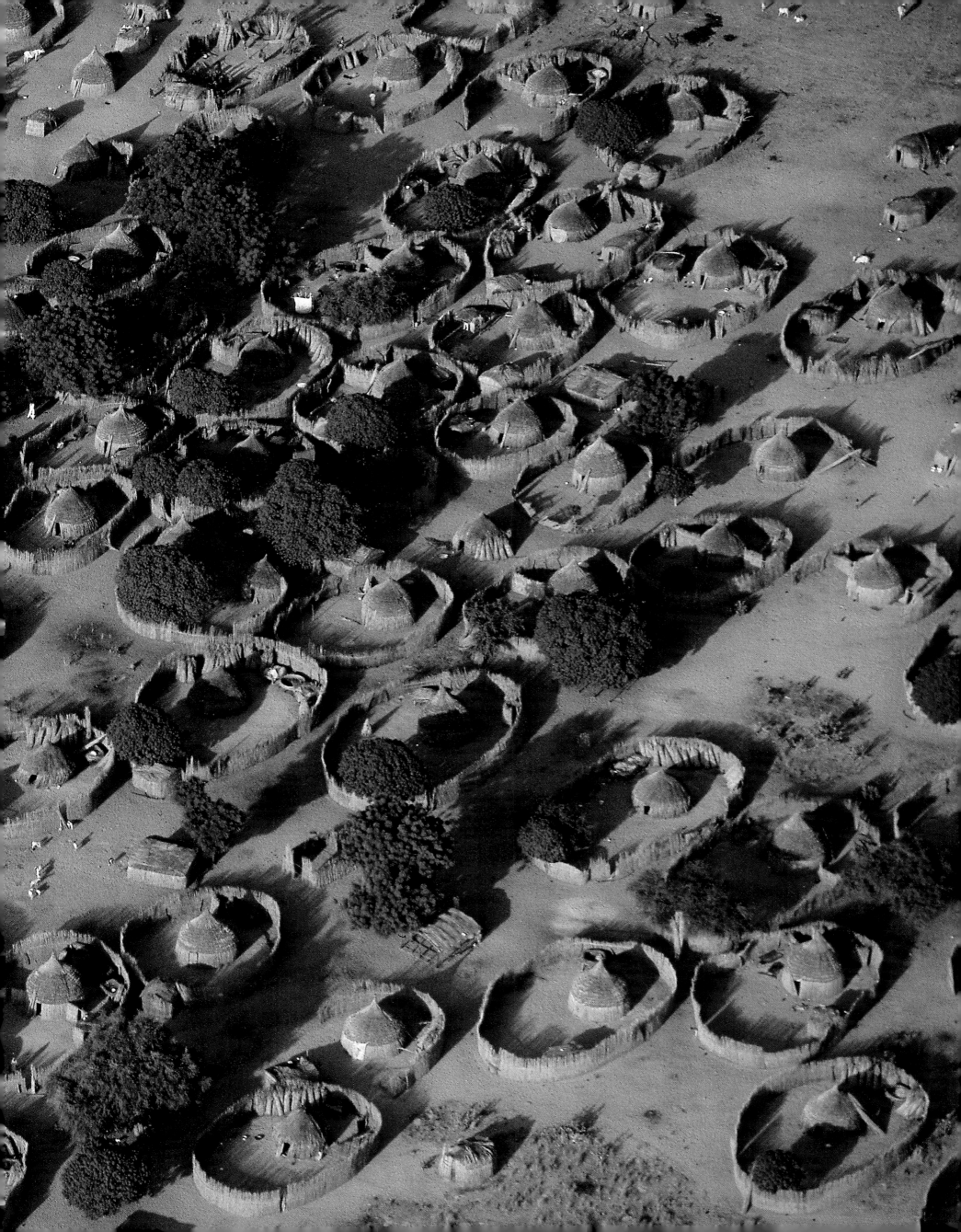

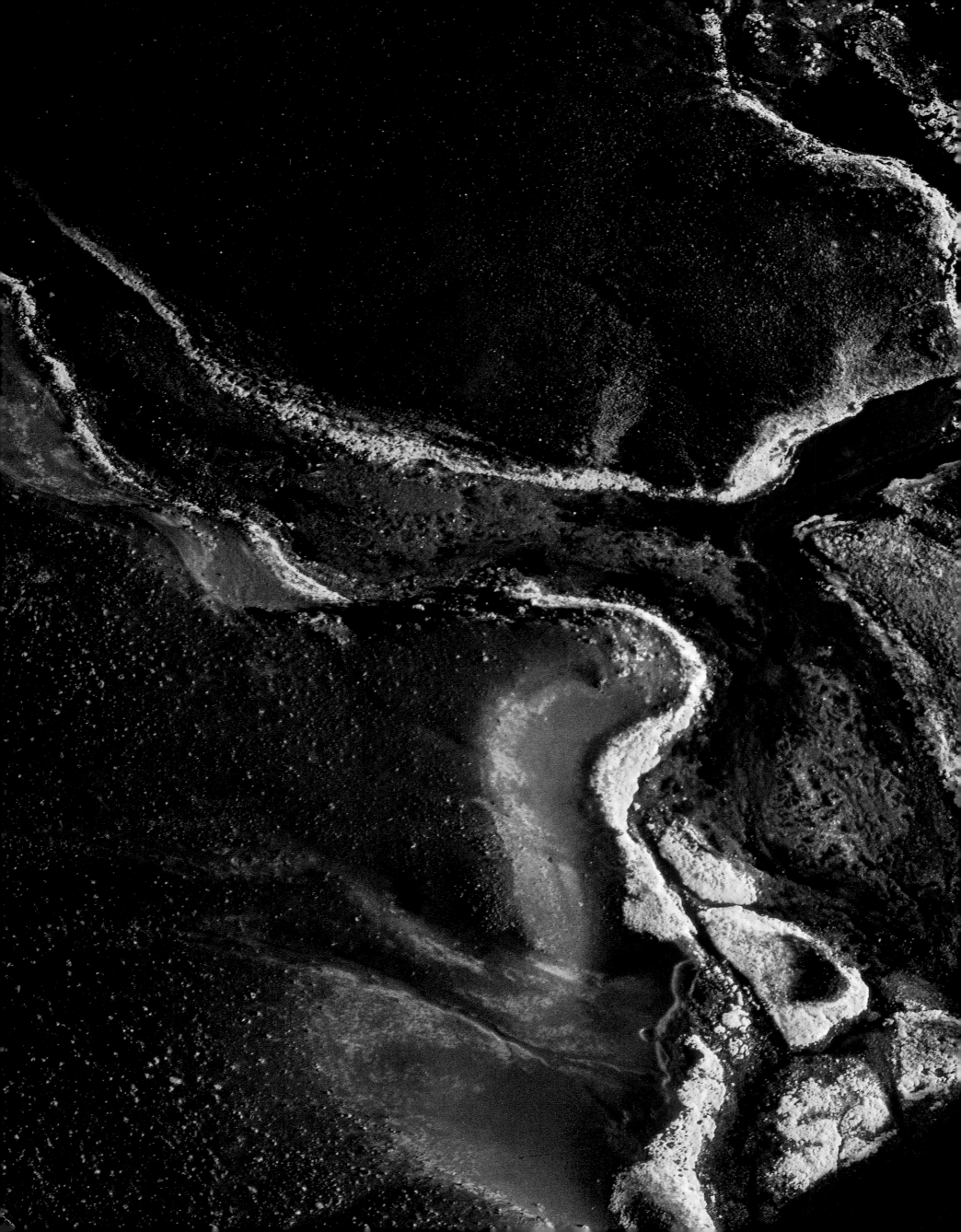

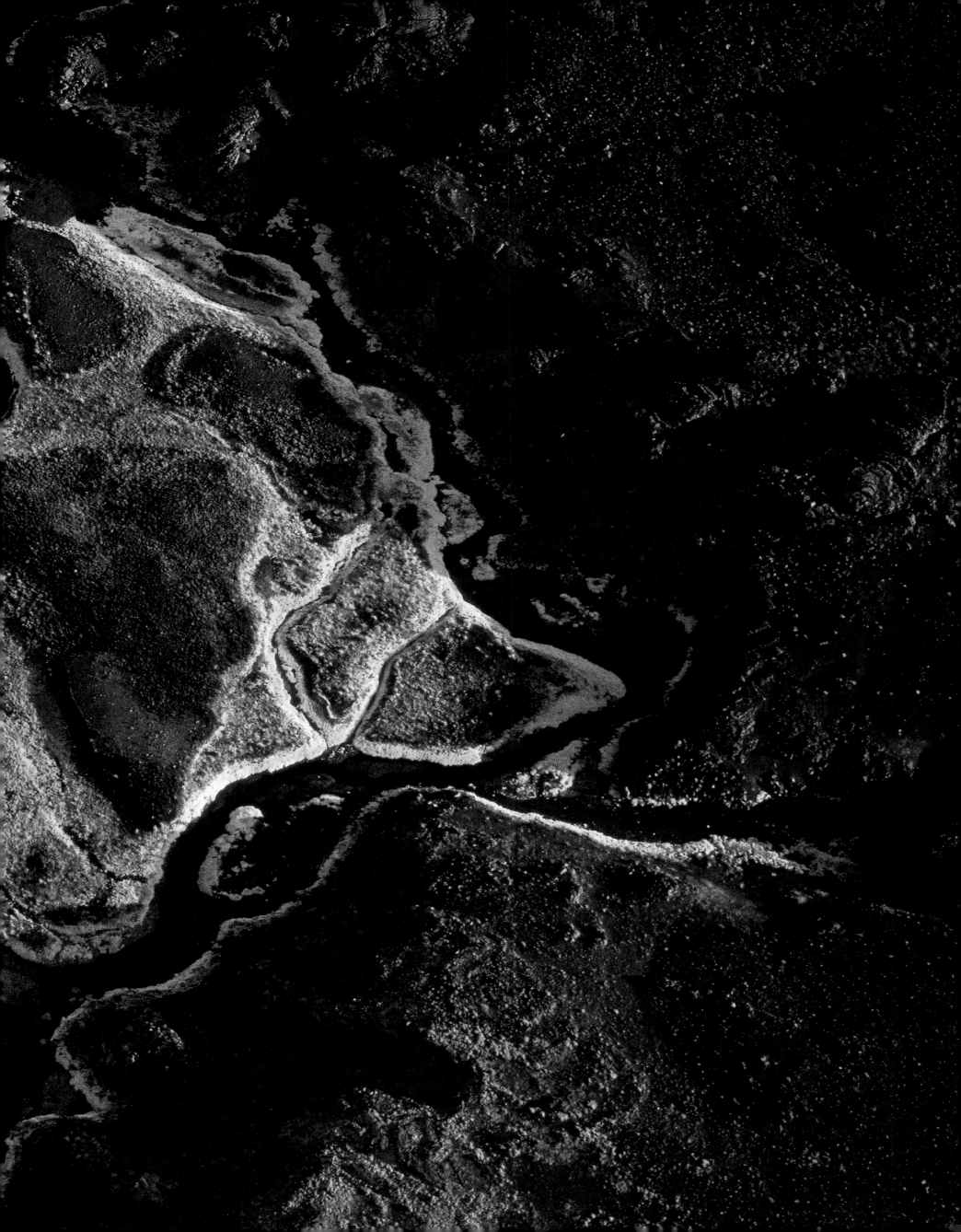

# RETHINKING THE WORLD'S ENERGY

While reserves of oil, gas, and coal are declining, renewable sources of energy—although still a closely guarded secret on a global level—are enjoying spectacular growth in those countries that have made them a political priority. A new era of energy is taking shape, inspired partly by the increasing scarcity of fossil fuels and their impact on the climate, and partly by the emergence of new countries on the stage of world energy. The train has already left the station, and some countries are already on board, but others are being left behind.

Over the course of the 20th century, oil and other fossil fuels provided the energy necessary to build a modern society and to enable the world's economy, as we knew it, to function. But the same fuels that helped to create our modern world are also weakening it. From the soaring price of petroleum and gas, which suggests that production is about to reach its peak around the world, to the 25 billion tons of carbon dioxide discharged every year into the atmosphere and posing a grave threat to the climate, our energy system is now a danger to the safety of the planet.

Major changes are rare in the field of energy. The last one took place a hundred years ago, when electricity and oil products replaced coal, wood, and animal fuels, which had dominated the scene until the 20th century. This change was brought about by a combination of economic, social, and technological factors—and we find ourselves faced with a similar combination today. The world's energy system has reached an impasse, and this situation could result in a radical transformation during the next few decades, guaranteeing a future with cleaner, more efficient, more reliable power by exploiting the Earth's vast resources of renewable energy.

Across the planet, energy consumption is increasing at an alarming rate. On an economic level, the ratio between consumption and GDP is being reduced, and during the last few decades, energy has been used more efficiently. Nevertheless, despite such encouraging progress, the demand for energy is rising in all sectors of the economy, from construction to transport—the latter being the principal consumer of the world's oil in terms of both quantity and rate of consumption.

It is scarcely surprising that consumption is now also rising in the developing countries, where the majority of people had previously never aspired to drive an automobile, use air conditioning, watch TV, or cook with any fuel other than wood or animal waste. It is perhaps more surprising that it also continues to rise in many countries that are already industrialized. But here people now drive bigger cars, build bigger houses, and buy more and more domestic appliances.

This ceaseless upward trend in the amount of energy used is not viable for several reasons. First, reserves of fossil fuels—especially oil—are insufficient to meet a demand that will continue to grow for the next hundred years. According to geologists, half the resources of usable oil have already been extracted. During the last thirty years, world economies have been using oil at a faster rate than that at which new reserves have been discovered, and production has either leveled out or been reduced in 33 of the 48 main oil-producing countries.

In the next ten years, production may reach its peak before entering into decline. But this imminent threat comes at a time when, in countries like China and India, more than a billion individuals are on the verge of embracing those elements of economic development that are most demanding of energy: modern conveniences such as central heating, air conditioning, refrigerators, and motor vehicles.

Fossil fuels are not only too scarce to meet the growing needs predicted for this century, but they also impose unacceptable costs on present and future generations at various levels—economic, health, social, and also that of security. Of all the imminent dangers, however, the most important and most alarming of all is climate change.

The increasing levels of carbon dioxide in the atmosphere—and the attendant risk of a sudden change in the climate—are now demanding everyone's attention, from town planners to the strategists in the Pentagon. Evidence continues to accumulate that global warming is already affecting humans, animals, and plant life all over the world with an impact that is accelerating at a rate unforeseen even by the climatologists. According to estimates made by the WHO (World Health Organization), climate change is responsible for 160,000 deaths a year worldwide. A large number of animal species have been driven north or to higher altitudes as a result of global warming, which has also caused the glaciers to melt and sea levels to rise all over the world.

Over the course of the next hundred years, the effects of global warming could wreck almost every ecosystem on the planet, causing more frequent and more serious floods and droughts, destroying food

◁ **FAVELAS IN RIO DE JANEIRO, BRAZIL** (22°55' S, 43°15' W)

Some 1.5 million *cariocas*—that is to say, one in seven residents of Rio de Janeiro—live in the city's 600 shantytowns, known as *favelas*, which have grown rapidly since the turn of the 20th century and are wracked by crime. Primarily perched on hillsides, these poor, underequipped neighborhoods regularly experience fatal landslides during heavy rains. Downhill from the *favelas*, the city's comfortable middle classes occupy the residential districts along the oceanfront. This social contrast marks all of Brazil, where 10 percent of the population controls the majority of the wealth while nearly half of the country lives below the poverty level. Worldwide, almost a billion people, or 32 percent of the world's urban population, live in slums. Since 1996, Rio's local government has gradually begun to urbanize the *favelas*, by taking charge of the infrastructure (road building, garbage collection, electricity and water supplies, sewers) and also by setting up job agencies.

These lower domestic costs even more rapidly and substantially in proportion to the manner in which the countries concerned develop their industries for creating, installing, and maintaining their renewable energy systems, using local labor and equipment. Thus countries which do not yet have major industries of their own can obtain impressive reductions in cost during the first few years after the introduction of efficient policies.

One day, historians will look back on the three-hundred-year exploitation of fossil fuels as an important, but transient period of human history—a period of technological, social, and economic development which provided a bridge between the Dark Ages and the age of clean and abundant forms of energy. The faster the world's economies accomplish the transition to renewable energy, the better it will be for everyone. With a political will for change and suitable measures targeted at creating lasting and structured growth, this transition can take place more rapidly than many people imagine. For the majority of developing countries which are poor in fossil fuels but rich in labor and renewable resources, the latter offer the perfect solution, creating millions of jobs and at the same time cutting the vast costs of importing fossil fuels.

The transition does require enormous investments up front, but experts have shown that these investments, carried out over an initial period of ten years with a view to making the renewable fuels competitive at world level within twenty years, would still be considerably lower than the costs engendered through a simple 10 percent increase in the price of oil. Just as the United States have dominated the oil economy over the last hundred years, countries which invest early in renewable energy technology will find themselves in a position to reap the economic rewards from this rapidly growing sector.

Today, much of the world remains trapped in a system of fossil fuels inherited from policies and investment decisions made long ago. It will not be easy to break with this tradition. But several countries have already shown that the change is genuinely possible, and that it can happen at speed if governments are willing to implement ambitious, coherent policies to ensure the future creation of firm markets for renewable energy, placing it at the forefront of the energy system.

CHRISTOPHER FLAVIN
JANET SAWIN

creating, installing, and maintaining systems of energy renewal. The aim must be to establish the conditions necessary for the energy industry to function permanently and profitably. It will then increase its capacity and production, and will cut its costs. To this end, long-term commitment by governments is essential to create new markets and guarantee profits to satisfy investors.

Consistent and reliable markets allow the development of the small and medium-sized businesses that lie at the heart of major technological innovations. Experience shows that in addition to the "worldwide learning curve," which keeps technological costs down at an international level, countries with established and sustainable markets for renewable energy succeed in achieving "national learning curves."

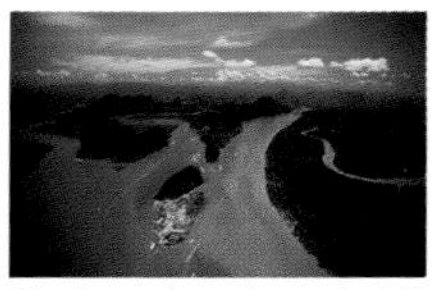

**PAGES 320–321**
VILLAGE OF KOH PANNYI, PHANG NGA BAY, THAILAND
(8°12' N, 98°35' W)

The jagged west coast of Thailand has a series of bays bordered by many islands in the Andaman Sea. The largest of these islands is Phuket, situated off the coast of the Malay Peninsula. Formerly an arid region, the Phang Nga Bay was created 18,000 years ago when the great glaciers melted, and the receding waters uncovered only the peaks of the chalky mountains, which soon grew tropical vegetation. The bay was declared a marine park in 1981. This floating village of "sea gypsies" was built on stilts 200 years ago by Muslim fishermen who originally came from Indonesia. The people live primarily on the products of traditional fishing, but the rock has become a favorite stopover for tourist boats as the neighboring island to Ko Ping Gan, or "James Bond Island," where *The Man with the Golden Gun* was filmed. Because of its irregular shape, the bay was not as severely affected as most of its neighbors by the tsunami of December 2004.

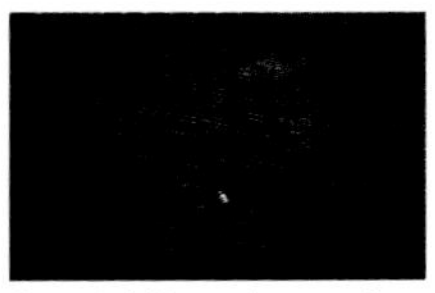

**PAGES 322–323**
PEASANT WORKING HIS FIELD, LASSITHI REGION, CRETE, GREECE
(35°09' N, 25°35' E)

Crete's hilly, rocky terrain creates problems for agriculture and also makes access to the fields difficult. The donkey, a traditional mode of travel, transport, and towing, is the animal best suited to the topography of the island. It remains widely used today, as in this fertile plain of the Lassithi plateau. The local climate, considered one of the healthiest and gentlest in Europe, may favor the exceptional longevity of the inhabitants of Crete. Yet the virtues of the Cretan diet, in which olives and olive oil reign supreme, surely also play a role. Cretans, however, are not the only group of people who commonly live a full century; the Vilcabamba Valley in Ecuador also has many centenarians. Medical progress and improved health conditions around the world are gradually extending the average human life expectancy, which now stands at 66 years. But the duration of life on Earth remains very uneven; in Japan and Canada, people on average live to the age of 80, whereas in the least developed countries three out of four people die before the age of 50.

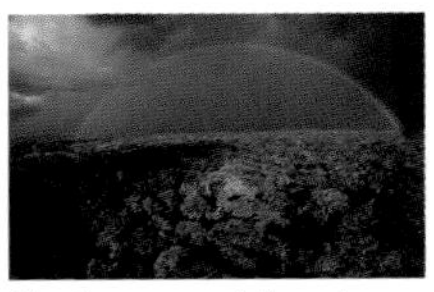

**PAGES 324–325**
STORM OVER THE AMAZON RAINFOREST NEAR TÉFÉ, AMAZONAS STATE, BRAZIL
(3°32' S, 64°53' W)

The Amazon rainforest covers 64 percent of Brazil's land area. The Amazon is the most extensive tropical forest ecosystem in the world, covering 1.4 million square miles (3.7 million km²), comprising one-third of the tropical forests in the world. These forests shelter 90 percent of the world's biological heritage, making them the richest regions of the globe. The inventory of animal and plant lifeforms on the planet, however, is far from complete, especially in tropical regions, and it is estimated that 12.5 million species are yet to be discovered. This research is of particular interest to the pharmaceutical industry; in fact, more than half of all medicines used today contain as an active ingredient a natural substance extracted from plants or animals. Every day, nearly 78 square miles (200 km²) of forest disappear forever from the face of the Earth, taking with them an inestimable number of species whose secrets will never be known.

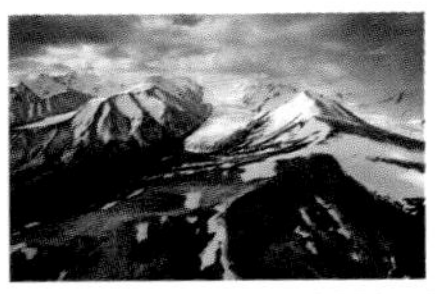

**PAGES 326–327**
GLACIER NEAR MOUNT IT-TISH, YSYK-KÖL REGION, KYRGYZSTAN
(41°50' N, 78°10' E)

There are some 3,000 glaciers in this region of Kyrgyzstan, and they cover such a wide area—(2,500 square miles, or 6,500 km²)—that some of them have not even been named. Their slow descent hollows out valleys in the Tien Shan mountain chain, which has the largest number of peaks in the world after the Himalayas. The highest of these, Pik Pobedy, reaches 24,406 ft (7,439 m). Right in the heart of Central Asia, surrounded by Uzbekistan, Tajikistan, Kazakhstan, and China, Kyrgyzstan lies at an average height of 9,800 ft (3,000 m). Steep, craggy mountains cover 95 percent of the land, leaving very little space for agricultural settlements. Because of this, there is a tradition of nomadism which has continued through to the present day.

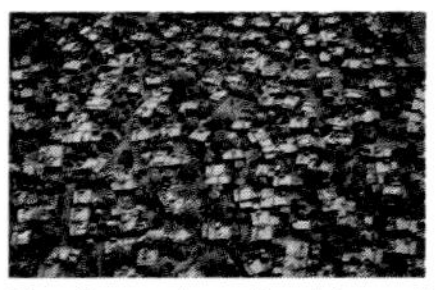

**PAGES 328–329**
DOGON VILLAGE NEAR BANDIAGARA, MALI
(14°23' N, 3°39' W)

The Dogon have lived in northeastern Mali for more than five centuries. They are sedentary farmers who originally fled to the region bordering the cliff of Bandiagara, near Mopti, in order to escape the spread of Islam. Their villages are made up of walled residences, each of which houses one family. Built of *banco* (a mixture of earth and straw), the homes are rectangular in shape and without windows, and they feature terraced roofs used for drying harvests. Each residence has several seed lofts for storing grain reserves, raised on stones, usually cylindrical, and covered with cone-shaped straw roofs. The Dogon, who number as many as 300,000, are known for their craftsmanship as well as their animist practices. The wealth of traditional Dogon culture led to the inclusion of the cliff of Bandiagara on the UNESCO list of World Heritage sites in 1989.

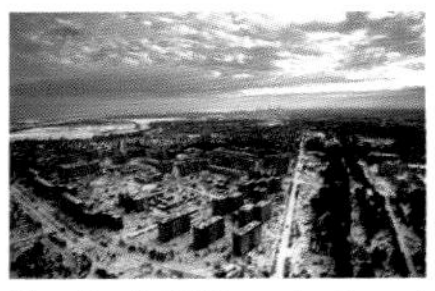

**PAGES 330–331**
ABANDONED CITY OF PRIPIAT, NEAR THE NUCLEAR POWER PLANT AT CHERNOBYL, UKRAINE
(51°21' N, 30°09' E)

The April 1986 explosion of a reactor at the Chernobyl power plant in Ukraine caused the worst civilian nuclear catastrophe of all time. A radioactive cloud escaped from the destroyed reactor and contaminated wide expanses in a spotted pattern, not only in Ukraine but also in Belarus and nearby Russia. The 120 closest neighboring localities, including Pripiat (2 miles from the epicenter, population 50,000), were evacuated, although not until some time after the accident. The cloud, pushed by winds, spread over Europe. Today the exact number of victims is not certain, but it is estimated that several million people suffer from illnesses linked to the radiation, such as deformities, cancers, and immune deficiencies. In December 2000 the last reactor of the power station, kept in operation to produce 9 percent of the country's electricity, was finally shut down, in exchange for Western aid of $2.3 billion for the construction of two other nuclear stations. The nuclear industry has yet to solve the problem of disposing of highly radioactive, long-lasting waste products, generated by 442 reactors in 35 countries, which are accumulating in stockpiling centers.

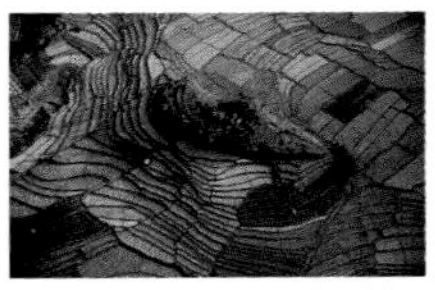

**PAGES 332–333**
ISLET IN THE TERRACED RICE FIELDS OF BALI, INDONESIA
(8°34' S, 115°13' E)

The Balinese, organized into *subaks* (farming cooperatives), have exploited the volcanic landscape and the approximately 150 waterways of their island by erecting a vast irrigation system, allowing them to grow rice. Water retained in the hills is directed into the terraced fields through a network of canals. Rice is considered by the Indonesian farmers to be a gift of the gods. Temples are erected in the middle of the rice fields and, at each stage in the harvest, offerings are made in honor of Dewi Sri, the goddess of rice. The introduction of a new, rapid-growing variety of rice in the 1970s and the (often heavy) use of fertilizers and pesticides has increased the number of annual harvests from two to three, making Indonesia the third-leading producer of rice in the world, after China and India. In 2001 Indonesia produced 51 million metric tons, 11.8 percent of the total world production. Rice is the staple food for over half of the population of the world.

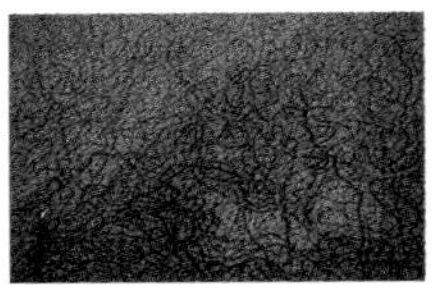

**PAGES 334–335**
COW IN A SWAMPY RIVER, RABAT, MOROCCO
(33°57' N, 6°48' W)

The region of Rabat, around the capital city, like the whole northern area of Morocco's Atlantic coast, enjoys relatively abundant precipitation (as much as 30 inches, or 800 mm, per year). In this part of the country the November and March rains feed the rivers and cause major flooding. However, from May onward a warm, dry, southeast wind, the *chergui*, gradually dries out the riverbeds. The beds become swampy and are covered with a short-lived carpet of grasses and flowers, which attract a few cows that have drifted away from neighboring herds searching for food. Cattle-rearing, made up largely of local breeds raised for both their milk and their meat, is relatively small-scale in Morocco, with just 2.6 million head. As in many Mediterranean countries, the populations of goat (5.2 million) and sheep (16.7 million) are far greater.

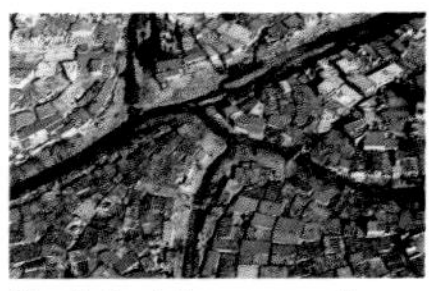

**PAGES 336–337**
SHANTYTOWN, PORT-AU-PRINCE, HAITI
(18°32' N, 72°20' W)

Capital of the poorest country in the world, Port-au-Prince has always known destitution and violence. In this small and densely populated land, 80 percent of the people live below the poverty line and more than 5 percent have been affected by Aids, but it attracts very little international aid from a world that is weary of its ever-present political corruption. Haiti is a hub of the drug trade and is in a state of permanent armed conflict, with around one hundred people killed every month. The country is effectively at the mercy of the *chimères*, armed gangs that live in the shantytowns and terrorize the population. Out of 1 billion poor people in the world, 750 million live in urban areas without homes and basic utilities, as is the case here, where sewers run down the middle of the road. Such extreme conditions can lead to exceptional initiatives, and this has happened in Port-au-Prince, where the people have banded together to counteract the deficiencies of the state: as best they can, they arrange for garbage to be collected and disposed of, and they try to look after their own security by setting up associations for mutual protection.

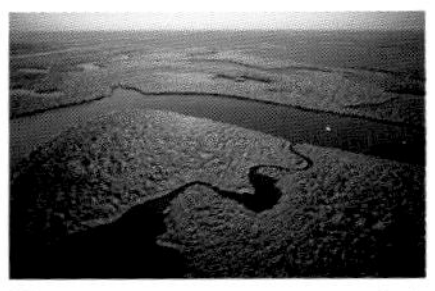

**PAGES 338–339**
MANGROVES IN EVERGLADES NATIONAL PARK, FLORIDA, UNITED STATES (25°27' N, 80°53' W)

The mangrove swamps of the Everglades, situated at the extreme southern tip of Florida, lie at the point of convergence of the fresh water from Lake Okeechobee and the salt water from the Gulf of Mexico. The Everglades have already been reduced by half in size by drainage and diking which began in 1880 to create greater urban and agricultural spaces. Since 1947 the 2,300 square miles (6,000 km²) of Everglades National Park have protected one-fifth of the original wetland. Numerous and diverse fauna takes refuge there, particularly 40 species of mammals including the endangered manatee, and 347 species of birds. The biological importance of the site is unanimously recognized: a Biosphere Reserve since 1976, a UNESCO World Heritage site since 1979, and a Wetland of International Importance since 1987. Despite this recognition, the Everglades were placed on UNESCO's World Heritage in Danger List in 1993. Population growth (900 people move to Florida every day) and industrial, urban, and agricultural pollution have overwhelmed this outstanding site. To avoid an ecological and economic disaster, an ambitious and comprehensive program is working to restore the ecosystem, providing drinking water for the region and preventing seawater from entering the overexploited groundwater supply.

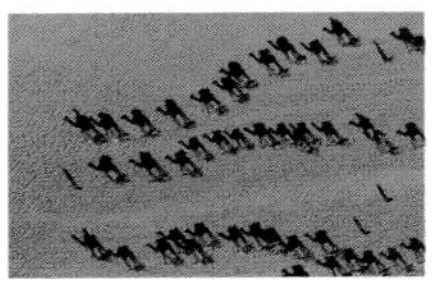

**PAGES 340–341**
DROMEDARY CARAVANS NEAR FACHI, TÉNÉRÉ DESERT, NIGER
(18°14' N, 11°40' E)

For decades the Tuareg have traded salt by driving camel caravans over the 485 miles (785 km) between the city of Agadez and the Bilma salt marshes. The camels, ridden in single file, travel in convoys at a rate of 25 miles (40 km) per day, despite temperatures reaching 114.8°F (46°C) in the shade, and loads of nearly 220 pounds (100 kg) per animal. Fachi, the only major town on the Azalaï (salt caravan) route, is an indispensable stop. Caravans, at one time made up of as many as 20,000 camels, generally are limited today to 100 animals; they are gradually being replaced by trucks. The drop in caravans and camel-breeding, the droughts of the 1970s and 1980s that took a heavy toll on livestock, and the conflicts of the 1990s have heralded the slow settlement of the Tuareg peoples. The Aïr and Ténéré reserves—an outstanding collection of landscapes, plant life (more than 350 species), and animals (at least 40 different mammal species)—where most of them live are seriously affected by poaching and overexploitation.

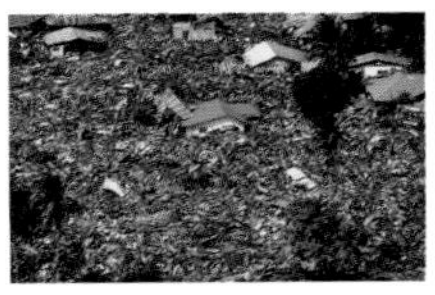

**PAGES 342–343**
BANDA ACEH AFTER THE TSUNAMI OF DECEMBER 26, 2004, SUMATRA, INDONESIA
(5°32' N, 95°19' E)

On December 26, 2004, the Indo-Australian tectonic plate slid violently beneath the Indonesian plate, causing an earthquake measuring 9 on the Richter scale—the energy equivalent to 30,000 atomic bombs. The shockwaves traveled with the speed of a jet plane across the Indian Ocean and, as it approached the coast, the quake took the form of a tsunami, a colossal wave which in some places was over 30 feet (10 meters) high. The coasts of Sri Lanka, Thailand, India, Burma, Indonesia, and the Maldives were ravaged, and 295,000 people lost their lives in the disaster. It created an unprecedented burst of solidarity, uniting governments and people all over the world. Money, materials, expertise, and transport flooded in, and no tragedy has ever roused compassion on such a large scale. This may have been due partly to media coverage of the catastrophe, partly to the fact that the countries affected were known to so many tourists, and partly to our renewed fear of the power of nature. We might well ask, however, why a disaster such as the Tangshan earthquake in China in July 1976, which caused the deaths of 242,000 people, did not have the same impact on the world's emotions.

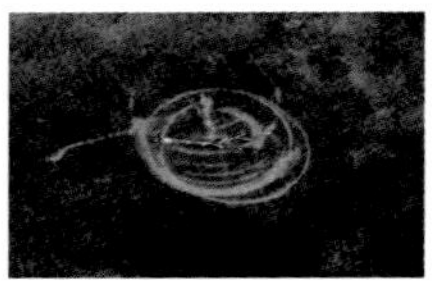

**PAGES 344–345**
TREE TRUNK IN A CORAL REEF, DOMINICAN REPUBLIC
(18°20' N, 68°55' W)

In the Caribbean Sea, between the islands of Saona and Catalina, a tree trunk caught in the coral reefs spins around, tracing these unusual patterns. The Dominican Republic is situated in the eastern part of Hispaniola, an island in the Greater Antilles. The southern coast of the island is bordered by the Caribbean with its 10,000 square miles (26,000 km²) of coral reefs. These form natural barriers that are vital to life in the region, particularly as they provide protection against hurricanes. However, these reefs are subject to ever greater threats, not only from the increasing number of hurricanes, but also from the impact of agricultural pollution as well as that caused by hydrocarbon emissions from pleasure boats. Coastal fishing is not an issue here, as it is not well developed owing to a lack of infrastructure. It is estimated that two-thirds of the region's coral reefs are now in danger, and if the pollution continues, the whole economy will suffer. The Dominican Republic, which is the region's prime tourist resort, draws most of its revenue from the two million visitors who come here every year, mainly to enjoy the beaches and the wonders of its marine life.

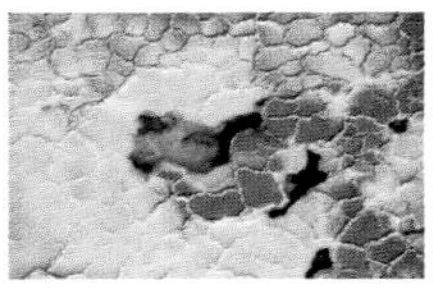

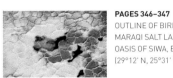

**PAGES 346–347**
OUTLINE OF BIRKET MARAQI SALT LAKE IN THE OASIS OF SIWA, EGYPT
(29°12' N, 25°31' E)

Under the burning sun of northwest Egypt, the evaporation of water from the shallower parts of this salt lake has cracked its bed of sand and mud, forming these extremely hard, rounded wrinkles. Here and there salt forms a white crust, tracing the outline of the bluish, stagnant pool. The salt concentration in the water is so high that no living organism can survive. However, the shores of these lakes are shaded by palm trees and olive trees, fed by the oasis's 230 freshwater springs. Thus, Siwa's 15,000 inhabitants grow 300,000 date palms and 70,000 olive trees. Fresh water is one of the scarcest resources on the planet, accounting for only 2.5 percent of the total volume of water on the Earth, and of that proportion, 77 percent is trapped as ice at the poles and in glaciers. Liquid fresh water is unequally distributed, being rare in the tropics but plentiful on the equator and in temperate regions. Even where it is abundant, it is still precious. Its quality is constantly deteriorating as a result of contamination from excess organic matter, fertilizers, and other chemicals released by agriculture, industry, and the general population.

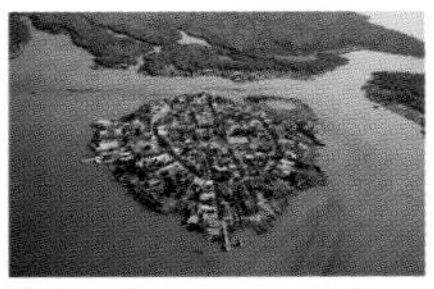

**PAGES 348–349**
MEXCALTITÁN, NAYARIT STATE, MEXICO
(21°54' N, 105°28' W)

Rising from the marshy meanders of a vast coastal lagoon, the village of Mexcaltitán rests on an isolated spit of sand 1,300 feet (400 m) long on the northwest Pacific coast of Mexico in the state of Nayarit. In September, toward the end of the rainy season, the waters of the lagoon flood the village streets, forcing the inhabitants to travel by canoe and giving the place the look of a "Mexican Venice." Some historians see the village as the mythical island of Aztlán, where the Aztecs reputedly originated. Half land, half water, Mexcaltitán reflects the rich natural heritage that surrounds it—a network of canals threads through the mangroves, home to more than 300 species of birds. Mexico's biodiversity is among the richest on the planet. With just 1.4 percent of the world's land surface, it has more mammal species than any other country (450). Mexico is also home to 10 percent of the known species of each animal and vegetable genus.

supplies, and accelerating the spread of infectious diseases. It is the relative stability of the climate during the last few millennia that has made human civilization possible, but this stability—unusual in terms of geological history—is now at risk, primarily because of the use of fossil fuels in industrial production and energy consumption. This is why more and more people in authority all over the world are sounding the alarm. According to Sir David King, the British government's Chief Scientific Advisor, climate change is "the most severe problem we are facing today—more serious even than the threat of terrorism."

The scientific foundations of a new energy system have been laid over the last thirty years. Technologies now exist for exploiting abundant and renewable sources of energy—wind, sun, geothermal power, bio-energy—and using them in the framework of a highly efficient infrastructure that will substantially reduce the amount of waste inherent in our current systems. Advances in all areas—from composite plastics to electronics and biotechnology—are now being adapted with a view to creating a new system of permanent energy supply, and the commercial results are promising.

In the last five years, wind energy has advanced at an annual average rate of 28 percent, solar energy at a rate of 30 percent, which means that production is being virtually doubled every two and a half years. These new forms of energy could have a revolutionary impact. Among the immediate effects are a substantial reduction in the cost of technological progress, economic growth, and widespread political support, all of which in turn pave the way for other political reforms and for increased growth.

The champions of fossil fuels tend to ignore the rapid expansion of what they consider to be minor industries. However, such growth rates can swiftly transform a new industry from playing a minor role to becoming a market leader, thereby completely changing the balance of power.

The solar energy industry continues to develop, while wind energy is now claiming its place among the principal suppliers—in some places, it is even competing cost-wise with conventional electricity. The impact of these industries is far from negligible, and they represent an annual investment of more than $30 billion. Today the worldwide capacity of the wind industry is sufficient to supply electricity to more than 22 million homes in Europe. According to some estimates, these new renewable sources of energy are actually fulfilling the domestic electricity requirements of more than 300 million people.

Biological fuels are also enjoying a dynamic increase in growth. Worldwide production of ethanol for energy purposes has increased at an annual rate of almost 17 percent since 2000. Ethanol is derived from sugar cane, and it now provides 30 percent of the fuel used by cars in Brazil, where its retail price is often lower than that of petrol. Worldwide production of biodiesel increased by 18 percent between 2002 and 2003. The EU has set itself a target of 20 percent renewable fuels for transport by 2020, and between 2001 and 2003 its production of biofuels increased by 43 percent.

Although these "new renewable" forms of energy (excluding traditional forms of hydraulic and biomass power) still constitute only a modest 2 percent of the world's consumption, solar, wind, geothermal, and bio forms of energy are vastly more abundant than fossil fuels, and are potentially in a far stronger position to meet the world's requirements. Renewable sources can produce electricity, can power all systems of heating and freezing, can drive machines like water pumps, and can provide fuel—in other words, they can replace all conventional forms of energy.

Furthermore, they are already sufficiently developed to enter the market now. The $25 billion invested in renewable energy in 2004 is the equivalent of about one-sixth of worldwide investments in all electrical installations. These industries are also attracting some of the leading companies in the international field, including BP, General Electric, Mitsubishi, Royal Dutch/Shell, and Siemens.

The vast potential of these renewable sources is evident from the rate of growth over the last ten years, due mainly to the efforts of eight countries which together constitute 80 percent of the world market for wind and solar energy and liquid biofuels. These eight leaders are as follows: Brazil for biofuel; China for small-scale hydraulics, biofuel, and solar heating; Denmark for wind and biofuel; Germany for wind and solar power; India for wind and biofuel; Japan for solar power; Spain for wind; the US for wind and biofuel.

Unlike oil and coal production, the development of renewable forms of energy over the last ten years reflects a series of political decisions as opposed to simple location of resources. Among the successful measures taken by these eight leading countries are availability of electricity at an attractive price, low-cost financing, reduced taxes and other forms of subsidy, fixed standards, and a heightened public awareness. At the other end of the spectrum, countries such as Canada, France, Russia, and the United Kingdom, all of whom have abundant renewable resources, have scarcely begun to explore their own potential owing to a lack of any coherent national policy.

While public investment in research and development (R&D) of these new technologies is of vital importance, it is only by creating markets that the techniques and economics of production can advance and thereby bring down the costs. These are very limited compared to the gains, with billions of dollars being invested in R&D and in equipment by the private sector.

The eight leading countries have shown that it is possible to create a rapidly developing market for renewable energy. Laws aimed at promoting this have been permanently introduced into various countries: at the beginning of 2005, China passed a law favoring renewable fuels for electricity, heating, and transport, the objective being that they should meet 17 percent of the nation's requirements by 2020. It is still too soon to know whether China will achieve this ambitious aim, but many of its experts are optimistic. If it does succeed, low-cost technology linked to renewable sources of energy in Chinese factories could change the world.

The growing number of countries—from Mexico to the Philippines —that are now on the verge of following the example of major states like China and India will soon take the market in renewable energy to a point at which it is certain to dominate just as oil did a hundred years ago. Legislation in several countries during the last two years will lead to further progress, and the only remaining question is when and how fast these policies will succeed, and whether these alternatives will take off on a global level.

If renewable forms of energy are to help strengthen the economy, create jobs, reduce dependence on fossil fuels, improve health, and limit the emission of greenhouse gases, it is essential to improve technological efficiency, reduce costs, and develop industrial means of

314

**UNFINISHED NUCLEAR POWER STATION, ARMINTZA, BASQUE COUNTRY, SPAIN**
(43°25' N, 2°54' W)

In 1984, Spain put a moratorium on the building of new nuclear power stations and on completing those under construction. Renewed in 1992, the moratorium left five plants, including that of Armintza, in an unfinished state. The country has nine nuclear power stations, which meet 30 percent of its electricity needs. European countries remain divided over the nuclear question. France, which with fifty-nine has the most nuclear reactors, has committed itself to this energy source, which provides 72 percent of its electricity. Austria, Denmark, and Italy, on the other hand, have virtually abandoned it. In the United States, nuclear power is the primary source for 15 percent of electricity generated. Although nuclear energy allows emissions of greenhouse gas to be reduced while renewable energy sources are developed, it comes with a variety of other risks, such as those related to radioactive waste, nuclear accidents, and terrorist attack. Whatever policy is adopted, the uranium that powers nuclear reactors is not renewable. If we want to significantly reduce greenhouse gas emissions—which could triple by 2100 and quadruple by 2150 if nothing is done—we must reduce our energy consumption.

## ⟩ THE STATE OF THE WORLD

**ENERGY SUPPLY DOMINATED BY FOSSIL FUELS**
Fossil fuels (oil, coal, natural gas): **79.6%**
Nuclear: **6.8%**
Renewable and waste materials: **10.9%**
Hydraulic: **2.2%**
Other renewable sources (solar, wind, geothermal): **0.5%**

**GROWING DEMAND**
Demand for energy is growing by **2%** per year.
The amount of oil consumed in less than **7 weeks**
today is the same as that consumed in **1 year** in **1950**.
If there is no change in the rate of energy consumption, world
demand will have increased by **65%** between **1995** and **2020**.

**THE FORGOTTEN PEOPLE**
In **2003**, almost **1.6 billion** had no access to electricity.

## ⟩ WHAT ENERGY SOURCES WILL SATISFY FUTURE NEEDS?

The only source of natural energy received
by the Earth is the sun. The other renewable
source of energy is enclosed within the
Earth: geothermal.

**THE REIGN OF OIL IS LIMITED**
A source that is easy to transport: oil accounts for **95%**
of energy consumption in the transport sector.
The most powerful energy potential: **1 ton of gasoline**
= 42 billion J (joules), **1 ton of biofuel** = 2 to 15 billion J,
**1 ton of waste** = 7 billion J
At the present rate of consumption, there is no guarantee that
nations now dependent on oil will be able to afford it in the future.

**AN IMMINENT AND IRREVERSIBLE BREAK IN THE PATTERN OF
ENERGY SUPPLY: A PEAK IN THE WORLD'S PRODUCTION OF OIL**
It will not be long before half the world's oil resources will have
been consumed. Oil production will then have reached its peak.
After that, production will no longer be able to meet demand,
and will decline until reserves are exhausted.
This scenario is already the case in the USA: oil production peaked
in **1970**, and since then the amount extracted has been in
decline; in **30 years** production has fallen by more than **30%**.

**RENEWABLE SOURCES: REAL POTENTIAL WITH NO RISK
OF EXHAUSTION**
Biomass: depending on the species, wood renews itself in
**5 to 200 years**
The sun: the energy produced by **11** days of sunshine on the
Earth's surface is equivalent to the entire estimated reserves
of fossil fuels (oil, gas, coal). But as a source of energy it is
intermittent and diffuse.

## ⟩ MAINTAINING ACCESS TO ENERGY IN THE NORTH AND GIVING IT TO THE SOUTH

**OIL RESERVES CONCENTRATED AND CONTROLLED**
The energy market is dominated by a small number of companies
which share oil deposits but are themselves dependent on a small
number of oil-producing countries.
**65.4%** of oil reserves are in the Middle East, and control over
access to these reserves is and will remain a source of
geopolitical tension.

**RENEWABLE SOURCES OF ENERGY, DECENTRALIZED AND
ACCESSIBLE TO SUITABLE TECHNOLOGY**
Deposits of renewable energy not necessarily comparable to oil,
but more equitably distributed.
Forms of energy available in sufficient quantities to meet
**25%** of current requirements.
At present only **15%** of technically exploitable forms
of renewable energy are being used.

## ⟩ ADAPTING TO INCREASINGLY LESS ACCESSIBLE ENERGY

**THE PRICE OF OIL WILL CONTINUE TO RISE.**
Once oil production has peaked, the gap between supply
and demand will result in ever-rising prices.
This constant rise in the price of a barrel will automatically
reduce the number of people who can afford it.

**COMPETITIVENESS OF RENEWABLE ENERGY**
Competitive renewable forms of energy currently cost
from **$50** per barrel.
In the last **30 years**, the price of photovoltaic solar energy
has dropped around **50%** every **10 years**.

## ⟩ A CARBON-FREE ECONOMY

In a situation where energy supplies are
increasingly difficult to access, activities
that do not depend on fossil fuels will be
at an advantage. Such alternative models
already exist.

**BEDZED: AN EXPERIMENTAL HOUSING DEVELOPMENT
IN SOUTH LONDON**
No fossil fuels = no $CO_2$ emissions
Local building materials = lower transport costs
Total energy consumption: **-70%**
Use of renewable energy forms

**ROCKY MOUNTAINS INSTITUTE: AN ULTRA-ECONOMICAL
RESEARCH CENTER IN COLORADO, US**
Altitude: **7,200 ft (2,200 m)** in the Rocky Mountains
Energy saving: **90%** on electricity, **99%** on heating
Stores heat from the air
Return on investment in **10 months** (average market price)

**THE POSITIVE HOUSE**
Average energy consumption in French homes is
**278 kWh per m² per year**. A few years ago, the Swiss and
the Germans launched the *Positiv Haus*, which produces its own
energy through its design and use of renewable sources.

**SHELL ECO MARATHON: ANNUAL RACE AT NOGARO (FRANCE)
FOR HIGH-PERFORMANCE VEHICLES OF THE FUTURE**
The winner covers the greatest distance on one liter of gasoline.
The record is **3,500 km** on one liter of gasoline, which is
**245 times** better than a small family saloon car.
The vehicles are currently unsuitable for daily use but they show
the potential for improvement (some **10 times** better than
ordinary cars).

---

⟩ **GREAT BARRIER REEF, QUEENSLAND, AUSTRALIA** (16°55' S, 146°03' E)

Extending over an area of 89,000 square miles (230,000 km²), the Great Barrier Reef is the world's largest coral reef. Coral
formations, the world's only relief that is biological in nature, are polyps that live symbiotically with photosensitive algae,
zooxanthellae, which allow their hosts to form calcareous skeletons. One of the most fragile and most complex systems
of biodiversity, coral reefs are now at risk from a large number of potentially devastating threats: population growth, global
warming (the coral is sensitive to increases in water temperature), and pressures from human sources (intensive fishing,
urbanization of coastal areas, the dumping of refuse, and chemical products used in farming). Today 20 percent of the world's
coral reefs have been destroyed, 24 percent are at serious risk of destruction, and another 26 percent are at potential future
risk. Thanks to severe protective measures and bans on coral removal, some affected coral colonies are starting to regenerate,
like those of the Great Barrier. But these reefs are still very much in the minority.

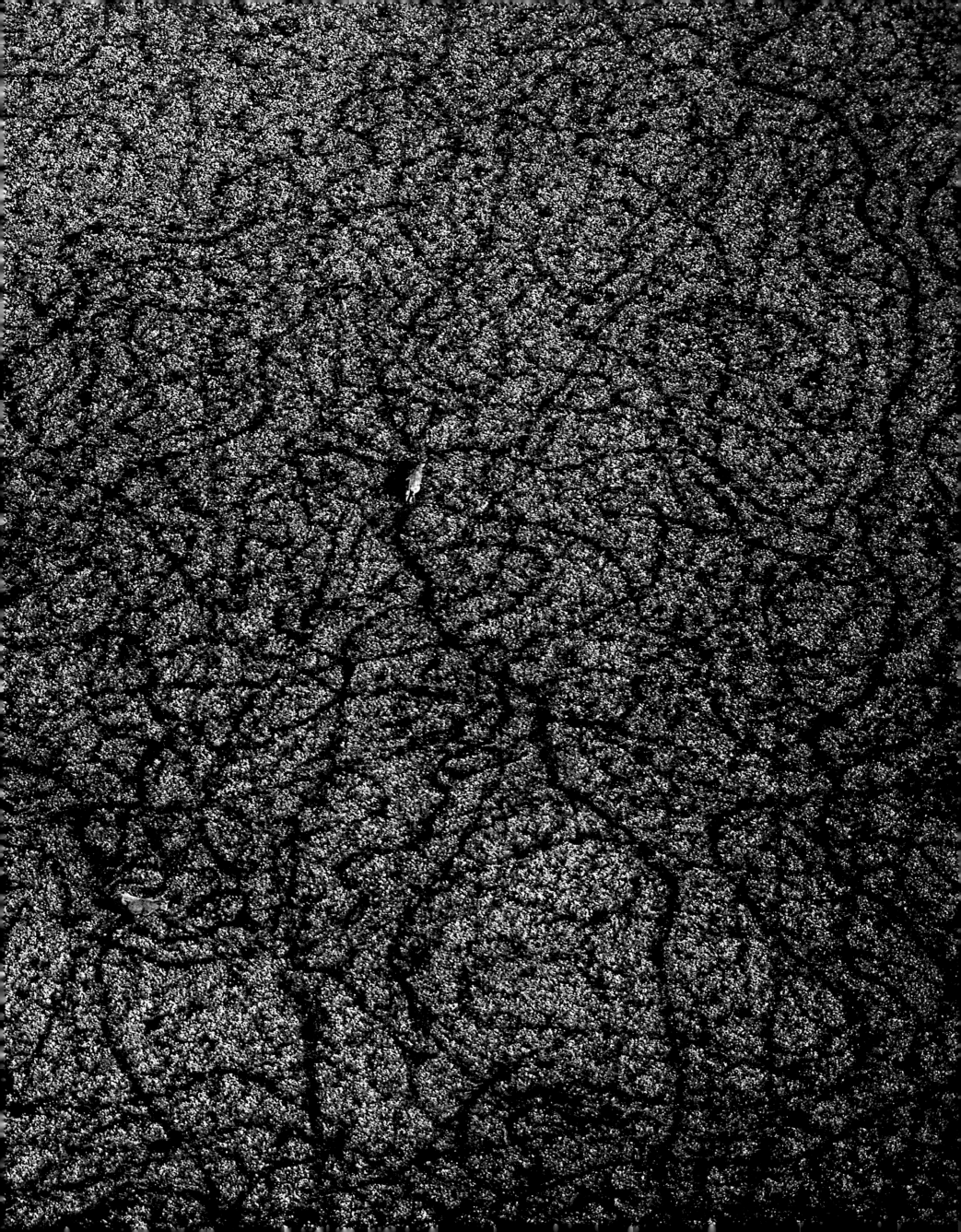

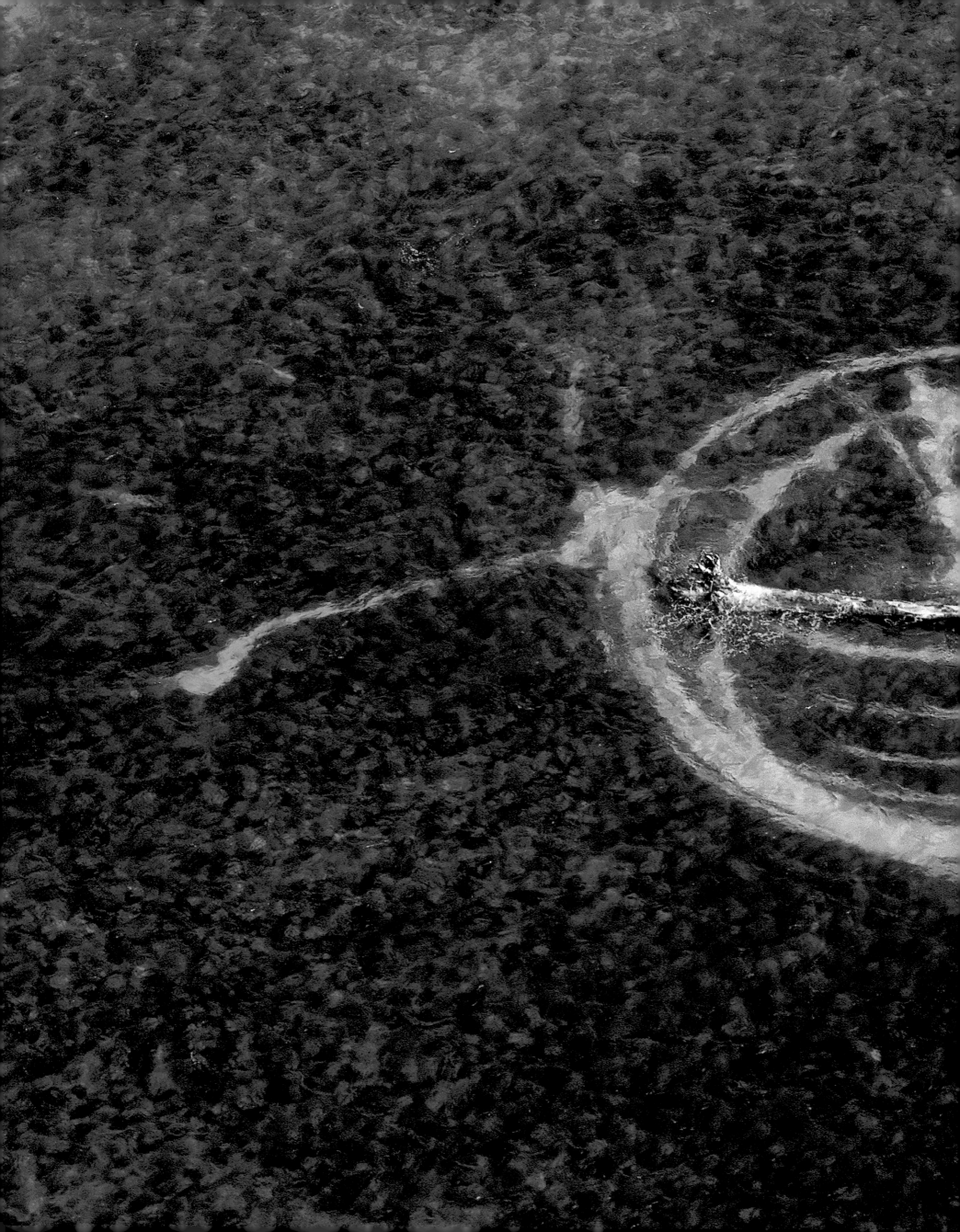

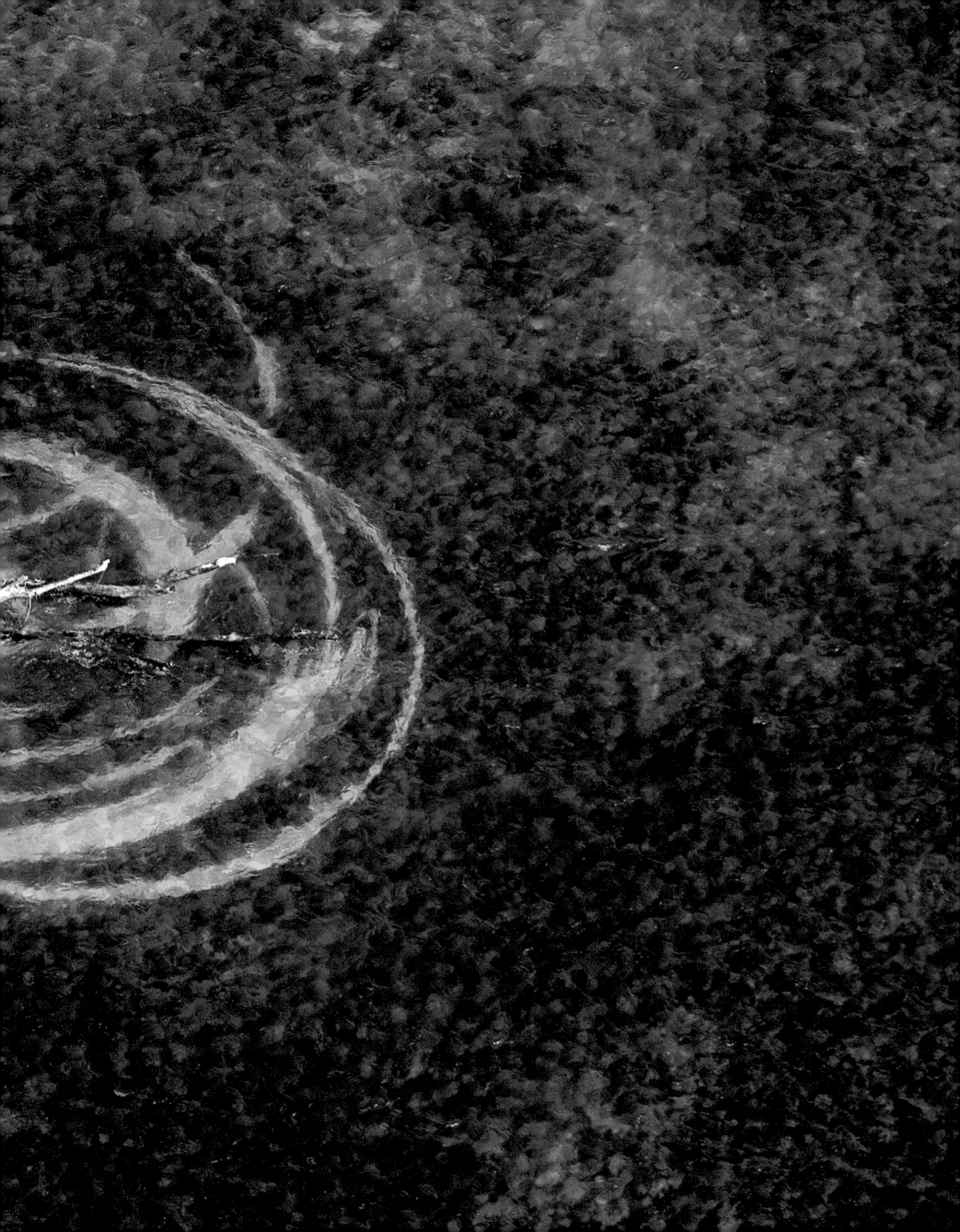

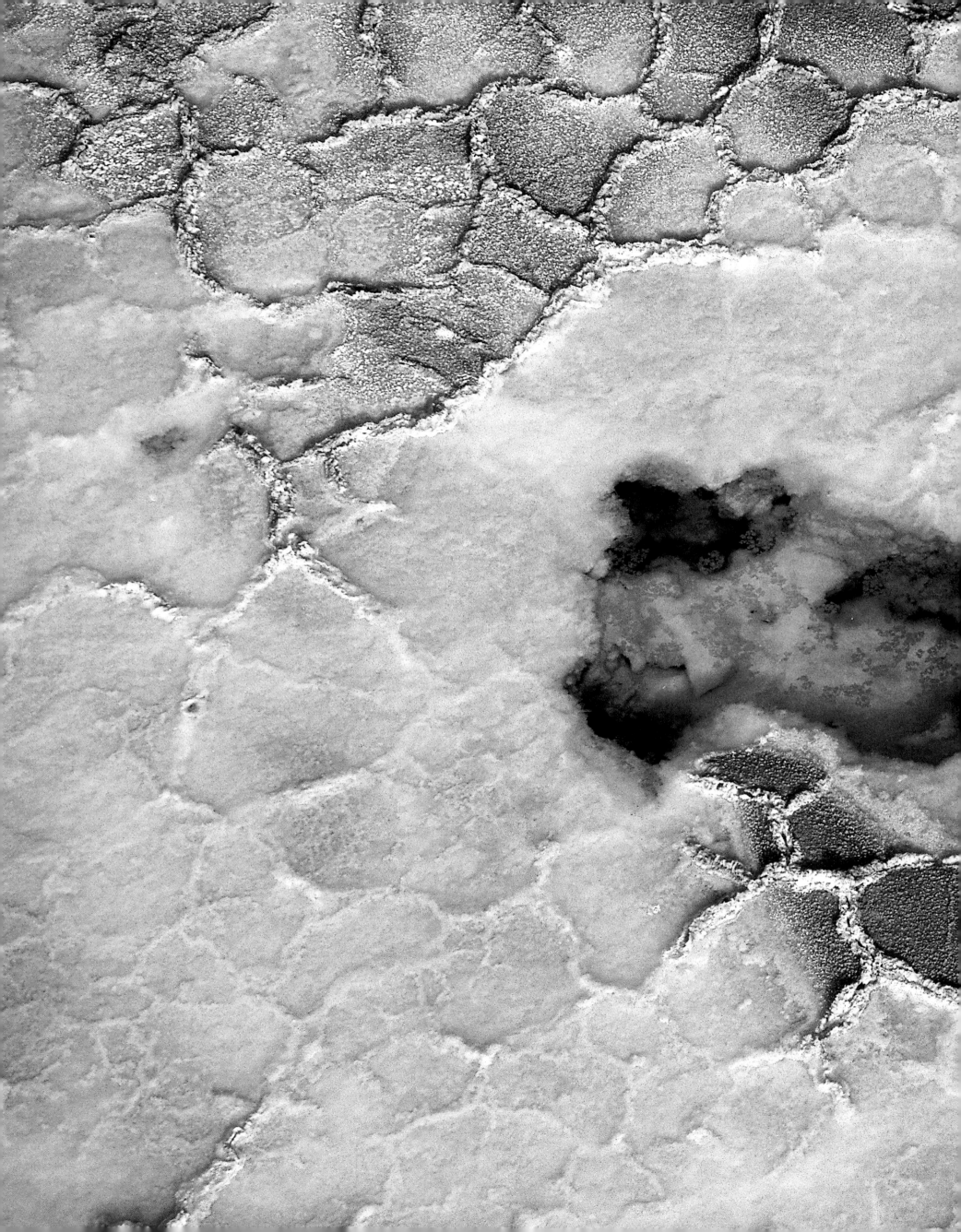

# SUSTAINABLE DEVELOPMENT

The need for food, energy, and consumer products is constantly growing along with the world's population. The pressure on our ecosystems from modern methods of production and consumption is a threat to the ecological resources that provide the bulk of what we consume. Industrialized countries bear the major responsibility because of their impact on the environment, but there is a risk that countries in transition are doing their best to imitate them. A policy of sustainable development requires changes both in international relations and institutions and in the responsibilities of the individual. New obligations must be imposed on states, on local authorities, on businesses, and ultimately—at the very end of this chain—on consumers themselves.

Neil Armstrong's first step on the moon in July 1969 was ultimately less significant than the view it gave him of Earth—a small, fragile, blue ball. The metaphor of the spacecraft in which all resources must be used sparingly is the exact opposite of the cowboy economy, which knows no limits in its exploitation of the land expanding endlessly toward the west. This is the global vision that has imprinted itself on the human mind. But to move from awareness of problems to the implementation of solutions requires a more discerning and detailed approach. The views of the world that are presented in this book take the perspective that is required to showcase the variety of landscapes and the many different ways in which the interaction between mankind and nature can be seen, and above all the omnipresent human pressure that is threatening the delicate balance of the biosphere.

During the 1970s, there was a degree of interest in the pollution caused by a small number of industrial concerns, though their impact was only local. During the 1980s, whole continents were affected by acid rain and by radiation from the Chernobyl disaster. Then finally, protection of the ozone layer and the battle against climate change took the environmental battle onto a worldwide level.

Paradoxically, the rise of the environment as a global issue has been accompanied by a reappraisal of less intense forms of pollution whose accumulative effects are proving to be as serious locally as globally, and which will have an increasing long-term impact on future generations. Overfarming threatens the quality of water and the biological equilibrium; road traffic contaminates the air and contributes to the greenhouse effect; domestic households produce vast quantities of waste. And it is by distinguishing these different forms of pollution that we come to see just how dependent we are on our environment.

The Millennium Ecosystem Assessment (MA) undertaken by more than 1,300 experts and published in March 2005 recognized the intrinsic importance of biodiversity and ecosystems, and it showed how vital their roles are to human wellbeing and to the reduction of poverty.

These "ecosystem services" may be divided into different categories. They are characterized by self-maintenance and ensure the continued basic functioning of the systems on which everything else depends: the food cycle, the constitution of the soil, and primary plant production. Provisioning services provide directly for human consumption—food, fresh water, wood, materials, fuels. Regulating services ensure the regulation of the climate, water, diseases, and water purification. And finally, cultural services deal with matters aesthetic, spiritual, and educational. Of the 24 services evaluated, 15—or more than 60 percent—are degraded or are being used in an unsustainable manner. The continuation of current practices and the general adoption of Western modes of development by the developing countries can only accelerate the process of degradation during the coming years. The environment is not a luxury—it is the foundation of all development, and this can only be viable in the long term if new and far-reaching policies are adopted.

For example, the field of biological production—that of the ecosystems that provide the ecological services—is measured by an indicator called the "ecological footprint." This indicator is increasing at an annual rate of 2.5 percent in a world whose area is, of course, limited. This expansion is at the expense of natural spaces which ensure the reproduction of life and a natural balance. According to some experts, the tolerable threshold is around 2.1 hectares per person, and this has been reduced ever since the 1970s. Today, owing to the increase in the world's population, it stands at 1.9 hectares per person. The average American takes up six times this area, the average European three times, whereas half the people on the planet are still below even this mark. However, their aspirations may lead them as well to step over the threshold if they adopt the Western style of development.

For this reason, in 1997 the General Assembly of the United Nations called for more rational and above all more efficient use of the Earth's natural resources. Such an aim can only be achieved through a massive revolution in technology and social structure. This would involve the separation of economic growth from the consumption of

Not far from Braunschweig, in northern Germany, an avalanche of mineral water, beer, fruit juice, and carbonated drinks of all kinds is spread out in a grocery store's warehouse lot. Bottled water, estimated as a $22 billion market per year, leads all competitors in the world beverage industry. This most basic of bottled drinks is increasingly successful; world consumption is growing by 12 percent a year. One and a half million metric tons of plastic are used to contain the 23.5 billion gallons (89 billion liters) of mineral water distributed in the world every year. Europe alone consumes 46 percent of bottled water. Although consumption of bottled water is justified in countries where water is unsafe to drink (much of Africa, Latin America, and Asia), this is not the case in the Western world, where tap water is an equally healthy and much more eco-friendly alternative. Four-fifths of plastic bottles are not recycled and so are piling up all over the planet.

development. As regulations passed at State level cannot always control what the multinationals do, and some countries are also reluctant to adhere to international law, the United Nations have opened a dialogue directly with the business world. Kofi Annan, Secretary General of the UN, launched an initiative in 1999, the "Global Compact," proposing that the economic world should commit itself to a set of values in the domains of working rights, human rights, the fight against corruption, and environmental practices. But such changes cannot simply be imposed from on high. Necessary though they are, these initiatives will have no effect if consumers and investors fail to adopt a more ethical approach, favoring products and companies that genuinely adhere to the principles of sustainable development.

Ordinary citizens can put pressure on their country, and consumers can put pressure on those who supply the goods. In order to give official status to this "good relationship" between new forms of production and new modes of consumption, certain standards and labels have been

introduced, such as fair trade, organic food, and certification that wood is taken from sustainable forests. In March 2005, the International Organization for Standardization (ISO) set to work on a three-year program to define guidelines concerning social responsibility and sustainable development.

It would, however, be a mistake to see these problems only from the standpoint of constraint. Sustainable development offers huge economic and industrial opportunities. Environmental industries now constitute a separate economic sector, based on an ecological concept of products and services that favors reduced pollution and sensible use of resources, and is based on the complete life cycle of products starting with the raw materials.

The purchasing policies of the state and of local authorities, which amount to nearly 15 percent of GDP, can strengthen the market force of products and investments that are economically and socially sound.

Certain things based on local resources and a way of life anchored in local culture, such as local products and good quality tourism, can provide a healthy link between development and the environment. It is, after all, the main objective of sustainable development to preserve everything while both promoting and exploiting diversity.

Finally, the key to all this lies within each of us. We must find a way of binding together our various aspirations: ecological, social and economic. Human beings must renew their links with Nature. People must be made aware of and sensitive to the situation they are in, and they must also be allowed to participate in the decisions that involve them. Consumers should have at their disposal both the information

---

⌂ **GAMLA STAN, STOCKHOLM, SWEDEN** (59°20' N, 18°03' E)

Where the graceful city of Stockholm stands, the fresh waters of Lake Mälaren run into the salty undertow of the Baltic, and the land looks as if it has been torn into shreds. For the Swedish novelist Selma Lagerlöf, Stockholm is "the city that floats on the water." Indeed, the capital is built on fourteen islands, linked by forty bridges and countless ferries. These islands belong to the vast Skärgården archipelago, whose 24,000 islands are scattered over the Baltic. This photograph immortalizes Stockholm's 750th anniversary, which thousands of its 750,000 inhabitants flooded the cobbled streets of Gamla Stan to celebrate in the spring of 2002. The old town, the city's medieval heart, contains the royal palace (*Kungliga Slottet*), whose imposing square shape is visible. In 1972, Stockholm hosted the first United Nations conference on the environment. Since then, humans have still not given up many practices and policies that are unviable in the long term and which, in attacking the environment, "affect the well-being of populations and economic development throughout the world."

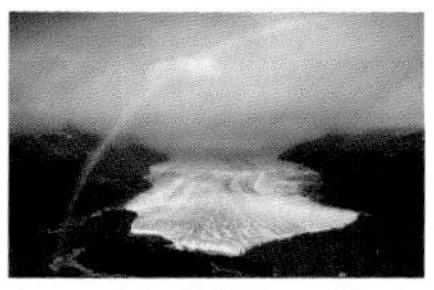

**PAGES 358–359**
PERITO MORENO GLACIER, SANTA CRUZ, ARGENTINA
(50°27' S, 73°10' W)

Created in 1937, Los Glaciares National Park is located in southern Patagonia, near the border of Chile. This protected zone, declared a UNESCO World Heritage site in 1981, contains 47 glaciers that originated from the continental glacial covering of Patagonia, the largest in the world after Antarctica and Greenland. With a frontal width of 2.5 miles (4 km) and a height of 147 feet (60 m), Perito Moreno extends for 32 miles (52 km) and moves along one of the arms of Lake Argentino, dragging rock debris torn from the banks in its wake, which erodes and shapes the landscape. Periodically, at the confluence of the two arms of the lake, the glacier interrupts the water's flow. The growing pressure of the water against the ice barrier ends up breaking it, producing an explosion that can be heard from several miles away. This phenomenon occurred sixteen times during the 20th century, and once again in March 2004. Glaciers and ice caps make up 9 percent of the Earth's land surface. Global warming may melt the ice, raising the level of the oceans by an average of 50 cm (20 inches) before the end of the 21st century and drowning the fertile shore areas.

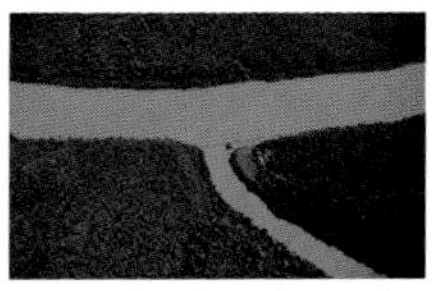

**PAGES 360–361**
CONFLUENCE OF THE RÍO URUGUAY AND A TRIBUTARY, MISIONES PROVINCE, ARGENTINA
(27°15' S, 54°03' W)

Drastically cleared to make way for farming, the tropical rainforest of Argentina is now in some areas a less effective defense against erosion than it was in the past. The heavy rains in the province of Misiones (79 inches, or 2,000 mm, per year) wash the soil and carry off significant quantities of iron-rich earth into the Río Uruguay, turning the waters a dark, reddish ocher. Carried by the river, this sediment is dumped in the estuary of the Río de la Plata—the largest on Earth—and accumulates in the access channels to the port of Buenos Aires. In 1997, to combat the sanding-up of the estuary and the pollution generated by the city, the Argentinian government and local authorities set up the EcoPlata project for the ecological and economic management of the estuary.

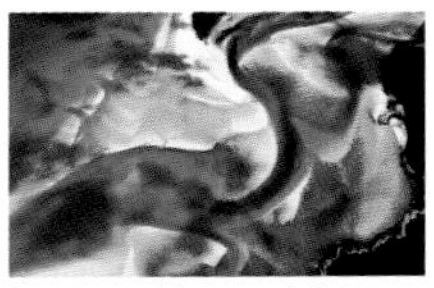

**PAGES 362–363**
SANDBANK ON THE COAST OF WHITSUNDAY ISLAND, QUEENSLAND, AUSTRALIA
(20°17' S, 148°59' E)

Innumerable coral islets and continental islands are sprinkled over the narrow corridor separating the coasts of Queensland, in northeastern Australia, from the Great Barrier Reef about 20 miles (30 km) offshore. Whitsunday Island, 43 square miles (109 km²) in area, is the largest of the 74 islands that make up the archipelago of the same name, baptized by British explorer James Cook, who discovered the islands in 1770 on Whitsunday (the Sunday of Pentecost). As seen here on Whitehaven beach, the islands' shoreline is marked by the exceptional whiteness of its sand, made up of coral sediment. This site is part of Great Barrier Marine Park, which receives more than 2 million visitors each year. Tourism, tightly regulated, has only a slight impact on this sensitive site, unlike coastal pollution and the repeated, unexplained invasions of crown-of-thorns starfish, a marine species that has damaged close to 20 percent of the reefs in the past thirty years.

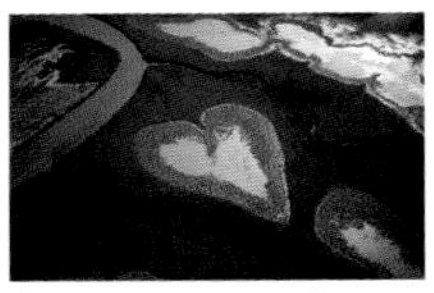

**PAGES 364–365**
HEART IN VOH, NEW CALEDONIA (FRENCH OVERSEAS TERRITORY)
(20°57' S, 164°41' E)

A mangrove swamp is a semi-aquatic forest common to muddy tropical coastlines with fluctuating tides. Made up of halophytes (plants that can grow in a saline environment), with a predominance of mangroves, these swamps cover almost one-quarter of tropical coasts and a total of some 56,000 square miles (15 million hectares) worldwide. This represents only half of their original extent, because these fragile swamps are continually shrinking due to the overexploitation of resources, agricultural and urban expansion, the creation of shrimp farms, and pollution. The mangrove nonetheless remains as indispensable to sea fauna and to the equilibrium of the shoreline as it is to the local economy. New Caledonia, a group of Pacific islands covering 7,000 square miles (18,575 km²), has 80 square miles (200 km²) of a fairly low (25 to 33 feet, or 8 to 10 m) but very dense mangrove swamp, primarily on the west coast of the largest island, Grande Terre. At certain spots in the interior that are not reached by seawater except at high tides, vegetation gives way to bare, oversalted stretches called "tannes," such as this one near the town of Voh, where nature has carved this clearing in the form of a heart.

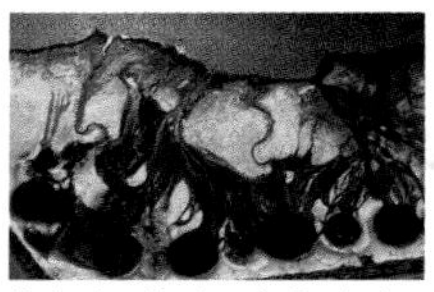

**PAGES 366–367**
URANIUM MINE IN KAKADU NATIONAL PARK, NORTHERN TERRITORY, AUSTRALIA
(12°41' S, 132°53' E)

Kakadu National Park is a rich source of uranium, making up 10 percent of the world's resources. It is divided into three plots in Aboriginal territory, Ranger, Jabiluka, and Koongarra, which are enclosed in the protected park (a UNESCO World Heritage site since 1981) but are statutorily excluded. The plan to open a mine on Jabiluka, reputed to be the richest uranium deposit in the world, was abandoned after five years of legal wrangling between the mining companies and the Mirrar Aboriginal people, the traditional owners of these sacred lands. Ranger is the only one of the three deposits that is authorized for mining. In this waste zone, large sprinklers water the marsh banks to increase evaporation and reduce the risk of dust buildup, leaving sulfate deposits. Australia also has two other large deposits of uranium, and in 2000 the country produced more than 20 percent of the uranium extracted in the world (34,400 metric tons). Uranium provides fuel for the world's nuclear sites, divided primarily between the United States, France, and Japan.

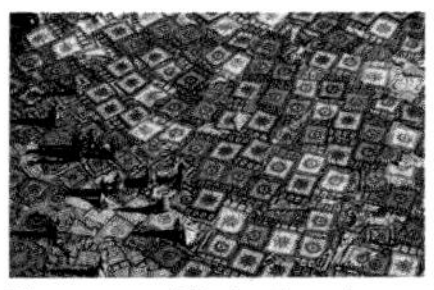

**PAGES 368–369**
COTTON FABRICS DRYING IN THE SUN IN JAIPUR, RAJASTHAN, INDIA
(26°55' N, 75°49' W)

The state of Rajasthan in northeastern India is an important center of textile production, renowned for centuries for the crafts of dyeing and printing on cotton and silk fabrics. This work is highly prized by tourists and is carried out by women. Indian women bear the brunt of the extreme poverty that affects 25 percent of the population, and traditionally Indians have a strong preference for boys, who represent the future of the name and the family, no matter how humble. They look after their parents in old age, and see to it that when they die the religious rites of cremation are properly performed. By contrast, girls leave their family when they get married and the parents have to provide a dowry, so they are often regarded as a burden. The abortion of female foetuses (now illegal but still widespread), the sudden death of baby girls, and saris that catch fire (rarely by accident) occur at all levels of society. It has been established that in certain states there are now less than 800 women to every 1,000 men, and the increase in such incidents is a source of concern for the government, which is trying to implement new legislation.

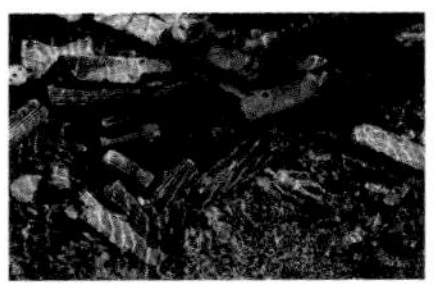

**PAGES 370–371**
TOURIST IN A SWIMMING POOL IN PAMUKKALE, ANATOLIA, TURKEY
(37°58' N, 29°19' E)

The city of Pamukkale in western Anatolia has warm-water springs that are rich in mineral salts, celebrated since antiquity for their curative properties. In 129 BC the Romans founded the city of Hierapolis here. It suffered four earthquakes and was rebuilt several times before its decline under the Byzantine Empire. Today the archaeological site of Hierapolis attracts many visitors. A hotel was built on the ruins of an ancient holy fountain; its pool, the bottom of which is littered with fragments of Roman columns, is a favorite with tourists. Hierapolis-Pamukkale was declared a World Heritage site by UNESCO in 1988, but its landscape was disfigured for a long time by a large number of tourist developments. The demolition of a number of hotels, and of the road that crossed the white travertine terraces, as well as the construction of a new thermal water distribution system, have returned the former luster to this site with its dreamlike landscape of frozen stone waterfalls.

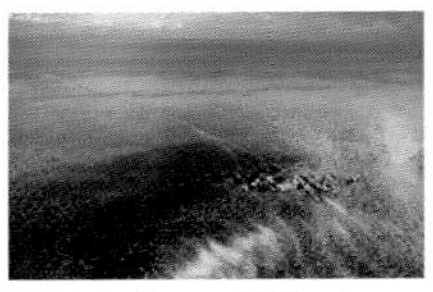

**PAGES 372–373**
VILLAGE ON STILTS IN TONGKIL, SAMALES ISLANDS, PHILIPPINES
(6°07' N, 121°81' E)

The southern Philippines, and in particular the Sulu Archipelago that includes the Samales Islands, is home to the Badjaos. Known as "sea gypsies," they fish and harvest shellfish and pearl oysters, and they live in villages on stilts. A channel carved out of the coral reef allows them to reach the open sea. The Badjaos belong to a Muslim minority who make up 5 percent of the Philippine population and are concentrated mostly in the south of the country. The region is attractive to the tourist trade but this is now on the point of dying out completely due to armed Communist insurrections and Muslim separatist movements in the south. These conflicts have shaken the country since the early 1970s, claiming 120,000 victims over three decades. Periods of violence alternate with talks and ceasefires in this land where 40 percent of the population lives below the poverty line, where the birth rate is the highest in Asia, and where the economy relies heavily on the diaspora.

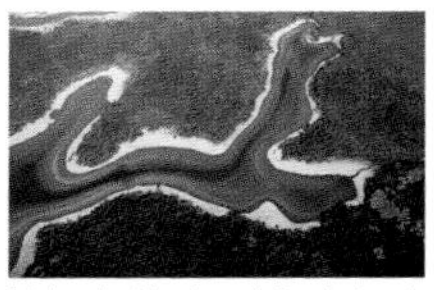

**PAGES 374–375**
KAKADU NATIONAL PARK, NORTHERN TERRITORY, AUSTRALIA
(13°00' S, 132°30' E)

Kakadu National Park in the Northern Territory has an area of nearly 7,800 square miles (20,000 km²), making it one of the largest parks in Australia. Declared a World Heritage site by UNESCO in 1981 because of its cultural and natural importance, it is ethnologically and archaeologically priceless because it has been continuously inhabited for 40,000 years. Its many Aboriginal cave art sites (over 7,000) are testimony to the close relationship between people and nature. Kakadu also contains an amazing collection of ecosystems that are home to many rare or endemic plant and animal species. Because Australia separated from the rest of the world 150 million years ago, many species developed there and on neighboring islands that do not exist on any other continent; these include most of the marsupials, such as the kangaroo and koala. Kakadu alone can count 128 reptile species, 280 birds, 64 mammals, and 1,700 plants, as well as over 10,000 insects. New species are frequently discovered. Some animals are under threat, including the vampire bat, the estuary crocodile, and several species of turtles.

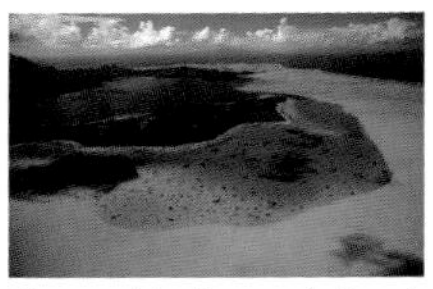

**PAGES 376–377**
BORA BORA, FRENCH POLYNESIA
(16°30' S, 151°44' W)

The archipelago of the Leeward Islands in French Polynesia, a French overseas territory since 1946, includes this island of 15 square miles (38 km²), whose name means "first born" in Polynesian. It is made up of the emerged portion of the crater of a 7-million-year-old volcano and surrounded by a coral barrier reef. *Motus*, small coral islands with beaches and vegetation that consists mainly of coconut trees, have developed along the reef. The lagoon's only opening to the sea is Teavanui Pass, which is deep enough to allow cargo and warships to enter. The island was used as a military base by the United States between 1942 and 1946. All of the coral formations of the planet cover only 110,000 square miles (284,000 km²) of the sea bed, less than 0.06 percent of the Earth's surface, but these areas still contain a remarkable biological diversity: about 100,000 plant and animal species have been classified there. The situation of coral is worrying—more than 60 percent of the world's reefs are under threat—but it is not yet desperate: despite the damage caused by pollution, overfishing, and rising temperatures that have affected many reefs, it has been observed that the surface regeneration of coral is increasing.

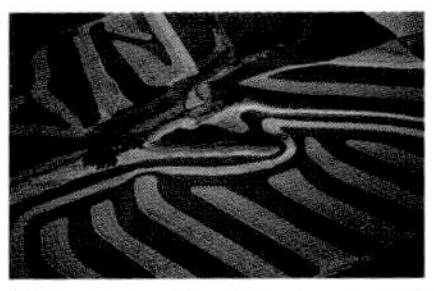

**PAGES 378–379**
FARMING NEAR PULLMAN, WASHINGTON, UNITED STATES
(46°42' N, 117°12' W)

Known as the Evergreen State, Washington has been raising wheat for decades, striving to adapt the grain in order to protect a soil made fragile by the erosive agricultural practices of earlier times. The development of "agrobusiness," an alliance of agriculture, industry, science, and financial investment, encourages technological innovations aimed at improving productivity and helps keep the United States the leading exporter of cereals (about 35 percent of the total) as well as corn (40 percent) and soya (nearly half of world production). The use of biotechnologies, especially in the production of corn and soya, has led to the creation of varieties that are resistant to parasites, and herbicides that are believed to increase yield. Controversial because little is known about the extent of their side effects on health and the environment, the cultivation of genetically modified organisms (GMOs) is nonetheless on the increase worldwide. In 2004, the area that they occupy rose by another 20 percent, particularly in the countries of the southern hemisphere.

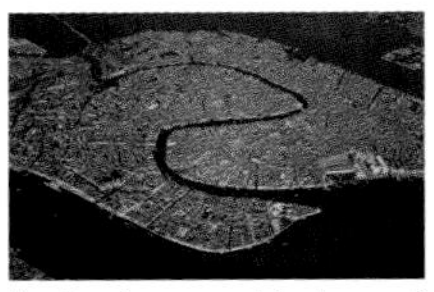

**PAGES 380–381**
VIEW OF VENICE, VENETO, ITALY
(45°35' N, 12°34' E)

Venice is an archipelago of 118 islands that are separated by 160 canals spanned by more than 400 bridges. The Grand Canal—Venice's main artery—is lined with the city's most beautiful buildings. A hundred or so Renaissance and Baroque palaces were built on the banks of the Grand Canal by rich Venetian merchants. They bear witness to the wealth these traders earned when Venice opened up to the outside world. The city dominated the Adriatic from AD 1000, extending this dominance to the entire Mediterranean and establishing a number of trading posts, until the end of the 17th century, when trade by land supplanted trade by sea, eclipsing Venice on the international trade scene. Today, the eclipse risks becoming total. "La Serenissima" could vanish under the waves, a victim of the floods that have increased as a result of canal widening, the sinking of the ground on which Venice is built, and the rise in sea level (0.24 inches, or 6 mm per year). In 2002, an ambitious and expensive plan called the Moses Project was chosen to build a damming system to protect the city from high tides. Almost 80 moveable steel barriers are to be installed and operational by 2011.

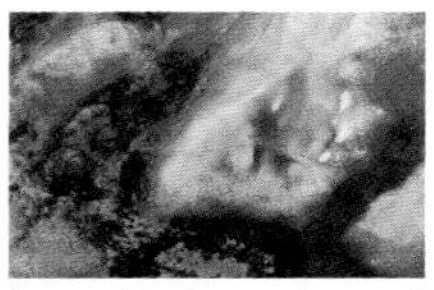

**PAGES 382–383**
LAKE ENRIQUILLO, DOMINICAN REPUBLIC
(18°30' N, 71°35' W)

Located in the southwest of the Dominican Republic, on the border with Haiti, Lake Enriquillo is the largest saltwater lake in the Caribbean (102 square miles, or 265 km²). Lying 130 feet (40 meters) below sea level, the lake was created during the glacial era, when the falling sea level removed the bay that divided the island in two, and created a huge saltwater basin, now isolated from the Caribbean Sea. From this distant past, Lake Enriquillo retains coral, the shells of sea animals, and a salinity that is three times greater than the ocean. Its wildlife is exceptional: it is home to 200 wild American crocodiles (an endangered species), as well as the spectacular rhinoceros iguana. In the center of the lake lies the national park of Isla Cabritos, which is visited by several dozen species of migratory birds, including the greater flamingo. A UNESCO World Heritage site and a Biosphere Reserve since 2002, Lake Enriquillo is currently the subject of an ecotourism plan being developed by the state of Haiti and the Dominican Republic, despite their longtime dispute over this shared natural site.

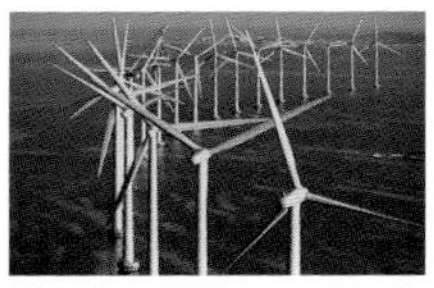

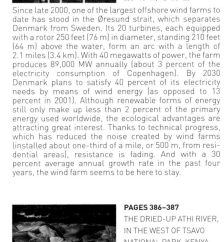

**PAGES 384–385**
MIDDELGRUNDEN OFFSHORE WIND FARM, NEAR COPENHAGEN, DENMARK
(55°40' N, 12°38' E)

Since late 2000, one of the largest offshore wind farms to date has stood in the Øresund strait, which separates Denmark from Sweden. Its 20 turbines, each equipped with a rotor 250 feet (76 m) in diameter, standing 210 feet (64 m) above the water, form an arc with a length of 2.1 miles (3.4 km). With 40 megawatts of power, the farm produces 89,000 MW annually (about 3 percent of the electricity consumption of Copenhagen). By 2030 Denmark plans to satisfy 40 percent of its electricity needs by means of wind energy (as opposed to 13 percent in 2001). Although renewable forms of energy still only make up less than 2 percent of the primary energy used worldwide, the ecological advantages are attracting great interest. Thanks to technical progress, which has reduced the noise created by wind farms (installed about one-third of a mile, or 500 m, from residential areas), resistance is fading. And with a 30 percent average annual growth rate in the past four years, the wind farm seems to be here to stay.

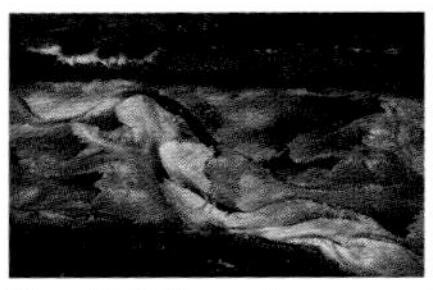

**PAGES 386–387**
THE DRIED-UP ATHI RIVER, IN THE WEST OF TSAVO NATIONAL PARK, KENYA
(2°59' S, 38°31' E)

The Athi River, the second-largest in Kenya, hurtles down from the high mountains in the center of the country. Its waters have sculpted its bed with great force, creating a spectacular landscape, and when it dries up—as it has done here in the Tsavo National Park—the nomads bring their cattle to drink from the holes that still retain the precious liquid. The pollutants carried by the river once it has passed through the capital Nairobi and the agricultural plateau regions that it irrigates, together with frequent and devastating droughts, are the reason for this seasonal drying, and desertification is a serious threat. The Tsavo National Park is one of the largest in the world, and contains large herds of elephants, hippos, and rhinos, among other species. With its mixture of plain, savanna, bush, lakes, rocky outcrops, ancient lava flows, and semi-desert, this immensely rich landscape is one of the country's major resources, and carefully regulated tourism is an important source of revenue.

resources, not by restricting and reducing human welfare, but by finding other and better ways of producing and utilizing the limited reserves that we possess.

This analysis has led to the proposal of a new concept: sustainable development, which is based in equal measure on social equity, economic efficiency, and the conservation of the environment and its resources. Although most of these elements were first formulated during the 1970s, the concept of sustainability only acquired its political status in 1987, in the report delivered by the World Commission on Environment and Development, presided over by the then Prime Minister of Norway, Gro Harlem Brundtland. Its definition serves now as a reference point for most international, European, and national policies: "development that meets the needs of the present without compromising the ability of future generations to meet their own needs." This entails providing for basic human needs, particularly for those who are most deprived, and working out how our technology and our social structure limit the capacity of the environment to cater to those needs now and in the future.

Sustainable development has been an integral part of international communiqués since the Rio Earth Summit in 1992, which included on its agenda: "That human beings are at the center of concerns for sustainable development. They are entitled to a healthy and productive life in harmony with nature." This is a principle that leads to a reappraisal of the social contract, promoting a new concept of citizenship with rights that are paid for by obligations toward the biosphere.

But the consensus that seems to be forming in relation to sustainable development is all too often based on ignorance of the scale of change necessary, and also of the constraints that have to be lifted. It is not enough merely to perform a few virtuous, isolated deeds and then tell everyone about them. Every organization needs to change its global impact, to put sustainable development at the very heart of its policies, and to mobilize all its creative powers to this end. The general consensus that we have now conceals far too many ambiguities and conflicting interests.

The first conflict is between the people of today and future generations, who will inherit the problems created by the exhaustion of fuel reserves and mineral deposits, the accumulation of pollutants in the atmosphere, and the destruction of ecosystems. This affects the very concept of progress, since the fate of future generations risks being less propitious than that of the present generation. The second conflict is between the rich and the poor, most notably between the countries of the northern hemisphere and those of the south. The third conflict has mankind on one side and nature (including all other living creatures) on the other. But generally these opposing interests—the southern hemisphere, future generations, nature—tend to be forgotten, because what counts in international politics and economics is the balance of power, and so these additional factors have little influence on or indeed are completely absent from the political debate.

Another absentee from many public decision-making processes is knowledge. Indeed, the diagnosis set out by scientists and other experts has found very little response among the political powers-that-be. This is exacerbated by the fact that scientific analysis has not yet achieved the degree of certainty necessary for serious and irreversible risks to be taken, whereas politicians have to take decisions now and are bound to follow the path of caution. The main obstacle, though, is surely the lack of political will to adopt the principles of sustainable development, together with the fact that there is no overall framework within which such a political will might be expressed.

On an international level, institutions lay great emphasis on two principles laid down in Rio: the sovereignty of states, and the special responsibility of the industrialized nations, and these principles require the establishment of multilateral relations based on negotiation and cooperation. Any international agreement, even if it has been negotiated under the aegis of the United Nations, can only come into force in those countries that have ratified it. Any protocol added to an agreement must also be ratified in the same way. This is why the United States, although they signed up to the agreement on climatic change in 1992, did not ratify the Kyoto Treaty of 1997 and are therefore not bound by its terms.

The Rio Conference was also an opportunity for a genuine contract between the countries of the south and the countries of the north, binding environmental policies to development and aid policies. But some southern countries are concerned about environmental constraints which northern countries do not apply to themselves, while also not fulfilling their commitment to devote 0.7 percent of their GNP to development aid.

The problem is one of quality as well as quantity. The southern countries must be allowed access to expertise and technology so that they can develop their own, adapted to their requirements. This is also the conclusion of the report drawn up by the MA. The importance of cultural diversity is generally recognized today, to the point of being the fourth pillar of sustainable development, beside the environment, economics, and society.

At last there are now many countries seeking to strengthen the framework of international environmental institutions under the aegis of UNEP (United Nations Environment Program), which could enforce environmental and social regulations and if necessary impose them on the WTO (World Trade Organization).

In Johannesburg in 2002, many countries committed themselves to implementing their own programs for sustainable development before 2005. But by 2003, only 12 percent of them had such a program in operation, 2 percent had obtained government approval, and 22 percent were working on it. A closer look at the strategies adopted reveals that these programs are often sector-specific and rarely envisage a brake on the speed of development. However, local authorities are being encouraged to put into operation Agenda 21, which entails strategies of sustainable development on a local level.

At all levels, innovation is essential—perfecting new processes that will involve society in general as well as private individuals. "Governance" is a key word to describe the processes of decision-making and cooperation, but everyone has a role to play: the State must fashion the right political environment and legal framework, the private sector must create jobs and produce revenue, and finally the civil sector must facilitate political and social interaction, inspiring groups to participate in economic, social, and political activities. The private and civil sectors and non-governmental organizations must make their voices heard at international gatherings.

The attitude of the private sector is crucial. The actions of businesses, particularly the multinationals, play a massive role in sustainable and the products that will enable them to make responsible use of their purchasing powers. Investors too must have access to information about the attitude of different companies toward the principle of sustainable development.

Could it be, however, that the dislocation of our aspirations, this apparent schizophrenia within us, comes from the structure of our brains? In the left hemisphere are our powers of logical thinking and abstraction; in the right lie our concrete thoughts and images. The success of the human species may rest on the dominance of the left hemisphere, but its limitations become apparent when abstraction and ideology begin to develop at the cost of our ability to perceive concrete problems. Let us hope that the power of the images contained in this book, appealing to our right hemisphere, will help to redress the balance necessary for the survival of humanity, so that the 21st century may become one of ecocitizenship, with a lessening of the violence done both to mankind and to nature, and in its place a new respect of one for the other.

CHRISTIAN BRODHAG

355

**DADES GORGE, MOROCCO** (30°55' N, 6°47' W)

The slender watercourse that flows between the High Atlas and the Anti-Atlas feeds many Berber villages, which huddle against the rocky walls of the Dades river valley. Built out of *pisé* (a mixture of packed earth and straw), the houses melt into the rocky scenery around them. Yet human presence does not go unnoticed: a multitude of delicate green gardens softens this rocky landscape. Most are tiny fields of grain or potatoes for local consumption. A product typical of this valley is the damask rose, whose flowers are distilled into rose water by a cooperative. By grouping together in this way, farmers can sell their produce at fair prices; if they worked individually, they would have to sell at rock-bottom prices in the local souk, or simply to the first middleman they could find. However, this system has remained limited to rose-growers, many villagers not feeling the need to change.

## ⟩ INCREASING AND EXCESSIVE CONSUMPTION OF RESOURCES

**ANNUAL CONSUMPTION OF ENERGY WORLDWIDE**
On an average day, coal consumption per person is the equivalent of **1 kg** of oil, oil itself is **1.5 kg**, and natural gas is the equivalent of **1 kg** of oil.

**ANNUAL CONSUMPTION OF METALS**
Since **1930**, the consumption of aluminum has increased more than **15** times and copper more than **10** times.

**REFUSE PRODUCTION**
Americans are the biggest producers of waste in the world: in the US, each person produces an average of **1,600 lb (720 kg)** of domestic refuse per year, or **4 lb (2 kg)** per day.

## ⟩ CAN CONSUMPTION CONTINUE AT THE SAME RATE?

**LIMITED AVAILABLE RESOURCES**
Renewable sources: mankind only has one planet available for the production and renewal of resources.
Non-renewable resources: it has taken nature **180 million** years to transform the atmosphere's $CO_2$ into subterranean reserves of fossilized carbon (oil, coal).

**ECOLOGICAL FOOTPRINTS: A WARNING SIGN**
In **2001**, humanity's ecological footprint was **2.5 times** larger than in **1961** and had exceeded the planet's capacity for renewal and for the absorption of pollutants by **20%**.
These excesses are reducing the natural reserves of the Earth and can only continue for a limited period of time or for a limited population. If the US model were adopted by the rest of humanity, the planet would need to be **5.3 times** richer than it is.

## ⟩ AN EVER-RICHER WORLD WITH EVER-INCREASING INEQUALITIES

**THE WORLD'S GDP CONTINUES TO GROW**
Since **1950**, the world's GDP has increased by an average of **3.9%** a year, reaching the equivalent of **$7,714** per person in **2002**.

**BEHIND THE GDP GROWTH LIE MAJOR DISPARITIES**
The three richest families in the world own a fortune greater than the entire GDP of the **48** poorest developing countries.
In **1971**, there were **27** countries whose GNP per person was less than **$900** per year. Today there are **49** such countries, **34** of which are in Africa.
**80%** of the world's wealth is owned by **15%** of the people in the richest countries.

**EVER-INCREASING DEBTS: A TAX ON FUTURE GENERATIONS**
The foreign debts of developing countries have multiplied more than sixfold since **1970**, reaching **$2,800 billion** in **1999**. These debts are just **5%** of those of the richest countries. Debts are not the only cause of problems in these countries, but they worsen existing problems: in **1995**, Mozambique spent **3.3%** of its budget on health, **7.9%** on education, and **33%** to service its debts. It is to be hoped that the historic decision taken by the G7 countries in June 2005 to cancel the debts of the poorest nations will have a beneficial effect on their economies.

## ⟩ DEVELOPMENT IS ONLY MEASURED BY WEALTH AND PROGRESS AT ALL COSTS

HDI: As wealth is only one way of raising the quality of life, the UNDP (United Nations Development Program) has worked out a Human Development Index (HDI) to measure the average level of a country's progress in terms of three criteria: longevity, knowledge, and standard of living.

Between **1975** and **2004**, the HDI has improved from predominantly "average to low" to "average to high."

**EDUCATION: PROGRESS WHICH MUST BE MAINTAINED**
Between **1990** and **2004**, the rate of adult literacy improved from **75.4%** to **81.7%**.
Today, nearly **20%** of people over the age of 15 are illiterate, **98%** of them in the southern hemisphere. Almost two-thirds of them are female.

**HEALTH: STILL A LONG WAY TO GO**
**17 million** people a year die of infectious diseases (malaria, Aids, tuberculosis), and **90%** of these deaths take place in the developing countries.
**82.6%** of the world's pharmaceutical industry is owned by North America (**40.2%**), Europe (**26.6%**), and Japan (**15.8%**).

## ⟩ ECONOMICS, HUMAN BEINGS, AND THE ENVIRONMENT: A DIFFICULT PARTNERSHIP

Our apparent wealth resides in economic growth, whose indicators ignore the state of our natural resources (for instance, deforestation is counted as a form of "wealth creation").

Since the **1970s**, the natural wealth of the Earth has been reduced by one-third due to human intervention.

With indicators such as the "ecological footprint" and HDI, a level of lasting development might be defined as:
Average footprint: **1.8 hectares** per person
Average HDI: **0.8**

**CURRENTLY NO COUNTRY HAS ACHIEVED SUSTAINABLE DEVELOPMENT**
"Emerging" countries in South America and Asia (e.g. Turkey) already have a larger ecological footprint of **1.8 hectares** hectares per person, but have not reached an HDI of **0.8**.
Rich countries (US, Australia, Canada, Europe) have a satisfactory HDI of around **0.9**, but their ecological footprint is far too great, at between **3** and **10 hectares** per person.
"Emergent" countries in North Africa and the Middle East, and developing countries in Asia and Africa have an ecological footprint of less than **1.8 hectares** per person, but their HDI is too low (less than **0.8**, and even as low as **0.4**).

---

⟩ **HYDRAULIC DRILLING STATION IN A VILLAGE NEAR DOROPO, CÔTE D'IVOIRE** [9°47' N, 3°19' W]

Throughout Africa the task of collecting water is assigned to women, as seen here near the regions of Doropo and Bouna, in northern Côte d'Ivoire. Hydraulic drilling stations, equipped with pumps that are usually manual, are gradually replacing the traditional village wells, and containers of plastic, enameled metal, or aluminum are supplanting canaris (large terra-cotta jugs) and gourds for transporting the precious resource. The water of these pits is more sanitary than that of traditional wells, 70 percent of which is unfit for drinking. Today 20 percent of the world population is without drinkable water. In Africa this is true for two out of five people, but more than half of the population in rural areas have no access to clean water. Illnesses from unhealthy water are falling, but are still the major cause of infant mortality in developing nations: diarrhea kills over 1.5 million children below the age of five. In Africa and Asia improved access to clean drinking water will be one of the major challenges of the coming decades, as their populations grow.

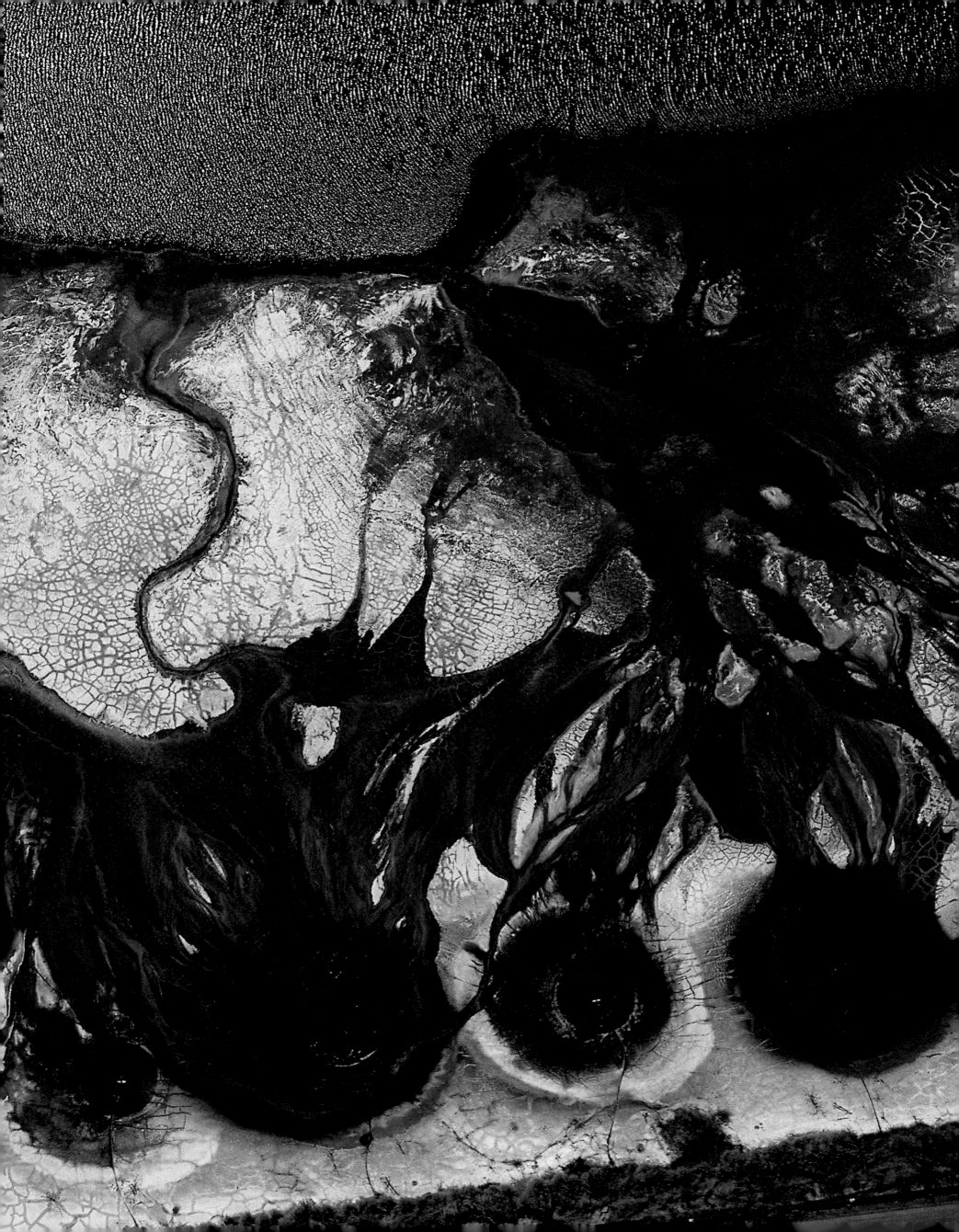

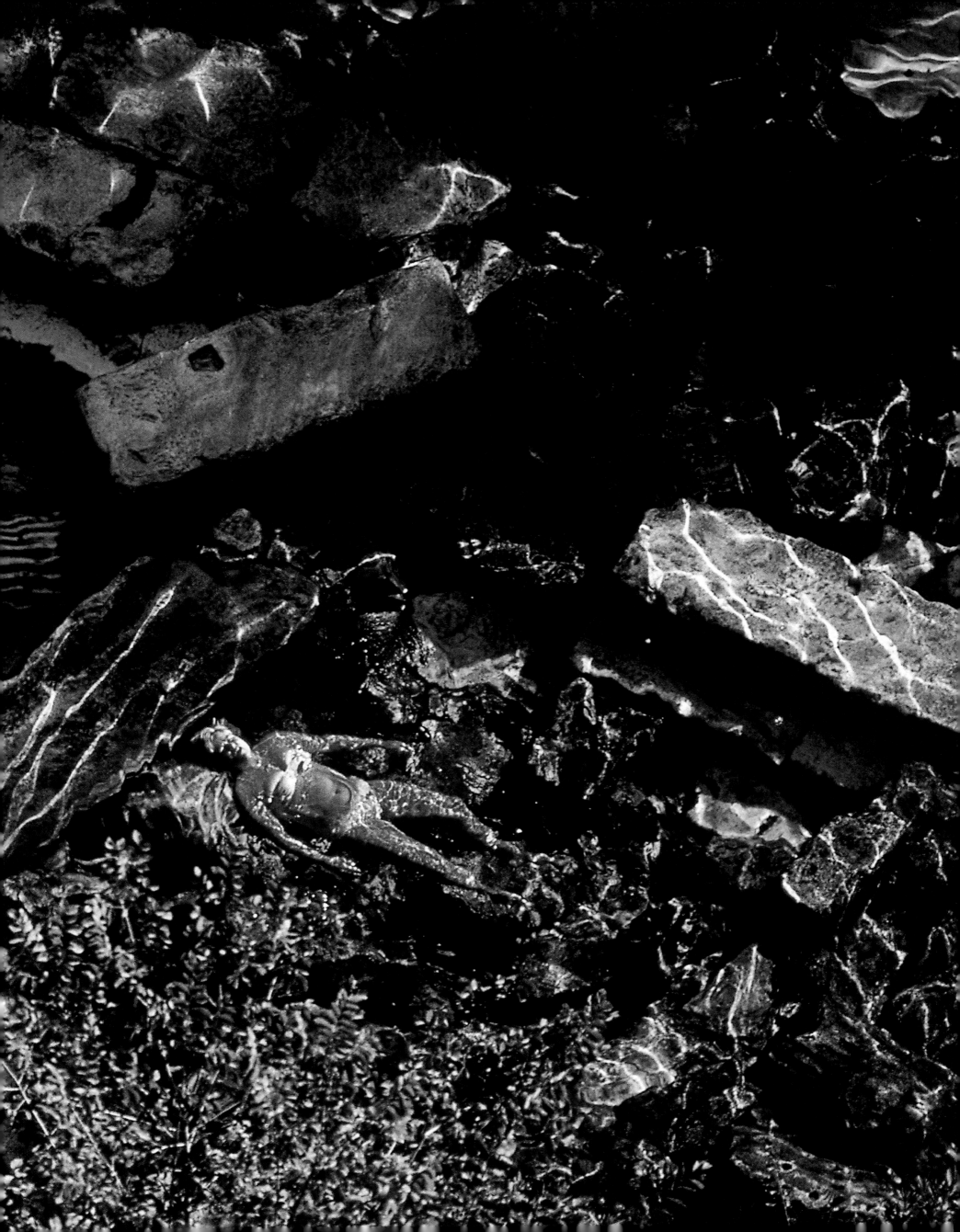

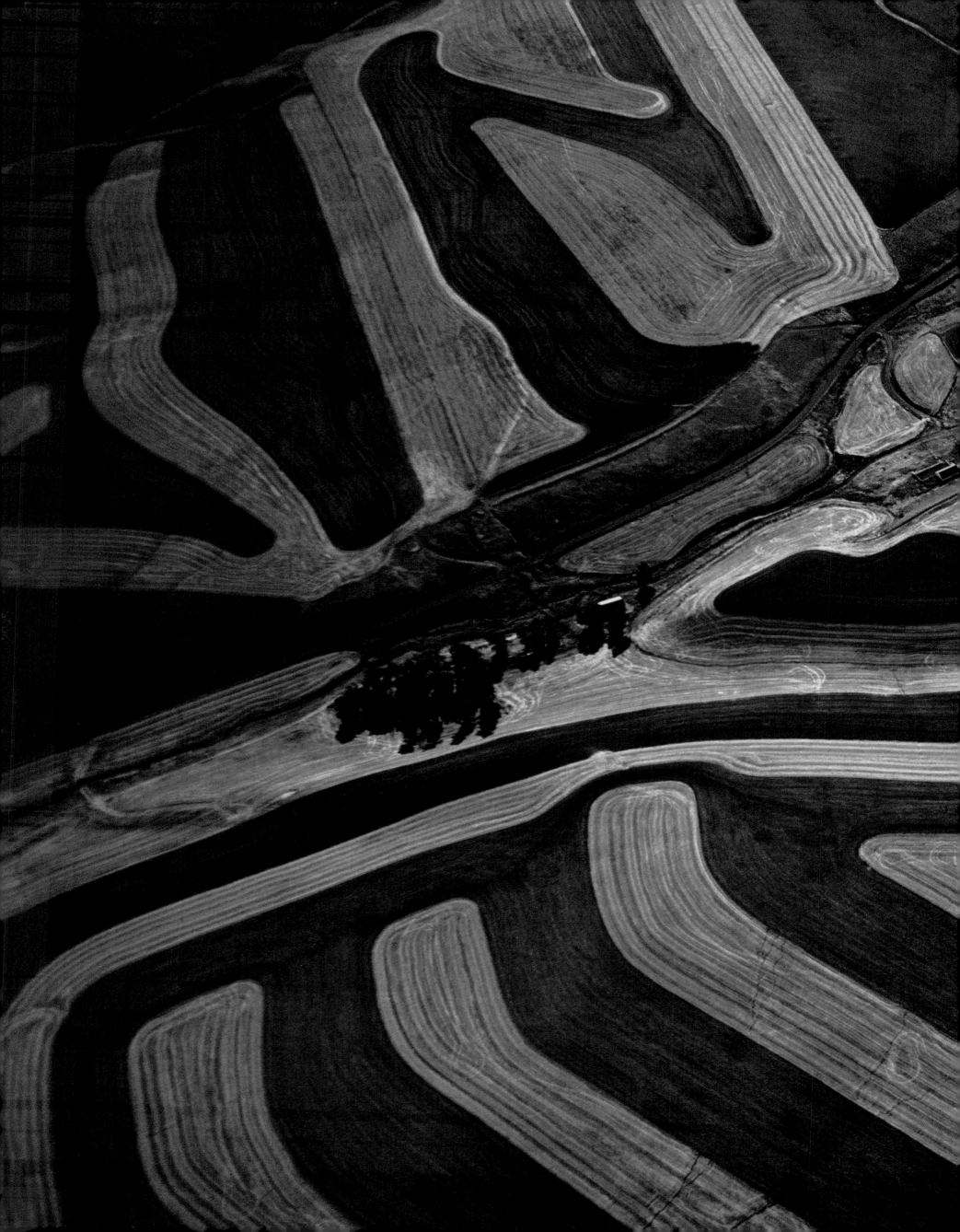

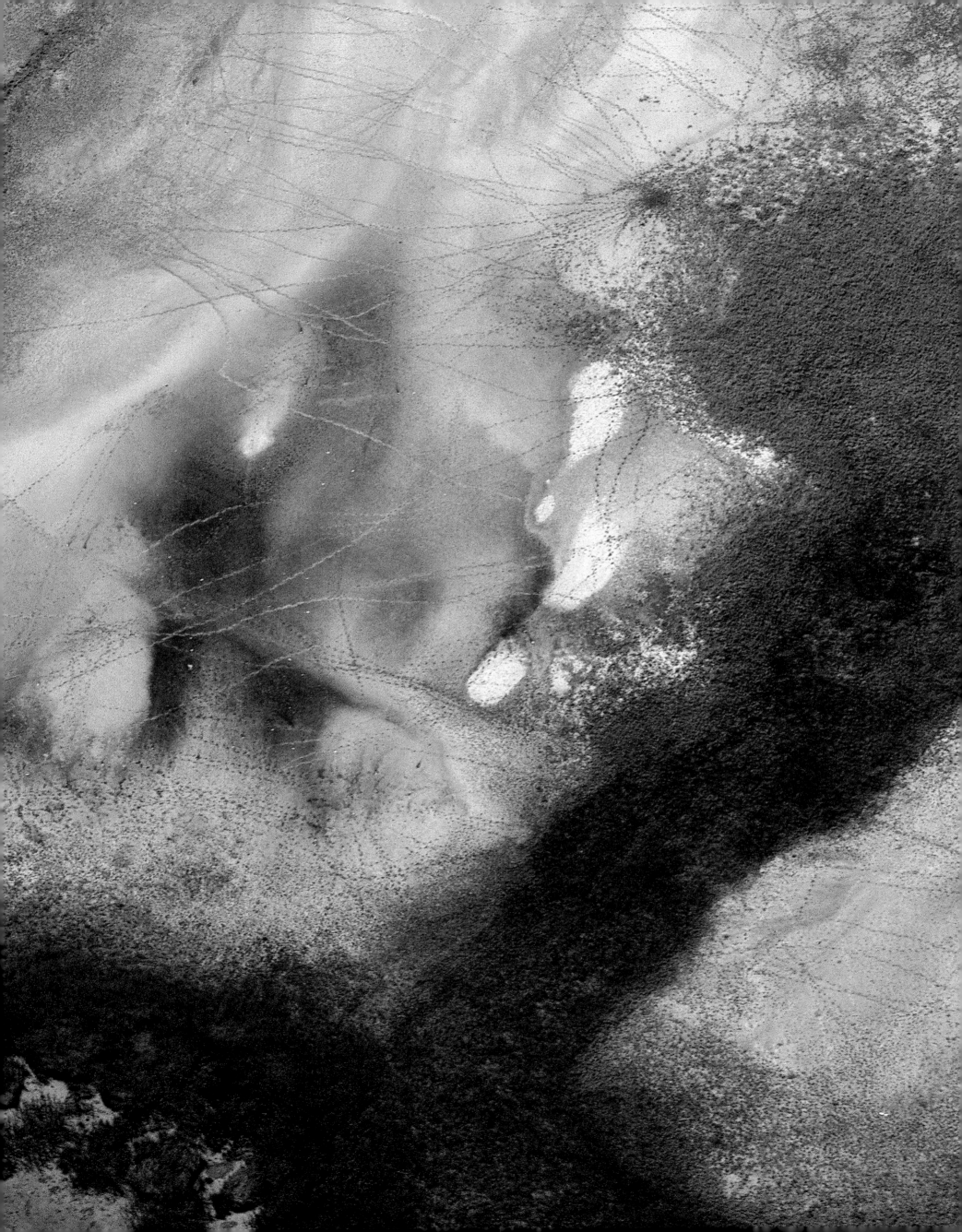

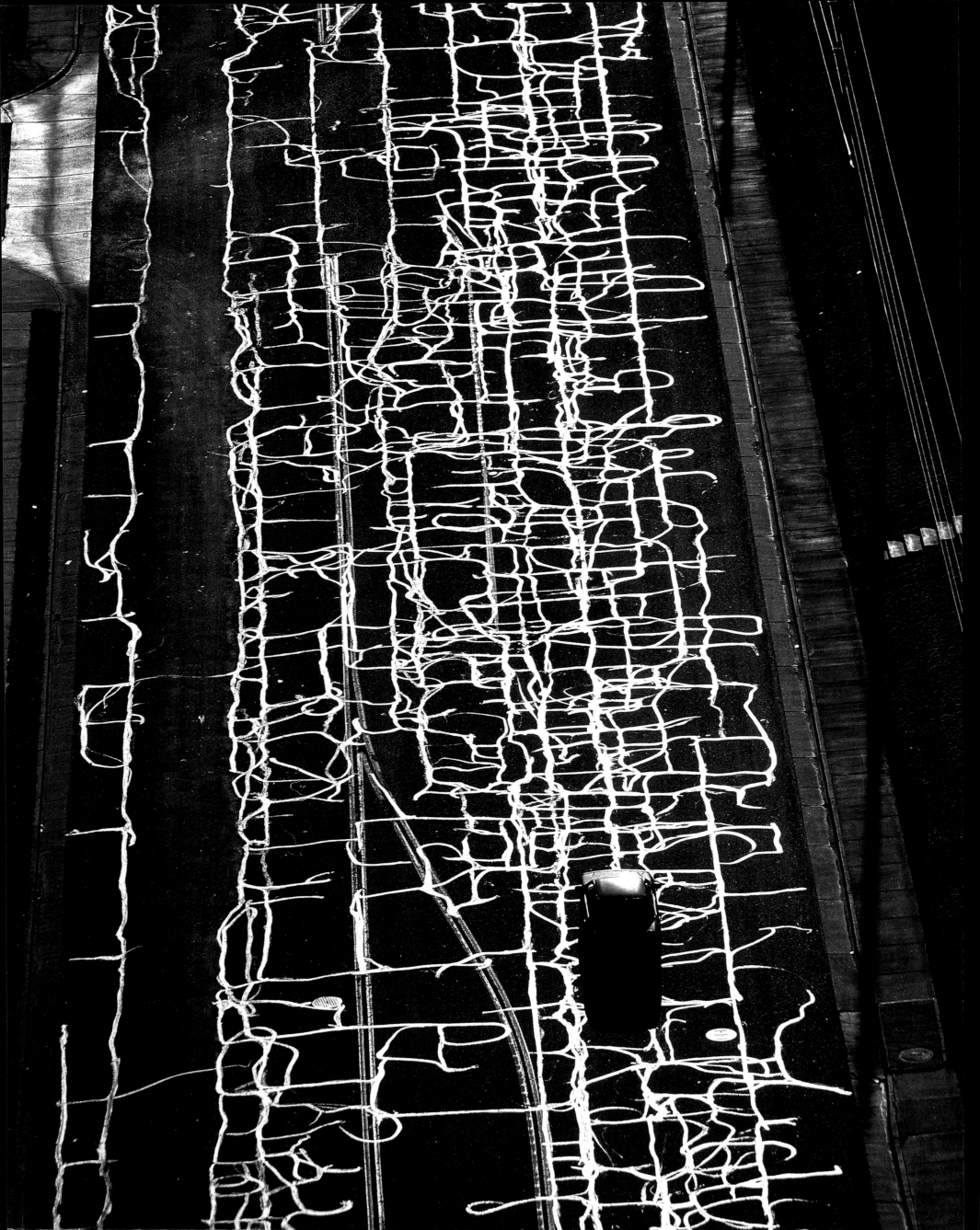

# MICROCREDIT AND
# THE FUTURE OF POVERTY

Two billion people, one-third of the world's population, are today affected by poverty. If nothing is done, this figure will double in thirty years. In order to wage war on this scourge, the countries of the north must fulfill their aid obligations, and the countries of the south must develop toward full democracy—the only guaranteed way to ensure efficient action. Finally, all the adults in the world should be given enough credit to buy the tools they need for work. This is the role of microfinance, which has already enabled 80 million people to escape from poverty.

Of all the challenges confronting the human race today, poverty is unquestionably the most complex: it prevents one-third of humanity not only from getting enough to eat, but also from gaining access to knowledge, to health care, to community life, and to the decision-making processes that will shape the future of their children and of the whole world.

More than 2 billion people are suffering from hunger, 200 million of these being children under the age of 5. Asia is the continent most affected (526 million people undernourished, with India the worst at 204 million), but it is in Africa that the proportion of people suffering from malnutrition is the highest. Forty-three developing countries have seen their infant mortality rate either stagnate or increase. 3.3 million children a year die at birth, 4 million in the month that follows their birth, and 6.6 million before they have celebrated their fifth birthday. Malnutrition kills one child somewhere in the world every five seconds.

Some 121 million children have never been to school. The proportion of children in education is 43 percent in the poorest countries, 60 percent in developing countries, and 93 percent in member states of the OECD (Organization for Economic Cooperation and Development). Furthermore, the growing concentration of people in urban zones where there are no sanitation facilities and a frightening increase in air and water pollution, means that a vast proportion of the Earth's inhabitants live in complete material destitution, while many of them are also without jobs and without freedom, not to mention their political and cultural deprivations.

Faced with this situation, the aid offered by the rich countries is already low and continues to shrink. The means at the disposal of the international agencies seem derisory, and are often used counterproductively. Everyone seems to think that the marketplace will do all that is necessary to reduce poverty. The old political solutions, such as liberalism and Communism, no longer carry any weight, and there is no government in the south that has made any serious inroads into the problem—even if growth has created a significant middle class, particularly in India and China, which now has access to consumer goods. Globalization seems to be worsening poverty by concentrating wealth

---

◁ **REPAIRS ON A ROAD NEAR DENVER, COLORADO, UNITED STATES** [39°45' N, 105°00' W]

Like an electronic circuit board, the "bandages" on this old road weave a pattern on the tarmac, their smooth, dark bands reflecting the light. Applied to repair cracks in the road surface, they bear witness to a long, hard life at the mercy of car tires. In the United States, the expansion of urban areas is not a recent phenomenon—but it is not over yet, either. Expansion is even speeding up as the population grows and the middle classes move to the residential suburbs. Thus cities continue to stretch out their tentacles, eating up almost 3,600 square miles (9,320 km²) of farmland each year. Worldwide, they gnaw into countryside, but they also wipe out any forests and wetlands that stand in their way. Their growth is a threat to both biodiversity and air quality. The building of higher-density neighborhoods, however, along with downtown revitalization of city centers that are often decaying and inhabited by the poor, can help limit the impact of urban growth on the environment while also encouraging a more diverse social mix.

△ **PIROGUES ON THE RIVER NIGER IN GAO, MALI** [16°16' N, 0°03' W]

The Niger is a major communication artery in Mali, linking trade between the region of Bamako, the capital city, and Gao in the north of the country (a distance of 870 miles, or 1,400 km). However, ships of average size can travel the river only during the high-water season, between July and December; only boats with light draft can navigate the Niger all year long. The Bozo people, traditionally fishermen, have become the masters of the river by handling local transport in their fishing boats. These large pirogues sail back and forth to the port of Gao; although fragile in appearance, they can carry several tons of merchandise. In particular, they transport great quantities of *bourgou*, a grass found in the waters of the river that is fed to the region's migratory livestock.

(MFIs), or "banks for the poor," set up by pioneers such as Muhammad Yunus with his Grameen Bank in Bangladesh, have offered the poorest people the opportunity to borrow small sums without any guarantee or collateral, in order to start up their own businesses.

These loans are very small and are generally for a period of less than a year, and they are at a rate of interest that will allow the microfinancial institutions to break even. Frequently, the borrowers are also encouraged to save by making regular deposits which earn a fixed rate of interest. Sometimes borrowers group together, with each member acting as a moral guarantor for the others. The Grameen Bank, for example, grants loans to groups of five.

Today there are some 10,000 MFIs worldwide. They take various forms, depending on their size, age, and country of operation: they may be commercial, cooperative, non-governmental. Some have just 300 members, and others several million. They are to be found in almost all southern hemisphere countries as well as in the north, but the bulk of them are in East Asia, Subaharan Africa, Latin America, China, and India. Over two-thirds of the beneficiaries are women, and although the loans are not interest-free, the rates are low. These men and women buy animals, farming tools and products, raw materials, and equipment for transport, trade or small workshops. They may work in towns or in the country. The MFIs offer not only microloans but also other services: microinsurance, microcredit for accommodation, education, health. They often help their customers to obtain training, and it is with their help that children can go to school, families can look after themselves, and democracy can function better. Every year, more than 5 percent of the customers earn enough to be regarded as middle class.

A few examples: in the Philippines, on the island of Mindanao—one of the poorest areas in the country—lives a young widow with a child, Natividad Monticello, who makes and sells rice cakes. Finding it difficult to survive, she needed to increase her income and so she borrowed $27 from BABA's Foundation, an MFI created in 1988, which enabled her to buy more rice and raise her production level from 2 kg to 5 kg a day; this in turn allowed her to send her child to school. In Peru, a young grandmother, Candelaria Ferrel Hurtado, has been selling fruit for twenty years; she has to look after her grandson, because his father—her son—lives a long way away. In order to do this properly, she borrowed $490 (without guarantee) from Ispeda, another MFI which grants loans mainly to women in the semi-urban areas of the Abancay region. Candelaria was then able to buy more fruit from different places, and the increase in her income enabled her to obtain a better education for her grandson. At Oujda in Morocco, Fatiha Hiouane, a

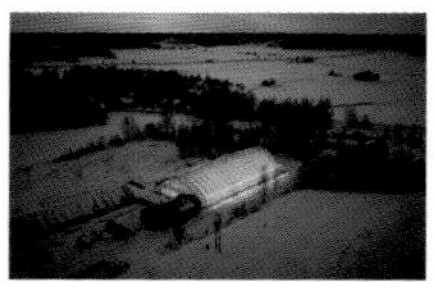

**PAGES 396–397**
ILLUMINATED GREENHOUSE NEAR SAUVO, VARSINAIS-SUOMI REGION, FINLAND
(60°18' N, 22°36' E)

Finland occupies the most northerly position in Europe, with one-quarter of its territory located above the Arctic Circle. At such high latitudes agriculture faces natural challenges; in winter, night lasts uninterrupted for nearly two months in the north, while in the south the sun does not appear for more than six hours daily. In this premature twilight the snow is scattered with gleaming greenhouses, where the daily duration of photosynthesis is extended by artificial lighting, as here near Sauvo, in the southwestern part of the country. Using this method, Finland manages to produce 35,500 tons of tomatoes per year; but its greatest field of exploitation remains timber. It exploits pine and birch forests that cover 70 percent of its land and provide more than one-third of its export revenues. Residue from the timber industry and waste from cutting trees serve as fuel, an important source of renewable energy that covers 20 percent of the country's energy consumption and 10 percent of its electricity consumption.

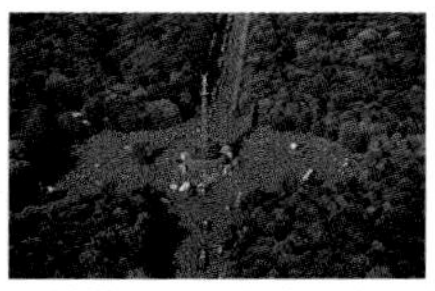

**PAGES 398–399**
"LOVE PARADE" IN TIERGARTEN PARK, BERLIN, GERMANY
(52°31' N, 13°25' E)

In 1989, shortly before the fall of the Berlin Wall, a Berlin disk jockey named Dr. Motte brought together 150 fans of electronic music for a modest street party in name of "tolerance, respect, and mutual understanding." The "Love Parade," now an enormous festival, draws over a million people together every year to dance to the beat of techno music from some fifty carnival floats. The Berlin Love Parade has been imitated in Paris, Zurich, Geneva, and Tel Aviv, and a Love Parade was even planned for Moscow in 2001, but the mayor's office canceled it. Often misunderstood—many confuse it with the Gay Pride Parade, founded in 1997—or criticized by ecologists because of the mountain of trash it creates, it was eventually for financial reasons that the Love Parade was unable to celebrate its fifteenth anniversary in 2004. The organizers, however, are optimistic that the event will be successfully revived in years to come.

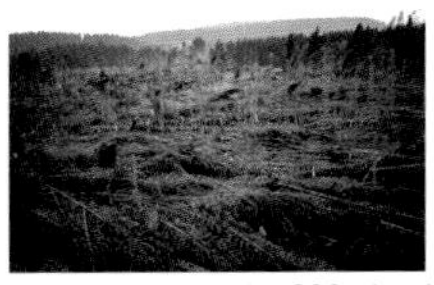

**PAGES 400–401**
TREES DOWNED BY STORMS IN THE FOREST OF THE VOSGES MOUNTAINS, FRANCE
(48°39' N, 7°14' E)

On December 26, 1999, the department of Vosges awoke to find 348 of its 515 towns and villages without electric power, 10 percent of its forests leveled, railway traffic totally at a stop, and 60,000 telephone lines cut. The following day, a second depression from the Loire region, also traveling at 62 miles per hour (100 km/h), crossed France in twelve hours. Violent winds cut down more than 300 million trees throughout the country, and the toll was high: 88 deaths, 3.5 million homes without electricity, and damage costing between 9 and 15 billion euros ($11.5–19 billion). The forests of France, which have been state-managed since the 17th century, had never known such destruction. The French National Forest Service, which set out to replace these woods, now promotes forests that are more resistant by nature, without endangering the timber industry, by favoring biological diversity (more adaptive and diverse species) and avoiding systematic alignment of trees. From this perspective, not all the consequences of the catastrophe have been negative.

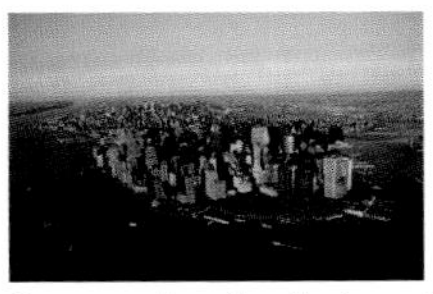

**PAGES 402–403**
FINANCIAL DISTRICT, MANHATTAN, NEW YORK, UNITED STATES
(40°45' N, 73°59'O)

Four months after the terrorist attacks of September 11, 2001, destroyed the World Trade Center, a great empty space, entirely cleared of the debris of the twin towers, was opened up in the heart of Lower Manhattan, the nerve center of New York. Despite its wounds, the city is determined to bounce back. Chicago and San Francisco have both been ravaged by fire in the past, and New York itself suffered two terrible fires, in 1776 and 1835. Each time the areas destroyed by the flames were rebuilt, as Manhattan's financial district will be. Soon after the attacks, a group of architects, town planners, and historians began to submit proposals to the city authorities. In February 2003, an architectural project by Daniel Libeskind was selected. Leaving an empty space where the twin towers stood and surrounding it with new blocks with broken lines, the new construction will pay homage to the thousands of Americans and others who died there.

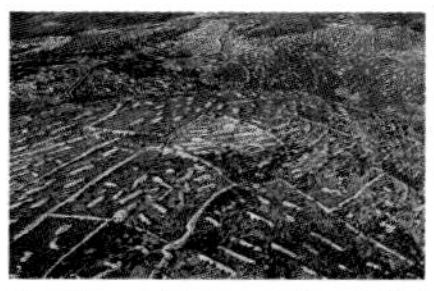

**PAGES 404–405**
PATTERN OF SMALL WALLS ON THE ISLAND OF DUGI OTOK, CROATIA
(43°58' N, 15°04' E)

The bare ridges of Dugi Otok are fluted by kilometers of dry stones. These lines of walls tell the history of livestock grazing and farming on the islands of the Adriatic Sea. Sheep farming, which was widespread until the beginning of the 20th century, led to serious deforestation. The walls were built not only to limit grazing areas (or plots where vines and olive trees still grow) but also to protect the hillsides from wind erosion and to reduce the amount of soil that rain washes away. Since the decline of sheep farming and agriculture in general, vegetation has been recolonizing this bare grassland. But this crowding of the environment is causing the disappearance of plant species adapted to this degraded "steppe" habitat typical of the Mediterranean region, where ecosystems have been shaped by human activity since the earliest times. Certain organisms have thus evolved in step with the changes made to the natural environment by agricultural ecosystems, sometimes called agrosystems.

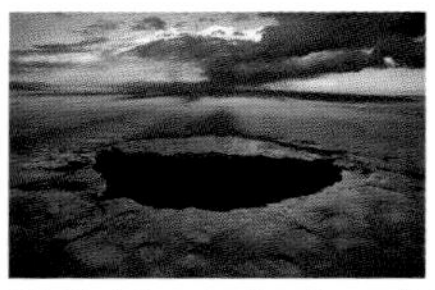

**PAGES 406–407**
BARRINGER CRATER, NEAR FLAGSTAFF, NORTHERN ARIZONA, UNITED STATES
(35°02' N, 111°01' W)

All that is missing from this lunar landscape are the astronauts. In fact, NASA uses this site for training because the topography closely resembles that of the moon. The crater interrupts the rocky, desertlike plain that stretches out around Winslow, Arizona, in the American Southwest. This cosmic scar, discovered in 1871, is 558 feet (170 m) deep and three-quarters of a mile (1.2 km) in diameter. It is the point of impact of a meteorite that collided with the Earth 50,000 years ago at a speed of 39,000 miles per hour (64,000 kph). The shock created by the impact of this mass of ferrous metal, some 160 feet (50 m) in diameter, would have resulted in an earthquake measuring over 5.5 on the Richter scale. The falling meteorite would also have caused a rise in temperature and atmospheric pressure that would have destroyed all life within a radius of 2.5 miles (4 km).

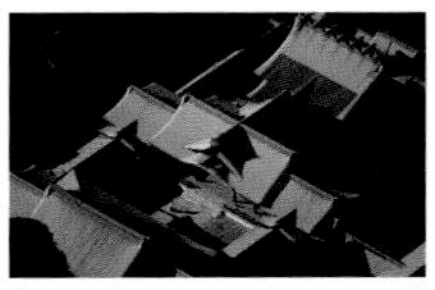

**PAGES 408–409**
SHINTO TEMPLE OF MEIJI-JINGU, TOKYO, HONSHU, JAPAN
(35°42' N, 139°46' E)

Severely battered by earthquakes and World War II bombing, Tokyo's religious heritage has been reduced to a few temples. One of those is Meiji-Jingu, a Shinto sanctuary that was built on the orders of the emperor Meiji and completed in 1920. This is where Tokyo residents gather to celebrate the New Year. The Shinto religion consists of rituals, ceremonies, and various customs associated with *kami*, spirits that protect communities and people, and which inhabit places in the urban or rural landscape that are considered sacred. Shinto establishes a simple relationship between people and the natural or manmade objects that surround them. It coexists easily with Buddhism, which is more metaphysical in character and was brought to Japan in the 6th century. Many Japanese incorporate both religions into their daily lives.

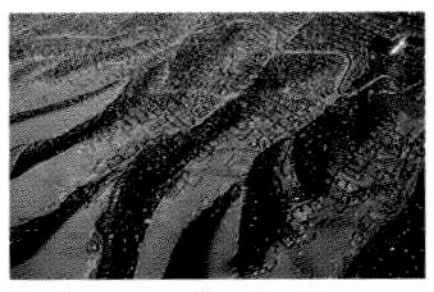

**PAGES 410–411**
YURTS ON THE OUTSKIRTS OF ULAANBAATAR (ULAN BATOR), MONGOLIA
(47°55' N, 106°53' E)

As large as Spain, France, Germany, and Portugal put together, Mongolia has only 2.7 million inhabitants. Ulaanbaatar, the capital, is set in the heart of the steppes, southwest of the Hentii mountain range. One-fourth of the Mongolian population is concentrated there, compared with one-eighth ten years ago. Tens of thousands of nomadic herders have settled in the city, driven off the land where their herds once grazed by desertification. Mongolia suffers from an extreme weather phenomenon called the *zud*, which causes severe summer and autumn droughts with extremely harsh winters. The *zud* used to be episodic, but has now been uninterrupted since 2000. Now over one-third of livestock have perished and the land is drained. Former nomads have pitched their traditional yurts—circular tents made from wool stretched over a wooden framework—around the outskirts of Ulaanbaatar, creating a huge shantytown of white points. Faced with this widespread phenomenon, the government has placed a ban on horses and goats. Living conditions are appalling, and alcoholism is a growing problem among the population that have been torn away from their steppe homelands. It now seems as if the nomadic way of life may not survive into the next generation.

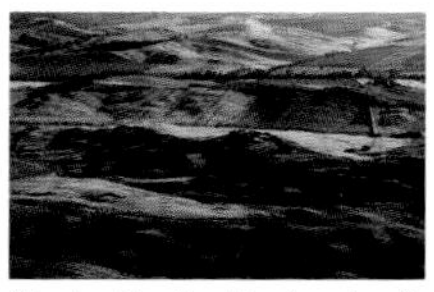

**PAGES 412–413**
COUNTRYSIDE AROUND SIENA, TUSCANY, ITALY
(43°19' N, 11°19' E)

Washed by the Tyrrhenian Sea, Tuscany in central Italy is one of the loveliest regions of the entire peninsula. Tuscany owes part of its fame to its hills, covered with vineyards, olive trees, corn and barley fields, and dotted with medieval villages. The hills also built the towns of the region, supplying the distinctive yellow-red clay whose color is still known as sienna. Aware of the advantages of living in harmony with the landscape, and of the potential risks of property development, mass tourism (60 million visitors in 2003), and industrialization, Tuscans developed ecotourism at an early date. Local businesses, especially craftspeople (leatherwork, marble, textiles, furniture), now adhere to Social Accountability 8000 (SA8000), a voluntary standard that ensures that economic development occurs through the ethical sourcing of goods and services.

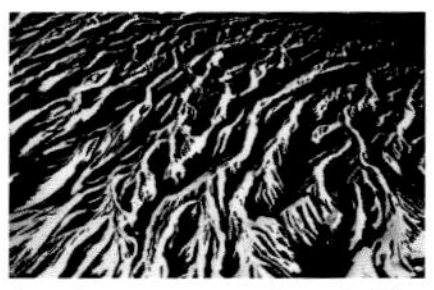

**PAGES 414–415**
SNOW-COVERED FLANKS OF KRONOTSKAYA VOLCANO, KAMCHATKA PENINSULA, RUSSIA
(56°00' N, 160°00' E)

At the eastern tip of Siberia, Kamchatka Peninsula spreads over nearly 145,000 square miles (370,000 km$^2$). This region of Russia is ruled by nature, and humankind is barely present (the population density is below 1 person per km$^2$). The peninsula is geologically very young (less than 1 million years) and has 160 volcanoes, including thirty that remain active; they were declared a UNESCO World Heritage site in 1996. Kronotskaya Volcano is one of the highest, at 11,570 feet (3,528 m). The 3,500 square miles (9,000 km$^2$) of the Kronotski Reserve are home to several protected species: the Kamchatka brown bear, lynx, sable, and fox. Facing Kamchatka across the Bering Strait, Alaska offers a similar landscape. Twenty-six thousand years ago small groups of people crossed the strait, at that time dry land, and gradually populated all of the Americas. The Sioux, the Inca, and the Guarani are all descendants of the people of Kamchatka.

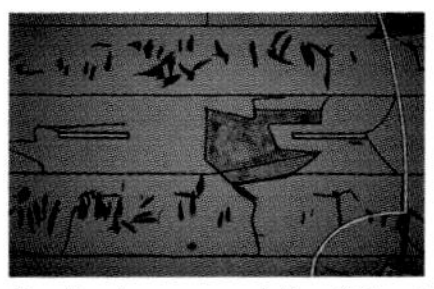

**PAGES 416–417**
DETAIL OF THE RUNWAY AT GIBRALTAR AIRFIELD, GIBRALTAR (BRITISH OVERSEAS TERRITORY)
(36°08' N, 05°21' W)

On the tarmac of the Gibraltar airfield, at the southern tip of the Iberian peninsula, a chance combination of geometric markings and repairs in the asphalt created this strange piece of abstract art. The air-transport sector, with 28 million jobs and an estimated value of $1.4 trillion, figures prominently in the world economy and is still expanding. Air routes carry one hundred times more passengers than they did fifty years ago, and two hundred times more goods. Outside of temporary drops in demand due to the fear of terrorist attacks, air traffic has shown an average regular growth of 6 percent per year for the past ten years; 1.5 billion tickets were sold in 2000. If this trend continues, by 2010 some 20,000 planes will crowd the skies to transport 2.3 billion travelers. But exploring the world by plane is costly in energy terms, and currently produces 3.5 percent of greenhouse gas emissions. This will rise to 15 percent by 2050 if the volume of air traffic continues to increase at its present rate.

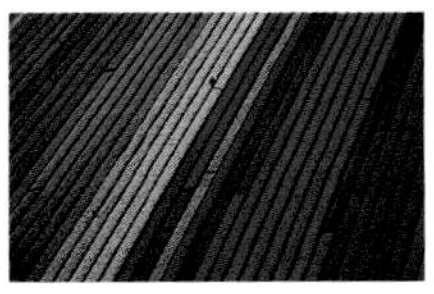

**PAGES 418–419**
FIELDS OF TULIPS NEAR LISSE, NEAR AMSTERDAM, NETHERLANDS
(52°15' N, 4°37' E)

In April and May of every year, the Dutch countryside briefly dons a multicolored garb. Since the first flowering in 1594 of bulbs brought back from the Ottoman Empire by the Austrian ambassador, four centuries of selection have led to the development of more than 800 varieties of tulip. On more than 50,000 acres (20,000 hectares), half devoted to tulips and one-quarter to lilies, the Netherlands produce 65 percent of the world production of flowering bulbs (or some 10 billion bulbs). But this success has been obtained at a high environmental price: in the 1990s, Dutch pesticide usage was the highest in Europe. Both the public and private sectors have therefore signed agreements regulating the use of chemical products, waste, and energy, and farmers have begun to make use of natural predators to protect their crops. Organic agriculture is expanding in the Netherlands and is now becoming big business. Similar environmentally conscious initiatives are happening worldwide; in several Canadian cities, as well as the town of Rennes in France, local councils have prohibited the use of chemical pesticides in public parks.

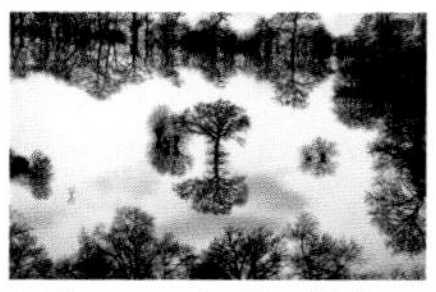

**PAGES 420–421**
TREES AMID THE WATERS NEAR TAPONAS, RHÔNE REGION, FRANCE
(46°07' N, 4°45' W)

In Taponas, in the Rhône region between the hills of Beaujolais and the hundreds of ponds scattered among the swampy Dombes area, the Saône River overflowed in March 2001. This is a recurring natural phenomenon in the low-lying zone downhill from the confluence of the Saône and the Doubs Rivers. The series of floods in several areas in eastern and central France was caused by torrential rains that fell on ground that was already waterlogged and on underground water tables saturated by recent rains. However, capricious climate conditions were not the only cause. Human action also played its part with construction in flood-prone areas, obstacles to water drainage (urban and transport infrastructure), poor river maintenance, and deforestation. With the threat of global warming, we must now adapt to these phenomena, which cannot be avoided: laws may now oblige local authorities and private owners to keep their buildings maintained or risk losing compensation, information on flood-risk areas will be more widely available, and collectives could be formed to help local people with tasks such as maintenance and evacuation.

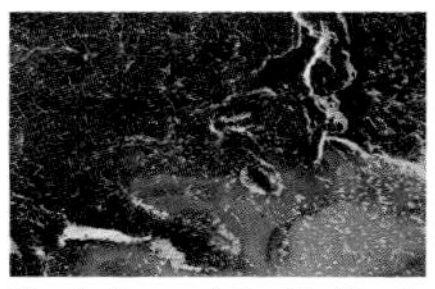

**PAGES 422–423**
POLYGONAL PATTERNED GROUND IN BEACON VALLEY, MCMURDO DRY VALLEYS, ANTARCTICA
(77°50' S, 160°40' E)

The bottom of the McMurdo Dry Valleys, one of the very few iceless regions in this continent, is strewn with polygonal ground patterns rather like holes in a dried-up pond. The extreme variations of temperature between summer and winter, when Antarctica is enveloped in six months of night and the temperature drops some 90°F (50°C), cause the ice deep down in the soil alternately to freeze and melt, thus creating this extraordinary mineral tapestry. The reason for these polygonal formations has never been fully explained, but their location has been pinpointed very precisely: they occur where the ground is permanently frozen, both in Antarctica and in the Arctic. Planet Earth does not, however, have a monopoly on these designs: pictures of Mars taken by the Mars Global Surveyor and by the rovers Spirit and Opportunity strikingly reveal identical polygonal patterns in the polar regions of the Red Planet, but on a colossal scale; the polygons measure several miles across, compared to the 30 to 100 feet (10 to 30 m) of those on Earth.

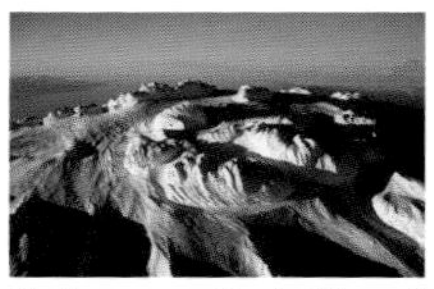

**PAGES 424–425**
ICE SCULPTED BY THE WIND ON TOP OF MOUNT DISCOVERY, ANTARCTICA
(78°20' S, 165°00' E)

At the summit of this extinct volcano (8,331 feet, or 2,681 m), the snow and ice have been sculpted by the katabatic winds that blow across the Transantarctic mountains. Very cold and extremely violent, these winds come from the top of the ice cap, and they gather speed (up to 198 mph, or 320 km/h) as they descend the slopes. In its climatic isolation, the Antarctic is covered by 8 million cubic miles (33 million km$^3$) of ice, in places 15,400 feet (4,700 meters) thick. The weight of this ice is so enormous that parts of the continent lie below sea level. This frozen crust together with the Antarctic Ocean, whose waters flow as far as the northern hemisphere, forms the world's largest climate control system. Antarctica is a land of paradox, for nowhere else on Earth is there such a vast quantity of fresh water (70 percent of the world's reserves), but because it is frozen it cannot be used, which makes this entire continent the driest desert in the world.

among the more affluent middle classes. In thirty years' time, more than 4 billion people—virtually half of humanity—will be living below the poverty line. In particular, this number will increase massively in Subsaharan Africa (400 million by 2015), and Central and Eastern Europe. Poverty will be concentrated mainly in the towns, which will increasingly become no-go areas, home to the poor but also a source of profit to the masters of the criminal underworld.

If poverty is to be tackled efficiently, new methods must be devised and combined. Firstly, the international community must provide more aid for the poorest nations and expand the debt relief program agreed by the G8 countries in July 2005; they must be prepared to finance the major infrastructures that are required—material, institutional, economic and social. The products of the poorest countries must be given

free access to the markets of the rich countries, but such developments must be made without disturbing the ecological balance and without accelerating the rate at which the planet's natural resources are being wasted.

The governments of poor countries must in turn reform their institutions: there can be no fight against injustice without democracy, for only an open society can uncover the inequalities and force those in power to act on behalf of the needy. Experience shows that the countries heading toward democracy are those where poverty is being best controlled. Of course, democracy is not just a matter of free elections, but also entails freedom of speech, of the press, of association—all essential to the opposition without which any election is a sham.

What is essential is that the poor must take control of their own destiny through being given the chance to work. To do this, they need the finance that will enable them to procure the necessary basics: land, an animal, a tool, raw materials. At present, however, the finance is not available, because commercial banks are not interested in customers who cannot offer the same guarantees as those who already own goods, property, or money.

This is where microfinance comes in. It allows the poorest people credit so that they can buy equipment and earn a living by way of free enterprise and the work that this can generate. Since the early 1980s, in Latin America and East Asia, the so-called Microfinance Institutions

married woman with five children, borrowed (without guarantee) $200 from the MFI Al Karama in order to set up a business making traditional garments. The institution itself gave her training in bookkeeping, and once again the investment proved to be a great success.

In total, the loans worldwide have now exceeded $8 billion. The rate of repayment is 98 percent, which is higher than that achieved by the commercial banks. These institutions are financed by both private and public donors, by the savings of their customers, and even by borrowing on the financial markets. But this amazing success is only in its early stages. Currently, more than 500 million people could benefit if only enough resources were available. For this to happen, the MFIs would need to develop still further, and governments should encourage and finance such programs, while the commercial banks should also look to help a clientele that is not only massive in scale but also potentially solvent. It will happen. Even now, the banks are beginning to take notice of this market of poor people. Of course, governments must take care that the beneficiaries do not saddle themselves with unnecessary debts and that their projects are viable. Every country needs to remain vigilant: the reduction of poverty must not be accompanied by an increase in the destruction of natural resources, and respect for human life must not be achieved by destroying nature. But then we shall see a real victory over poverty, and human charity will give way to human dignity.

JACQUES ATTALI

**TRADITIONAL VILLAGE NORTH OF ANTANANARIVO, MADAGASCAR** (18°49' S, 47°32' E)

393

Not only is Madagascar one of the world's fifteen poorest countries, but in 1998 it had the lowest levels of health spending in Africa, at $15 per person. Despite this inadequacy, Madagascar is one of the few countries in Subsaharan Africa that has largely escaped the HIV epidemic. This illness, now in its third decade, has taken on frightening proportions in the continent. In 2002, more than 39 million Africans were living with HIV, a number comprising 70 percent of the people infected in the world. In the same year, 2.4 million people in Africa died from it—compared with 8,000 in Western Europe. In four southern African countries, the rate of HIV infection in adults is climbing at alarming rates: 38.8 percent in Botswana, 31 percent in Lesotho, 33.4 percent in Swaziland, and 33.7 percent in Zimbabwe. Loss of life has been so high that it has affected the continent's economy and led to food crises. The HIV phenomenon has not yet reached its peak, and the international community—governments, nongovernmental organizations, media, and international institutions—has yet to find a way of dealing with this disaster.

## THE FIGHT AGAINST POVERTY

The poorest people are excluded from the banking system because they do not receive a salary, have no collateral, and are often illiterate: a priori they are not "profitable." Microcredit allows these men and women access to financial services (credit, savings) to start small-scale businesses that might generate income: a microbusiness.
The loan is paid back with income from this business, which sometimes also enables them to save money and to finance the education of their children.

**POVERTY IN THE WORLD**
**2.8 billion** people live on less than **$2** per day.
**1.2 billion** people live on less than **$1** per day.

**POTENTIAL OF MICROCREDIT**
It is estimated that microfinance could enable more than **500 million** of these people to start up their own small business and escape from poverty.

## THE BIRTH OF MICROCREDIT

Microcredit is a recent innovation, started 30 years ago in Bangladesh by the Grameen Bank project.

**PROMISING RESULTS IN LESS THAN 10 YEARS**
One-third of the Grameen Bank's customers have escaped from poverty. Another third have raised themselves to a level just below the poverty line.

**THE GRAMEEN BANK PROJECT**
This was started in **1976**, when Muhammad Yunus, head of the Economics department at Chittagong University, set up a research project on the possibility of a credit system designed for poor rural populations.
Between **1976** and **1979**, the project was tried and tested in several villages before being successfully extended.
In **1983**, the Grameen Bank became an independent bank.

**THE GRAMEEN BANK TODAY**
More than **3.7 million** borrowers, of whom **96%** are women
**1,267** branches
**46,000** villages have benefited, representing more than **68%** of the villages of Bangladesh
**90%** of the capital is held by the borrowers, and **10%** by the government

## MICROCREDIT TODAY

**AN INTERNATIONAL DEVELOPMENT**
There are microfinance institutions (MFIs) in over **130** countries, and a total of almost **7,000** MFIs worldwide.
Around **1,500** are recognized internationally and are supported by NGOs (non-governmental organizations).

**UNEQUAL ACCESS**
In Asia, **31%** of the poorest families have access to microfinance.
**9.1%** in Central and South America
**7.8%** in Africa and the Middle East
**1.7%** in Europe and in the newly independent states

**MORE AND MORE CUSTOMERS**
More than **80.9 million** clients have been helped worldwide.

**A MODEL THAT WORKS**
In Morocco in **2002**: 11 MFIs, **180,000** clients, rate of repayment **100%**
In Bangladesh: Grameen Bank rate of repayment over **97%**

## MICROFINANCE HELPS WOMEN

In most developing countries, women are excluded from political, economic, and social power, and rarely have access to education. But when they are able to work for profit, their entire family benefits (food, health, education).

**WOMEN IN THE WORLD**
Women make up **50%** of the world's population.
They do two-thirds of the world's working hours.
They only earn one-third of the world's income.
They own less than **10%** of the world's total resources.
They represent two-thirds of the world's illiterate population.
They represent two-thirds of the **1.2 billion** people who live on less than **$1** per day.

**WOMEN AND CREDIT: A MAJOR IMPACT**
Loans granted to women are most often repaid: in **98%** of cases.
Loans granted to women have a greater beneficial effect on children's quality of life, and consequently have greater social impact.
**82.5%** of the poorest customers that benefit from microfinance are women.

## THE OBJECTIVES OF THE MICROCREDIT SUMMIT CAMPAIGN

"Working to ensure that 100 million of the world's poorest families, especially the women of those families, are receiving credit for self-employment and other financial and business services by the year 2005."
*Declaration by the Microcredit Summit Campaign,* **1997**

**AN AMBITIOUS UNDERTAKING**
The campaign's starting point: at the end of 1997, **7.6 million** of the poorest families were given help.
Objective: to help **100 million** of the poorest families by 2005.
Growth rate required: **38%** per year

**WILL THE OBJECTIVE BE ACHIEVED?**
The final results will be announced at the World Microcredit Summit on November 12–15, **2006** in Halifax, Canada.

**SITUATION ON DECEMBER 31, 2003**
More than **80.9 million** customers helped, **54.8** of whom were among the poorest* when they were granted their first loan. Assuming an average of 5 persons per family, the help given to the **54.8 million** poorest customers by the end of 2003 would have extended directly to almost **278 million** people. The global expansion of the campaign rose to **621%** between **1997** and **2003**, and is running at an average rate of just under **39%** per year.

(*The Microcredit Summit Campaign defined "the poorest" as people in the lower half of those living below the poverty line, or those living on less than $1 per day at the time they enter the program.)

---

**NATIONAL MILITARY CEMETERY OF NOTRE DAME DE LORETTE, NEAR ABLAIN-SAINT-NAZAIRE, PAS-DE-CALAIS, FRANCE**
(50°23' N, 2°42' E)

Two major conflicts devastated Europe before the words of Victor Hugo (1802–1885) became a prophecy: "No more armies, no more frontiers, a single Continental currency.... The day will come when you will lay down your arms." Before unifying in peace, Europe had to go through two world wars; World War I cost 8 million lives, and World War II cost 45 million. The Battle of Lorette, from October 1914 to October 1915, in which the French and Germans struggled for possession of the strategic plateau of Artois, shed the blood of more than 100,000 victims on the fields of northern France. This military cemetery commemorates the fallen: 20,000 crosses are aligned across 30 acres, and eight ossuaries hold more than 22,000 unknown soldiers. Hugo also said, "The day will come when the only battlefields will be markets open to commerce and minds open to ideas." That day has come, but it is a battle whose outcome remains uncertain.

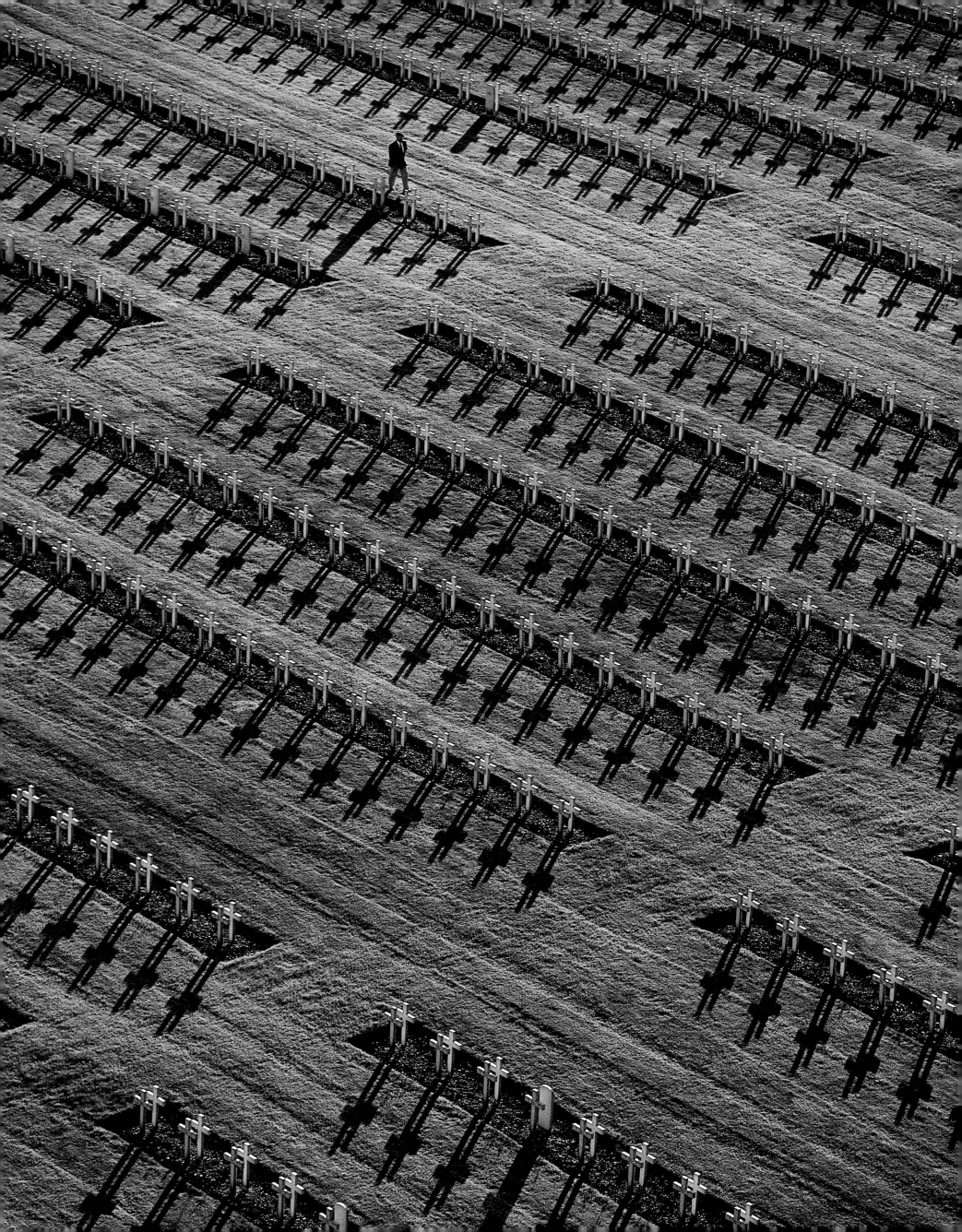

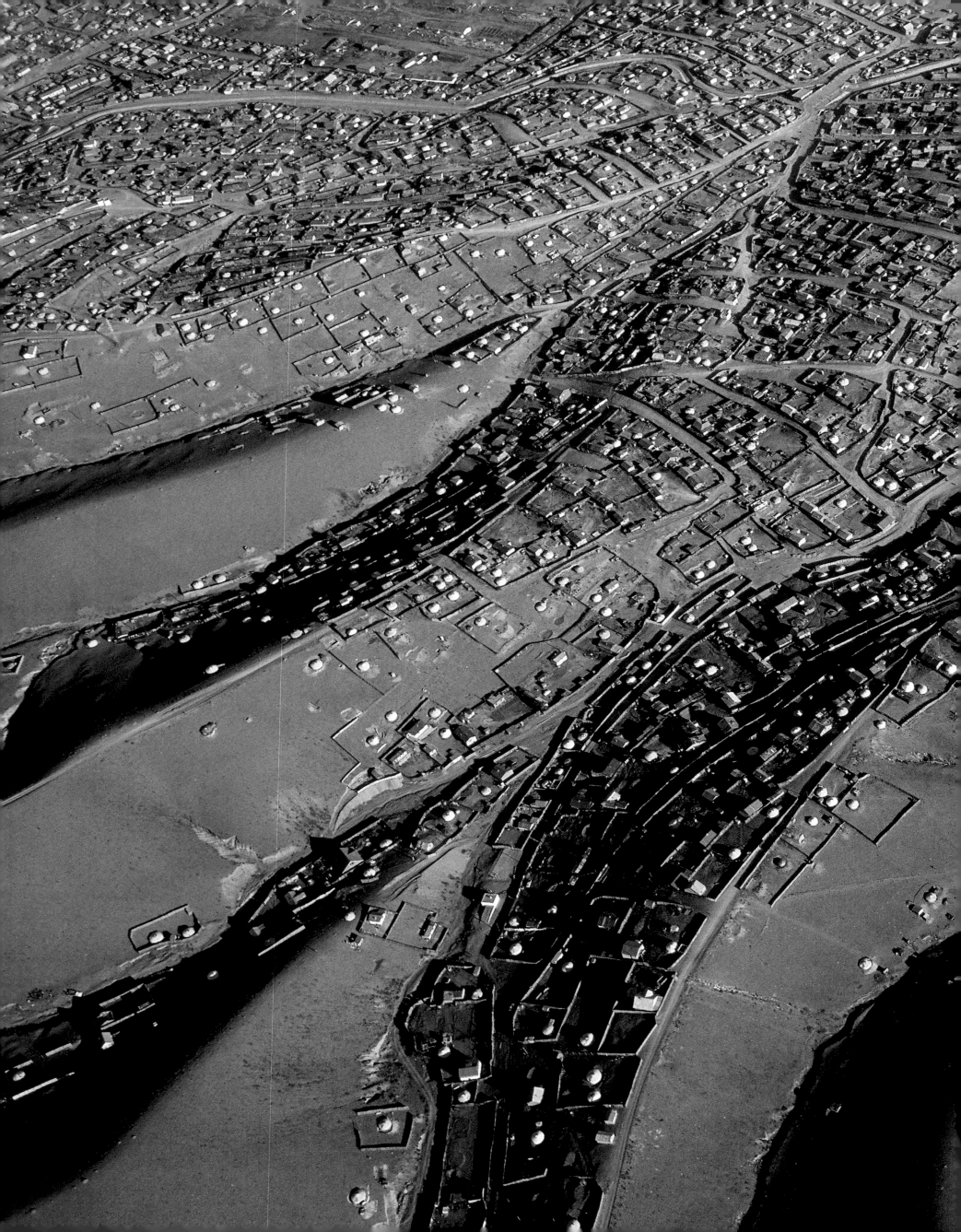

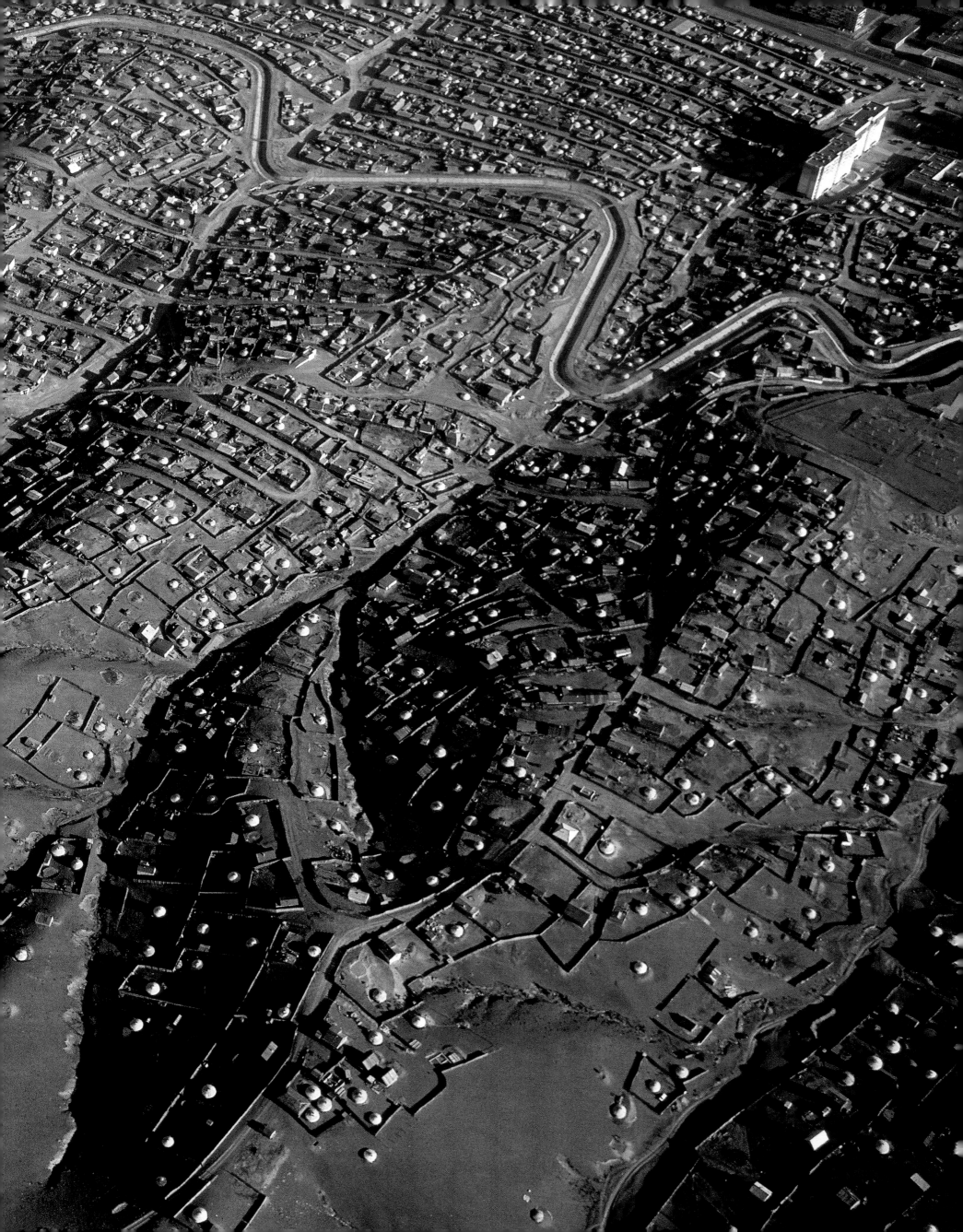

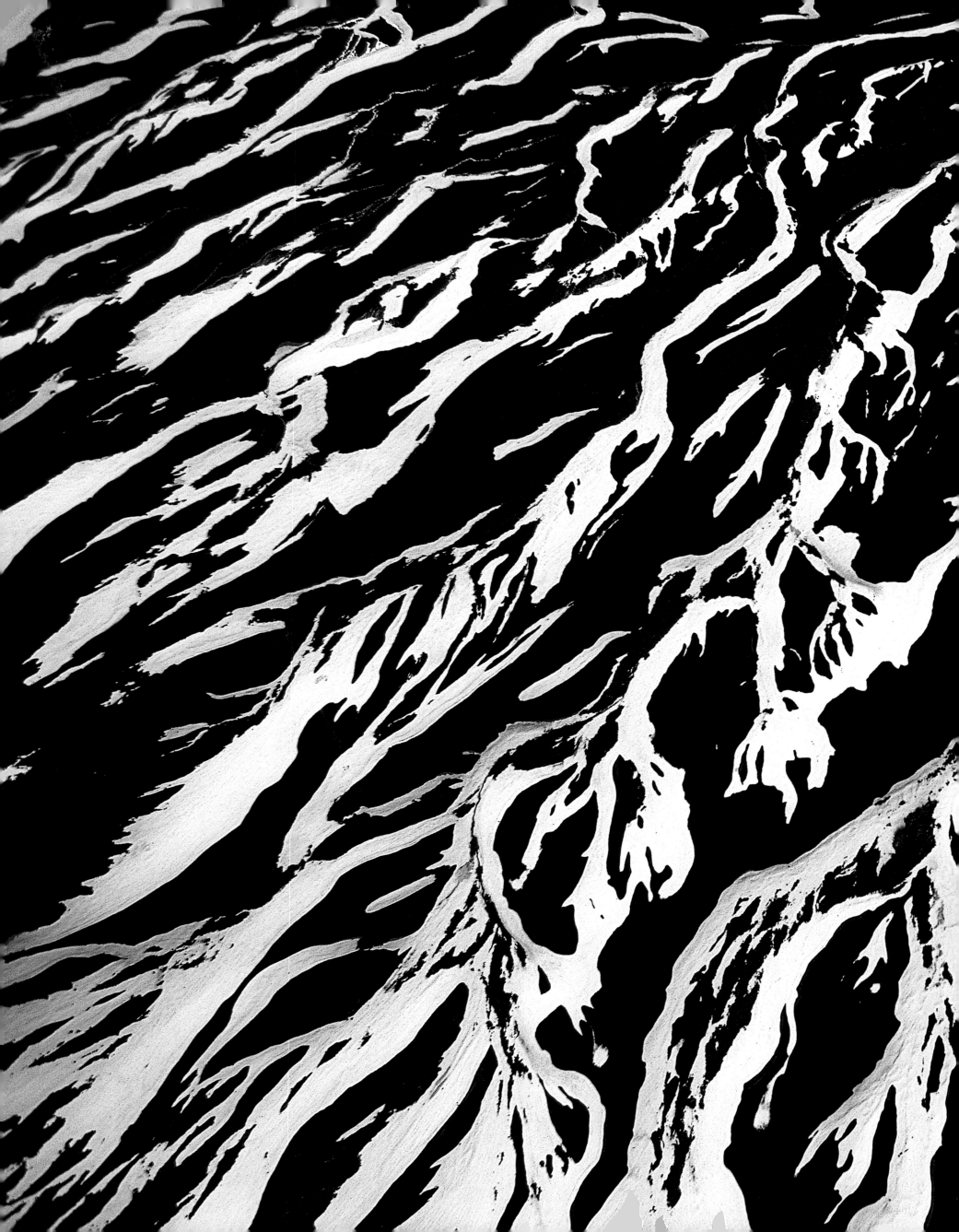

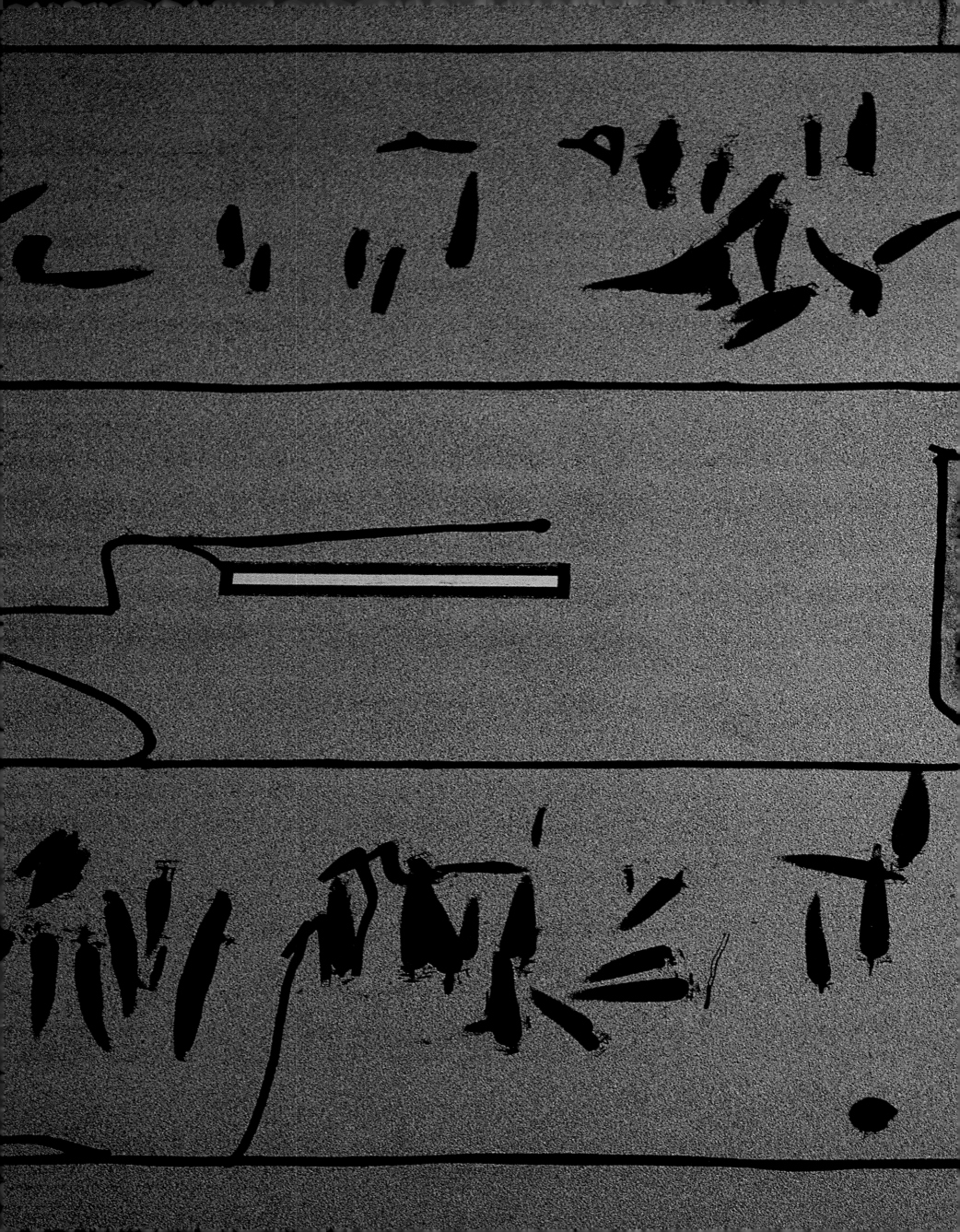

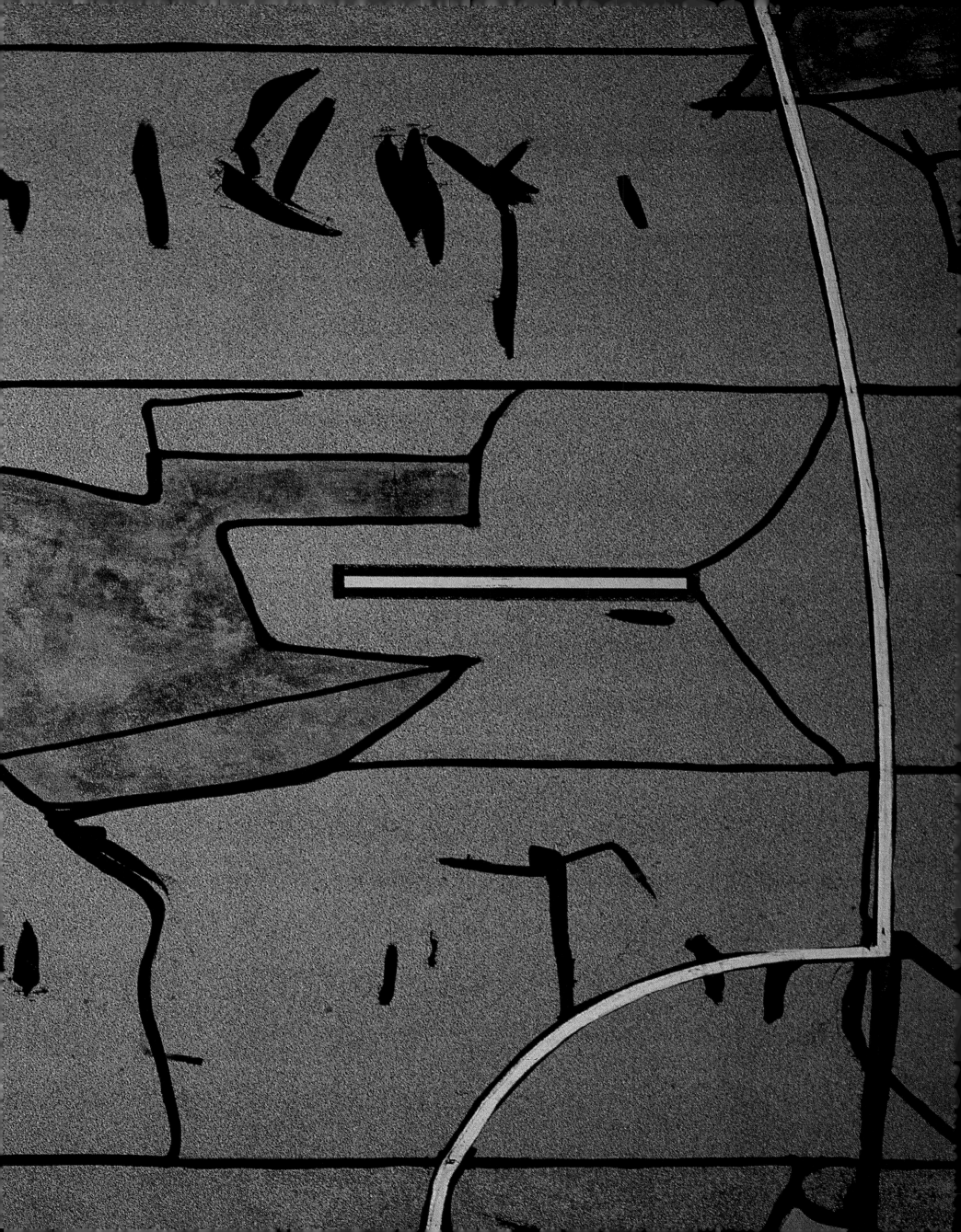

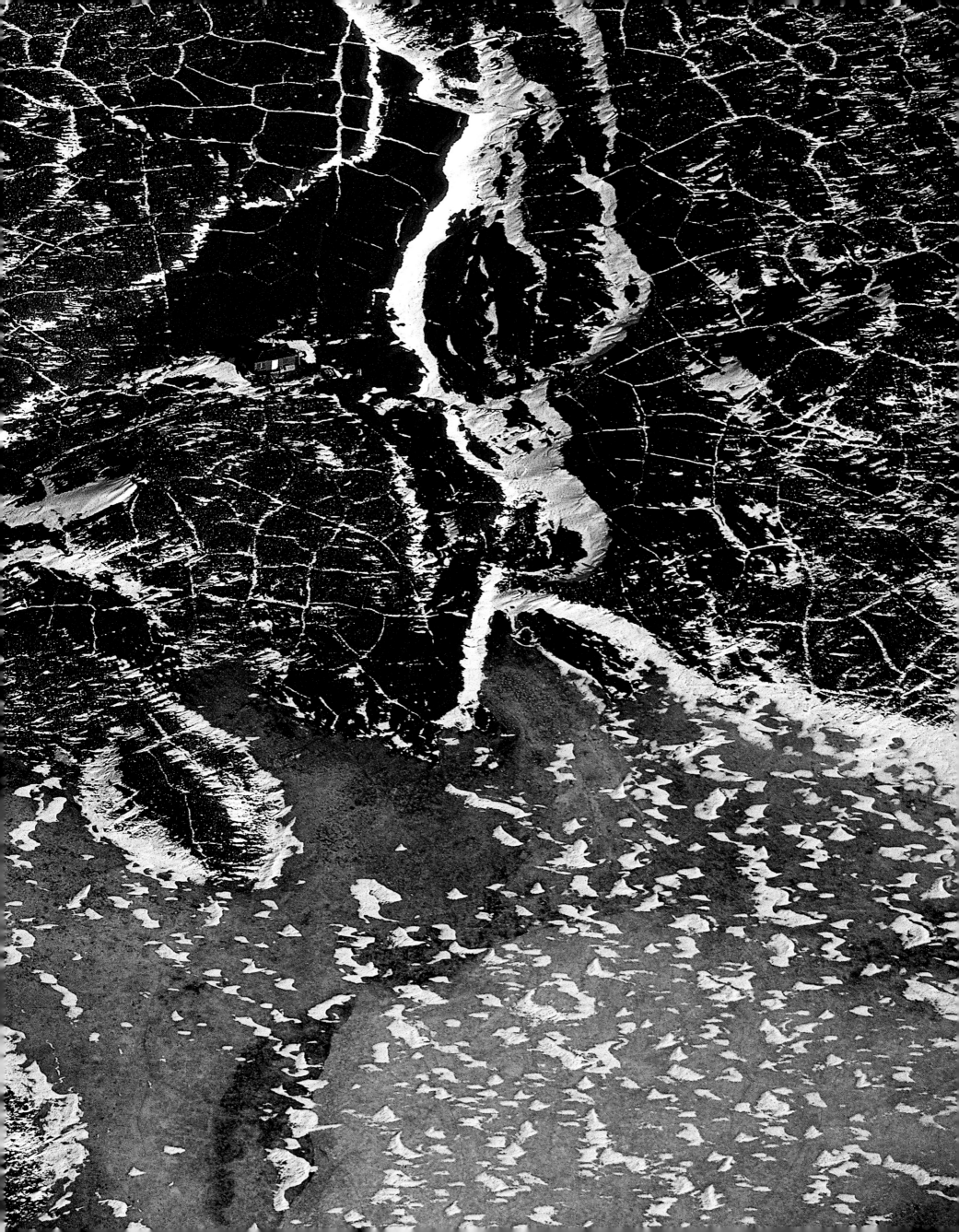

# ANTARCTICA:
# THE CONTINENT OF HOPE

Lost for millions of years at one end of the Earth, 98 percent of it covered
by an icy shell, Antarctica—a continent one and a half times the size of Europe—is as
fascinating as any remote and mysterious planet. Its immaculate white coat conceals
freshwater lakes, valleys, and mountains that no one has ever seen with their own eyes.
This polar continent belongs to no nation, and in 1991 it was declared a "natural reserve,
devoted to peace and science." This form of administration is unique, and makes
this realm of ice, rock, and wind an all too rare example of tolerance,
international cooperation and respect for the environment.

"Can you see that huge island of ice? That's B-15 A." Over the intercom, I was being kept informed by Frank Mendicino, co-pilot of the New York Air National Guard Hercules LC-130 which was taking me from Christchurch in New Zealand to the US McMurdo base on Ross Island in Antarctica. We were flying over the Ross Sea, along the coast of Victoria Land and the Transantarctic Mountains. Down in the dazzling white landscape almost 20,000 feet (6,000 m) below, the co-pilot was pointing to something that looked like a colossal raft of ice, floating flat in the deep blue sea. It was indeed the famous B-15 A, the biggest iceberg on the planet: 75 miles (120 km) long, with an area equivalent to that of Luxembourg. B-15 A was moving in the currents at a rate of 1.8 miles (3 km) a day, and it was heading straight for Drygalski, a spit of floating ice that is 43 miles (70 km) long and 9 miles (15 km) wide. The distance between them was just a matter of a few miles, and the world's media were holding their breath for the moment when the giant iceberg and the Drygalski glacier would collide. It finally happened on April 15, 2005, and was captured on satellite by the European Space Agency.

This, then, is Antarctica, a continent on the southernmost edge of our planet, in a solitude that is almost extraterrestrial. It is a country of all the extremes: the coldest, the driest, the windiest, the highest. The land of the most extraordinary icebergs on Earth, with massive glaciers—the largest is called Lambert, and is 300 miles (500 km) long and 50 miles (80 km) wide—inhabited by countless colonies of emperor penguins, the world champion bird divers (they can reach depths of some 2,000 feet, or 600 m). At the center of this continent, there is only one sunrise and sunset a year, and there is only one river—the Onyx, which flows through the Dry Valleys of McMurdo, where no land vertebrate has

a permanent home. "No one comes here casually," said the Canadian geologist John Tuzo Wilson, one of the great exponents of the tectonic plate theory. "It is a continent of extremes and of contrasts where there is no middle way."

You do not need a passport to go to Antarctica because, as we have seen, it does not belong to anyone—or, to be more precise, it belongs to the whole of mankind—but it took several decades as well as several major hiccups for the world to rouse its ecological conscience. The establishment of a nuclear reactor at McMurdo (closed down in 1972 with large areas of contamination) was one; the construction of a runway at the French base of Dumont D'Urville was another; and in 1957, a joint US and New Zealand scientific base was set up at Cape Hallett, right in the center of a huge colony of Adelie penguins (it was abandoned in 1973, and demolished in 2004–2005).

In 2003, McMurdo set up its own water purification system. Until then, its port was regarded as one of the most polluted in the world, but today the desire for change is clearly visible. Indeed, clean-up operations are going on at virtually all the bases on the continent.

Why is the example of Antarctica so important for the rest of the planet? One explanation may be that advanced by the meteorologist Edwin Mickleburgh: "The continent has become a symbol of our time. The test of man's willingness to pull back from the destruction of the Antarctic wilderness is the test also of his willingness to avert destruction globally. If he cannot succeed in Antarctica he has little chance of success elsewhere."

Antarctica, however, is far more than just a symbol of our will to protect the environment. It is also one of the main regulators of the Earth's climate, thanks to its ice caps, its belt of floes, and especially its circumpolar current (the great mass of water that flows round the continent with a range about 135 times further than that of all the world's rivers combined). The freezing, very dense waters that emanate from the circumpolar current sweep over the depths of the Pacific, Atlantic, and Indian oceans, mixing and cooling the waters of the Earth, and extending as far as the borders of the Arctic.

The ice continent is also the most extraordinary laboratory in the world. Here scientists study the physics of the atmosphere, the relationship

---

◁ **ICEBERGS OFF THE ADELIE COAST, ANTARCTICA** (67°00' S, 139°00' E)

These drifting icebergs recently detached from the glacial platforms of Antarctica, as can be seen from their flat shape and the ice strata that are still visible on their jagged sides. Like all 480 cubic miles (2,000 km³) of ice that detach every year from Antarctica, these icebergs will slowly be eroded by the winds and waves before disappearing. Antarctica is a place of extremes: temperatures reach as low as −129.3°F (−89.6°C), and winds reach speeds of 200 miles (300 km) an hour. The continent has an area of 5,500 square miles (14 million km²) and contains 90 percent of the ice and 70 percent of the freshwater reserves of the planet. Antarctica has been governed since 1959 by the Washington Treaty, which gives it international status and restricts its uses to scientific activities. Studies of the ice, which contains bubbles of air that were trapped as it formed, are particularly useful for insight into the origins of recent climate changes. The European EPICA program has allowed the ice to be examined down to a depth of over 2 miles (3,270 m), revealing a climatic archive that goes back some 900,000 years.

McMurdo, established by the Americans in 1955 on Ross Island, is the biggest of all the bases with 1,200 people in summer and 200 in winter. It is rather like a little mining town, and is known to the locals as "McTown." You need a map to find your way around. There is a post office, a fire station, and a greenhouse containing tomatoes, capsicums, and fresh herbs. McMurdo was Yann Arthus-Bertrand's base in October 2004 when, at the invitation of the National Science Foundation, he came to photograph Ross Island, the Erebus volcano, the giant iceberg B-15 A, and the polar desert of the Dry Valleys.

Covering an area approximately half the size of the island of Corsica, the McMurdo Dry Valleys (discovered in 1903 by Captain Scott) are the closest we can get on Earth to a Martian landscape. During the 1970s, this was where NASA came to put the finishing touches to preparations for the Voyager 1 and 2 missions. When you fly over this polar desert, you are astonished by the absence of ice and snow; the glaciers in the Taylor, Wright and Victoria valleys are surrounded by vast stretches of sand, stones and rocks sculpted by the wind. The contrast is simply spectacular. The bottom of these valleys is carpeted with strange mineral patterns—the result of extreme temperatures between winter and summer as the permafrost deep in the ground alternately freezes and thaws. This so-called polygonal patterned ground looks rather like a dried-up pond bed.

The biodiversity of the Dry Valleys is extremely limited: the only living things are bacteria (cyanobacteria), clusters of lichen that grow in the cracks of the rocks, unicellular algae (diatoms), microscopic insects,

and invertebrates such as rotifers, tardigrades, and nematodes (cylindrical worms), all of which are perfectly adapted to an infernal environment which marks the very limit of what can be survived on Earth. Scientists call them "extremophiles." When winter approaches, and temperatures fall to below −58°F (50°C), the nematodes dehydrate and enter into a state of dormancy, in which they can remain for years, like Sleeping Beauty, until the day when the right weather conditions arrive to give them the kiss of life. While they sleep, they may be caught in the violent winds that sweep the valleys, and transported far away. In June 2004, the Dry Valleys were designated an Antarctic Specially Managed Area (ASMA).

How is this vast no-man's-land governed? The system, as we have seen, is unique. Ratified in 1959 and implemented on June 23, 1961, the Antarctic Treaty regulates all international dealings and all activities on the continent and on the ice barriers south of the 60° parallel. Since 1961 it has been revised, with various agreements, protocols, and appendices, and is now known as the Atlantic Treaty System: it constitutes the sum total of all the laws that govern the 43 signatory states. Consultative meetings take place every year. The treaty also contained an agreement concerning the exploitation of Antarctic mineral resources (CRAMRA), but this was never implemented and was replaced by Article 7 in the protocol for the protection of the environment, which forbade all mining and oil exploitation for fifty years. What minerals lie hidden beneath the great crust of ice? Among those that have been discovered are iron, coal, uranium, gold, nickel, phosphates, and copper.

The heart of the treaty is the protocol for the protection of the environment (which came into force in 1998). This consists of 27 articles and 5 appendices, guaranteeing such protection. Waste is sorted and some of it processed on the spot, though most of it is exported. The bases should in principle be equipped with systems for treating dirty water, and when a scientific base is set up, it is obligatory even for toilet waste to be sent back home!

All scientific and logistical activities must be preceded by a detailed study on the environmental impact. However, one activity that has not yet been regulated by the treaty is bioprospecting—the search for sub-

## ⊡ AN EXTRAORDINARY CONTINENT

### LAND OF ICE
Area: **5,500,000 square miles (14,000,000 km²)**
(around one and a half times the area of the US)
Temperature: between **32°F (0°C)** (on the coasts)
and **–31°F (–35°C)** (inland) in summer and falling to **–31°F
(–35°C)** (coasts) and **–94°F (–70°C)** (inland) in winter

### HUMAN BEINGS
No permanent human settlements. Scientists and researchers:
around **1,000** in winter and **4,000** in summer
Tourists: **20,000** a year

### THE CONTINENT OF EXTREMES
The coldest: lowest temperature ever recorded:
**–129.28°F (–89.6°C)**
The driest: maximum annual rainfall **2 inches (50 mm)**,
comparable to that of the Sahara desert
The windiest: gusts of up to **199 mph (320 km/h)**
The highest: average height of **7,200 ft (2,200 m)**

### THE LAND
**98%** of the land has a permanent ice cap up to **15,400 ft
(4,700 m)** thick (four times the height of the Eiffel Tower).
There is only one river, the Onyx.
**77%** of the Earth's fresh water is contained in the ice.

### AN ISOLATED LAND
**2,200 miles (3,600 km)** from Africa
**1,800 miles (3,000 km)** from New Zealand
**1,400 miles (2,300 km)** from Tasmania
**590 miles (950 km)** from the tip of South America

## ⊡ BIODIVERSITY IN ANTARCTICA

### WILDLIFE
Around **350** species, mainly lichens, mosses, and algae
No land mammals live here permanently
**19** species of birds, including 5 species of penguins
**6** species of seals, including elephant seals and leopard seals
**2** species of higher plants: 1 grass and 1 variety of carnation;
no trees

### UNIQUE ORGANISMS
"Extremophile" organisms are able to resist extremes
of temperature, salinity, or aridity.
Antarctic fish have "antifreeze" proteins that enable them
to survive in temperatures below freezing.

### TREASURES ALREADY BEING HUNTED
Seals are hunted for their skin: in 1930 there were only a few left,
but today the population has risen to more than **1 million**.
The blue whale: more than **300,000** have been killed in
Antarctica, and today there are only **500** remaining.
More than **40** patents have been taken out worldwide on Antarctic
flora and fauna, and **90** additional applications
are said to have been filed with the US patents office.

429

## ⊡ A LAND FOR SCIENTISTS

### FIFTY YEARS OF RESEARCH
Systematic long-term exploration and scientific study of the
Antarctic began in **1957**, the International Geophysical Year (IGY).
12 nations set up more than 60 scientific bases in Antarctica
during the IGY, and explored most regions of the continent.
Today there are **47** scientific bases, of which **37** are permanent.

### AN INDICATOR OF CLIMATE CHANGE
Average temperature increase of **4.5°F (2.5°C)** over the
last 50 years—**5 times** greater than in the rest of the world.
Over the last 50 years, **87%** of glaciers have shrunk, and icebergs
melt earlier every year. Currently glaciers are shrinking an
average of **160 ft (50 m)** per year.
The fall of the West Antarctic ice cap into the sea as a result
of warming could raise sea levels by **23 ft (7 m)**.

## ⊡ ANTARCTIC EXPLORERS

### IN SEARCH OF THE SOUTHERN CONTINENT
James Cook: first explorer to go round the Antarctic Circle during
the **1770s**.
John Davis (American seal hunter): first-known landing on the
continent, February 7, **1821**.
It was not until the **1840s** that Antarctica was recognized
as a continent.

### THE BEGINNINGS OF SCIENTIFIC EXPLORATION
Evelyn Byrd (US): set up the first Antarctic base in Little
America, **1928**.

### EXPLORING THE ICE REGIONS
Dumont d'Urville (France): discovered the region of Adelie and
mapped the Pacific coast of the Antarctic in **1840**.
Clark Ross (Great Britain): pinpointed the position of the magnetic
South Pole in **1841**.
De Gerlache (Belgium): first truly scientific expedition, and first
to spend winter in Antarctica—the boat was trapped in the ice—
in **1898**.
Borchgrevink (Norway, with British crew): first team to spend
winter on land in **1899**.
Nordenskjöld (Sweden): discovered the first fossils on the
continent in October **1902**.

Charcot (France): mapped the west coast of the Antarctic
peninsula in **1903**.
Shackleton (Great Britain): first ascent of Mount Erebus (12,447 ft,
or 3,794 m), the highest volcano on the continent, with five other
explorers in **1908**.

### CONQUEST OF THE SOUTH POLE
Amundsen (Norway): first team to reach the South Pole,
**December 14, 1911**.
Scott (Great Britain): second team to reach the pole, January 18,
1912. Every member of Scott's expedition died on the return trip.

## ⊡ THE COMMON PROPERTY OF MANKIND

### THE ANTARCTIC TREATY (1959)
Signed by **12** countries; came into force in **1961**.
Regards Antarctica as being under international ownership;
all territorial claims are suspended.
Stipulates that Antarctica should be used exclusively for peaceful
scientific research.
Prohibits all military activities, nuclear explosions, and the
disposal of radioactive waste.
**45** signatory countries in **2003**

### THE MADRID PROTOCOL (1991)
Came into force in **1998**. Supplements the Antarctic Treaty.
Designates Antarctica as a "natural reserve, devoted to peace
and science."
Committed signatory countries to ensuring complete
protection of the Antarctic environment and its dependent
and associated ecosystems.
Prohibits all oil or mineral mining.

IN 1991, THE ANTARCTIC TREATY WAS EXTENDED FOR FIFTY
YEARS, TO RUN UNTIL 2041.

between solar activity and the Earth's magnetosphere, glaciology, oceanography, geology, volcanology, zoology, seismology, and especially astronomy, astrophysics, and cosmology. Dome C, home of the Franco-Italian base Concordia, is considered to be the best site on Earth for observing the stars.

It is on the southern polar ice cap, some 9,100 feet (2,800 m) thick, that IceCube—the biggest neutrino telescope in the world—is to be situated. Its construction began in January 2005, close to the US Amundsen-Scott base, and it is scheduled to be completed in 2012. IceCube's 4,200 "eyes" will be able to follow the paths of neutrinos, the most mysterious and ghostly elementary particles in the universe. This will enable astrophysicists to explain some great mysteries, such as the origin of gamma rays and the nature of dark matter—the invisible material that makes up 90 percent of the universe.

The ice of Antarctica is a remarkable archive of data: analysis of core samples extracted between 1999 and 2003 at the Franco-Italian Base C by EPICA (the European Project for Ice Coring in Antarctica) gave a great deal of insight into the way the climate has evolved over the last 740,000 years: during this period, the Earth has gone through eight climatic cycles. The warm periods of the last 420,000 years were characterized by temperatures similar to those of today, whereas earlier ages were colder and lasted longer. The longest warm period within these 740,000 years took place 420,000 years ago and lasted for about 28,000 years. It was analogous to the present age. These findings show that a new glaciation should not take place for another 16,000 years, but analysis of air bubbles trapped in the ice confirm that the current content of greenhouses is the highest in 440,000 years. The most recent core sample was extracted by EPICA on December 21, 2004 at a depth of 10,728 feet (3,270 m)—scarcely 15 feet (5 m) from the rock base. In all, the core samples taken at Dôme C will supply us with information about the climate over the last 900,000 years—the oldest ice ever obtained.

In order to go back even further in time, one would have to take samples of marine sediments from along the coasts: this is the aim of a very ambitious project called ANDRILL, financed by Germany, Great Britain, Italy, New Zealand, and the United States. From 2007 onward, teams from ANDRILL will be excavating in different locations below the glacial platform of Ross, in order to extract samples that will shed light on the climatic, tectonic, and glaciological history of Antarctica during the last 65 million years.

Cape Adare, at the eastern end of Victoria Land, is a long peninsula of volcanic origin, which is free of ice and snow. It is home to the largest colony of Adelie penguins in Antarctica: 500,000 birds come together here between early October and the end of January in order to breed. At this time, every square foot of ground is occupied by a nest. They are everywhere, even in the discarded barrels around the camp of the explorer Carsten Borchgrevink (the first man to spend the winter on the continent, 1899–1900). These nests consist of mounds of little pebbles, and the penguins' favorite pastime is to spend the whole day stealing stones from one another. The Adelies are one of five penguin species that reproduce in Antarctica (there are seventeen species altogether).

Some 35 to 40 million years ago, the South Seas were inhabited by some forty species of penguin, some of which were as big as a fully grown man, as was confirmed by the explorer Otto Nordenskjöld when on the island of Seymour, an Antarctic peninsula, he discovered the skeleton of a penguin 6 feet (1.8 m) tall, weighting about 297 pounds (135 kg). Beside the modern emperor penguin (4 feet, or 1.2 m, and weighing in at 55–90 pounds, or 25–40 kg), these giants, known as *Anthropornis nordenskjoeldi*, must have been truly impressive.

Antarctica is covered with a frozen crust of 30 million km³ of ice, each one weighing about a billion tons: the weight of the ice is so great that the Earth's crust lies half a mile (800 m) below sea level. This vast white coat contains 90 percent of the world's ice and 77 percent of its fresh water. If one could lift it up, one would discover mountain chains such as the Gamburtsev range, whose origin remains totally unknown, together with deep valleys and freshwater lakes—satellite radar altimeters have detected 140 of these. The largest, Vostok, is hidden beneath 1,300 feet (400 m) of ice, and it is thirty-two times the size of Lake Geneva.

In 2004, there were 36 scientific bases south of the 60° parallel. Port-Martin, the first French base, was built in 1950 in Adelie by Paul-Émile Victor's Expéditions Polaires Françaises. It was badly damaged by fire during the night of January 23, 1952, and so a second base was set up 50 miles (80 km) away, on the Pointe-Géologie archipelago. Today, the Dumont d'Urville (DDU in Antarctic jargon) houses around 80 people in summer and 20 in winter. It even has a post office. Along with the Italian Mario Zucchelli base at Terra Nova Bay (750 miles, or 1,200 km, to the west), DDU is the headquarters of the Franco-Italian Concordia base at Dôme C, at the very heart of the continent. From February to November 2005, Concordia welcomed its first group of 13 winter guests (11 French and 2 Italian).

> **GONDOLA RIDGE AND THE MACKAY GLACIER, DRY VALLEYS, ANTARCTICA**
(77°02' S, 161°50 W)

On the Earth there is one continent that is as fascinating and mysterious as another planet: Antarctica, the *Terra Australis Incognita* of explorers from the 17th to 19th centuries. It was not until 1899 that Carsten Borchgrevink became the first to winter on the continent. Today Antarctica is a world reserve dedicated to peace and science; it belongs to no other country and is regulated by the Antarctica Treaty signed in 1959 and expanded in 1991. From bioprospecting (searching for unknown organic molecules) to astronomy, almost all scientific disciplines run research programs here. For example, it was at the British-run Halley base that the "hole" in the ozone layer was discovered in the 1980s. At the US McMurdo base, they are studying the fossil evidence of the Big Bang, the gigantic explosion that preceded the creation of the universe, 15 billion years ago. Another important area of Antarctica research is the study of climate change, using bubbles of air that have been trapped inside the ice for hundreds of thousands of years.

stances and genetic resources that might be commercially exploited for food and cosmetic purposes by the pharmaceutical industry.

How will global warming affect the ice continent? The answers are contradictory. On the one hand, there are disturbing signs on the Antarctic peninsula, where temperatures have risen by 4.5°F (2.5°C) during the last fifty years, resulting in 75 percent of the 400 glaciers shrinking, while huge platforms of ice such as Larsen B have disintegrated (March 2002); on the other hand, data collected in eastern Antarctica show that temperatures are falling. The system is extremely complex (remember that this is a vast continent), and temperatures alone are not enough to indicate general trends. There can be marked variations from one year to the next, El Niño can have a major influence, and predictions differ according to the type of mathematical model used. How the continent will react to global change is one of the vital studies that will take place during International Polar Year in 2007–2008.

As for the future, could it be that eventually political and economic interests will override our desire to protect this, the last untouched territory on Earth? Let us hope not, and let us continue to believe in the words of the great American polar explorer Richard Byrd: "I am hopeful that Antarctica in its symbolic robe of white will shine forth as a continent of peace, as nations working together there in the cause of science set an example of international cooperation."

LUCIA SIMION

431

**⌄ A SPIT OF THE TAYLOR GLACIER REACHING INTO BEACON VALLEY, DRY VALLEYS, ANTARCTICA** [77°48' S, 160°50' E]

Antarctica is a vast and frozen continental land mass, one and a half times the size of Europe and covered with the biggest ice cap in the world. It is so thick and so extensive that it covers 98 percent of the continent and holds captive 70 percent of the planet's reserves of fresh water. Close to the American science base at McMurdo, the region of the Dry Valleys is one of the rare terrains that are not covered with ice. The katabatic winds that blow from the heart of the continent are so cold and so strong that snow cannot drift. The rocks are exposed, revealing sedimentary layers of ocher from rivers and lakes, interspersed with black basalt, which is volcanic in origin. There are some forms of life that have adapted themselves to these conditions: bacteria and unicellular algae, endolithic lichens that grow in the rocks themselves, and also nematodes (cylindrical worms), which dehydrate and go to sleep as winter approaches, but wake up again when weather conditions improve.

# THE STORY OF A PHOTOGRAPH

The Heart of Voh has become the symbol of a planet in urgent need of protection.
Thanks to Yann Arthus-Bertrand, this image has now been seen all over the world.
Twelve years after his original photograph, he returned to the same spot
to fly over the same mangrove swamp once again.

No, this clearing wasn't carved by human hands. Nor was it created with computer manipulation! Nature is the originator of this motif amid the mangrove swamps of New Caledonia. Many people have wondered about this enigmatic image, especially its size. To satisfy their curiosity, Yann Arthus-Bertrand took a second helicopter with him when he returned to the Heart of Voh in 2002. The light patch in the foliage at the bottom of the photo is a result of the blast of air from the second helicopter's blades. For Yann, returning to the Heart of Voh was rather like making a pilgrimage to the site of one of the earliest photographs of this entire project. The image was not planned in advance. During that original flight, the pilot simply said to Yann: "I want to show you something." It was not long before this image with its disturbing message became the symbol of the entire project. Between 1990 and 2002, the vegetation grew back inside the heart, where the salt had cleared almost 10 acres (4 hectares) of ground. These shapes are created by chance in the more elevated areas, which are less often flooded, causing salt to become concentrated by evaporation. If the salinity continues to drop, the mangrove may close up the heart completely. If the salination comes back, the heart will rebuild itself. Nature will decide. Perhaps the only way to find out will be to come back.

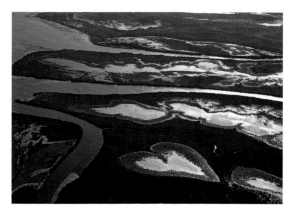

△ YANN'S FIRST SHOT OF THE HEART OF VOH, IN 1990

◁ (TOP) MANGROVE SWAMPS NEAR VOH, NEW CALEDONIA. PHOTO IGN, 1982

◁ THE HEART OF VOH, NEW CALEDONIA, FEBRUARY 2002

# THE STORY OF A BOOK

"What about Sicily?"

This impatient question is addressed to Yann Arthus-Bertrand, who has just entered the office of the Altitude agency in his usual energetic fashion. Sicily is no go, stubbornly hidden under clouds. A change in plans at the last minute made the more obliging Austria the subject of the latest European report. For the coming weekend the forecast is predicting clear skies over Finland. Good news, because that trip had already been put off twice. There's little time left to confirm airline tickets and an on-site helicopter rental. Not much time either for viewing the results of the last shoot. And still less for all the meetings crammed into the photographer's tight schedule.

An entire wall of the agency is taken up by a vast world map bristling with blue arrows to indicate countries already flown over, and red ones for those yet to be covered. It's not quite up to date, but it represents six years of frantic work on this project, struggles to obtain permission to fly through international air spaces, and globetrotting at the rate of two weeks of travel per month. The map testifies to the early stages of the saga, when each new blue arrow was a victory for the entire team. Yann, who drives the project, confirms it: "The author of this book is the whole team. When the project began I was very naive. I thought that five years would be enough. But in fact, this is the work of a lifetime and it's far from finished."

For Yann, the adventure of photography began in 1978. He was 32 years old, and left for Kenya with his wife, Anne, to study the behavior of a family of lions in the Masai Mara reserve. In those three years of patient research, Yann supplemented his written notes by taking photographs. "I soon realized that photographs give information in a completely different way than text." He was supposed to be writing a thesis, but it turned into a book: *Lions*, published in 1983.

At the same time, using his pilot's license to finance his long African project, he carried tourists in a hot-air balloon, offering them a new way of discovering the Kenyan grasslands. He himself was soon completely won over by this new and different way of seeing reality, that can reveal a huge expanse or a close-up view, depending on the range.

The foundations had been laid. In fact, those years in Kenya already contained all the ingredients that would make such a success not only of this book, but of all Yann's photographic work: a pronounced preference for long-term projects, a determination to describe every facet of a subject, and the association of the images with genuinely informative texts, written by scientists specializing in the topics concerned.

⌃ In 1978, Yann went to Kenya to spend three years studying lions. To earn a living while he was there, he took tourists on balloon trips, and his love of aerial photography was born.

⌃ Yann sometimes requires help from the armed forces to fly over troubled areas. This was the case during the tsunami of December 2004, when he flew in a helicopter chartered by the French army, based on the helicopter carrier *Jeanne d'Arc*, to see the devastation in Meulaboh, Indonesia.

◁ The arrival of the helicopter in remote locations often arouses the curiosity of local people. Children in particular come from all around and always want to climb inside the helicopter: this was the case in Côte d'Ivoire in February 1998.

With his team, Yann gradually developed the plan that would draw together all these components. "The idea was to show what the Earth looks like today," he says, "through pictures that could explain the world and alert people to important problems, current or future."

The goal of making a portrait of the planet in aerial photographs gradually took hold of him, but the scope of the task remained a stumbling block for his potential partners. Yet the photographer's enthusiasm, energy, and tenacity helped him convince several companies and governments to sponsor this titanic effort that would require colossal resources (one hour in a helicopter costs between $950 and $3,800). The blessings and support of UNESCO also helped, providing an effective door-opener that also unlocked quite a few air spaces.

The fact remains that in some sensitive countries, aerial photography is tantamount to espionage. So it took him three years to get permission to fly over India. But Yemen, Saudi Arabia, and China, for instance, have never relented. "Not yet," Yann corrects, showing that for him perseverance overcomes resistance.

But flight permission is just the first of many obstacles. The next is to find, on site, a means of flight (not easy in the Ténéré Desert), or else to bring one along, as he did for Easter Island. Although some photographs are taken from a plane, microlight, or paraglider, his preference is for the helicopter, a machine that can be manipulated, allowing every altitude and every angle.

"A helicopter is a wonderful tool," the photographer confirms. "You take it up, bring it down, orient it easily to find the best frame—just like a crane or a mobile tripod." That depends, of course, on having an experienced pilot at the controls. "He has to be able to place the helicopter as I tell him to. The pilot is really situated between the picture and me, so he has to know aerial photography, he's got to be really good."

The pilot also has to know the area and its sights; it's too expensive to make a reconnaissance flight beforehand to size things up. So Yann and his team have to trust maps and tourist guidebooks, which fill dozens of shelves in the agency offices, and then trust in the pilot. In New Caledonia, it was the pilot who led Yann to the

A worker rests on bales of cotton, Côte d'Ivoire.

Heart of Voh, which became the emblem for the entire project. It is also necessary to trust in chance, never relaxing attention and having a good eye: 80 percent of the photographs were not planned in advance!

And finally the last, indispensable requirement: good weather. Forecasts from Météo France Internationale have helped the team avoid many a disaster, but it's not unknown for a flight, after months of planning, to be canceled at the last minute because of cloud cover.

In the air, in the tight cabin of the helicopter, the assistant juggles with the flight log and seven cameras equipped with different lenses, responding to Yann's demands as he hovers restlessly in the doorway. He's ready at any minute to put on the red anorak that he always remembers to pack, so he can be put down, just long enough for a shot, on a monumental iceberg. Reduced to the status of a tiny red dot, he will provide the scale of the immense scope of nature.

Back from an assignment, he identifies the pictures with the precious information noted during the flight.

Between glass plating, filing, selection, numbering, archiving, it takes a long time to create a documentary archive. And sometimes, a very long time: approximately 10,000 photographs taken in India (90 percent of the work done there) have been blocked by the country since March 1999. Developed by the Indian army, then turned over to the authorities, they have never been returned.

This image database today has some 500,000 aerial views taken in more than 100 countries. Thanks to their geographic coordinates, it will be possible in a few years to record changes in the portrait of our ever evolving planet. For instance, since March 2000 the house at Keremma, in Brittany, no longer stands overlooking its fragile sand peninsula. Here and there, the face of the Earth has already visibly changed. And the captions that accompany the images, providing food

An aerial shot reveals the making of a photograph in Côte d'Ivoire.

for thought, have had to be updated between the first printing of the book and the present revised edition.

This book, as the author explains, is not only a collection of spectacular photographs: "A book is a goal, a direction, something that remains. It is an opportunity for a photographer, it keeps him from going off in all directions." And yet, he had to go off in many different directions in order to build every chapter of the great story he wanted to tell, the story of today's world. It is a reality that is at once historical, geographic, ecological, and human, a story that often cannot be seen from the ground. An opening that, from the surface, looks like a wide valley, when viewed from higher up becomes a slight scar on the Earth's skin.

People are present in almost every photo in this collection—if not physically, then through the traces they have left behind. Also, as their author explains, "Everyone seems at home in these photographs." We all consider ourselves, quite naturally, residents of the Earth. It is a feeling of disconcerting simplicity, which may have contributed to the book's worldwide success and the touching meetings with people at the book signings and exhibitions that followed publication. "People came up to hug me out of gratitude, some of them crying with emotion," Yann recalls. One pregnant young woman had me dedicate a book to her future child. I had never had contact with the public in this way before, and it was overwhelming."

Yann Arthus-Bertrand discusses sustainable development with the people of Kabul, April 2005.

An optimist, the photographer sees all of this as a sign that "today a global awareness is taking shape, the awareness that we all belong to the same unique planet and that it is being degraded." Almost 3 million people all over the world wanted to own this portrait of their planet in 440 pages (and 9 pounds in weight!), which has been translated into 24 languages including Chinese, Taiwanese, Japanese, Korean, Hungarian, Finnish, Slovakian, Catalan, and Arabic.

"This success surprised and encouraged me, but it's also beyond me. No one expected it. It's impressive, moving, encouraging. But it's also more difficult,

Above Mount Everest, at 16,500 feet, oxygen is necessary.

because you're in constant demand. That gives you the chance to do it better yet, to have a stronger ethic and truly follow your path with greater independence." Moreover, some countries that had previously been reluctant are ready to allow flights over their territory. China could become one of them sometime soon. And the team that accompanies the photographer today has been expanded to respond to new needs.

This great popularity with a public of all nationalities provided a unique opportunity to make the many admirers of this planet aware of the great ecological, economic, and human challenges of our century. This has become a major enterprise for the photographer, who, as a witness to his time, strives to give meaning to his work. His task has evolved from year to year. "Throughout these long hours spent flying over the Earth, talking to specialists, meeting people, I have moved from being an ecologist to a humanist. There can be no sustainable development unless we can learn to live together." For two years, Yann and his team have been working on a new project, the natural sequel to this one, but this time in video form: interviews with men and women from all over the world, expressing their own concepts of life and their own visions of the world.

In all his work, Yann tries to ask questions of us: it's up to every individual to decide what kind of planet we choose, every day, individually and collectively, to leave

Yann flies over Namibia with a Himba woman, who calmly points out her village.

More than 2 million people visited the exhibition at the Luxembourg Gardens in Paris, 2000, the first in a long series.

to our children and to future generations. Each one of us, according to his or her own sensitivity, will react individually. The authors accommodate this kind of individual response in the sections between Yann's photographs in this second new edition. Specialists from all over the world, they share their specific knowledge with the public at large, expounding their own viewpoints, in texts supported by statistics and examples, concerning the most disturbing ecological problems for the future of humankind.

When Yann decided to exhibit these photographs in public places and at no charge, to pass on his own convictions, the idea was met with almost unanimous skepticism. Only the Senate in Paris provided space for the exhibition, at the Luxembourg Museum. The show was originally booked for a month and a half starting in May 2000, but it ran until December, attracting a flood of excited visitors. The 150 large-format photographs were then displayed on the fences of the Luxembourg Gardens, finally granting Yann's dearest wish: to share with everyone this voyage above the Earth, to reach and amaze an audience of more than 2.5 million. Likewise, the book, which was sold at an accessible price at the wish of photographer and publisher, was within reach of almost every purse, especially among buyers not usually drawn to this type of work. They were fascinated with the book and in turn bought it as gifts for others. "This book is no innocent gift. You receive it and then buy another to give to someone else," Yann observes.

Contrary to predictions, the prints exhibited on the fences of the Luxembourg Gardens were not harmed. It was as if the beauty of the Earth, by itself, had inspired respect. When the exhibition ended, the prints were auctioned off for charity. "What surprised me most," explains Yann, "was that by holding an exhibition, I changed status in the eyes of the public, and turned from a photographer into an artist. But I'm still the same person."

Other prints, accompanied by a great global map on the ground, on which visitors had fun covering the world in a few steps, set out in turn to tour the world. They were magically integrated into the main square of Copenhagen, Denmark, as well as in the port of Hamburg, Germany. By day as well as by night, people

in Caracas admired a little corner of the Philippines, while people of São Paulo discovered a sampling of Japan, and in Ankara, Kabul, Doha, and Taipei, they marveled at the Netherlands. Hosted by more than 80 cities in more than 30 countries, the exhibition has already attracted some 60 million visitors, and it has been praised from St. Petersburg to Beijing. So let them prepare, in Ljubljana and Geneva, to offer a VIP welcome to the star of the event in person—the Earth.

Yann asks the people of a Madagascan village about locust swarms in the region.

# INDEX OF TOPICS

Page numbers in *italics* refer to illustrations.

# INDEX OF PLACES

*All references are to illustrations*

# ACKNOWLEDGMENTS

At the time of writing this page, which stirs good memories from all across the globe, we fear that we may have forgotten to mention some of you who have helped us to bring this project to life. If so, our sincere apologies and our warmest thanks. Our thoughts also go out to all the "anonymous" people who have contributed in one way or another to this crazy enterprise.

## UNESCO:
Federico Mayor, Director-General, Pierre Lasserre, director of the Ecological Sciences division, Mireille Jardin, Jane Robertson, Josette Gainche, Malcolm Hadley, Hélène Gosselin, Carlos Marquès, Vladislav Oudatchine, from the Bureau of Public Information, Francesco di Castri and Jeanne Barbière, from the environment team, as well as Gérard Huber for promoting our project to this organization.

## FUJIFILM:
Masayuki Muneyuki, President, Toshiyuki "Todd" Hirai, Minoru "Mick" Uranaka, of Fujifilm in Tokyo, Peter Samwell of Fujifilm Europe, and Doris Goertz, Mrs. Develey, Marc Héraud, François Rychelewski, Bruno Baudry, Hervé Chanaud, Franck Portelance, Piotr Fedorowicz, Françoise Moumaneix, and Anissa Auger of Fujifilm France

## AIR FRANCE:
François Brousse and Christine Micouleau, as well as Dominique Gimet, Mireille Queillé, and Bodo Ravoninjatovo

## EUROCOPTER:
Jean-François Bigay, Xavier Poupardin, Serge Durand, and Guislaine Cambournac

## AFGHANISTAN:
French Embassy, Colonel Daniel Chambon
The troops of ISAF:
General Ethem Erdagi, ISAF commander in Afghanistan
Commander Ozkan, chief of the ISAF Turkish helicopter detachment
Commander Volkan, ISAF air operations officer
Daniel Massat-Bourrat of the CCF and Helmand
Sultan Ahamad Bahee
The pilots of the Afghan army:
General Amir Djan
General Dawran
Mr. Loudin
Hamid Karzai and Jaoued Loudin
Zaher Mohammed Azimi

## ALBANIA:
ECPA, Ltd: Colonel Aussavy, DICOD, Colonel Baptiste, Capitaine Maranzana, and Capitaine Saint Léger SIRPA, Charles-Philippe d'Orléans, DETALAT, Capitaine Ludovic Janot; Teams from the French Air Force, Etienne Hoff, Cyril Vasquèz, Olivier Ouakel, José Trouille, Frédéric Le Mouillour, François Dughin, Christian Abgral, Patrice Comerier, Guillaume Maury, Franck Novak, pilots

## ALGERIA:
President of the Republic Abdel Aziz Bouteflika
Ministry for the Environment and Land Management:
Chérif Rahmani, Minister
Mohamed Si Youcef
Lylia Harchaoui
Farid Nezzar
All the Algerian states, state governors, and directors of the environment
French Embassy in Algiers:
Anis Nacrour
Michel Pierre
Tassili Airlines:
Mohamed Boucebci
Rachid Nouar
Pilot: Samir Rekibi

## ANTARCTICA:
French Institute for Polar Research and Technology; Gérard Jugie; L'Astrolabe, Capitaine Gérard R. Daudon, Sd Capitaine Alain Gaston; Heli Union France, Bruno Fiorese, pilot; Augusto Leri and Mario Zucchelli, Projetto Antartida, Italian Terra Nova base.
At the US McMurdo base, Raytheon:
Elaine Hood, Karen Yusko, Melba Gabriel
National Science Foundation: Guy Guthridge
Pilots: Dustin and Scott
Helicopter coordinators: Monika and Patrick
Mechanics: Bob, Ron, Bob, and Steve
Helicopter supplies: Wendy

## ARGENTINA:
Jean-Louis Larivière, Ediciones Larivière; Mémé and Marina Larivière; Felipe C. Larivière; Dudú von Thielman; Virginia Taylor de Fernández Beschtedt; Cdt Sergio Copertari, pilot, Emilio Yañez and Pedro Diamante, co-pilots, Eduardo Benítez, mechanic; Federal Police air division, Commissioner Norberto Edgardo Gaudiero; Capt. Roberto A. Ulloa, former governor of Salta Province; Orán Police, Salta Province, Cdt Daniel D. Pérez; Institute of Military Geography; Commissioner Rodolfo E. Pantanali; Aerolineas Argentinas

## ARMENIA:
Michel Pazoumian
Léon Bagdassarian of Saberatours
Armenian Embassy in France, especially Edward Nalbandian, ambassador, and Ruben Kharazian
French Embassy in Armenia, Henri Cuny, ambassador
Gérard Martin, cooperation attaché
Armenian Development Agency and Arthur Babayan
Armenian Ministry of Foreign Affairs, particularly Shahen Avakian and Hamlet Gasparian;
Christophe Kebabdjian and Max Sivaslian

## AUSTRALIA:
Helen Hiscocks; Australian Tourism Commission, Kate Kenward, Gemma Tisdell, Paul Gauger; Jairow Helicopters; Heliwork, Simon Eders; Thai Airways, Pascale Baret; Club Med in Lindeman Island and Byron Bay Beach

## AUSTRIA:
Hans Ostler, pilot

## BAHAMAS:
Club Med in Eleuthera, Paradise Island, and Columbus Isle

## BANGLADESH:
Hossain Kommol and Salahuddin Akbar, External Publicity Wing of the Ministry of Foreign Affairs; Tufail.K. Haider, Bangladeshi ambassador to Paris, and Chowdhury Ikthiar, first secretary; Renée Veyret, French ambassdor to Dhaka; Mohamed Ali and Amjad Hussain of Biman Bangladesh Airlines, as well as Vishawjeet, Mr. Nakada, Fujifilm in Singapore, Mr. Ezaher of the Fujifilm lab in Dhaka, Mizanur Rahman, director, Rune Karlsson, pilot, and J. Eldon. Gamble, technician, MAF Air Support, Muhiuddin Rashida, Sheraton Hotel in Dhaka, Mr. Minto

## BELGIUM:
Thierry Soumagne
Wim Robberechts
Daniel Maniquet
Bernard Séguy, pilot

## BOTSWANA:
Maas Müller, Chobe Helicopter

## BRAZIL:
Governo do Mato Grosso do Norte e do Sul; Fundação Pantanal, Erasmo Machado Filho and the Parcs Naturels Régionaux de France, Emmanuel Thévenin and Jean-Luc Sadorge; Fernando Lemos; Fernando Pedreira, Brazilian ambassador to UNESCO; Dr Iracema Alencar de Queiros, Instituto de Proteção Ambiental do Amazonas, and his son Alexandro; Brasilia Office of Tourism; Luis Carlos Burti, Editions Burti; Carlos Marquès, Office of Public Information, UNESCO; Ethel Leon, Anthea Communication; TV Globo; Golden Cross, José Augusto Wanderley and Juliana Marquès, Hotel Tropical in Manaus, VARIG

## CAMEROON:
Jacques Courbin, French ambassador to Chad; Yann Apert, cultural advisor; Sandra Chevalier-Lecadre and the offices of the French Embassy in Chad
Lael Weyenberg and "A Day in the Life of Africa"
Thierry Miaillier of RJM Aviation
Jean-Marie Six and Aviation Sans Frontières
Bruno Callabat and Guy Bardet, pilots
Gérard Roso

## CANADA:
Anne Zobenbuhler, Canadian ambassador in Paris; Canadian Tourism Commission, Barbara di Stefano and Laurent Beunier, Destination Québec; Cherry Kemp Kinnear, Nunavut Tourism; Huguette Parent and Chrystiane Galland, Air Canada; First Air; Air Transat; André Buteau, pilot, Essor Helicopters; Louis Drapeau, Canadian Helicopters; Canadian Airlines

## CHAD:
Jacques Courbin, French ambassador to Chad; Yann Apert, cultural advisor; Sandra Chevalier-Lecadre and the offices of the French Embassy in Chad.
Lael Weyenberg and "A Day in the Life of Africa"
Thierry Miaillier of RJM Aviation
Jean-Marie Six and Aviation Sans Frontières
Bruno Callabat and Guy Bardet, pilots
Gérard Roso
Colonel Kalibou
Aviation Sans Frontières:
Jean-Claude Gérin
Bruno Callabat
Thierry Miailler
COOPI:
Giacomo Franceschini

## CHILE:
Véronica Besnier
Luis Weinstein
Jean-Edouard Drouault of Eurocopter Chili
Capt. Fernando Perez of the Chilean Air Force
Capt. Carlos Lopez, pilot
Capt. Patricio Gallo, director of operations, Eurocopter Chili
Capt. Carlos Ruiz, pilot
Capt. Gonzalo Maturana, co-pilot
Capt. Yerko Woldarski, pilot
Capt. Hernán Soruco, co-pilot and Corporal David Espinoza

## CHINA:
Hong Kong Office of Tourism, Mr. Iskaros; Chinese Embassy in Paris, HE Caifangbo, Li Beifen; French Embassy in Beijing, Pierre Morel, French ambassador; Shi Guangeng of the Ministry of Foreign Affairs; Serge Nègre, kite expert; Yan Layma

## CÔTE D'IVOIRE:
Vitrail & Architecture; Pierre Fakhoury; Hugues Moreau and the pilots, Jean-Pierre Artifoni and Philippe Nallet, Ivoire Hélicoptères; Patricia Kriton and Mr. Kesada, Air Afrique

## CROATIA:
Franck Arrestier, pilot

## CYPRUS:
Sylvie Hartmann
Michel Morisseau
Cyprus Police:
Mario Mbouras, pilot

## DENMARK:
Weldon Owen Publishing, and the whole production team of *Over Europe*; Stine Norden

## DJIBOUTI
Ismail Omar Guelleh, President of the Republic of Djibouti
Osman Ahmed Moussa, Minister of Presidential Affairs
Fathi Ahmed Houssein, Division Head, Chief of State and Major General of the Armed Forces
Hassan Said Khaireh, Cabinet Chief of Defense
Mouna Musong, presidential advisor
Djibouti Office of Tourism

## DOMINICAN REPUBLIC:
Jean-Claude Moyret, French ambassador to the Dominican Republic
Dominique Dollone, cultural attaché
Marianne de Tolentino
Nestor Acosta, pilot

## EGYPT:
Rally of the Pharaohs, "Fenouil," organizer; Bernard Seguy, Michel Beaujard, and Christian Thévenet, pilots; the Paris-Dakar teams of 2003 and Etienne Lavigne of ASO.

## ECUADOR:
Loup Langton and Pablo Corral Vega, Descubriendo Ecuador; Claude Lara, Ecuadorian Minister of Foreign Affairs; Mr. Galarza, Ecuadorian consulate in France; Eliecer Cruz, Diego Bouilla, Robert Bensted-Smith, Galapagos National Park; Patrizia Schrank, Jennifer Stone, European Friends of Galapagos; Danilo Matamoros, Jaime and Cesar, Taxi Aero Inter Islas M.T.B.; Etienne Moine, Latitude 0°; Abdon Guerrero, San Cristobal airport

## FINLAND:
Dick Lindholm, pilot

## FRANCE:
Dominique Voynet, Minister for the Environment and Land Management; Ministry of Defense/SIRPA Parisian Police Force, Philippe Massoni, and Mrs. Seltzer; Montblanc Helicopters, Franck Arrestier and Alexandre Antunes, pilots; Corsican Office of Tourism, Xavier Olivieri; Auvergne Tourist Office, Cécile da Costa; Conseil Général de Côtes d'Armor, Charles Josselin and Gilles Pellan; Conseil Général de Savoie, Jean-Marc Eysserick; Conseil Général de Haute-Savoie, Georges Pacquetet and Laurent Guette; Conseil Général des Alpes-Maritimes, Sylvie Grosgojeat and Cécile Alziary; Conseil Général des Yvelines, Franck Borotra, president, Christine Boutin, Pascal Angenault and Odile Roussillon; Loire Tourist Office; Rémy Martin, Dominique Hériard-Dubreuil, Nicole Bru, Jacqueline Alexandre; Éditions du Chêne, Philippe Pierrelee, art director; Hachette, Jean Arcache; Moët et Chandon/Rallye GTO, Jean Berchon, and Philippe des Roys du Roure; Printemps de Cahors, Marie-Thérèse Perrin; Philippe Van Montagu and Willy Gouere, SAF helicopter pilot, Christophe Rosset, Hélifrance, Héli-Union, Europe Helicoptère Bretagne, Héli Bretagne, Héli-Océan, Héli Rhône-Alpes, Hélicos Légers Services, Figari Aviation, Aéro service, Héli air Monaco, Héli Perpignan, Ponair, Héli-inter, Héli Est; La Réunion: Tourist Office of La Réunion, René Barrieu and Michèle Bernard; Jean-Marie Lavèvre, pilot, Hélicoptères Helilagon; New Caledonia: Charles de Montesquieu, Daniel Pelleau of Hélicocéan, and Bruno Civet of Héli Tourisme; Antilles: Club Med in Les Boucaniers and La Caravelle; Alain Fanchette, pilot; French Polynesia: Club Med in Moorea; Haute-Garonne: Carole Schiff, Alexandre Antunès, pilot; Lyons and region: Béatrice Shawann, Christophe Schereich, Daniel Pujol (pilot for Saône floods, Taponas); Pyrénées-Atlantiques: DICOD and SIRPA.
CORSICA: Jacques Guillard, publisher
Marie-Joseph Arrighi-Landini, journalist
Jean Harixçalde, photographer
Gilbert Giacometti, pilot
TOULON: Admiral Jean-Louis Battet, Commander in Chief of the French Navy
French Navy, Maritime Méditerranée regional press office:
Capitaine de Corvette Antoine Goulley
Préfecture maritime de Méditerranée:
Vice Admiral of the Fleet Jean-Marie Huffel
Maître David Hourrier
Enseigne de Vaisseau Rousselet
Armoury Division, Centre d'Essais des Landes et de la Méditerranée:
Pierre Lusseyran
Jacques Pertois

## GERMANY:
Peter Becker, pilot
Ruth Eichhorn, Geneviève Teegler and all the team at GEO Germany
Wolfgang Mueller-Pietralla for Autostadt
Frank Müller-May and Tom Jacobi from *Stern Magazin*

## GIBRALTAR:
David Durie, Governor of Gibraltar
John Woodruffe from the Governor's Office
Colonel Purdom
Lieutenant Brian Phillips
Béatrice Quentin
Peggy Pere
Franck Arrestier, pilot
Jérôme Marx, mechanic

## GREECE:
Ministry of Culture, Athens,
Eleni Methodiou, Greek delegation to UNESCO; Greek National Tourism Organization; Club Med in Corfu Ipsos, Gregolimano, Helios Corfu, Kos, and Olympia; Olympic Airways; Interjet, Dimitrios Prokopis and Konstantinos Tsigkas, pilots, and Kimon Daniilidis; Meteo Center, Athens

## GUATEMALA & HONDURAS:
Giovanni Herrera, director, and Carlos Llarena, pilot, Aerofoto in Guatemala City; Rafael Sagastume, STP Villas in Guatemala City

## HUNGARY:
The staff of the French Embassy in Budapest,
The Mayor of Budapest
Institut Français, Budapest

**ICELAND:**
Bergur Gislason, Gisli Guestsson, Icephoto Thyriuthionustan Helicopters; Peter Samwell; Iceland Tourist Board, Paris

**INDIA:**
Indian Embassy in Paris, HE Kanwal Sibal, ambassador, Rahul Chhabra, first secretary, S.K. Solat, Chief of the Air Force; Mr. Lal; Mr. Kadyan, and Vivianne Tourret; Indian Ministry of Foreign Affairs, Tek. E. Prasad and Manjish Grover; N.K. Singh from the Prime Minister's Office; Mr. Chidambaram, member of Parliament; Air Headquarters, S. J. Kumaran, Mr. Pande; Mandoza Air Charters, Atul Jaidka, Indian International Airways, Capt. Sangha Pritvipath; French Embassy in New Delhi, Claude Blanchemaison, French ambassador, François Xavier Reymond, first secretary

**INDONESIA:**
Total Balikpapan, Ananda Idris, and Ilha Sutrisno; Mr. and Mrs. Didier Millet
French Navy:
Admiral Jean-Louis Battet, Commander in Chief of the French Navy
Anne Culler, Capitaine de Frégate
The crew of the helicopter carrier Jeanne d'Arc and the captain of the Marc de Briançon
The pilots of ALAT (Aviation Légère de l'Armée de Terre)

**IRELAND:**
Aer Lingus; Ireland Tourist Board; Capt. David Courtney, Irish Rescue Helicopters; David Hayes, Westair Aviation Ltd

**ITALY:**
French Embassy in Rome, Michel Benard, press office; Heli Frioula, Greco Gianfranco, Fanzin Stefano, and Godicio Pierino

**JAPAN:**
Eu Japan Festival, Shuji Kogi and Robert Delpire; Masako Sakata, IPJ; NHK TV; Japan Broadcasting Corp.; Asahi Shimbun Press Group, Teizo Umezu.

**JORDAN:**
Mrs. Sharaf, Anis Mouasher, Khaled Irani, and Khaldoun Kiwan, Royal Society for Conservation of Nature; Royal Airforces; Riad Sawalha, Royal Jordanian Regency Palace Hotel

**KAZAKHSTAN:**
Nourlan Danenov, Kazakhstan Ambassador in Paris; Alain Richard, French ambassador in Almaty, and Josette Floch; Professor René Letolle; Heli Asia Air and Mr. Anouar, pilot

**KENYA:**
Universal Safari Tours, Nairobi
Patrix Duffar; Transsafari, Irvin Rozental

**KUWAIT:**
Kuwait Centre for Research & Studies, Prof. Abdullah Al Ghunaim, Dr. Youssef; Kuwait National Commission for UNESCO, Sulaiman Al Onaizi; Kuwaiti Delegation to UNESCO, Dr. Al Salem, and Mr. Al Baghly; Kuwait Airforces, Squadron 32, Major Hussein Al-Mane, Capt. Emad Al-Momen; Kuwait Airways, Mr. Al Nafisy

**KYRGYZSTAN:**
René Cagnat

**LEBANON:**
Lucien George
Georges Salem
The Lebanese Armed Forces

**LITHUANIA:**
Lithuanian Border Guards
Neria Lejay
Hili Flights: Mr. Alguis

**LUXEMBOURG:**
Bernard Séguy, pilot

**MADAGASCAR:**
Riaz Barday and Normand Dicaire, pilot, Aéromarine; Sonja and Thierry Ranarivelo, Yersin Racerlyn; pilot, Madagascar Helicopters; Jeff Guidez and Lisbeth

**MALAYSIA:**
Club Med in Cherating

**MALDIVES:**
Club Med in Faru

**MALI:**
TSO, Paris–Dakar Rally, Hubert Auriol; Daniel Legrand, Arpèges Conseil, and Daniel Bouet, Cessna pilot

**MAURITANIA:**
TSO, Paris–Dakar Rally, Hubert Auriol; Daniel Legrand, Arpèges Conseil, and Daniel Bouet, Cessna pilot; Sidi Ould Kleib

**MEXICO:**
Club Med in Cancun, Sonora Bay, Huatulco, and Ixtapa

**MONACO:**
His Highness Prince Albert of Monaco
Colonel Lambelin
Colonel Jouan
Catherine Alestchenkoff, Grimaldi Forum
Patrick Lainé, pilot

**MONGOLIA:**
Jacques-Olivier Manent, French ambassador to Mongolia
Louzan Gctovdorjiin, Mongolian ambassador to France
Tuya de Mongolie Voyages
The Mongolian Armed Forces

**MOROCCO:**
Gendarmerie Royale Marocaine, General El Kadiri and Colonel Hamid Laanigri; François de Grossouvre

**NAMIBIA:**
Ministry of Fisheries; Mission Française de Coopération, Jean-Pierre Lahaye, Nicole Weill, Laurent Billet, and Jean Paul; Namibian Tourist Friend, A.mut Steinmester

**NEPAL:**
Nepalese Embassy in Paris; Terres d'Aventure, Patrick Oudin; Great Himalayan Adventures, Ashok Basnyet; Royal Nepal Airways, J.B. Rana; Mandala Trekking, Jérôme Edou, Bhuda Air; Maison de la Chine, Patricia Tartour-Jonathan, director, Colette Vaquier and Fabienne Leriche; Marina Tymen and Miranda Ford, Cathay Pacific

**NETHERLANDS:**
Paris-Match; Franck Arrestier, pilot

**NIGER:**
TSO, Paris–Dakar Rally, Hubert Auriol; Daniel Legrand, Arpèges Conseil, and Daniel Bouet, Cessna pilot

**NORWAY:**
Airlift A.S., Ted Juliussen, pilot, Henry Hogi, Arvid Auganaes, and Nils Myklebust

**OMAN:**
His Majesty Sultan Qaboos bin Said Al Said; The Oman Ministry of Defense, John Miller; Villa d'Alésia, William Perkins, and Isabelle de Larrocha

**PERU:**
Dr. Maria Reiche and Ana Maria Cogorno-Reiche; Ministry of Foreign Affairs, Juan Manuel Tirado; Policía Nacional del Perú; Faucett Airlines, Cecilia Raffo and Alfredo Barnechea; Eduardo Corrales, Aero Condor

**PHILIPPINES:**
Filipino Air Force; Seven Days in the Philippines, published by Editions Millet, Jill Laidlaw

**PORTUGAL:**
Club Med in Da Balaia
Ana Pessoa and ICEP
HeliFortugal and Margarida Simplício
IPPAR (Instituto Português do Património Arqu tectónico)

**QATAR:**
Qatar Foundation
Saeed Salem Al-Eida
The pilots of Gulf Helicopters

**RUSSIA:**
Yuri Vorobiov, Deputy Minister; Yuri Brazhnikov, Emercom; Nikolai Alexey Timoshenko, Emercom in Kamchatka; Valery Blatov, Russian Delegation to UNESCO

**SAINT VINCENT & GRENADINES:**
Paul Gravel, SVG Air; Jeanette Cadet, The Mustique Company; David Linley; Ali Medjahed, baker; Alain Fanchette

**SINGAPORE:**
The French Armed Forces
Eurocopter Singapore
Dider Millet
Antoine Monod
Nigel Tan

**SENEGAL:**
TSO, Paris-Dakar Rally, Hubert Auriol; Daniel Legrand, Arpèges Conseil, and Daniel Bouet, Cessna pilot; Club Med in Les Almadies and Cap Skirring

**SOMALILAND:**
Sheikh Saud Al-Thani of Qatar; Majdi Bustami, E. A. Paulson, and Osama, Office of Sheikh Saud Al-Thani; Fred Viljoen, pilot; Rachid J. Hussein, UNESCO-PEER, Hargeisa, Somaliland; Nureldin Satti, UNESCO-PEER, Nairobi, Kenya; Shadia Clot, Sheikh's representative in France; Waheed, Al Sadd travel agency, Qatar; Cécile and Karl, Emirates Airlines, Paris

**SOUTH AFRICA:**
SATOUR, Mrs. Salomone, South African Airways, Jean-Philippe de Ravel, Victoria Junction, Victoria Junction Hotel

**SOUTH KOREA:**
Miok and Hyungjoon
The South Korean Armed Forces:
Mooyeol Kim
Jongsun Park
Estelle Berruyer, cultural attaché to the French Embassy in Seoul
Colonel Loïc Frouard, defense attaché to the French Embassy in Seoul
Seongwoo Yoon
Chankgsik Kim

**SPAIN:**
Jesus Ezquerra, Spanish ambassador to UNESCO; Club Med in Don Miguel, Cadaquès, Porto Petro, and Ibiza, Canaries: Tomás Azcárate y Bang, Viceconsejería de Medio Ambiente; Fernando Clavijo, Protección Civil de las Islas Canarias; Jean-Pierre Sauvage and Gérard de Bercegol, Iberia; Elena Valdés and Marie Mar, Spanish Tourist Office; Basque Country: the office of the Basque government, Zuperia Bingen, director, Concha Dorronsoro and Nerea Antia, press office of the Basque government; Juan Carlos Aguirre Bilbao, chief of the Basque Police (Ertzaintza) helicopter fleet

**SWEDEN:**
Stine Norden

**TAIWAN:**
Helene Lai
The Civil Aviation Office of the Taiwanese Ministry of Transport

**THAILAND:**
Royal Forest Department, Viroj Pimanrojnagool, Pramote Kasemsap, Tawee Nootong, Amon Achapet; NTC Intergroup Ltd, Ruhn Phiama; Pascale Baret, Thai Airways; Tourism Authority of Thailand, Juthaporn Rerngronasa and Watcharee, Lucien Blacher, Satit Nilwong and Busatit Palacheewa; Fujifilm Bangkok, Mr. Supoj; Club Med in Phuket

**TUNISIA:**
President Zine Abdine Ben Ali; the Presidency of the Republic of Tunisia, Abdelwahad Abdallah and Haj Ali; Tunisian Air Force, Laouina Base, Colonel Mustafa Hermi; Tunisian Embassy in Paris, Mongi Bousnina, ambassador, and Mohamed Fendri; Tunisian Tourist Office, Raouf Jomni and Mamoud Khaznadar; Editions Cérès, Mohamed and Karim Ben Smail; The Residence Hotel, Jean-Pierre Auriol; Basma-Hôtel Club Paladien, Laurent Chauvin; Tunis Weather Center, Mohammed Allouche

**TURKEY:**
Turkish Airlines, Bulent Demirçi and Nasan Erol; Mach'Air Helicopters, Ali Izmet, Öztürk and Seçal Sahin, Karatas Gulsah; General Aviation, Vedat Seyhan, and Faruk, pilot; Club Med in Bodrum, Kusadasi, Palmiye, Kemer, and Foça

**UKRAINE:**
Olexander Demyanyuk, UNESCO Delegate; A. V. Grebenyuk, administrative director of the Chernobyl exclusion zone; Rima Kiselitza, attaché to Chornobylinterinform, Marie-Renée Tisné, Office for Protection Against Ionizing Radiation.

**UNITED KINGDOM:**
England: Aeromega and Mike Burns, pilot; David Linley; Philippe Achache; Environment Agency, Bob Davidson and David Palmer; Press Office of Buckingham Palace; Scotland: Paula O'Farrel and Doug Allsop of Total Oil Marine in Aberdeen; Iain Grindlay and Rod from Lothian Helicopters Ltd in Edinburgh.

**UNITED STATES:**
Wyoming: Yellowstone National Park, Marsha Karle and Stacey Churchwell; Utah: Classic Helicopters; Montana: Carisch Helicopters, Mike Carisch; California: Robin Petgrave of Bravo Helicopters, Los Angeles, and pilots Akiko K. Jones and Dennis Smith; Fred London, Cornerstone Elementary School; Nevada: John Sullivan and pilots Aaron Wainman and Matt Evans, Sundance Helicopters, Las Vegas; Louisiana: Suwest Helicopters and Steve Eckhardt; Arizona: Southwest Helicopters and Jim Mc Phail; New York: Liberty Helicopters and Daniel Veranazza; Mike Renz, Analar Helicopters, John Tauranac; Florida: Rick Cook, Everglades National Park, Rick and Todd, Bulldog Helicopters in Orlando, Chuck and Diana, Biscayne Helicopters, Miami, Club Med in Sand Piper; Alaska: Philippe Bourseiller, Yves Carmagnole, pilot; Denver: Elaine Hood of Raytheon Polar Services Company and Karen Wattenmaker

**UZBEKISTAN:**
(not flown over) Embassy of Uzbekistan in Paris, Mr. Mamagonov, ambassador, and Djoura Dekhanov, first secretary; Jean-Claude Richard, French ambassador to Uzbekistan, and Jean-Pierre Messiant, first secretary; René Cagnat and Natacha; Vincent Fourniau and Bruno Chauvel, Institut Français d'Etudes sur l'Asie Centrale (IFEAC)

**VENEZUELA:**
Centro de Estudios y Desarrollo, Nelson Prato Barbosa; Hoteles Intercontinental; Ultramar Express; Lagoven; Imparques; Icaro, Luis Gonzales

We would also like to thank the companies whose commissions and deals have allowed us to work:

**AÉROSPATIALE,** Patrice Kreis, Roger Benguigui, and Cotinaud
**AOM,** Françoise Dubois-Siegmund, Felicia Boisne-Noc, Christophe Cachera
**CANON,** Guy Bourreau, Pascal Briard, Service Pro, Jean-Pierre Colly, Guy d'Assonville, Jean-Claude Brouard, Philippe Joachim, Raphaël Rimoux, Bernard Thomas, and of course Daniel Quint and Annie Rémy who have helped us so often throughout this long project.
Canon Europe: Ian Lopez (manager of Canon Europe's Pro Imaging Department), Andrew Boag (director of communications, Canon Europe), Adelina Marghidan, Jacqueline Ripart
**CLUB MED,** Philippe Bourguignon, Henri de Bodinat, Sylvie Bourgeois, Preben Vestdam, Christian Thévenet
**CRIE,** worldwide express courier, Jérôme Lepert, and all his team
**DIA SERVICES,** Bernard Crepin
**FONDATION TOTAL,** Yves le Goff, and his assistant Nathalie Guillerme
**JANJAC,** Jacques and Olivier Bigot, Jean-François Bardy, and Eric Massé
**KONICA,** Dominique Brugière
**MÉTÉO FRANCE,** Mr. Foidart, Marie-Claire Rullière, Alain Mazoyer, and all the forecasters
**RUSH LABO,** Denis Cuisy, and all our friends at the lab
**WORLD ECONOMIC FORUM** in Davos, Klaus Schwab, Maryse Zwick and Agnès Stüder

**Yann Arthus-Bertrand's team at the Altitude agency:**

Photo assistants: Franck Charel, Françoise Jacquot, Sibylle d'Orgeval, Erwan Sourget, who were there throughout this project, as well as Frédéric Lenoir, who joined us recently, and all those who have helped me throughout these airborne years: Ambre Mayen, Denis Lardat, Arnaud Prade, Tristan Carné, Christophe Daguet, Stefan Christiansen, Pierre Cornevin, Olivier Jardon, Marc Lavaud, Franck Lechenet, Olivier Looren, Antonio López Palazuelo.

*Pilot of the Colibri EC 120 Eurocopter:* Wilfrid "Willy" Gouère

**Coordination office:**

*Production coordination:* Hélène de Bonis (1994–1999) and Françoise Le Roch'-Briquet
*Editorial coordination and captions:* Anne Jankeliowitch (2000–2002) and Isabelle Delannoy since 2002
*Exhibition organizers:* Catherine Arthus-Bertrand and Marie Charvet, Tiphanie Babinet and Jean Poderos (in 2002 and 2003)
*Production:* Antoine Verdet, Catherine Quilichini, Gloria-Céleste Raad for Russia
*Texts:* Danielle Laruelle, Judith Klein, Hugues Demeude, Sophie Hurel, and PRODIG,
geographic laboratory, Marie-Françoise Courel and Lydie Goeldner, Frédéric Bertrand
*Picture research:* Isabelle Bruneau, Isabelle Lechenet, Florence Frutoso, Claire Portaluppi

I would also like to take this opportunity to express my gratitude to my friend Hervé de La Martinière, and to the entire team, who worked on this book, especially Benoit Nacci, the art director, for his kind support, Céline Moulard, Sébastien Raimondi, Carole Daprey, Marianne Lassandro, Christel Durantin, Amaëlle Génot, Marie-Hélène Lafin, and Jeanne Castoriano.
A final word of thanks to Quadrilaser and its team for the photo engraving, Kapp-Lahure-Jombart for the printing, and SIRC for the binding.
For the 2005 edition: Isabelle Grison, Cécile Vandenbroucque, Téo Weber, and Marie Poitou
Graphic design and layout for the 2005 edition: 'Olo

**OUTSKIRTS OF MAR DEL PLATA, BUENOS AIRES PROVINCE, ARGENTINA** (38°00' S, 57°33' W)

This vast country—the second largest in South America after Brazil, covering an area of 1.04 million square miles (2.7 million km²)—has a population of less than 40 million. In the fertile pampas, agriculture and cattle breeding are practiced on a huge scale. Nothing here comes in a standard size—not even this sand graffiti, which bears witness to the official language of Spanish, which has wiped so many indigenous languages off the cultural map. Since the 1970s, however, hostility or indifference to these local languages has given way to renewed interest, although it is too late for many of them, as they are spoken by a mere handful of old people. Half of the world's 6,000 languages are similarly threatened, and a language effectively disappears every two weeks. And yet language, an intangible yet basic element of everyone's cultural heritage, is a vital symbol of a people's identity. Spanish—against which six languages are now fighting for survival in Argentina—is the third most widely spoken language in the world, with Mandarin Chinese in first place, although English is most common on the Internet (68.4 percent of all communications).

All of the photographs in this book were taken with Fuji Velvia film (50 ASA).
Yann Arthus-Bertrand worked primarily with CANON EOS 1N cameras and CANON L series lenses.
Some photographs were taken with a PENTAX 645N and the panoramic FUJI GX 617.

Yann Arthus-Bertrand's photographs are
distributed by the agency Altitude, Paris, France:
www.altitude-photo.com

Find out more from:
www.yannarthusbertrand.org